Y0-ABO-607

THE DICTIONARY OF
INTERNATIONAL
BUSINESS TERMS

JAE K. SHIM, PH.D.
JOEL G. SIEGEL, PH.D., CPA
MARC H. LEVINE, PH.D., CPA

GLENLAKE PUBLISHING COMPANY, LTD.
Chicago • London • New Delhi

FITZROY DEARBORN PUBLISHERS
Chicago and London

CHABOT COLLEGE LIBRARY

REF
HD
62.4
.S524
1998

© 1998 The Glenlake Publishing Company, Ltd.
ISBN: 1-888998-34-2

Library edition: Fitzroy Dearborn Publishers, Chicago and London
ISBN: 1-57958-001-7

All rights reserved. No part of this book may be reproduced in any form or by any means, electronic, mechanical, photocopying, recording, or otherwise without the prior written permission of the publisher.

Printed in the United States of America

GPCo
1261 West Glenlake
Chicago, Illinois 60660
glenlake@ix.netcom.com

Dedication

Chung Shim
Dedicated Wife

Roberta Siegel
Loving Wife, Colleague, and Partner

Carol Levine
Dedicated Wife and Friend

Reva and Daniel Levine
Loving Children

Tessie Levine
My Dear Mother

TABLE OF CONTENTS

ACKNOWLEDGMENTS

We wish to express our appreciation to Barbara Craig for the outstanding job she did on this project. We recognize her exceptional editorial efforts. Thanks also goes to Roberta M. Siegel for her expertise in international business.

ABOUT THE AUTHORS

Jae K. Shim, Ph.D., is a Professor of Business Administration at California State University, Long Beach. Dr. Shim received his Ph.D. from the University of California at Berkeley. He is President of the National Business Review Foundation, a management consulting firm. Dr. Shim has published approximately 50 articles in professional Journals, including Journal of Systems Management, Financial Management, Journal of Operations Research, Data Management, Management Accounting, Long Range Planning, Journal of Business Forecasting, Decision Sciences, Management Science, Michigan Business Review, Business Economics, Cost and Management, International Journal of Systems Science, International Journal of Management, and Econometrica. Dr. Shim has over 45 books to his credit and is a recipient of the Credit Research Foundation Award for his article on financial modeling. He is also recipient of a Ford Foundation Award, Mellon Research Fellowship, Arthur Andersen Research Grant, and an International Service Fellowship. For over 20 years, Dr. Shim has been an industrial consultant to international companies in such areas as systems development and applications, corporate planning and modeling, and business forecasting.

Joel G. Siegel, Ph.D., CPA, is a management consultant to international businesses and Professor of Accounting, Finance, and Information Systems at Queens College. He was previously associated with Coopers and Lybrand, CPAs and Arthur Andersen, CPAs. Dr. Siegel has served as a consultant to numerous organizations, including Citicorp, International Telephone and Telegraph, Person-Wolinsky Associates, and the American Institute of CPAs. Dr. Siegel is the author of 55 books. He has also authored approximately 200 articles on international business topics. His articles have appeared in such journals as Financial Executive, Computers in Accounting, Financial Analysts Journal, The CPA Journal, National Public Accountant, Practical Accountant, International Accountant, Business and Economic Dimensions, University of Michigan Business Review, European Journal of Accountancy, Long Range Planning, Managerial Planning, Personnel Management, Leadership and Organization Journal, Taxes, Journal of Corporate Accounting and Finance, and Ohio CPA. Dr. Siegel is the recipient of the Outstanding Educator of America Award. He is listed in "Who's Who Among Writers" and "Who's Who in the World." Dr. Siegel is the former chairperson of the National Oversight Board.

Marc H. Levine, Ph.D., CPA, is an accounting and financial consultant to multinational companies, and is a Professor of Accounting and Information Systems at Queens College. Dr. Levine has authored two books and numerous professional articles in such journals as The CPA Journal, National Public Accountant, Practical Accountant, Michigan CPA, Journal of Corporate Accounting, and Journal of International Management. Dr. Levine was previously associated with Deloitte and Touche, CPAs.

HOW TO USE THIS BOOK

In reading and using this book, the reader should note that alphabetization is by letter rather than by word. That is, multiple-word entries are treated as single words. Abbreviations or acronyms appear as entries and are referenced to the full spelling. Terms with several meanings appear in numbered sequence.

When a cross-reference appears within the text of a definition, the term is in **ALL CAPS** and is not repeated in the *see* or *see also* part of the definition. Italics are used for titles for publications. Cross-references at the end of a definition may refer to a related or contrasting term, or an abbreviation or acronym. Cross-references at the end of a definition are in **ALL CAPS.** *See* is used when a term is fully defined at another entity; *see also* is used when another related term is defined or a reference is made within the text of another definition.

This Dictionary is an invaluable reference for all business people involved in international business. Accountants, financial managers, business managers, marketing executives, attorneys, operations research managers, economists, investment portfolio managers, production managers, and others should have this book in their library for daily reference.

A

ABANDONMENT The intentional desertion of property by a owning or leasing entity without making provision for transferring the ownership or use to another. For example, a multinational company may divest itself of a segment of its business by abandonment. The measurement date of such a transaction is the day that the operations of the abandoned segment cease. The abandonment of the property by an owner or leasing entity does not negate any liability or responsibility that the entity may have relating to it. The property generally reverts back to the prior owner.

ABROGATION The abolishment, repeal, or annulment of an agreement or act. Insurance can be taken out to cover damages resulting from a nullifying or breach of a contract between a multinational company and foreign companies or a foreign government. Such coverage may include the expropriation of property overseas.

ABSOLUTE ADVANTAGE Ability to produce a good with fewer resources per unit or at a lower cost than that of a country's trading partners. It contrasts with **COMPARATIVE ADVANTAGE** in that the exporting country holds an absolute superiority in the availability and cost of certain products.

ABSOLUTE QUOTA A ceiling placed by a government on the number of general or specific imported products from one or more countries for a designated time period. For example, if the quota is 100,000 imported cars from Japan for 19X9, once that level is reached no additional imported cars will be allowed for that year. The objective of this policy might be to protect domestic industries.

ABSORPTION COSTING Under this costing method (also called full costing), all manufacturing costs (variable and fixed) that are incurred in the production process are considered inventory costs of the unit manufactured and become cost of goods sold when the unit is sold. Variable costs are those costs that fluctuate in direct proportion to production volume. They consist of direct materials, direct labor, and variable factory overhead (e.g., factory supplies). Fixed costs, on the other hand, remain constant as production volume changes. They consist of fixed factory overhead (e.g., factory rent). For external financial reporting, absorption costing must be followed for inventory valuation (disclosure) purposes in order to satisfy **GENERALLY ACCEPTED ACCOUNTING PRINCIPLES.** A special, modified form of absorption costing is allowed for tax purposes. In a variable costing system (direct costing method), only variable costs of the production process are charged to the product as inventory costs. Variable costing is used extensively for internal managerial reporting purposes in such areas as budget preparation, decision making and cost control.

However, it is neither acceptable for external financial reports nor tax purposes. *See also* **MANUFACTURING COST.**

ABSORPTION OF CHARGES **1.** The process of paying or "absorbing" charges that are assessed by others. For example, in shipping terms, a **FREE ON BOARD** shipping point means that the seller/shipper of goods is not responsible for shipping costs. Rather, the purchaser is responsible for all costs of shipment initiating from the seller's place of business. If a common **CARRIER** requires that the seller/shipper pay the cost of delivery to the purchaser in advance, then the purchaser must absorb these charges and pay the seller/shipper for them as part of the purchase price of the goods. **2.** Payment or absorption by a common **CARRIER** of related freight costs such as storage costs, wharfage, etc., on a shipment.

ABUSES Economic injuries intentionally perpetrated by one company over another as a result of a trade agreement or arrangement. For example, abuses may occur if a company sells its products with differing contractual stipulations for the purpose of putting one purchasing company at a trading disadvantage to that of another. Other examples include selling goods to countries at unfair, highly inflated selling prices, limiting production for the purpose of artificially inflating prices, limiting competition so that monopolistic conditions exist for purposes of price control, producing at substandard quality, etc. *See also* **PRICE CONTROLS.**

ACCELERATED TARIFF ELIMINATION An agreement between two or more countries to hasten the lowering of a **TARIFF** or tariffs between them. This may include an attempt to eliminate any tariff. The objective is to promote **INTERNATIONAL TRADE.**

ACCELERATION CLAUSE A contractual or agreed provision that upon the occurrence of a stipulated act or event, the multinational company's vested interest in a property will be earlier. An example is when an obligation owed to the company becomes immediately payable in full because of the debtor's nonpayment of an installment payment or some other violation of the agreement.

ACCEPTANCE **1.** A binding contract effected when one party to a business arrangement accepts the offer of the other. Acceptance may be implied or partial, oral or written, depending on the nature of the offer. **2.** A drawee's promise to pay either a **TIME DRAFT** or sight draft. Typically, the acceptor signs his/her name after writing "accepted" on the bill along with the date. An acceptance of a bill in effect makes it a **PROMISSORY NOTE;** the acceptor is the maker and the drawer is the endorser. *See* **BANKERS ACCEPTANCE.**

ACCEPTANCE ADVICE In **INTERNATIONAL TRADE,** a confirmation between banks that consummation of a transaction has occurred. Typically, in the transference of funds between banks, acceptance advice is sent by the bank that has

2

received funds to the bank that has sent the funds confirming the amount of collection, the account for which the collection was made, miscellaneous fees, charges, etc., relating to the transaction.

ACCEPTANCE FACILITY A credit line received from a financial institution such as a bank to finance a company's export or import of products or services. The bank may require and want to hold documentation of title to the goods such as a warehouse receipt.

ACCEPTANCE FINANCING A means used by exporters in **INTERNATIONAL TRADE** for the purpose of arranging financing, i.e., **EXPORT FINANCING.** For example, if an exporter needs short-term capital, the exporter will offer a draft for payment in advance of its specified date of **MATURITY.** When a bank accepts the draft, the exporter receives the discounted value of the draft (the discount rate may be the current bank rate or may be a rate based on the term of the draft and the risk associated with repayment). By accepting the draft through endorsement, the accepting bank guarantees payment of the draft.

ACCESSION The act of becoming a participant in a multinational agreement or treaty and as a result assenting to, agreeing to, and abiding by the contractual terms upon which the association is based. For example, accession occurs when a nation becomes a member of the **GENERAL AGREEMENT ON TARIFFS AND TRADE, EUROPEAN ECONOMIC COMMUNITY,** and other such trade agreements. The act of signing such a treaty signifies that a country will adhere to all the terms of the coalition agreement.

ACCESSORIAL SERVICE Additional services besides transportation provided by a carrier (e.g., packing, freezing, heating, assembling, mixing, and storing).

ACCIDENTAL EXPORTS Exports obtained with no effort or deliberate plan of the exporter.

ACCOMMODATING TRANSACTION Exchanges in the form of official reserve assets and foreign official assets used by a nation to correct imbalances in **INTERNATIONAL TRADE.** For example, if a company has a **TRADE DEFICIT** in a given period, it may use gold or its official currency reserves as an accommodating transaction to balance any deficiency relating to international cash flows. *See also* **BALANCE OF PAYMENTS.**

ACCOUNT In an accounting system, an account is the conventional method of measuring transactional changes in balance sheet and income statement categories affecting an entity's financial statements. Increases and decreases affecting an account are measured by increase or decrease indicators known as debits and credits. The specific account being analyzed will determine whether the increase or decrease will be accounted for with a debit or a credit. In a typical business, entity accounts are divided into assets, liabilities and stockholders' equity classifications.

In **INTERNATIONAL TRADE,** a summary of a country's credit and debit transactions with other trading countries are measured in an account termed **BALANCE OF PAYMENTS.** In this area, the two groups that encompass balance of payments transactions are the current account and the capital account. *See also* **BALANCE OF PAYMENTS ACCOUNTING.**

ACCOUNTANT'S INTERNATIONAL STUDY GROUP (AISG) The **AMERICAN ACCOUNTING ASSOCIATION,** in an attempt to study the diversity in international accounting theory and practice in 1966 established the AISG for the purpose of publishing comparative studies on accounting issues in the United Kingdom, Canada, and the United States. Towards this end, representatives from the **INSTITUTE OF CHARTERED ACCOUNTANTS IN ENGLAND, CANADIAN INSTITUTE OF CHARTERED ACCOUNTANTS,** and the **AMERICAN INSTITUTE OF CERTIFIED PUBLIC ACCOUNTANTS** meet to study issues of comparative international accounting.

ACCOUNTING EXPOSURE Accounting exposure, also called translation exposure, is the impact of an exchange rate change on the multinational firm's financial statements. An example would be the impact of a French Franc devaluation on a United States firm's reported income statement and balance sheet.

ACCOUNTING SYSTEM A system or procedure that processes financial transactions to provide scorekeeping, attention-directing, and decision-making information to management. Accounting is concerned with two kinds of management information: financial information and information generated from the processing of transaction data. The system is responsible for the preparation of financial information and the information obtained from transaction data for the purposes of: (1) internal reporting to managers for use in planning and controlling current and future operations and for nonroutine decision making and (2) external reporting to outside parties such as stockholders, creditors, and government.

ACCOUNTS RECEIVABLE (A/R) MANAGEMENT The technique used by a multinational company to adjust their A/R to reduce foreign exchange risk and optimally to time fund transfers. For example, in countries where currency values are likely to drop, financial managers of the subsidiaries should avoid giving excessive trade credit. If accounts receivable balances are outstanding for an extended time period, interest should be charged to absorb the loss in purchasing power. Note that a net asset position (i.e., assets minus liabilities) is not desirable in a weak or potentially depreciating currency. In this case, you should expedite the disposal of the asset. By the same token, you should lag or delay the collection against a net asset position in a strong currency.

ACHIEVEMENT MOTIVATION The desire of managers or employees to achieve their goals and objectives.

ACROSS THE BOARD A reference to include or encompass all units or members of a group, class, or association. In **INTERNATIONAL TRADE,** a reference is sometimes made to "across the board tariff reductions." This means that all countries that had signed the **GENERAL AGREEMENT ON TARIFFS AND TRADE,** for example, would agree to reduce tariffs across the board by a predetermined uniform amount rather than have to negotiate specific tariff reductions among themselves. An across the board decrease in the prices of securities means most securities (e.g., stocks, bonds) are decreasing in price. An across the board change in price may also apply to products or services. Employees may receive the same percentage pay raise.

ACT OF STATE DOCTRINE In international law, the fact that each country has its own control of what takes place within its territory.

ACTIVE MARKET A reference to the fact that the volume in a given trading market has been high. Any market such as foreign exchange, bond, stock, commodity, etc., may experience high volume of buying and selling in either in a given day or period.

ACTUAL VALUE 1. Measure used by customs agents for assessing import duties based on items of a similar nature that could be purchased or sold in an open market. **2.** Value of a shipment transported by a carrier. 3. Utility or worth of an asset at the current time. The actual value of an asset is measured by its **FAIR MARKET VALUE** which may be estimated by the amount of money that would be received upon the sale of the item in a normal (unforced liquidation) market. When an asset is initially acquired, its purchase price or cost is generally its market value, actual value, or current worth. *See also* **FAIR VALUE.**

ACTUALS In a business merchandising environment, actuals are the inventory or merchandise that an entity purchases and then sells as part of its primary business function.

ACU. *See* **ASIAN CURRENCY UNIT.**

ADB. *See* **ASIAN DEVELOPMENT BANK.**

ADAPTATION An adjustment of a multinational company to new circumstances in **INTERNATIONAL TRADE** such as changing tastes for goods or services in a foreign region or country. This change in focus may require a modification in the company's policy of pricing, promotion, packaging, and warranty.

ADF. *See* **AFRICAN DEVELOPMENT FUND.**

ADJUDICATION The legal process to resolve international disputes between companies in a court of law. In the proceeding, evidence is presented, witnesses testify as to the issues, and a legal judgment is reached based on the facts.

ADJUSTABLE PEG Between trading nations, an adjustable peg refers to a system of fixed, locked exchange rates that are set by the governments directly involved or by multigovernmental agreement in the international currency exchange markets. These rates may be modified, however, when a participating nation has a highly unfavorable **BALANCE OF PAYMENTS.** In this situation, the nation would attempt to reduce the imbalance by devaluing its currency thus causing the fixed rate to change. *See also* **PEGGED EXCHANGE RATE.**

ADJUSTABLE RATE MORTGAGE (ARM) A mortgage having an interest rate that varies depending on the change in some outside standard such as the prime interest rate, the interest rate on United States treasury securities, or the **INFLATION** rate, for example, as measured by the Consumer Price Index (CPI). The lender can increase or decrease the interest rate on the mortgage at specified intervals based on changing market conditions. The mortgage agreement specifies when the interest rate may change and any limits imposed.

ADJUSTMENT APPROACH The methodology or policies taken by a government to reduce its **BALANCE OF PAYMENTS** deficit. This can be done through: (1) monetary modifications by affecting changes in governmental spending and taxes; (2) currency exchange controls by direct intervention over foreign exchange; (3) fiscal modifications by influencing the country's interest rates and its money supply; (4) governmental regulations that affect tariffs, quotas, and other protective restrictions; (5) multinational negotiated actions such as voluntary export restraint(s), **INTERNATIONAL COMMODITY AGREEMENT(s), and ORDER MARKETING AGREEMENT(s);** etc. *See also,* **BALANCE OF PAYMENTS ADJUSTMENT.**

ADMINISTRATIVE EXCEPTION Member nations of the **COORDINATING COMMITTEE FOR MULTILATERAL EXPORT CONTROLS (COCOM)** were an organization of 17 western nations which agreed to monitor and restrict the exports of high technology products, products having military potential, atomic energy applications, etc., to the communist nations. In addition to the 17 western nations, other nations around the world were classified as cooperating countries. As part of the **COCOM** agreement, a member country could alone decide on the commodities that they would export. That is, through the act of administrative exception, a member nation could unilaterally decide on its export commodities and was only required to notify the member nations of **COCOM** of its decision. The **COCOM** organization ended in 1994.

ADMINISTRATIVE PRICING RULE A concept of pricing based on a seller's control of the market with the resulting ability to independently set prices. In this environment, market forces of supply and demand do not determine the selling price as they would under the assumption of competition.

ADMINISTRATOR AD COLLIGENDUM An individual or entity selected judicially or otherwise to handle the proceeds received from selling foreign assets.

ADOPTION NOTICE A written or oral agreement by a carrier that it is accepting a duty of a preceding party (e.g., multinational company, prior shipping company). An example is the carrier's acceptance of freight charges or tariffs.

ADR. *See* **AMERICAN DEPOSITARY RECEIPT.** *See also* **ADVANCE DETERMINATION RULING**

AD VALOREM A Latin term that means relating to value.

AD VALOREM DUTY A duty levied as a proportion of the price or value of an import commodity.

ADVANCE AGAINST DOCUMENTS In **INTERNATIONAL TRADE,** a form of **EXPORT FINANCING** in which an importer sends the exporter an advance based on future payment for goods being sold. The advanced payment (i.e., the loan) is securitized by the documentation covering the shipment of goods.

ADVANCE BILL 1. A written order to pay drawn prior to the shipment of goods by an importer (the drawer) on the importer's bank (the drawee) requiring that a specific sum be paid to an exporter (the payee) in a given currency. The **DRAFT** that is drawn in this situation is a sight draft requiring immediate payment upon presentation by the exporter. **2.** Invoice presented prior to the receipt of merchandise or services.

ADVANCE DETERMINATION RULING (ADR) Issued by the **INTERNAL REVENUE SERVICE (IRS).** As a means of insuring sound tax compliance, the national office of the IRS and the taxpayer's district director may decide to respond to inquiries of organizations and/or individuals regarding prospective transactions and completed transactions before the inquirer's return is completed. Requests on prospective transactions are handled by the national office while requests on completed transactions are administered by the taxpayer's district director. Advance rulings, however, are generally not issued if the problem is currently present in a return of the taxpayer for a prior year for which a current audit or examination by a district office or branch office of the Appellate Division is currently taking place. An ADR may be sought regarding a transfer pricing question involving a multinational business.

ADVANCED CHARGE A **FREIGHT** charge or other miscellaneous cost that is advanced by one common carrier to another in the process of shipping a good. The advanced charge is ultimately paid for and collected from the entity (the consignee) receiving the goods. (The common carriers are reimbursed for all charges incurred during shipment.)

ADVERTISING The promotion of a company's products or services to stimulate demand. The objective is to improve the company's **MARKET SHARE** and profitability. The trend in the ratio of sales to advertising indicates advertising effectiveness in generating revenue.

ADVISORY CAPACITY The inability or lack of authorization to make changes or adjustments without the approval or agreement of those in authority. For example, in **INTERNATIONAL TRADE,** an agent of the shipper, acting in an advisory capacity, would not have the authority to change a sales order without the express permission of the selling entity.

AFDB. *See* **AFRICAN DEVELOPMENT BANK.**

AFFIDAVIT A written swearing as to a matter or set of facts before a notary public or other duly authorized individual. Types of affidavits include: (1) Those which serve as evidence in a court of law so that a proper legal judgment can be made; (2) Those which state that an individual has been served with notice that they are a party to a pending lawsuit; and (3) Those which give a statement of facts to public officials so that an individual can be arrested.

AFFILIATE A partly or fully owned unit of a multinational company. Affiliates include a wholly owned branch, foreign-incorporated subsidiary, **JOINT VENTURE,** and any other legal foreign operation.

AFFIRMATIVE DUMPING DECISION A country's decision to allow for the intentional selling of products below their normal selling price to a foreign country. As a result, penalties may be assessed against the country.

AFFREIGHTMENT A contractual agreement between a multinational company and carrier to ship products overseas or domestically.

AFLOAT In maritime trade, a reference to the fact that goods have not reached their destination and are still in the process of being transported by sea. Goods that have arrived and have not been unloaded by longshoremen are not deemed to be afloat.

AFRICAN DEVELOPMENT BANK (AfDB) The AfDB was established to provide African countries with capital and financing for the purpose of fostering the economic growth and expansion of its member nations. The AfDB, operating in association with the **UNITED NATIONS DEVELOPMENT PROGRAM (UNDP),** attempts to provide economic support to member countries by granting loans and arranging for technical assistance for projects and programs that stimulate economic development and raise current standards of living. Development projects are financed in such areas as agriculture, public health, transportation, manufacturing, public health, commerce, banking, energy, communications and public utilities. Currently, all African countries, except for the Republic of South Africa, are members. Administratively, the AfDB consists of the AfDB itself, the **AFRICAN DEVELOPMENT FUND,** and the **NIGERIAN TRUST FUND.**

AFRICAN DEVELOPMENT FUND (ADF) A source of financing without interest to African nations for approved programs that stimulate or enhance the social or political well-being, or economic condition, in those countries. The source of funding is through the **AFRICAN DEVELOPMENT BANK.**

AFTER DATE A term used in business and **INTERNATIONAL TRADE** which indicates the **MATURITY DATE** of a credit instrument such as a note or bill of exchange (time draft). The clause "due 45 days after date" written on a **PROMISSORY NOTE** would mean that the note is payable 45 days after the date of the note. For example, a note dated May 1st would mature and be payable on June 15th. *See also* **AFTER SIGHT.**

AFTER MARKET **1.** Trading of securities and money market instruments in secondary financial markets. That is, trading of securities in organized stock exchanges and in the **OVER-THE-COUNTER** markets after the original issuance of the securities has taken place (primary market). **2.** Trading of financial instruments directly among investors. **3.** Purchase and sale of retail merchandise related to large-ticket item sales or events. For example, automobiles, boats, and blockbuster movies all have large after market sales.

AFTER SIGHT A term used in business and **INTERNATIONAL TRADE** which indicates the **MATURITY DATE** of a credit instrument such as a note or bill of exchange (time draft). The clause "due 30 days after sight" written on a **PROMISSORY NOTE** would mean that the note is payable 30 days after the note is presented for payment. For example, a note presented and accepted on May 1st would mature and be payable on May 31st. *See also* **AFTER DATE.**

AGAINST ALL RISK In **INTERNATIONAL TRADE** (especially in maritime commerce) insuring against all risk refers to insuring against the generally expected standard risks recognized by the industry.

AGENCY COSTS **1.** Costs, such as a reduced stock price, that stem from conflicts between managers and stockholders and between stockholders and bondholders. **2.** Fees payable to the agent of a shipping company.

AGENCY/DISTRIBUTOR SERVICE Agent for American exporters registered with the **INTERNATIONAL TRADE ADMINISTRATION** of the United States **DEPARTMENT OF COMMERCE.** The service locates distributors and import agents who are interested in selling and promoting American goods and products abroad.

AGENCY FOR INTERNATIONAL DEVELOPMENT (AID) An agency of the United States government founded by President Kennedy in 1961 whose mission has been to foster social and economic development in the **THIRD**

WORLD. AID has the following initiatives: (1) assisting transition to a **MAR-KET-BASED ECONOMY** in Eastern Europe; (2) establishment of a regulatory framework for securities markets in Indonesia, Jordan, Sri Lanka; (3) road construction and maintenance in Latin America and Southern Asia; and (4) agricultural research and farm credits worldwide. AID fields workers worldwide and administrative officers in Washington identify worthy projects and then ask United States industry to submit proposals. The winners receive government support. The payoff for winning bidders can be significant, including profitable business from a reliable customer-the federal government-and safe entry into international markets. In 1997, AID had $2.5 billion a year in contracts and grants for U.S companies and individual Americans to bid on for its Third World missions. It plays a central role in promoting United States interests in 78 countries worldwide, from Albania to Zimbabwe.

AGENT 1. Under the **LAW OF AGENCY**, an agent is an individual who is authorized to transact business for a person (the principal) on behalf of another (third party). In such a relationship, the actions of the agent fully obligates the principal to the third party and correspondingly give the principal legal rights against the third party. A company, attempting to establish a market for its products abroad, may engage a foreign sales agent who is a bona fide representative of the entity in all contractual negotiations relating to its selling activities. 2. Representative of a government agency (e.g., the **INTERNAL REVENUE SERVICE** or the **SECURITIES EXCHANGE COMMISSION**).

AGGREGATE LIMIT OF LIABILITY In the United States, the maximum an insurance company will cover an insured in a given period of time (e.g., a year, a lifetime, etc.) regardless of the number of claims submitted to the insurance company during that period. The limit is clearly delineated in the insurance policy and is either predetermined by company policy or is determined by negotiations between the insurance company and the insured.

AGGREGATED SHIPMENT A cargo destined for one buyer that has been aggregated by the carrier from smaller lots received from various suppliers. When aggregated, the full lot is transported to the destination point.

AGREED WEIGHT AND VALUATION Amounts that are decided upon by a shipper and common **CARRIER** in a typical shipping contract. The weight of the shipment will determine its transportation costs and the manner best suited for transportation. The valuation of the shipment will determine its rating and classification for insurance purposes.

AGREEMENT A mutual assent between individuals, companies, or countries such as in a legally enforceable contract between competent parties. It is a coming together of two or more minds on a given set of facts with respect to their rights and duties concerning certain past, present, or future facts and performances and rights of the contracting parties.

AGREEMENT CORPORATION Corporation chartered by a state to engage in international banking; so named because the corporation enters into an "agreement" with the **FEDERAL RESERVE BOARD OF GOVERNORS** (United States) to limit its activities to those permitted an Edge Act Corporation. *See also* **EDGE ACT AND AGREEMENT CORPORATION.**

AGRICULTURAL MARKETING SERVICE (AMS) A service of the United States government to assure foreign purchasers of United States goods that they satisfy quality standards and contractual commitments.

AICPA. *See* **AMERICAN INSTITUTE OF CERTIFIED PUBLIC ACCOUNTANTS.**

AID. *See* **AGENCY FOR INTERNATIONAL DEVELOPMENT.**

AIRWAY BILL A document corresponding to the **BILL OF LADING** in land surface transport or of a marine bill of lading in water transport. It is used for goods shipped by air transport.

AISG. *See* **ACCOUNTANT'S INTERNATIONAL STUDY GROUP.**

ALEATORY CONTRACT The performance of one party to a contract depends on some contingent occurrence. An example is a fire insurance policy payable in the event of an uncertain fire at the company's plant.

ALIEN A citizen of a foreign nation currently living in another country without citizenship in that country.

ALIEN CORPORATION A company that is incorporated under the laws and regulations of a foreign nation doing business in a country other than the one in which it was incorporated. Some use the term synonymously with a **FOREIGN CORPORATION.** However, the term foreign corporation more commonly refers (in the United States) to a corporation that is incorporated in one state but does business in another.

ALIENATION The problem in modern industrial societies that some workers become disenchanted with their jobs due to boredom, lack of incentive, lack of motivation, etc.

ALL-EQUITY DISCOUNT RATE An interest rate that is used in **CAPITAL BUDGETING** for discounting future cash flows generated by the project if the project were financed entirely with owners' or stockholders' equity.

ALL IN In transporting goods, a common **CARRIER** commonly quotes a price that incorporates all cargo costs and related charges.

ALLOCATE In accounting, the process of assigning a portion of costs, expenditures, or revenues to those departments, products, customers, processes, or activities responsible for incurring or generating them. The assignment is generally performed on either a proportional basis or other reasonable means of distribution. For example, if three departments occupy a building, the annual **DEPRECIATION** on the building might be allocated to each department based on the square footage that each department utilizes. If a company purchases a group of assets at a **LIQUIDATION** sale, it might choose to allocate the lump sum payment proportionally to each asset purchased (i.e., to the land, building, machinery, etc.) based on their relative component **FAIR MARKET VALUE**(s).

ALL OR NONE 1. A term used by investment banking institutions in bidding for underwriting rights. It indicates the decision to either underwrite the entire issue of an entity's newly issued securities or not participate in the underwriting at all. Alternatively, the investment banking institution may be willing to underwrite the entire issue or any portion that is made available to sell (all or any part). **2.** An investor may execute an all or none order in which his broker is directed to either purchase or sell an order of securities totally or none at all.

ALL RISK INSURANCE COVERAGE A comprehensive type of property insurance that includes coverage for any physical loss or damage to property other than losses specifically excluded. Because of its broad-based nature, all risk insurance begins with the assumption that all losses are covered with the exception of those caused by circumstances enumerated in the policy as exclusions. All risk insurance coverage is commonly used in international maritime trade.

ALONGSIDE The placement of freight next to a carrier ship (e.g., on the dock) so it may be loaded on to the vessel.

ALTERNATIVE RATES Choosing the lowest rate when comparing two or more alternatives for the purposes of deriving the best price.

ALWAYS ACCESSIBLE A port facility's indication to a common **CARRIER** that there will be a provision (at all times) for loading and unloading its freight when it arrives.

AMEND To change or alter for the better. That is, to make modifications that improve. For example, if an international environmental protection agreement is amended by the preagreed number of parties to the original accord, the changes that are made generally have the same status as those in the original agreement and must be adhered to by all contracting parties. *See also* **AMENDMENT.**

AMENDMENT A change or alteration to a contract, agreement, law, or other document. For example, an amendment to a trade agreement will modify the original agreement and require that the participating contracting nations adhere to the modified form of the agreement unless otherwise stipulated. Also, the **GENERAL AGREEMENT ON TARIFFS AND TRADE (GATT)** allows for amendments to be binding only on those countries that accept the modification(s). **GATT** amendments become effective when two-thirds of the participating nations accept them. *See also* **AMEND.**

AMERICAN ACCOUNTING ASSOCIATION (AAA) A national organization of accounting academicians that influences the development of the **GENERALLY ACCEPTED ACCOUNTING PRINCIPLES** through the theoretical research of its professorial membership. Research is disseminated through its committee reports, bulletins (Accounting Education News) and the renowned quarterly national journal, The Accounting Review.

AMERICAN BASIS. *See* **AMERICAN TERM.**

AMERICAN DEPOSITARY RECEIPTS (ADR) Certificates that represent stock in foreign companies. A foreign company places shares in trust with a United States bank, which in turn issues depositary receipts to United States investors. The ADRs, then are claims to shares of stock, and are essentially the same as shares. The depository bank performs all clerical functions-issuing annual reports, keeping a shareholder ledger, paying and maintaining dividend records, and what not-allowing the ADRs to trade in markets just like domestic securities trade. ADRs are traded on the **NEW YORK STOCK EXCHANGE, AMERICAN STOCK EXCHANGE,** and **OVER-THE-COUNTER** markets as a share in stock, minus voting rights. Examples of ADRs are Hanson, Cannon, and Smithkline Beecham. ADRs have become an increasingly convenient and popular vehicle for investing internationally. Investors do not have to go through foreign brokers and information on company operations is usually available in English. Therefore, ADRs are good substitutes for direct foreign investment. They are bought and sold with United States dollars and pay their dividends in dollars. Further, the trading and settlement costs are waived that apply in some foreign markets. The certificates are issued by depository banks (e.g., the Bank of New York). ADRs, however, are not for everyone. Disadvantages include: (1) ADRs carry an element of currency risk. For example, an ADR based on the stock of a British company would tend to lose in value when the dollar strengthens against the British pound, if other factors were held constant. This is because as the pound weakens, less United States dollars are required to buy the same shares of a U.K. company. (2) Some thinly traded ADRs can be harder to buy and sell. This could make them more expensive to purchase than the quoted price. (3) Problems may occur in obtaining reliable information on the foreign companies. It may be difficult to research the selected foreign stocks. For one thing, there may be a shortage of data: the annual report may be all that is available, and its reliability questionable. Furthermore, in many instances, non-United States financial reporting and accounting standards are substantially different from those accepted in the United States. (4) ADRs can be either sponsored or unsponsored. Many ADRs are not sponsored by the underlying companies. Non-sponsored ADRs oblige the purchaser to pay certain fees to the depository bank. The return is reduced accordingly. (5) There are a limited number of issues available for only a small fraction of the foreign stocks traded internationally. Many interesting and rewarding investment opportunities exist in shares with no ADRs.

AMERICAN INSTITUTE OF CERTIFIED PUBLIC ACCOUNTANTS (AICPA) A national organization of practicing Certified Public Accountants. Prior to the **FINANCIAL ACCOUNTING STANDARDS BOARD (FASB),** the Institute provided the national leadership in the development of **GENERALLY ACCEPTED ACCOUNTING PRINCIPLES** through the work of its Accounting Principles Board and its Committee on Accounting Procedure. (The Committee on Accounting Procedure was dissolved in 1959 and the Accounting Principles Board was replaced by the FASB in 1973.) More recently, the institute has established the Accounting Standards Executive Committee to represent it in the area of financial accounting and reporting. The AICPA generates a myriad of publications in accounting, tax, auditing, and management advisory services for its members. It also publishes the prestigious The Journal of Accountancy each month. *See also* **CANADIAN INSTITUTE OF CHARTERED ACCOUNTANTS; INSTITUTE OF CHARTERED ACCOUNTANTS IN ENGLAND.**

AMERICAN QUOTE. *See* **AMERICAN TERM.**

AMERICAN SELLING PRICE (ASP) The price used, for customs purposes, as a tax base for determining import duties. Under this system, the domestic price of competing goods in the U.S is used for this purpose. Since this price is commonly above the actual foreign price, this system is often construed as a projectionist device.

AMERICAN SHARES Shares of equity securities (stocks) of American companies trading on foreign financial markets.

AMERICAN STOCK EXCHANGE (AMEX) The stock exchange located at 86 Trinity Place, New York City, NY 10006-1881. The **AMEX** is known as the Curb Exchange. It generally trades stocks and bonds of small to medium-sized companies, as compared to those of large companies traded on the **NEW YORK STOCK EXCHANGE.**

AMERICAN TERM Also called American basis or American quote, foreign exchange quotations for the United States dollar, expressed as the number of United States dollars per unit of non-United States currency. For example, United States $0.0086956/yen is an American term.

AMEX. *See* **AMERICAN STOCK EXCHANGE.**

AMORTIZATION **1.** Gradual reduction of an amount over time such as the paying off of a debt. **2.** The process followed in allocating the cost of long-lived assets to the periods in which their benefits are derived. Examples are amortized expenses on intangible assets such as **GOODWILL** and organization costs of a firm. For fixed assets, the amortization is called **DEPRECIATION,** but for natural resources, it is called **DEPLETION EXPENSE.**

AMS. *See* **AGRICULTURAL MARKETING SERVICE.**

ANALYSIS The breakup or decomposition of data or information for the purpose of understanding or determining it nature, cause, or reasonableness. For example, a nation might analyze its current **BALANCE OF PAYMENTS** deficit for the purpose of determining why the deficit has increased so much over the last period. An accountant may prepare an analysis of a particular company for the purpose of ascertaining whether investment in the entity is wise. An auditor might prepare an analysis of particular accounts during the course of an audit to make sure that they are properly stated and free from material misstatement. A manager of a multinational company may evaluate **FOREIGN RISK(s),** pricing and quality of products or services, market position, demand/supply relationships, and emerging trends in politics and the marketplace.

ANCHORAGE 1. An anchoring or being anchored. **2.** Fee charged to anchor in the port. **3.** Location where a ship awaits its berth.

ANNUAL PERCENTAGE RATE. DEFINE *See also* **EFFECTIVE INTEREST RATE.**

ANDEAN PACT An agreement made in 1969 between Bolivia, Chile, Columbia, Ecuador, and Peru to form a **CUSTOMS UNION.**

ANNUITY A series of equal periodic payments or receipts. Examples of an annuity are semiannual interest receipts from a bond investment and cash dividends from a preferred stock. There are two types of an annuity: (1) **ORDINARY ANNUITY,** where payments or receipts occur at the end of the period, (2) **ANNUITY DUE,** where payments or receipts are made at the beginning of the period.

ANNUITY DUE. *See* **ANNUITY.**

ANTIDUMPING RESTRICTIONS A government regulation or law to prevent or correct a dumping of products or services by a multinational company in a **FOREIGN MARKET.** For example, the foreign country might outlaw a particular multinational company from engaging in such practice within its borders. Alternatively, the foreign country might assess a very high tariff on dumping and the resulting price disparity.

ANTITRUST Government prevention of anti-competitive practices of companies. For example, the government may block a merger of companies that would have made it a monopoly.

ANTITRUST LAWS Federal statutes making it illegal for companies to prevent competition by engaging in price discrimination, collusion with other companies to control quantity, and other practices to restrain trade in the market for the company's goods or services.

A/P. *See* **AUTHORITY TO PAY.**

APPRECIATION An increase in the worth of real or financial assets over a specified time period. For example, if General Motors stock is bought at $50 per share and now has a market price of $60 per share, the stock has increased in value by $10 per share.

APPRECIATION OF THE DOLLAR Also called, strong dollar or **REVALUATION.** A rise in the foreign exchange value of the dollar. A strong dollar makes Americans' cash go further overseas and reduces import prices-generally good for United States consumers and for foreign manufacturers. If the dollar is overvalued, United States products are harder to sell abroad and at home, where they compete with low-cost imports. This helps give the United States its huge **TRADE DEFICIT.** A weak dollar can restore competitiveness to American products by making foreign goods comparatively more expensive. But too weak a dollar can spawn **INFLATION,** first through higher import prices and then through spiraling prices for all goods. Even worse, a falling dollar can drive foreign investors away from United States securities, which lose value along with the dollar. A strong dollar can be induced by interest rates. Relatively higher interest rates abroad will attract dollar-denominated investments which will raise the value of the dollar. The following table summarizes the impacts of changes in foreign exchange rates on the multinational company's products and services. See also **DEPRECIATION OF THE DOLLAR.**

THE IMPACTS OF CHANGES IN FOREIGN EXCHANGE RATES		
	Weak Currency (Depreciation)	**Strong Currency (Appreciation)**
Imports	More expensive	Cheaper
Exports	Cheaper	More expensive
Payables	More expensive	Cheaper
Receivables	Cheaper	More expensive
Inflation	Fuel inflation by making imports more costly	Low inflation
Foreign investment	Discourage foreign investment. Lower return on investments by international investors.	High interest rates could attract foreign investors.
The effect	Raising interests could slow down the economy.	Reduced exports could trigger a trade deficit.

APPROPRIATE **1.** Foreign government seizes a multinational company's property with or without full or partial reimbursement. **2.** Assigning property for a specific use.

APPROPRIATE TECHNOLOGY The technology-whether advanced, intermediate, or undeveloped, or whether labor intensive, intermediate, or capital intensive-that fits best for the distribution of the factors of production for the country using it. For example, in countries where labor is relatively cheap and abundant, appropriate technology would be labor-intensive.

A/R. *See* **ACCOUNTS RECEIVABLE.**

ARBITRAGE The purchase and sale of the identical security or commodity at the same time in different markets. Arbitrage attempts to profit from market inefficiencies. The arbitrager sells the security on the exchange with the higher price and buys the security on the exchange with the lower price. The following formula is used:

$$\text{Profit} = (\text{Higher price - Lower price}) \times \text{Quantity}$$

EXAMPLE
ABC Company is at $25 per share on the **NEW YORK STOCK EXCHANGE (NYSE)** and $25.25 per share on the **TOKYO STOCK EXCHANGE (TSE).** If the company's investment manager buys 1,000,000 shares on the NYSE and sells the same number of shares on the TSE, the profit equals:

$$\text{Profit} = (\$25.25 - \$25) \times 1,000,000 \text{ shares} = \$250,000$$

This effect continues until the prices on the exchanges become in parity.

ARBITRAGEUR An individual or business that practices **ARBITRAGE.**

ARBITRATION **1.** An independent party (or parties) formulates a judgment after listening to the issues and disputes between management and labor. The arbitrator's decision is binding on the parties. **2.** A third party (or parties) decides on the merits of a dispute between companies and makes a "finding" decision.

ARBITRATION OF EXCHANGE The cost of foreign currency varies from country to country. When an international importer purchases goods from an exporter, it may be in the importer's best interests to purchase a **BILL OF EXCHANGE (DRAFT)** in a different country to pay the exporter. Doing this would enable the importer to take advantage of a relative favorable currency exchange in that country for payment in another.

ARM. *See* **ADJUSTABLE RATE MORTGAGE.**

ARRANGEMENT FOR SUPPORTED EXPORT CREDITS One agreement that exists among the 23 participating **ORGANIZATION FOR ECONOMIC COOPERATION AND DEVELOPMENT** countries is an arrangement effecting the general guidelines relating to supported export credits. The considerations that are incorporated into the agreement include required cash down payments, interest rates, and repayment terms. Although these guidelines are voluntary and cannot be enforced, they are generally adhered to by the members of the group.

ARM'S LENGTH PRICE A price set in an arm's length transaction, which is entered into by unrelated parties, both acting in their own self-interests. It is assumed that in this type of transaction the price used is the **FAIR MARKET VALUE** of the product or service being transferred in the transaction.

ARM'S LENGTH TRANSACTION. *See* **ARM'S LENGTH PRICE.**

ARRIVAL DRAFT A financial instrument that has to be accepted about the same time the shipment is received at its destination. The draft is typically paid at that time.

ASCRIBED GROUP A membership in an organization or affiliation based on a cultural classification such as age, sexual preference, or religion.

ASEAN. *See* **ASSOCIATION OF SOUTHEAST ASIAN NATIONS.**

ASIAN CURRENCY UNIT (ACU) A unit of a Singaporean bank that deals in foreign currency deposits and loans.

ASIAN DEVELOPMENT BANK (ADB) A multilateral development finance institution whose capital stock is owned by 56 member countries. The bank is engaged in promoting the economic and social progress of its developing member countries (DMCs) in the Asian and Pacific region. Its headquarters are in Manila, Philippines. The bank began operations in December 1966. It is owned by the governments of 40 countries from the region and 16 countries from outside the region. During the past 30 years, the bank has been a catalyst in promoting the development of the most populous and fastest-growing region in the world. The bank makes loans and equity investments. It provides technical assistance grants for the preparation and execution of development projects and programs, and also for advisory purposes. It promotes investment of public and private capital for development purposes. It responds to requests for assistance in coordinating development policies and plans of DMCs. The bank gives special attention to the needs of the smaller and **LESS DEVELOPED COUNTRIES.** It gives priority to regional, subregional, and national projects and programs which contribute to the harmonious economic growth of the region as a whole and which promote regional cooperation. The bank's ordinary capital resources (OCRs) consist of subscribed capital, reserves, and funds raised through borrowings. It has special funds, made up of contributions from member countries, accumulated net income, and amounts previously set aside from paid-in capital. Loans from OCRs on nonconcessional terms account for about 70 percent of cumulative bank lending. These loans are generally made to member countries which have reached a somewhat higher level of economic development.

ASIAN-DOLLARS Dollar-denominated deposits held in Asian-based banks.

ASK PRICE Also called **OFFER PRICE**. The price at which a dealer is willing to sell foreign exchange securities or commodities.

ASP. *See* **AMERICAN SELLING PRICE**.

ASSEMBLY SERVICE A CARRIER provides its terminal as a location for it to assemble the multinational company's cargo such as merging smaller lots of items into one larger one.

ASSESSMENT 1. Percentage allocation of a cost to an activity or program. **2.** Fee due a foreign government for some activity or valuation. An example is a tax on the value of imported products. **3.** Penalty charged such as a foreign government's penalty fee on a multinational company for dumping its products on a foreign market. **4.** Appraising the importance of something such as the effectiveness of an advertising campaign for certain products in the Asian markets.

ASSIGNMENT 1. Transfer of something from one party to another such as property, securities, and legal rights. For example, the assignor may transfer to the assignee an interest in land, a title to a bill, or transfer of an interest in an invention. An assignment for the benefit of creditors is an assignment of the property of an insolvent debtor to a trustee who will use it to pay the debtor's creditors. **2.** Process of writing a **PROMISSORY NOTE with ACCOUNTS RECEIVABLE** as collateral. **3.** Transferring rights under an insurance policy to another. **4.** Transferring the lessee's entire interest in a lease to another. However, if the assignee does not pay, the original lessee is typically required to do so.

ASSISTS Reference to American manufactured component parts that are shipped to foreign manufacturing plants for incorporation into products that are assembled there for subsequent export back to the United States. A duty assessed by the United States **CUSTOMS SERVICE** is levied on these components when they are imported back into the United States as part of the completed finished goods.

ASSOCIATION AGREEMENT An agreement between or among countries to assist each other economically and financially.

ASSOCIATION OF SOUTHEAST ASIAN NATIONS (ASEAN) An association set up in 1967 designed to establish a free trade area between Brunei, Indonesia, Malaysia, the Philippines, Singapore, and Thailand.

ASTRAY FREIGHT 1. Enroute shipment to a specified buyer. **2.** Shipping going off the right path in error.

AT BEST An order given to a broker or representative that the securities or goods being bought or sold should be transacted at the current market price (i.e., at the best possible price that the market will bear). *See also* **AT OR BETTER**.

AT OR BETTER An order given a broker or representative that the securities or goods being bought or sold should be transacted at the price requested by the client or better. For example, if securities are being purchased, the broker will attempt to purchase the securities at the price requested or lower. On the other hand, if securities are being sold, the broker will attempt to sell them for the price requested or greater. *See also* **AT BEST.**

AT RISK A tax concept (United States) that limits the deductibility of losses from business and income-producing activities. At risk limits apply to individuals and closely-held corporations and were established to prevent the deductibility of losses in excess of the actual amount of the investment that was made. Under current United States **INTERNAL REVENUE SERVICE** rules, the amount an individual may deduct in a given taxable year is limited to the amount at risk. This amount is defined as being the total of: (1) the adjusted basis of the property and cash contributed to the investment activity and (2) amounts that are borrowed (for which an individual is personally liable) or property pledged as security property not being used in the investment. The at risk limit is increased each year by the taxpayer's share of net income in the activity or decreased by his share of its losses. For example, if an individual incurs a combined cash investment and personal debt of $150,000 in a partnership venture and has taxable income from the activity of $25,000, then his at risk limit is $175,000.

AT SIGHT A designation indicating the fact that a negotiable instrument or **DRAFT** is payable on demand upon presentation or sight. Alternatively, a **TIME DRAFT** is generally payable at a future time after acceptance. *See also* **AFTER SIGHT, BILL OF EXCHANGE, NOTE.**

ATTACHMENT **1.** Addendum to an insurance policy (United States) indicating additional coverage or exclusions to primary coverage that was purchased. For example, a policy covering fire and theft may contain attachments indicating augmented coverage for replacement cost, vandalism, etc. The term attachment is synonymous to **RIDER** or **ENDORSEMENT.** **2.** A court order taking a defendant's property to pay a debt due the plaintiff.

AUTARKY A self-sufficient economy in which a country reduces as much as possible its importation of products and services. Instead, domestic manufacturing is emphasized, and the country seeks to isolate itself from **INTERNATIONAL TRADE** and relationships. In almost all cases, such a policy proves to be short-lived.

AUTHORITY **1.** Having the power or right to command and direct. For example, a corporation that owns more than 50 percent of the voting stock of another company has sufficient equity to maintain total control and authority over the investee. **2.** An agency of a government or corporation that has the power to administer a function or program. For example, the Port Authority of New York administers, among other things, all the bridges and tunnels in the New York City area.

AUTHORITY TO PAY **1.** A document issued by a bank, used in **INTERNATION-AL TRADE** (especially in the Far East), which commits the bank to acquire **DRAFT**(s) up to a designated amount drawn on an importer. When this document is presented to a seller of goods, the bank's credit is substituted for the importer's credit. This virtually eliminates any risk on the part of the seller in selling goods to the importer. *See also* **LETTER OF CREDIT.** **2.** A right granted another to purchase goods on the entity's behalf.

AUTHORITY TO PURCHASE. *See* **AUTHORITY TO PAY.**

AUTOMATIC ADJUSTMENT MECHANISM The automatic response of an economy that is triggered when **BALANCE OF PAYMENTS** imbalance occurs. When a **TRADE DEFICIT** exists under **FLEXIBLE EXCHANGE RATES,** a **CURRENCY DEVALUATION** generally occurs to invigorate exports and lessen imports. Under **FIXED EXCHANGE RATES,** domestic **INFLATION** is anticipated to be below a foreign counterpart, which leads to relatively cheaper domestic products, thereby increasing exports and reducing imports.

AUTOMATION The use of the latest technology in the manufacturing process to increase productivity, improve quality, and lower costs. An example is using robots instead of people.

AUTONOMOUS A tax charged on a multinational company by a foreign government.

AVERAGE **1.** The arithmetic mean computed by deriving the sum of the numbers being evaluated and dividing it by the count of numbers in the sum. For example, the simple average of foreign earnings of $150,000 in 1999, $200,000 in 1998, and $140,000 in 1997 is $163,333 ($150,000 + $200,000 + $140,000 = $490,000/3 years). **2.** Synonymous with the term particular average as used in the maritime insurance industry. It refers to a loss associated with maritime insurance coverage by damage caused by an accident on the high seas. **3.** A measure of central tendency.

AVERAGE EXCHANGE RATE. *See* **EFFECTIVE EXCHANGE RATE.**

AVERAGE HAUL The average distance a ton is transported by a **CARRIER.** For example, if 20 tons of freight travel 200 miles, the average haul equals 10 miles per ton. *See also* **AVERAGE LOAD.**

AVERAGE LOAD The average tons of freight per vehicle (e.g., ship, truck) transporting it. For example, if 50 tons are transported by five trucks, the average load is 10 tons per truck. *See also* **AVERAGE HAUL.**

AVERAGE TAX RATE Also called effective tax rate, the tax rate applicable to all taxable income. It is computed as follows:

Total tax liability ÷ Taxable income

EXAMPLE

If XYZ Corporation has $160,000 in taxable income, the tax obligation is calculated as follows:

Income($)	x	Marginal Tax Rate	=	Taxes($)
50,000	x	15 percent		$7,500
25,000	x	25 percent		6,250
85,000	x	34 percent		28,900
60,000	x	5 percent		(surcharge) 3,000
				$45,650

The average tax rate then is $45,650/$160,000 = 28.53 percent. This contrasts with **MARGINAL TAX RATE.**

AWAY Quoted price differing from the prevailing market price for a particular product or service.

B

BACK DRAFT The process of dating a draft, check, or bill of exchange earlier than the date on which it is drawn. *See also* **DRAFTS** and **BILL OF EXCHANGE.**

BACKGROUND NOTES A publication of the United States State Department that provides trade and economic information on countries that trade with the United States.

BACKSPREAD A minimal difference between the price of a security that is selling in two different financial markets (e.g., the **NEW YORK STOCK EXCHANGE** and the **TORONTO STOCK EXCHANGE**) at the same time. This phenomenon results in **SECURITIES ARBITRAGING.** Securities arbitraging is the buying and selling of the same security at the same time in different markets for the purpose of taking advantage of a small price difference. The practice of arbitraging results in the minimization of price differences throughout world markets. *See also* **ARBITRAGE.**

BACK-TO-BACK FINANCING A system of financing used in **INTERNATIONAL TRADE** between importer and exporter. An exporter will make use of back-to-back financing generally when obtaining credit in its own country is either too difficult or expensive (e.g., high interest rates). An importer makes a deposit of funds in a bank or otherwise guarantees a loan in favor of an exporter with whom he does business who is located in another country. The exporter is now able to go to a local branch of the bank in which the importer deposited funds or guaranteed the loan and borrow funds in his country's currency. When the loan matures and is paid by the exporter, the importer is able to withdraw the funds that were deposited or withdraw the guarantee of funds that was made.

BACK-TO-BACK LETTER OF CREDIT A form of **PRETRADE FINANCING** in which the exporter employs the importer's **LETTER OF CREDIT** as a means for obtaining credit from a bank, which in turn supports its letter of credit to the exporter.

BACK-TO-BACK LOANS Also called link financing, parallel loans, or fronting loans. **1.** An intercompany loan in which two affiliates located in separate nations borrow each other's currency for a specific period of time, and repay the other's currency at an agreed maturity. These loans are frequently channeled through a bank. Back-to-back loans are often used to finance affiliates located in countries with high interest rates or restricted **CAPITAL MARKETS** or with a danger of **CURRENCY CONTROLS** and different tax rates applied to loans from a bank. They contrast with a **DIRECT INTERCOMPANY LOAN** which is direct and does not involve an intermediate bank. The loan process is depicted below.

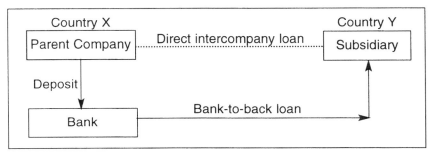

2. A loan in which two multinational companies in separate countries borrow each other's currency for a specific period of time, and repay the other's currency at an agreed maturity. The loan is conducted outside the **FOREIGN EXCHANGE MARKET** and often channeled through a bank as an **INTERMEDIARY.**

BACKWARDATION A pricing system for **FUTURES** contracts in commodities in which the cost of the contract decreases as the **MATURITY DATES** increase.

BAHT Thailand's currency.

BAILEE RECEIPT A bailee is a party that has temporary control and custody of the property of another. A bailee receipt which indicates title to the property is frequently used in financing arrangements in which the custodial property is the collateral.

BAILMENT The transferring of possession and control of property or goods for some designated purpose but not title to it. It is held in trust. After the designated purpose has been fulfilled, the property or goods are returned. Examples are the consignment of goods from the consignor to consignee, and a bank retaining collateral from a borrower. The deliverer is termed the bailer and the receiver is called the bailee. The bailee, when in possession of the property, must exercise reasonable care regarding the safety of the article.

BALANCE **1.** A portfolio concept implying that risk needs to be weighted against return in order to pick the right kind of investment. **2.** Difference between total debits and credits in an account. 3. Balance of a loan or a bank account.

BALANCE OF PAYMENTS (BOP) A systematic record of a country's receipts from, or payments to, other countries. In a way, it is like the balance sheets for businesses, only on a national level. The reference you see in the media to the **BALANCE OF TRADE** usually refer to goods within the goods and services category of the current account. It is also known as **MERCHANDISE TRADE** or **VISIBLE TRADE** because it consists of tangibles like foodstuffs, manufactured goods, and raw materials. "Services," the other part of the category, is known as **INVISIBLE TRADE** and consists of intangibles such as interest or dividends, technology transfers, services (such as insurance, transportation, financial), and so forth. When the net result of both the current account and the **CAPITAL ACCOUNT** yields more credits than debits, the country is said to have a surplus in its balance of payments. When there are more debits than credits, the country has a deficit in the balance of payments. The following figure presents the components of each and their interrelationships. Data are collected by the United States Customs Service. Figures are reported in seasonally adjusted volumes and dollar amounts. It is the only non-survey, non-judgmental report produced by the United States **DEPARTMENT OF COMMERCE**. The balance of payments appears in **SURVEY OF CURRENT BUSINESS**. *See also* **ADJUSTMENT APPROACH**.

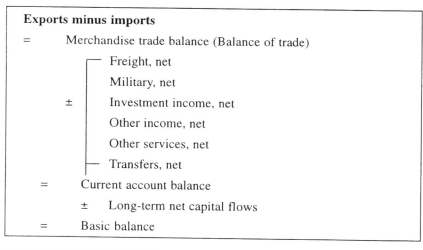

BALANCE OF PAYMENTS (BOP) ACCOUNTING A double-entry bookkeeping system that is used to record transactions that appear in the **BALANCE OF PAYMENTS**. Every transaction is recorded as if it consisted of an exchange of something for something else-that is, both as a debit and a credit. In the case of merchandise imports, for example, goods are normally acquired for money or debt. Imports are recorded as a debit and payment as a credit. By the same token, exports are recorded as a credit and payment as a debit. Where items are given rather than exchanged, special types of counterpart entries are made in order to furnish the required offsets. Just as in accounting, the words **DEBITS** and **CREDITS** have no value-laden meaning-either good or bad. They are merely rules or conventions; they are not economic truths. Under the conventions of double-entry bookkeeping, an increase in the assets of an entity is always recorded as a debit and an increase in liabilities as a credit. Thus, a debit records (1) the import of goods and services, (2) increase in assets, or (3) reductions in liabilities. A credit records (1) the export of goods and services, (2) a decrease in assets, or (3) increases in liabilities.

BALANCE OF PAYMENTS (BOP) ADJUSTMENT An adjustment that is necessary to correct an imbalance (a disequilibrium) of payments. There are three major ways of doing this: (1) the use of fiscal and monetary policies to vary the prices of domestically produced goods and services vis-á-vis those made by other countries so as to make exports relatively cheaper (or more expensive) and imports more expensive (or cheaper) in foreign currency terms. (2) changes in the exchange rate between currencies so as to make exports cheaper (or more expensive) and imports more expensive (or cheaper) in foreign currency terms. (3) the use of tariffs, quotas, controls, and the like, to affect the price and availability of goods and services. *See also* **ADJUSTMENT APPROACH; BALANCE OF PAYMENTS.**

BALANCE OF TRADE Also called **VISIBLE TRADE** or **MERCHANDISE TRADE BALANCE,** an entry in the **BALANCE OF PAYMENTS** measuring net flows of merchandise (exports minus imports) between countries. Thus if exports of goods exceed imports the trade balance is said to be 'favorable,' or to have a trade surplus, whereas an excess of imports over exports yields an 'unfavorable' trade balance or a trade deficit. The balance of trade is an important item in calculating balance of payments.

BALANCE ON CURRENT ACCOUNT. *See* **CURRENT ACCOUNT BALANCE.**

BALANCE SHEET Also known as the Statement of Financial Position, the balance sheet describes the status of the firm's assets, liabilities, and stockholders' equity cumulatively as of a specific date. An entity's balance sheet is generally classified into three major categories: assets, liabilities, and stockholders' equity. These three categories are, in turn, classified into other balance sheet categories. For example, assets are made of current assets and long-term assets; liabilities consist of current liabilities and long-term liabilities. Stockholders' equity consists of paid-in capital accounts and retained earnings. The balance sheet formula is considered to be the primary accounting equation. The formula is:

$$\text{Assets} = \text{Liabilities} + \text{Stockholders' equity}$$

Assets are the economic resources owned by the business. Liabilities are the entities to whom the business' resources are owed. Stockholders' equity is the ownership interest.

BALANCE SHEET EXPOSURE. *See* **ACCOUNTING EXPOSURE.**

BALANCE SHEET HEDGING The strategy of a multinational company of using **HEDGING** (such as a **FORWARD CONTRACT**) to avoid international risk (i.e., **TRANSLATION EXPOSURE, TRANSACTION EXPOSURE,** and/or **OPERATING EXPOSURE)** that would potentially adversely affect the company's balance sheet. This strategy involves bringing exposed assets equal to exposed liabilities. If the goal is protection against translation exposure, the procedure is to have monetary assets in a specific currency equal monetary liabilities in that currency. If the goal is to reduce transactions or economic exposure, the strategy is to denominate debt in a currency whose change in value will offset the change in value of future cash receipts.

BALANCED ECONOMY The economic condition in which a nation's value of imports equals its exports. *See also* **BALANCE OF TRADE.**

BALLOON A large final payment made at the end of a series of payments on a loan or other long-term obligation such as on a commercial property mortgage or bond which fully satisfies the debt. For example, a schedule of repayments for a borrower may require 59 monthly payments of $10,000 and a balloon payment of $50,000 in the last (or 60th) month.

BALTIC FREIGHT INDEX (BFI) An index derived from a specified number of cargo shipments weighted based on market importance. It is used to determine the trend in prices for commercial shipping. The index is published in the **JOURNAL OF COMMERCE**.

BAND The range in which a currency is within a freely floating exchange rate.

BANK CLEARING. *See* **CLEARING.**

BANK DRAFT A DRAFT addressed to a bank. It is the instrument used for payment in foreign trade. The draft may be a **SIGHT DRAFT,** i.e., payable on presentation when received, or a **TIME DRAFT,** payable at the time specified on the document itself -normally 30, 60, 90, or 120 days.

BANK GUARANTEE Comparable to a **LETTER OF CREDIT** issued by a bank which guarantees the payment of its customer's drafts up to a stated amount for a certain period of time. The customer is usually a local importer who needs the bank guarantee so that a foreign exporter will ship goods to him without fear of default. The bank guarantee provides the exporter with the assurance that the bank cover any of its customer's (importer) drafts. This guarantee effectively eliminates any selling risk on the part of the exporter.

BANK LOAN SWAP An arrangement structured to protect an amount of principal from future changes in the **FOREIGN EXCHANGE RATE**. It consists of the purchase of a foreign currency which remains on deposit in the bank (with accrued interest) with the simultaneous forward sale of the same foreign currency on deposit at a future date that occurs on the same date as the **MATURITY DATE** of the deposit.

BANK RELEASE A bank release occurs as a result of the acceptance by the bank of a **TIME DRAFT** drawn on it by an exporter allowing the purchaser (importer) of the goods to take delivery. However, it may be necessary for others to approve the release as well. For example, clearance from Federal Customs or other governmental agencies may be required before the goods may be unequivocally released to the importer. A bank release improves the credit standing of the importer by putting the bank upon which the time draft is drawn behind the transaction.

BANK SWAP A SWAP made between banks to avoid foreign exchange risk. Swaps are popular with banks since it is difficult to avoid risk when trading in many specific future dates and in many different currencies.

BANKER'S ACCEPTANCE A **TIME DRAFT** drawn by a business firm whose payment is guaranteed by the bank's "acceptance" of it. It is especially important in foreign trade when the seller of goods can be certain that the buyer's **DRAFT** will actually have funds behind it. Banker's acceptances are money market instruments actively traded in the **SECONDARY MARKET.**

BANKER'S BILL In **INTERNATIONAL TRADE,** a **BILL OF EXCHANGE** drawn by an exporter directly on the importer's bank in payment for goods and services sold.

BARGAINING UNIT A union representing employees with the employer or representatives of management engaging in contractual negotiations and implementation.

BARRIERS TO ENTRY A company (monopoly) or companies in an industry create obstacles for new companies trying to enter the industry such as underpricing their goods or controlling the availability of raw materials.

BARTER The exchange without cash of merchandise or services between two entities. In accounting and taxes, the transaction should be accounted for at fair market value. An example of a barter exchange is a TV station giving "air time" in exchange for electronic equipment provided by a supplier.

BASE CURRENCY The national currency that is used to quote the comparative exchange rate of another national currency. It is used in quoting the number of units of one currency that may be exchanged for one unit of another. The base currency usually represents the denominator of the comparative ratio. For example, if $7.9010 Mexican Pesos may be exchanged for one United States Dollar, the United States Dollar is considered the base currency and the Mexican Peso is termed the quoted currency.

BASE MONEY The amount of money required by the United States Federal Reserve System that a bank must hold on reserve. The requirement is quoted in the form of a percentage of its deposits.

BASIC BALANCE In a **BALANCE OF PAYMENTS,** all of the current account items plus the net exports of long-term capital during a given time period.

BASIS For tax purposes, the value of an asset used for calculating **DEPRECIATION, DEPLETION, AMORTIZATION,** and gain and loss on sale or exchange. The basis of an asset is initially established by its acquisition cost.

BASIS POINT A unit of measure for the change in interest rates for bonds and notes. One basis point is equal to 1/100th of a percent, that is, 0.01 percent. Thus 100 basis points is equal to 1 percent. For example, an increase in a bond's yield from 6.0 percent to 6.5 percent is a rise of 50 basis points.

BASKET PEGGER A foreign nation using **FIXED EXCHANGE RATES** based on a mix of two or more foreign currencies.

B/E. See **BILL OF EXCHANGE.**

BEAR SQUEEZE Short sellers of securities, commodities, or currencies hoping that prices will drop must sell their positions at losses because prices in fact are increasing. *See also* **SELLING SHORT.**

BEARER BOND **1.** A **TIME DRAFT** drawn by a business firm whose payment is guaranteed by the bank's "acceptance" of it. It is especially important in foreign trade, when the seller of goods can be certain that the buyer's **DRAFT** will actually have funds behind it. A **BANKER'S ACCEPTANCE** is a money market instrument actively traded in the **SECONDARY MARKET.** **2.** A **BOND** which does not have the owner's name recorded; its coupons can be clipped and cashed by any holder.

BEARER SECURITIES Securities that are not registered in the name of the individual or entity who owns them. Ownership is determined by physical possession. For example, the person who presents the coupons of a bearer bond (sometimes called a coupon bond) for payment is entitled to the interest payments. Upon maturity, the person presenting the bearer bond for repayment is entitled to its principal. *See also* **COUPON.**

BEGGAR-MY-NEIGHBOR POLICIES Economic measures taken by one country unilaterally to improve its domestic economic status, which may negatively impact the position of other countries located by it. The measures include **CURRENCY DEVALUATION** or trade protection. For example, a country may increase domestic employment by increasing exports or reducing imports by devaluing its currency or exerting **TARIFFS, QUOTAS,** or **EXPORT SUBSIDIES.** The benefit which it acquires is at the expense of some other country which experiences lower exports or increased imports and a consequent lower level of employment. Such a country may then be forced to retaliate by a similar type of measure. To avoid confrontation of this kind, various international organizations have been set up to regulate the conduct of **INTERNATIONAL TRADE.**

BENCHMARK COUNTRY A country used for purposes of comparing measurable variables such as economic performance, product or process evaluation, marketing strategies, etc., with that of other countries. Such an analysis enables the country making the comparison with the benchmark country to ascertain what it is doing incorrectly or determine what changes have to be made so that improvement may be achieved. A country may be chosen as a benchmark because of the success it has achieved in a given area.

BENEFICIARY **1.** The entity or person to whom annuity benefits or insurance proceeds are payable. **2.** A reference to the exporter in an **INTERNATIONAL TRADE** arrangement. **3.** The seller for whose benefit a **LETTER OF CREDIT** is issued. **4.** The entity or person in a trust agreement for whose benefit assets or property are held.

BERTH TERMS The owner of the shipping vessel is responsible for the loading and discharging fees.

BEST EFFORTS A commitment in the offering of a new security issuance (e.g., stock) to the public by **UNDERWRITERS** or **INVESTMENT BANKERS** to use their "best efforts" to successfully sell the entire issue by a given promised date.

BETA COEFFICIENTS A measure of a security's (or mutual fund's) volatility relative to an average security (or market portfolio). Put it another way, it is a measure of a security's return over time to that of the overall market. For example, if ABC's beta is 2.0, it means that if the stock market goes up 10 percent, ABC's common stock goes up 20 percent; if the market goes down 10 percent, ABC goes down 20 percent. Here is a guide for how to read betas:

Beta	What It Means
0	The security's return is independent of the market. An example is a risk-free security such as a T-bill.
0.5	The security is only half as responsive as the market.
1.0	The security has the same responsive or risk as the market (i.e., average risk). This is the beta value of the market portfolio such as **STANDARD & POOR'S 500 (S&P500).**
2.0	The security is twice as responsive, or risky, as the market.

Beta of a particular stock is useful in predicting how much the security will go up or down, provided that investors know which way the market will go. Beta helps to figure out risk and expected (required) return.

Expected (required) return = risk-free rate + beta x (market return - risk-free rate) .The higher the beta for a security, the greater the return expected (or demanded) by the investor.

EXAMPLE

ABC stock actually returned 8 percent. Assume that the risk-free rate (e.g., the return on a T-bill) = 5.5 percent, market return (for example, the return on the S&P 500) = 9 percent, and ABC's beta =1.2. Then the return on ABC stock required by investors would be:

Expected (or required) return = 5.5 percent + 1.2 (9 percent - 5.5 percent)
= 5.5 percent + 4.2 percent
= 9.7 percent

Since the actual return (8 percent) is less than the required return (9.7 percent), you would not be willing to buy the stock. Betas for stocks (and mutual funds) are widely available in many investment newsletters and directories. Below is a list of some selected betas:

Stocks	Betas
Philip Morris	1.20
Charles Schwab	2.20
Dow Chemical	1.00
Exxon	0.65
Pfizer	1.10
General Motors	1.15
Coca-Cola	1.10

Source: Value Line Investment Survey, (April-May 1997), published by Value Line, Inc., 711 3rd Avenue, New York, NY 10017.

BFI. *See* **BALTIC FREIGHT INDEX.**

BID Also called a **QUOTATION** or **QUOTE.** The highest price anyone has declared that he wants to pay for a security or property at a particular time.

BID-ASK SPREAD The spread between the bid and the asked price which is the lowest price anyone will take at the same time.

BIG BANG 1. The liberalization of the London capital markets that took place in the month of October, 1986. **2.** Those advocating very significant changes in the policies of a country or multinational company.

BILATERAL AGREEMENT 1. Contract involving mutual commitment between two parties. **2.** An agreement between two nations. Commonly, this agreement is in the area of trade, i.e., relating to the exchange of goods and services between two participating nations. *See also* **BILATERAL TRADE.**

BILATERAL MONOPOLY There is only one seller and one buyer in the market for a product or service.

BILATERAL TRADE The sale and reciprocal purchase flow of goods and services between the two countries that have agreed to this exchange for the purpose of mutually improving their trade relations. *See also* **BILATERAL AGREEMENT.**

BILL OF CREDIT A written statement generated by a person or entity requesting that its bank honor the payment of a specific amount of money to the bearer of the note to be drawn against the writer's account or available credit.

BILL OF EXCHANGE (B/E) Also called a **DRAFT,** an order written by an exporter instructing an importer or an importer's agent such as a bank to pay a specified amount of money at a specified time. The individual or business initiating the bill of exchange is called the maker, while the party to whom the bill is presented is called the drawee. *See also* **ARBITRATION OF EXCHANGE.**

BILL OF LADING (B/L) A **TIME DRAFT** drawn by a multinational company whose payment is guaranteed by the bank's "acceptance" of it. It is especially important in **INTERNATIONAL TRADE,** when the seller of goods can be certain that the buyer's **DRAFT** will actually have funds behind it. **BANKER'S ACCEPTANCES** are money market instruments actively traded in the **SECONDARY MARKET.**

BILL OF SALE A written document which transfers goods, title or other interests from a seller to a buyer and specifies the terms and conditions of the transaction.

BIND 1. During trade negotiations, a country may agree to bind or not to change the level of a given tariff. That is, the country may commit itself not to increase a given tariff and thus maintain the status quo. **2.** A course of action committed to by a company.

BINDER 1. A deposit on the purchase of property in order to hold it. The deposit may or may not be refundable depending on the terms. For example, a binder based on third-party approval may be refundable if such approval is not given. **2.** Temporary insurance coverage pending a regular policy.

B/L. *See* **BILL OF LADING.**

BLACK MARKET 1. An illegal or underground **FOREIGN EXCHANGE MARKET.** **2.** A sort of underground market where products or services are traded in violation of law or at the price exceeding the legally acceptable one. The situation occurs usually when there exist limited supply and strong demand for certain items.

BLACKLISTED 1. A group of individuals or organizations that have been found to be unacceptable for a particular function, event, activity, or operation. For example, a business organization may decide not to buy any goods from a par-

ticular foreign company because of perceived quality deficiencies, discrimination policies, or questionable business policies. **2.** The government of a country may preclude any its domestic companies from buying or selling goods to
companies of another country because of political considerations. This ban
may extend to traveling to the other nation as well. A recent example is when
the United States government placed restrictions on foreign companies that do
business with Iran. **3.** A list of those censured.

BLACK-SCHOLES OPTION PRICING MODEL (OPM) An option pricing
equation developed in 1973 by Fischer Black and Myron Scholes. It is used to
price OTC options and value option portfolios, or evaluate option trading on
exchanges. The model provides the relationship between call option value and
the five factors that determine the premium of an option's market value over
its expiration value: **1.** Time to maturity. The longer the option period, the
greater the value of the option. **2.** Stock price volatility. The greater the volatility of the underlying stock's price, the greater its value. **3.** Exercise price. The
lower the exercise price, the greater the value. **4.** Stock price. The higher the
price of the underlying stock, the greater the value. **5.** Risk-free rate. The higher the risk-free rate, the higher the value. The formula is:

$$V = P[N(d_1)] - Xe^{-rt}[N(d_2)]$$

where V = Current value of a call option
P = current price of the underlying stock
$N(d)$ = cumulative normal probability density function = probability
that a deviation less than d will occur in a standard normal distribution.
X = exercise or strike price of the option
t = time to exercise date
(For example, 3 months means $t = 3/12 = 1/4 = 0.25$)
r = (continuously compounded) risk-free rate of interest
$e = 2.71828$

$$d_1 = \frac{\ln(P/X) + [r + s^2/2]t}{s\sqrt{t}}$$

$$d_2 = \frac{\ln(P/X) + [r + s^2/2]t}{s\sqrt{t}} \quad or = d_1 - s\sqrt{t}$$

s^2 = variance per period of (continuously compounded) rate of return
on the stock

The formula, while somewhat imposing, actually requires readily available
input data, with the exception of s^2, or volatility. P, X, r, and t are easily
obtained.

The implications of the option model are the following:
1. The value of the option increases with the level of stock price relative to
the exercise price (P/X), the time to expiration times the interest rate (rt),
and the time to expiration times the stock's variability (s^2t).
2. Other properties:
a. The option price is always less than the stock price.

b. The option price never falls below the payoff to immediate exercise (P - EX or zero, whichever is larger).

c. If the stock is worthless, the option is worthless.

d. As the stock price becomes very large, the option price approaches the stock price less the present value of the exercise price.

EXAMPLE

You are evaluating a call option which has a $20 exercise price and sells for $1.60. It has 3 months to expiration. The underlying stock price is also $20 and its variance is 0.16. The risk free rate is 12 percent. The option's value is:

First, calculate d1 and d2:

$$d_1 = \frac{\ln(P/X) + [r + s^2/2]t}{s\sqrt{t}}$$

$$= \frac{\ln(\$20/\$20) + [0.12 + (0.16/2)](0.25)}{(0.40)\sqrt{0.25}}$$

$$\frac{0 + 0.05}{0.20} = 0.25$$

$$d_2 = d_1 - s\sqrt{t} = 0.25 - 0.20 = 0.05$$

Next, look up the values for $N(d_1)$ and $N(d_2)$:

$N(d_1) = N(0.25) = 1 - 0.4013 = 0.5987$
$N(d_2) = N(0.05) = 1 - 0.4801 = 0.5199$

Finally, use those values to find the option's value:

$V = P[N(d_1)] - Xe^{-rt}[N(d_2)]$

$= \$20[0.5987] - \$20e^{(-0.12)(0.25)}[0.5199]$
$= \$11.97 - \$19.41(0.5199)$
$= \$11.97 - \$10.09 = \$1.88$

At $1.60, the option is undervalued according to the Black-Scholes model. The rational investor would buy one option and sell .5987 shares of stock short.

BLANKET CERTIFICATE A written government declaration that is filled out by an exporter who intends to make continuous shipments of goods to a particular importer. This certificate (also known as a blanket certificate of origin) is filed in lieu of separate certificates for each shipment. *See also* **CERTIFICATE OF ORIGIN.**

BLANKET RATE An across-the-board rate applying uniformity to all items of a group of goods, to all shipments from one location to another, etc. For example, in order to protect a fledgling domestic industry from cheaper competitive goods, a government may assess a blanket tariff rate on all imports (worldwide) that may threaten that industry's survival and growth.

BLOCK A significant number of shares or bonds owned or traded. A trade of 10,000 or more shares is typically the guideline.

BLOCK EXCHANGE. *See* **EUROPEAN UNIT OF ACCOUNT.**

BLOCKED CURRENCY A currency which is illegal to convert to another specified one. There is a government restriction on the transfer of the currency for some reason such as economic or political.

BLOCKED FUNDS Funds in one nation's currency that may not be exchanged without restriction for foreign currencies due to exchange controls or other reasons.

BOARD OF SUPERVISION The group of elected individuals who pass the laws and regulations of a small municipality, town, city, hamlet, etc., representing an important part of the governing body of the entity.

BOILERPLATE A uniform and standardized wording usually in fine print in contracts such as in insurance, rentals, or sales agreements. The provisions are typically to benefit the preparer of the document.

BOLIVAR Venezuela's currency.

BOLIVIANO Bolivia's currency.

BONA FIDE Acting in good faith and genuinely without deceit or fraud. An example is a legitimate international transaction for goods.

BONA FIDE RESIDENT An individual who legally resides in a foreign country, has a legal right, and meets the foreign residency requirements of the home country.

BONDED 1. The condition of having secured insurance coverage protecting an entity from all losses that may be incurred due to the acts of its employees. **2.** In **INTERNATIONAL TRADE,** the status of imported goods being stored in a government commissioned warehouse until all required duties are paid. The goods, known as "bonded goods" may not be removed until the duty payments are made. **3.** Status of having posted a bond providing security that a tax will be paid when due. 4. Debt in the form of a bond. **5.** Currency not easily convertible into others.

BONDED EXEMPTION An exemption on certain goods of government **IMPORT DUTIES** (or the rebate of previously paid duties) if the goods are utilized in the production of another product that is subsequently exported.

BOOK VALUE 1. The net assets (total assets minus total liabilities), divided by the number of common shares outstanding. Book value of a business may be substantially different from market value. **2.** The net assets minus the value of the preferred stock. This provides the book value of the common stockholders' equity. **3.** The net amount of a fixed asset (such as plant, machinery and equipment) equal to the gross cost minus accumulated **DEPRECIATION.** For example, if a firm buys a piece of equipment for $200,000 with a 10-year life and no salvage value and straight line depreciation is employed, the depreciation per year will be $20,000 ($200,000/10 years). The book value of the machine at the end of the first year is $180,000 ($200,000 - $20,000).

BOOKING NUMBER A number assigned to something **(INVOICE, BILL OF LAD-ING,** contract) reflecting a transaction so that reference may be made to it, if needed.

BOOM The condition of experiencing a rapid expansion (growth) in all phases of business activity. The expansion may show itself in the stock market and/or in the overall economy and commonly results in an increased demand for goods and services and inflationary pressure on prices.

BOOMERANG EFFECT 1. A situation where technology sold to firms in one nation is used against the seller of the technology. This is one reason why firms often fear to sell their technology abroad and face the competition later. **2.** Taking steps to reduce the effect of product **DUMPING.**

BORDER BARRIERS The physical restrictions at a country's borders to monitor and control imported products. They may be designed to restrict import flows of certain products, enable the assignment of different duties depending on the country the product is received from or quantity involved, and stop products or property representing a health hazard.

BORDER TAX ADJUSTMENTS The provision in the **GENERAL AGREEMENT ON TARIFFS AND TRADE,** under which imported goods are subject to some or all of the tax levied in the importing country and reexported goods are duty free.

BOTTOM-FISHING An investment strategy of buying securities that are very undervalued at their low prices. The expectation is that the securities will recover in value and should be bought. In some cases, investors look for financially troubled companies which are about to turnaround.

BOYCOTT Singularly or collectively unifying others (individuals, groups, nations, etc.) with the refusal to buy the products or services sold by one or many individuals, groups, organizations, or nations for the purpose of punishing or coercing that individual or entity. For example, boycotts are frequently used by consumers in an effort to lower the prices of certain goods.

BRANCH 1. A foreign operation not incorporated in the **HOST COUNTRY,** in contrast to a **SUBSIDIARY. 2.** An office of a company geographically situated away from the headquarter's main location.

BRAND LOYALTY Customers' repurchase of goods because of the goods' brand name association.

BRAND NAME Also called **TRADE NAME**. The spoken or visible version of the brand identification, often protected by a trademark (e.g., Coke, Tide, MasterCard). It can be a name, symbol, design, or other element that identifies one multinational company's product and differentiates it from other competitive products. The brand or trade name may, over time, get to hint high quality and dependable service and be the reason for the buyers' loyalty to the product.

BREACH The failure to fulfill a contractual promise, perform some agreed-upon act, or comply with a legal duty to society. Examples are when a government or a party to a contract unilaterally violates a legal agreement or commitment. Damages may be sought by the aggrieved party. An anticipatory breach is the refusal to perform in the future some pre-existing contractual obligation.

BREAK 1. A significant reduction in the sales price of a good or service. For example, an advertised "price break" **(DISCOUNT)**. **2.** A sudden and profound drop in the price of a singular security or group of securities (commonly relating to a particular industry or group). For example, an across the board stock price break for banks occurred when the Federal Reserve decided to raise interest rates to control inflationary pressures. **3.** To cause an individual, company, or other entity to declare bankruptcy. **4.** Breaking down a large shipment into smaller ones. **5.** Stroke of good luck for a business. **6.** Discrepancy in the accounts of a business.

BREAK BULK The breaking down of a large cargo into smaller ones destined for a particular buyer. It may be done to facilitate the shipment, lower insurance premiums, or improve safety.

BREAKOUT 1. The increase in the price of a stock or bond above a previous highest price **(RESISTANCE LEVEL)** or a decrease in the price of the security below a previous lowest price **(SUPPORT LEVEL)**. In a breakout, there is a continuous upward or downward movement. A graph showing a breakout follows:

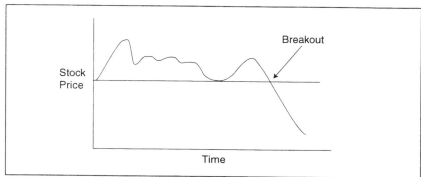

2. Penetration of the price of a security into a range that was not expected. For example, a breakout occurs when the price of a particular security significantly increases even though the other prices of securities in the industry have dropped due to selling pressures.

BRETTON WOODS AGREEMENT A 1944 agreement at an international conference with representatives of 40 countries in Bretton Woods, New Hampshire, that established the **INTERNATIONAL MONETARY SYSTEM** in effect from 1945 to 1971. Each member government pledged to maintain a fixed, or pegged, exchange rate for its currency versus the dollar or gold. These **FIXED EXCHANGE RATES** were designed to reduce the riskiness of international transactions, thus promoting growth in global trade.

BRETTON WOODS CONFERENCE A conference in 1944 in which representatives of 40 nations got together to map a new **INTERNATIONAL MONETARY SYSTEM.**

BRIEF A written summary and analysis of testimony and arguments in a judicial matter. It covers legal points, statutes, and precedents in prior cases. The brief is filed in connection with a motion, trial, or appeal.

BROADLINE GLOBAL COMPETITION The **COMPETITIVE STRATEGY** that involves diverse product lines manufactured in one or more industries with sales in many nations. *See also* **PRODUCT LINE.**

BROKER An individual that represents a buying or selling party for the purpose of effecting a purchase or sale without actually entering into the transaction itself. For example, a securities broker will purchase or sell the securities of its clients for a **COMMISSION.** An insurance broker acts as an **INTERMEDIARY** between the insurance company and insured. In **INTERNATIONAL TRADE,** a freight or customs broker will contract with interested third parties on behalf of its clients. *See also* **BROKERAGE FEE.**

BROKERAGE FEE The **COMMISSION** or fees charged by a **BROKER** or brokerage firm for the performance of its services. For example, a broker charges a $50 fee for the purchase of 100 shares of AT&T for its client.

BROKERS' MARKET The market for exchange of financial instruments between any two parties using a **BROKER** as an **INTERMEDIARY** or agent. The brokers' market in the case of foreign exchange typically involves a huge portion of the trades that involve two commercial banks as buyer and seller.

BROWN ITEM **1.** Durable goods. **2.** Furniture.

BRUSSELS TARIFF NOMENCLATURE. *See* **CUSTOMS COOPERATION COUNCIL NOMENCLATURE.**

BUDGETING A process of developing a quantitative plan of activities and programs expressed in terms of the assets, equities, revenues, and expenses which will be involved in carrying out the plans, or in other quantitative terms such as units of product or service. The budget expresses the organizational goals in terms of specific financial and operating objectives. Advantages of budget preparation are planning, communicating company-wide goals to subunits, fostering cooperation between departments, control by evaluating actual figures to budget figures, and revealing the interrelationship of one function to another.

BULK SHIPMENT Unpackaged, unbound goods being transported. An example is grain.

BULLDOGS Foreign bonds sold in the United Kingdom. See also FOREIGN BOND.

BULLET A loan taken out by a multinational company to be repaid in a lump sum at the **MATURITY DATE.**

BUNDESBANK The German central bank equivalent to the Federal Reserve Bank of the United States. Its primary goals are to (1) set the discount rate, known as the **LOMBARD RATE,** (2) monitor the money supply, and (3) assist economic policies.

BUSINESS A commercial enterprise structured in the form of a sole proprietorship, **PARTNERSHIP,** or **CORPORATION** whose primary purpose is to earn a profit on the money and resources contributed by its owners. The business, which is considered independent and separate from its owners (from an accounting prospective) sells goods, provides services, or performs some other function for the purpose of earning net income. During the operation of the business, the investments made by the owners of the business are totally at risk. If the business incurs losses, the owners' investments will be reduced. If, on the other hand, the business is successful and generates net income, the owners' investment will increase.

BUSINESS AMERICA A publication of the United States Department of Commerce providing important information on **INTERNATIONAL TRADE** and marketing. It is published biweekly and is available on request from the United States Printing Office in Washington, DC.

BUSINESS CYCLE The regular pattern of expansion (recovery) and contraction **(RECESSION)** in aggregate economic activity around the path of trend growth, with effects on growth, employment, and inflation. At the peak of the cycle, economic activity is high relative to trend, while at the trough (valley) of the cycle, the low point in economic activity is reached. In cycles, we see movements in GNP, unemployment, prices, and profits, although the movements are not so regular and predictable. A first clue to the source of business cycles is found in the large amplitude of fluctuations of investment or durable CAPITAL GOODS. Although most economists agree on this fact, they differ in their emphasis upon external or internal factors. Increasingly, however, they lean toward a synthesis of external and internal factors. The business cycle tends to have an impact on corporate earnings, cash flow, and expansion. Forecasting the business cycle is still difficult and inexact. Today, the most successful forecasters use medium-to large-scale computer models, based on statistical estimates, to forecast future changes in the economy.

BUSINESS ENVIRONMENT RISK INDEX An index measuring the uncertainty associated with the business conditions in many foreign countries. It is issued every 3 months.

BUSINESS INTERRUPTION INSURANCE Insurance protection to reimburse a company for lost profits due to a catastrophe. An example was the payment to businesses damaged in the World Trade Center bombing during the reconstruction period. Such coverage is advisable to reduce risk of multinational companies.

BUSINESS UNIONISM A union view that seeks to maximize economic returns to union members rather than social reforms to benefit working classes.

BUY AMERICAN POLICY A variation of "buy-local policy," a policy used particularly by the United States government to urge the public to buy American-made goods. Governments, buyers, and sellers themselves, have the power to shun or foster **INTERNATIONAL TRADE** in ways not available to private firms and are free to do so as they like in their purchases for their own use. The international **TOKYO ROUND OF MULTILATERAL NEGOTIATIONS** trade pact signed in 1979, however, calls for more open international competition in bidding for government contracts.

BUY AT BEST An instruction given to a **BROKER** indicating that the quantity requested be filled without regard to price. That is, the broker is ordered to bid whatever price it will take (without limit) to purchase the quantity demanded by the client.

BUYBACK A multinational company repurchases its stock (called treasury stock) or bonds in the open market. The company may buy its stock back for several possible reasons such as to increase market price per share of its stock held by the public or to prevent a takeover by having less shares outstanding. A multinational company may retire its bonds before maturity if the interest rate on the bond is higher than prevailing market interest rates.

BUYBACK AGREEMENT In **COUNTERTRADE,** a contract between the exporter and importer in which the initial export sale is for **CAPITAL GOODS** that is used to manufacture products that are at a later date used as payment by the importer.

BUYER'S MARKET The ability of the buyer to significantly influence price due to excess supply or glut. This market situation may occur in a certain sector or in the entire economy. The buyer has leverage and can obtain a bargain price and/or terms.

C

CABLE TRANSFER In **INTERNATIONAL TRADE,** the process of transferring funds, by cablegram, from one individual (or entity) to another located overseas. The transfer is usually made bank to bank in the form of a **DRAFT.** For example, a customer deposits money in his bank account and requests his bank to cable transfer the funds, for a fee, to another individual's account in a bank in a foreign country. When the funds are transferred, they are available for use by the recipient.

CALENDAR SPREADING The concurrent purchase and sale of options of the same category having differing expiration dates. *See also* **EXPIRATION DATE.**

CAD. *See* **CASH AGAINST DOCUMENTS.**

CALL 1. An option to buy (or "call") an asset at a specified price within a specified period. **2.** The right to buy 100 shares of stock at a specified price within a specified price. See also **OPTIONS. 3.** The process of redeeming a bond or preferred stock issue before its normal **MATURITY.** A security with a call provision typically is issued at an interest rate higher than one without a call provision. This is because investors demand it-they look at yield-to-call rather than **YIELD-TO-MATURITY. 4.** A **CALL LOAN** payable upon notice of the lender.

CALL LOAN Loan made by brokers from banks to cover required security positions of their clients. Rates for call loans are commonly quoted in the newspapers as an indicator of short-term borrowing rates.

CALL MONEY 1. Also called **DAY-TO-DAY MONEY** or **DEMAND MONEY,** interest-bearing deposits payable upon demand. An example is Euromarket deposits. **2.** Money loaned by banks to brokers, payable at call, on demand.

CALL OPTION. *See* **CALL.**

CALL PRICE The amount of money that investors of a callable bond or preferred stock will receive when they must involuntarily redeem their securities to the issuing entity. The call decision rests solely with the issuer. The call price is generally set at a slightly higher amount than par or liquidation price of the security. An issuing corporation will generally "call" its callable bond or preferred stock issue when the market rate of interest falls below the rate that the security is paying. For example, a company may choose to call a bond that has an eight percent stated rate of interest if the market rate of interest has fallen to six percent.

CALL PROVISIONS. *See also* **EUROBONDS.**

CALLABLE BOND A bond that is issued with a contractual provision allowing the issuer of the bond to redeem it from the investor. The call provision may be outstanding for the full term of the bond or a portion of it. Generally, the issuer must pay a **PREMIUM** (an amount above par) in the redemption.

CALVO DOCTRINE The assertion that legal disputes arising from international affairs affecting a multinational company are handled by the judicial system in the foreign country.

CAMBISM The business of selling or buying foreign currency.

CANADIAN INSTITUTE OF CHARTERED ACCOUNTANTS National organization of Canadian Chartered Accountants. The Chartered Accountant (CA) license designation in Canada is equivalent to the Certified Public Accountant (CPA) license designation in the United States. The Canadian Institute of Chartered Accountants, like its American counterpart, the American Institute of Certified Public Accountants in the US, supports research and professional projects and publishes the monthly prestigious journal, CA Magazine, for its readership. Topics commonly covered in the journal include: all areas of accounting, auditing, information systems, international accounting, professional ethics, estate planning, taxation, and financial management. See also **AMERICAN INSTITUTE OF CERTIFIED PUBLIC ACCOUNTANTS; CERTIFIED PUBLIC ACCOUNTANT.**

CAP The maximum limit of interest generally associated with adjustable rate mortgages. Several caps exists in an adjustable rate mortgage. For example, a life-of-loan cap refers to the maximum interest rate that the mortgage can have over the entire life of the loan. The annual adjustment cap refers to the maximum amount of interest rate increases that can occur in a given year.

CAPACITY 1. Upper limit of production constrained by such variables as labor, materials, capital, and plant and equipment. Capacity limits, defined in terms of units, man hours, dollars, etc., are developed by management for current control and planning purposes. There are several measures of capacity that require explanation. Measurements of capacity begin with maximum capacity. This level assumes that ideal conditions exist in the factory and that production of output is occurring all (100 percent) of the time. Practical capacity is derived by subtracting downtime, repair time, weekend time, holidays, etc., in which no production takes place. This level represents the maximum level of production at which acceptable efficiency can be achieved. Normal capacity is a level of production (less than practical capacity) that will satisfy demand for the entity's products over a sufficiently long period that considers seasonal, cyclical, and trend variation. Budgeted capacity is the level of production that will satisfy next year's use. An index of **CAPACITY UTILIZATION** and capability equal to the ratio of actual output to potential output. **2.** Weight restriction for cargo of a transporting vehicle (e.g., delivery truck). **3.** Legal competency to act as a representative of a multinational company.

CAPACITY UTILIZATION The ratio of units produced to the capacity level of the production facility. A high ratio reflects manufacturing productivity.

CAPITAL ACCOUNT A balance of payment account that records transactions involving the purchase or sale of capital assets. *See* **BALANCE OF PAYMENTS.**

CAPITAL ASSET PRICING MODEL (CAPM) A model stating that the expected return on a security is a function of (1) the risk-free rate, (2) the security's **SYSTEMATIC RISK,** and (3) the expected **RISK PREMIUM** in the market. A security risk consists of two components:diversifiable risk and nondiversifiable (or systematic) risk. Diversifiable risk, sometimes called controllable risk or unsystematic risk, represents the portion of a security's risk that can be controlled through diversification. This type of risk is unique to a given security. Business risk, liquidity risk, and default risk fall into this category. Nondiversifiable risk, sometimes referred to as noncontrollable risk or systematic risk, results from forces outside of the firm's control and is therefore not unique to the given security. Purchasing power risk, interest rate risk, and market risk fall into this category. Nondiversifiable risk is assessed relative to the risk of a diversified portfolio of securities, or the market portfolio. This type of risk is measured by the beta coefficient. The capital asset pricing model (CAPM) relates the risk measured by beta to the level of expected or required rate of return on a security. The model, also called the security market line (SML) (See the following figure), is given as follows: $rj = rf + b (rm - rf)$ where ri = the expected (or required) return on security I, rf = the risk-free security (such as a T-bill), rm = the expected return on the market portfolio (such as Standard & Poor's 500 Stock Composite Index) , and b = Beta, an index of nondiversifiable (noncontrollable, systematic) risk. In words, the CAPM or (SML) equation shows that the required (expected) rate of return on a given security (rj) is equal to the return required for securities that have no risk (rf) plus a risk premium required by investors for assuming a given level of risk. The higher the degree of systematic risk (b), the higher the return on a given security demanded by investors. *See also* **BETA COEFFICIENT.**

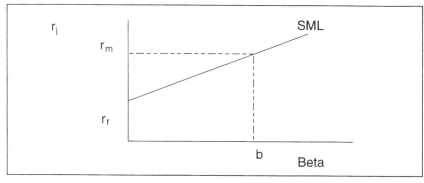

CAPITAL BUDGETING The process of deciding whether or not to commit resources to a project whose benefits will be spread over several time periods. There are typically two types of investments: **1.** Selection decisions in terms of obtaining new facilities or expanding existing facilities. Examples include: (a) Investments in long-term assets such as property, plant, and equipment. (b) Resource commitments in the form of new product development, market research, refunding of long-term debt, introduction of a computer, etc. **2.** Replacement decisions in terms of replacing existing facilities. Examples include replacing a manual bookkeeping system with a computerized system and replacing an inefficient lathe with one that is numerically controlled. As such, capital budgeting decisions are a key factor in the long-term profitability of a firm. To make wise investment decisions, managers need tools at their disposal which will guide them in comparing the benefits and costs of various investment alternatives.

CAPITAL CONTROLS Partial controls over outflows of short-term and long-term capital often used (1) to achieve balance of payment equilibrium, at desired exchange rate level, (2) execute economic development priorities, (3) to support various foreign policy goals, and (4) affect the patterns and size of international business operations in a country. These controls restrict not only capital outflows but imports as well. *See also* **BALANCE OF PAYMENTS; CAPITAL INFLOW/OUTFLOW.**

CAPITAL EXPORTS. *See* **CAPITAL FLIGHT.**

CAPITAL FLIGHT Also called capital exports, the export or movement of capital resources out of a country, typically for fear of **ECONOMIC RISK** or **POLITICAL RISK.**

CAPITAL GOODS Long-lived assets that are purchased for use in the operation of the firm rather than being held for resale as inventory. Capital goods consist of land, buildings, equipment, natural resources, intangibles (e.g., patents, copyrights, trademarks) etc., used by the entity to perform its primary business function(s).

CAPITAL INFLOW/OUTFLOW A decrease (increase) in the assets of a nation held by others outside the country or an increase (decrease) in the foreign assets of a nation held by individuals or entities in the country.

CAPITAL INTENSIVE An industry or company with primarily property, plant and equipment (capital) rather than labor. A capital intensive business usually has a high ratio of fixed costs to total costs. It has risk in an economic downturn because if revenue declines it cannot reduce fixed costs (which are constant) in the short-term. As a result, profitability decreases. Examples of capital intensive industries are airlines and auto manufacturers. *See also* **LABOR INTENSIVE.**

CAPITAL MARKETS The markets for long-term debt and corporate stocks. The **NEW YORK STOCK EXCHANGE (NYSE),** which trades the stocks of many of the larger corporations, is a prime example of a capital market. The **AMERICAN**

STOCK EXCHANGE and the regional stock exchanges are also examples. In addition, securities are issued and traded through the thousands of brokers and dealers on the over-the-counter market. The capital market is the major source of long-term financing for business and governments. It is an increasingly international one and in any country is not one institution but all those institutions that canalize the supply and demand for long-term sources of capital, e.g. the stock exchanges, underwriters, investment bankers, banks, and insurance companies.

CAPITAL OUTFLOW. *See* **CAPITAL INFLOW/OUTFLOW.**

CAPITAL STOCK Equity shares in a corporation that are issued for cash or other assets paid into the business by its owners. Capital stock consists of all the classes of stock issued by a business entity, e.g., **COMMON STOCK** and **PREFERRED STOCK** issues. However, if only one class of securities exist, it must be voting common stock. If there are more than one class of stock, the additional classes represent stock that have some preference or restriction of basic rights.

CAPITALISM A system in which capital is privately owned. It is a social and economic system in which individuals are free to own the means of production (land, buildings, equipment and other materials, etc.) of goods and services for consumption by society.

CAPITALISTIC ECONOMIC SYSTEM. *See* **ECONOMIC SYSTEM.**

CAPM. *See* **CAPITAL ASSET PRICING MODEL.**

CARGO A shipment of freight being transported such as by ship, truck, or airplane.

CARGO INSURANCE Insurance protection against loss or damage to goods that is incurred during transportation by a common carrier at sea. The owner of the goods generally must collect from the common carrier first. Any excess loss is then recoverable under the policy from the insurance company. War zone coverage, loss due to delay of shipment, loss of market, and damages due to dampness are generally excluded in a standard cargo insurance policy. However, cargo war risk coverage protecting the goods during their transportation by sea or air while in a war zone may be separately purchased from the insurance company. In general, cargo insurance coverage may be purchased for all shipments of goods that are made (most commonly purchased by shippers) or may be purchased for a single shipment only. *See also* **MARINE CARGO INSURANCE.**

CARGO TONNAGE The weight ton of freight. In the United States, it is about 2,000 to 2,240 pounds.

CARIBBEAN BASIN INITIATIVE (CBI) A United States government policy established in 1983 aiming at stimulating private-sector business in Central America and the Caribbean through tariff reductions and other incentives.

CARIBBEAN COMMON MARKET (CARICOM) An association of English-speaking Caribbean nations forming a customs union.

CARICOM. *See* **CARIBBEAN COMMON MARKET.**

CARNET A form allowing the temporary importation of specific products without a duty charged used in some countries. It may apply to samples of products used for sales promotion purposes.

CARRIAGE CHARACTER The carrier's fee for transporting freight.

CARRIER 1. The company that transports cargo and freight for others by ship, airplane, train or truck. Generally referred to as the common carrier. 2. A company that is engaged in the transportation of people for compensation. For example, American Airlines is one of the largest airline carriers in the world today.

CARRIER'S CERTIFICATE A statement from a common carrier to customs agents attesting that the imported goods to which it relates are bona fide and may be cleared through customs. In addition, the document certifies that the individual or entity named on the document is duly entitled to receive the merchandise being shipped.

CARRY 1. To convey or transport from one place to another. 2. In margin stock acquisitions, the loaning of money by a broker to a customer in order to pay for the securities. The broker will ultimately be repaid with interest. 3. To maintain in one's accounting records. 4. The interest charge when financing the acquisition of securities. 5. To hold merchandise. 6. To support or subsidize a product or service.

CARTAGE The charge to transport merchandise by a moving vehicle (e.g., trucks, carts).

CARTEL A producer association that controls the supply, pricing, and marketing policies of its members to restrict competition and maximize their gains. The **ORGANIZATION OF PETROLEUM EXPORTING COUNTRIES** is a prime example of a cartel.

CASH AGAINST DOCUMENTS As an **INTERNATIONAL TRADE** term, payment given upon presentation of the **BILL OF LADING.**

CASH DELIVERY A brokerage term referring to the delivery of securities on the same day of the trade.

CASH IN ADVANCE The prepayment for freight prior to shipping, or if shipped, before delivery. This arrangement might be suitable for smaller orders or for custom-made products.

CASH POOLING The combining of cash from various sources for some common benefit or purpose.

CASH POSITION **1.** The amount of cash held by an entity at a given point in time. Cash is often expressed as a percentage of current assets and/or total assets. The cash position of an entity is very important in evaluating its **LIQUIDITY** and financial flexibility. **2.** In foreign currency transactions, the amount of cash at the disposal of the trader for use in acquisitions and other needs.

CASH WITH ORDER (CWO) Purchase of merchandise in which the buyer pays for the goods when the goods are ordered rather than when they are received. Such an acquisition represents a bona fide transaction and is binding on both buyer and seller.

CATALOG EXHIBITS A small, inexpensive exhibit of a smaller multinational company's catalogs and videos used to promote and evaluate the items' market appeal to foreigners. Companies may want to contact the **INTERNATIONAL TRADE ADMINISTRATION** for guidance and referrals (e.g., qualified foreign personnel to make presentations).

CAUSE OF ACTION A legal claim giving rise to the right to sue another such as one party's failure to abide by the terms of a contract.

CBI. *See* **CARIBBEAN BASIN INITIATIVE.**

CCC. *See* **CUSTOMS COOPERATION COUNCIL.**

CCCN. *See* **CUSTOMS COOPERATION COUNCIL NOMENCLATURE.**

CEASE AND DESIST ORDER A court order prohibiting a company from continuing an action or conducting an operation in which it is currently engaged. An example of this is an illegal activity such as a company's violation of government pollution control standards.

CENTRAL BANKS Government institutions with authority over the size and growth of the nation's money supply. They commonly regulate commercial banks and are architects of the nation's monetary policy. Central banks frequently intervene in the foreign exchange markets to smooth fluctuations. For example, the **BUNDESBANK** is a central bank of Germany while the **FEDERAL RESERVE SYSTEM** is the central bank in the United States

CENTRAL BANK SWAPS Central banks of nations exchange their currencies to maintain international transferability and protect themselves against changes in foreign exchange rates. Exchanges or swaps between these two nations occur at the official exchange rate and enables a country to obtain a source of foreign exchange to be used when it needs another nation's currency to support its own currency's relative value during times of crises or other contingencies. See also **FOREIGN EXCHANGE RATE.**

CENTRALIZATION A method of structuring the flow of authority and control in a country or business organization in which decision making is relegated to the upper levels of the entity rather than the lower levels. In this type of organization, delegation of authority is minimized and the flow of information is from the top down rather than from the bottom up as would occur in a decentralized entity. The greater the amount of entity centralization, the higher the level in which the decision making resides. It provides greater uniformity within the business.

CENTRALIZED CASH MANAGEMENT The management practice used by a multinational company to place the responsibility for managing corporate cash balances from all affiliates under the custody of a single, central office-commonly in New York or London.

CERTIFICATE An official or sworn document that conveys some fact. For example, a certificate of registry of a ship indicates that the ship has been legally registered in a given country. A stock certificate shows that an entity has a bona fide investment in some corporation. A bond certificate evidences a company's indebtedness. A diploma is a certificate attesting to the successful completion of a course of study by an individual.

CERTIFICATE OF ANALYSIS Attestation required by a governmental agency or an importer indicating that overseas purchased goods meet minimum standards of quality.

CERTIFICATE OF HEALTH An attestation document required by nations importing goods that the commodities being exported meet minimum standards of cleanliness, quality, and purity. Exporters must arrange to have the certificate of health completed.

CERTIFICATE OF MANUFACTURE An attestation document used with a **LETTER OF CREDIT in INTERNATIONAL TRADE.** The certificate is completed by the producer of the merchandise and is signed by the exporter. It indicates that the merchandise that has been ordered by the importer has been duly completed and made available for shipment.

CERTIFICATE OF ORIGIN A shipping document that states the country of origin (manufacture) of goods. The certificate is often received from an organization (e.g., chamber of commerce). Upon presentation of such certificate, a lower import duty may be assessed or trade restrictions relaxed.

CERTIFICATE OF WEIGHT Attestation document used in **INTERNATIONAL TRADE** indicating the weight of a given shipment of goods.

CET. *See* **COMMON EXTERNAL TARIFF.**

C&F. *See* COST AND FREIGHT.

CFC. *See* COMMON FUND FOR COMMODITIES; CONTROLLED FOREIGN CORPORATION.

CHAMBER OF COMMERCE A council or association of business individuals who have come together for the purpose of promoting their business interests. A chamber of commerce is most commonly formed at the local level but may also be established at higher levels. For example, the International Chamber of Commerce is a private organization made up of the national trade councils of 60 nations established for the purpose of promoting private enterprise and the interests of businesses at the national and international level.

CHANNEL MANAGER 1. The company that has a significant influence in a marketing system that controls the channel of distribution of particular goods and services. The channel of distribution represents the organizational structure used by an entity in the vertical transfer of merchandise from the manufacturing level to the final user. The channel manager is the company in the system that dominates decisions such as what goods and services are developed and marketed (as well as how they are marketed) through the channel. *See also* **CHANNEL OF DISTRIBUTION. 2.** A corporate manager responsible for keeping price increases to the lowest possible level.

CHANNEL OF DISTRIBUTION The structure that an entity utilizes in vertically transferring goods from the manufacturing level to the final user. Intermediary or middlemen levels situated throughout the channel include: (1) Merchants defined as middlemen who take legal title to the inventory and then resell it as a means of generating profit for themselves. Examples of merchant middlemen include wholesalers and retailers. (2) Agents defined as middlemen who do not take legal title to the goods but act as agents in the sale of the inventory. Examples of agent middlemen include sales agents, brokers, and manufacturers' representatives. *See also* **AGENT; BROKER.**

CHARGES FORWARD Costs incurred in the exportation of goods into a country. Such costs include: brokerage fees, legal costs, vessel captain fees, trade commission fees, etc. *See also* **BROKERAGE FEE.**

CHARTERING AGENT The broker specializing in obtaining availability on shipping vessels for freight.

CHEAP DOLLAR. *See* APPRECIATION OF THE DOLLAR.

CHECK RATE The primary rate used to compute all other rates used in foreign exchange trades.

CHIPS. *See* CLEARINGHOUSE INTERBANK PAYMENT SYSTEM.

CIF. *See* **COST, INSURANCE, AND FREIGHT.**

CIP. *See* **COMMODITY IMPORT PROGRAM.**

CKD. *See* **COMPLETELY KNOCKED DOWN.**

CLAIM 1. In **INTERNATIONAL TRADE,** the monetary assertion by an individual against a common carrier for reimbursement of losses incurred in the process of transporting goods from one location to another. **2.** The demand by an individual against an insurance company for reimbursement for losses incurred to insured property. **3.** An assertion of a right to property or money.

CLASSIFICATION (FREIGHT) Reference to a publication of categories and classes of commercial ships afloat (Lloyd's Registry) regarding size, quality, condition, etc. for insurance purposes (applying class rates) and employment.

CLEAN BILL OF LADING Certificate issued by a common carrier indicating a receipt of goods in good condition without any apparent damages or missing items. If the condition of the goods is questionable or it is clear that part of the shipment is missing, such a document cannot be issued.

CLEAN COLLECTION A means of collecting funds by an exporter from a sale of goods by submitting to the bank only the importer's draft with instructions for collection. In essence, a clean collection is nothing more than a means of financing exportation.

CLEAN FLOAT Unrestricted changes in foreign currency exchange rates as a result of market conditions unobstructed by governmental restrictions. *See also* **FLOATING EXCHANGE RATES.**

CLEAN LETTER OF CREDIT. *See* **NONDOCUMENTARY LETTER OF CREDIT.**

CLEAN REPORT OF FINDINGS A certificate issued by a reputable examining or investigative agency indicating that the inspected items are in order and within the parameters of acceptability.

CLEAR CUSTOMS The process of preparing imported goods for customs clearance into a country. The procedure consists of filing appropriate forms, providing the requisite documents, having the goods inspected and valued for customs duty assessments, paying those duties, etc., and finally obtaining full clearance if all requirements have been met. This process may also be performed by utilizing the services of a **CUSTOMS BROKER.**

CLEAR RECORD A record indicating that a shipment of goods successfully reached its destination without any destruction or damage.

CLEARANCE **1.** A document issued by customs agents indicating that permission has been granted to a ship, truck, or airplane to enter or leave a port, airport, or other location as a result of satisfying all customs requirements. **2.** The granting of access to an individual to a restricted area. **3.** The passage of bank drafts or checks through a clearinghouse. *See also* **BANK DRAFT. 4.** The act of being cleared through customs. **5.** A special sale of a particular type of merchandise so as to reduce inventory levels.

CLEARING **1.** The exchange of checks and drafts that occurs between banking institutions with the resulting accounting and adjustments for differences that arise therefrom. Bank clearing generally occurs in a facility known as a clearinghouse. **2.** A clearinghouse technique of protecting buyers and sellers of **FUTURES** contracts against loss by assuring performance on each contract. In this process, the clearinghouse becomes a buyer to each seller and a seller to each buyer.

CLEARINGHOUSE INTERBANK PAYMENT SYSTEM (CHIPS) A computerized clearing network system for transfer of international dollar payments and settlement of interbank foreign exchange obligations, connecting some 140 depository institutions that have offices or affiliates in the City of New York.

CLOSE **1.** In a mortgage contract, the final consummation of the agreement marked by the seller's transfer of the real property and deed to the buyer and the payment of the remaining purchase price (original purchase price less deposit) by the buyer to the seller. **2.** In bookkeeping, the process of transferring the balances of the nominal accounts of an entity to the capital account in a sole proprietorship or partnership or to retained earnings in a corporation. **3.** To finalize a business transaction. **4.** The ending price of a security for the day.

CLOSED ECONOMY An economic system that is completely self-sufficient. It has no **INTERNATIONAL TRADE** (no imports or exports), as opposed to an **OPEN ECONOMY.**

CMEA. *See* **COUNCIL FOR MUTUAL ECONOMIC ASSISTANCE.**

CODE OF SUBSIDIES AND COUNTERVAILING DUTIES The Agreement on Subsidies and Countervailing Measures (SCM Agreement) that disciplines the provision of subsidies (e.g., grants, below-market-rate loans, tax credits and over-valued equity infusions) by governments to specific enterprises or industries. The SCM Agreement sets up a three-class framework. Subsidies contingent on export performance and certain other egregious subsidies are prohibited. Three types of government assistance (aid for research and development, aid to disadvantaged regions, and aid for environmental adaptation) are non-actionable when strict conditions and criteria are satisfied. All other subsidies may be challenged in either World Trade Organization (WTO) dispute settlement or a domestic countervailing duty proceeding if they cause adverse trade effects. The disciplines of the SCM Agreement will apply to all WTO members after transition periods ranging up to ten years for developing countries and for countries in transition from planned to market economies.

COLLATERAL Property in the form of real estate, stocks, bonds, etc., representing the security to one's obligation to satisfy a debt in case of default. For example, in the purchase of real property, the mortgage note is collateralized by the real property that is purchased. If the debt is not paid, the lender may sell the property to pay off the loan.

COCOM, *See* **COORDINATING COMMITTEE ON MULTILATERAL EXPORT CONTROLS.** *See also* **ADMINISTRATIVE EXCEPTION.**

CODE OF CONDUCT ON TRANSNATIONAL CORPORATIONS An intergovernmental agreement sponsored by the United Nations, in 1987, aiming at spelling out the rules of good corporate behavior for multinational companies in host and home countries.

CODETERMINATION A trend of significance to the multinational companies in which national laws in many nations give workers a voice in management through workers' councils and representation on the board of directors. It is predicated on the notion that labor as well as shareholders have a vested interest in the business firm. Thus, in codetermination countries, labor participates in management decisions affecting both the global operations of locally based multinational companies and the local operations of foreign-owned subsidiaries.

COINSURANCE A practice under which the insured and insurer share proportionately in the payment of a loss or expenses incurred.

COLLAR OPTION As a form of mixture option, the simultaneous purchase of a put option and sale of a call option, or vice versa. See also CALL; PUT.

COLLUSION Private agreement between two or more persons for the purpose of circumventing the law, defrauding another, or committing some other wrongful act.

COLUMN RATES Import tariff charges set by the United States. They include rates for most favored nation status.

COMBINATION RATE A combining of two or more varying tariff fees or percentages.

COMBINED TRANSPORT DOCUMENT A document corresponding to the **BILL OF LADING** but used for shipping in case more than one form of transport is involved.

COMBO A carrier that can transport multiple cargoes (e.g., wheat and gold).

COMECON The now-defunct economic association of Eastern European Communist block countries headed by the former **USSR**. *See* **COUNCIL FOR MUTUAL ECONOMIC ASSISTANCE.**

COMITY PRINCIPLE Countries engaged with each other in **INTERNATIONAL TRADE** agree to consider their interests in making contractual agreements and fulfilling their responsibilities. An example is taking into account unfair competition.

COMMAND ECONOMIC SYSTEM. *See* **ECONOMIC SYSTEM.**

COMMAND ECONOMY An economic system in which the allocation of economic resources in terms of what and how much is to be produced is planned by the government.

COMMERCE 1. Large-scale purchase and sale of materials, products, services, etc., among nations, states, companies, or communities. The Interstate Commerce Commission is the United States governmental agency charged with regulating commerce between states. The United States Department of Commerce is charged with promoting both domestic and foreign trade. **2.** Mercantile activities between nations and states.

COMMERCIAL ACTIVITY REPORT An economic report generated componentially by American embassies in many countries across the world in which the United States Department of Commerce does not operate in. The Commercial Activity Report analyzes the business opportunities and activities of the country it is reporting on as well as the political implications of the current government to present and future United States trade and economic issues.

COMMERCIAL BILL In **INTERNATIONAL TRADE, a BILL OF EXCHANGE** or bank check generated in the sale of goods and services.

COMMERCIAL CONTROLS In **INTERNATIONAL TRADE,** restrictions placed by countries on the trading of goods and services.

COMMERCIAL INVOICE The exporter's **BILL OF SALE** that describes closely the merchandise, price, and terms of sale. This is one of the principal types of documents involved in export transactions. The other two are the **BILL OF LADING** and insurance certification. *See also* **INSURANCE CERTIFICATE.**

COMMERCIAL LAW The judicial law dealing with commerce and other profitable pursuits among businesses and those parties related thereto. It includes consideration of legal rights and duties of individuals such as under the Uniform Commercial Code (UCC). An example is an action brought because of an unfair trade practice.

COMMERCIAL PAPER Short-term, unsecured bearer obligations issued principally by high quality industrial corporations, finance companies, and commercial factors at a discount from face value (although some may be interest bearing). Issuing commercial paper is less costly than taking out a bank loan. Commercial paper is generally issued in denominations ranging from $100,000 to $1,000,000 for terms ranging from two to 270 days. It is secured only by the creditworthiness of the issuer and is traded prevalently in the United States.

COMMERCIAL POLICIES The laws, regulations, and guidelines affecting a nation's interaction and involvement in **INTERNATIONAL TRADE**. Disputes relating to trade among nations may be arbitrated with the International Commerce Commission (ICC).

COMMERCIAL RISK **1.** Also called **BUSINESS RISK,** the likelihood of loss or uncertain variations in earnings of a business due to change in demand and business operations. **2.** In banking, the chance that a foreign debtor will not be able to repay its loans because of adverse business conditions. **3.** In connection with **EXPORT-IMPORT BANK** guarantees, failure of repayment caused by other than political factors, such as bankruptcy. **4.** Uncertainty existing that the exporter may not be paid for goods or services.

COMMERCIAL TREATY An agreement between two or more nations describing the parameters under which commercial activity may be transacted. Such an agreement typically enumerates tariff requirements or exemptions thereto, shipping terms (when the transfer of goods takes place, e.g., FOB destination or shipping point), arbitration of commercial trade disputes, etc. *See also* **FREE ON BOARD.**

COMMINGLING **1.** The combination of products having varying tariffs associated with them in the same shipment and where it is difficult for the customs agent to make a distinction between them. In such a case, the tariff assessed may be the highest one applicable to one product for all the goods. Therefore, an attempt at segregating the component parts of the shipment or package should be made by the multinational company. **2.** A trustee mixing his funds with that of a customer or client. It is usually illegal because of conflict of interest. **3.** The combination of monies in two or more funds into a single account.

COMMISSION **1.** A fee or a percentage paid to an agent or salesperson for services performed. For example, a real estate broker may charge the seller of a house a commission of 7.5 percent of the sales price as a fee for arranging for the sale. **2.** Authorization or command to act in a specified way to accomplish a particular goal. **3.** A regulatory body such as the Interstate Commerce Commission (ICC) which oversees trade among the states. *See* **TRADE AMONG THE STATES.**

COMMISSION AGENT An individual who purchases inventories and goods in his own country on behalf of large foreign private companies or governmental agencies who want to import them. A commission fee is paid by these entities for this service. *See also* **PURCHASING AGENT.**

COMMISSION FEE. *See* **COMMISSION AGENT.**

COMMITMENT Legal obligation or pledge to perform some act. For example, a mortgage commitment represents a contractual obligation on the part of a lender to loan funds to another in accordance with prearranged specifications. A purchaser may enter into an agreement with a supplier to purchase goods at a fixed price for a specified amount of time in the future. The agreement establishes a commitment to purchase and sell the goods at the prearranged price and therefore fully binds both buyer and seller. The buyer must purchase the goods at the contracted price even if prices fall and the supplier must sell at the given price even if prices rise.

COMMITMENT FEE The fee charged by a lender for making funds available to a borrower. For example, a borrower is charged a commitment fee when a mortgage commitment is secured for the right to borrow when financing a real estate purchase.

COMMODITIES FUTURES An agreement to either buy or sell a specific amount of a commodity (usually a quantity of standardized units) at a given price by a certain date. A commodities futures contract obligates the buyer to purchase the commodity or the seller to sell it unless the contract is sold before its **EXPIRATION DATE.** The term of a commodities future contract is usually less than a year.

COMMODITIES FUTURES CONTRACT. *See* **COMMODITIES FUTURES.**

COMMODITY Any good traded, i.e., bought or sold in commerce. Commodities are generally traded on commodities exchanges and include a wide range of products such as petroleum, lumber, livestock, meat, grains, metals, financial instruments, foods, etc. Commodities are also traded on spot markets.

COMMODITY GROUPINGS United States Bureau of Census classification system of grouping imports and exports. The system is numerically based and has broader categories than the United States **INTERNATIONAL TRADE COMMISSION's** tariff schedules. *See also* **TARIFF SCHEDULE.**

COMMODITY IMPORT PROGRAM (CIP) A financing program of the United States government designed to expedite the payment for essential commodities to countries receiving United States economic aid. The program is administered by the **AGENCY FOR INTERNATIONAL DEVELOPMENT.** The CIP makes money available on a loan or grant for basic commodities and equipment (non-military, non-police, non-luxury products) that are needed by United States aid recipients. The commodities and products that are sent are exported from the

United States and generally consist of such items as: foodstuffs; raw materials; chemicals; agricultural, transportation, and construction equipment; etc.

COMMODITY TERMS OF TRADE A fractional comparison of a country's export price index (price index of the country's exports) to its import price index multiplied by 100. (The numerator of the ratio represents the nation's export price index, and the denominator represents its import price index.)

COMMON EXTERNAL TARIFF (CET) The uniform level of tariffs levied by countries on all goods imported from other nations in the same group, such as the **EUROPEAN COMMUNITY** under an agreement.

COMMON FUND FOR COMMODITIES (CFC) A fund provided for International Commodity Organizations established by the **UNITED NATIONS CONFERENCE ON TRADE AND DEVELOPMENT** whose goal is to regulate prices and assure adequate supplies of goods through an integrated approach rather than on an ad hoc basis. The fund is headquartered in Switzerland, consisting of a governing body, an executive group, and a consultative committee.

COMMON MARKET A high degree of **REGIONAL ECONOMIC INTEGRATION.** It involves: (1). Eliminating internal trade barriers and establishing a common external tariff. (2) Removing national restrictions on the movement of labor and capital among participating nations and the right of establishment for business firms. (3) The pursuit of a common external trade policy. The best known is the European Common Market. *See also* **CARIBBEAN COMMON MARKET; EUROPEAN COMMUNITY; EUROPEAN ECONOMIC COMMUNITY.**

COMMON STOCK Common stock represents the primary equity portion of a public or privately held corporation. Each share represents one unit of ownership. Preferred stock holders also represent a pseudo- equity interest in the corporation, but their risk of loss is limited to the liquidation value of the preferred stock in the event that the company declares bankruptcy and makes a distribution of the corporate assets. Common stockholders assume the primary risk of the business. That is, if the business does well (e.g., net income has risen significantly relative to last period) the resulting rise in stock price will accrue to the benefit of the common stockholders. On the other hand, if the business does poorly (e.g., net income has materially dropped relative to last period) then the resulting reduction in stock price will adversely effect the common stock' holdings. One must examine the articles of incorporation of a given corporation as well as stock certificates and applicable state law to determine the exact rights of any class of stock. However, if there are no restrictive provisions relating to the common stockholders' of a corporation, it can be assumed that a share of common stock provides the following basic rights relating to ownership:

- The right to share in the profits and losses of the corporation.
- The right to share in the management of the corporation, i.e., the right to vote for the corporation's board of directors.

- The right to proportionately share in the corporation's assets upon liquidation.
- The right to maintain one's proportionate share in the ownership of the entity when new shares are being issued. The pre-emptive right allow shareholders the right to share proportionally in the new issue to prevent any dilution of their ownership in the corporation.

COMMON-SIZE ANALYSIS. *See* **VERTICAL ANALYSIS.**

COMPARABILITY The ease with which two or more companies may be compared and analyzed to each other with respect to financial considerations. The comparability of the financial statements of two or more companies is enhanced with respect to each other if, for example, they utilize the same financial accounting formats, structure their disclosures identically, employ the same accounting principles, and use similar measurement techniques.

COMPARATIVE ADVANTAGE A doctrine that every country gains if each country specializes in the products that can be made relatively more efficiently and cheaply and then trades for goods in which it has the greatest comparative disadvantage. By emphasizing a comparative rather than an **ABSOLUTE ADVANTAGE,** the doctrine supports **FREE TRADE** arguments that every country has a basis for trade.

COMPARATIVE COST THEORY Also known as the Heckscher-Ohlin theory, an explanation of trade patterns, offered by the Swedish economist Bertil Heckscher and subsequently developed by his pupil, Eli Ohlin, that contends that **INTERNATIONAL TRADE** is based on differences in comparative costs but attempts to explain the factors which make for differences in comparative costs. Different goods require different factor proportions, and different counties have different relative factor endowments; countries will tend to have comparative advantages in producing the goods that use their abundant factors more intensively; for this reason each country will end up exporting its abundant factor goods in exchange for imported goods that use its scarce factors more intensively. For example, a country which has an abundance of, say, labor will specialize in the production and export of goods, which are intensive in the use of labor, and import goods which are intensive in the use of the country's scarce factors of production.

COMPENSATION DEAL A bartering arrangement in which goods are purchased partially with cash and partially by trading with other goods and services.

COMPENSATION The amount paid or property given to workers for their labors. The payment may be based on a fixed salary rate, hours worked, or performance achieved (e.g., units produced).

COMPENSATORY SUSPENSION The retaliation by a nation for having its trading concessions and allowances canceled by its trading partner. In response, the nation suspends the trade concessions granted to the trading partner.

COMPETITIVE ADVANTAGE Any attribute possessed by a multinational company that allows it to achieve lower costs, higher revenues, or less risk than its competition. This feature is needed especially in a highly competitive global market.

COMPETITIVE DEVALUATION The devaluation by a country of its currency (relative to other world currencies) for the purpose of making its products less expensive in the international market. The objective of this action is to give the nation a competitive trading advantage in the exportation of its goods.

COMPETITIVE STRATEGY A policy formulated by a multinational company so it can successfully compete with the products and/or services offered by a competitor. Such strategy may take the form of an aggressive advertising promotion emphasizing the quality of the company's goods and how such goods best satisfy customer needs at a reasonable price. On the other hand, the promotion may seek to discredit the competitor in some way.

COMPLEMENTARY GOODS Products or services consumed together. For example, if a person orders a book he would also likely order the accompanying software package.

COMPLETELY KNOCKED DOWN (CKD) Parts or components shipped into a country for assembly there. It is frequently used in the automobile industry.

COMPOUND DUTY A form of import duty with a combination of an ad valorem duty and a specific duty. Specific duties are levied on the basis of some physical units such as dollars per meter or per bushel.

CONCENTRATION POLICY A strategy adopted by a multinational entity of selecting countries and markets for investing and committing material amounts of resources for the purpose of establishing a long-term influence and interest in those areas. See also DIRECT FOREIGN INVESTMENT.

CONCESSION **1.** A right to undertake and profit by a specific activity in exchange for services. **2.** An agreement between a host country and a company in which the country gives the company the right to explore for, extract, and sell, oil in return for specified taxes, fees, and other charges. **3.** A reduction in selling price to boost sales. **4.** Per-share commission for the investment banker's underwriting service in a new security issue. **5.** A decrease in the tariff, relaxing of trade barriers, or other reduction in import quotas, in reciprocation for concessions granted by another country.

CONCESSION AGREEMENT **1.** Agreement between a foreign company and a country that wants the company to invest, commit resources, and do business within its borders. The specific concessions that the country is willing to make to entice the foreign company (i.e., asset donations, tax abatements, etc.,) is usually agreed to before any investment takes place. **2.** Lower fee or rental charged typically in the early time period of a contract often as an incentive. **3.** Right to use property.

CONCILIATION The attempt to bring a labor union and management together to rectify and solve their problems and issues. By meeting face-to-face viable solutions can be offered and relationships strengthened. Typically, an independent party serves as a mediator. It is a less formal approach than arbitration.

CONDITION PRECEDENT A provision in a written contractual agreement that responsibilities to act occur once a specified event or happening takes place. For example, a multinational company must perform its duties once a foreign distributor agrees to market the product.

CONDITION SUBSEQUENT An act after a contractual breach forgiving the legal damages arising from that breach. An example is when a multinational company forgives a supplier for failure to deliver merchandise on the due date if it agrees to supply other merchandise in limited demand in the future.

CONDITIONAL CONTRACT A stipulation that the parties shall enter into a binding agreement based upon the happening of some specified event. The specified event, called a condition precedent, precedes the creation of the binding obligation. Such words as subject to, as soon as, and on condition, indicates that a potential contract is based upon the happening of some specified event. An example is a multinational company's agreeing to buy machinery from a foreign company contingent on the machinery passing inspection of the United States company's maintenance and production staff.

CONFIRMED LETTER OF CREDIT A letter of credit issued by one bank (a foreign bank) with its authenticity substantiated by another bank (a United States bank), obligating both banks to honor any drafts drawn in compliance. An exporter who requires a confirmed letter of credit from the buyer is guaranteed payment from the United States bank in case the foreign buyer or bank defaults. It reads, for example, "we hereby confirm this credit and undertake to pay drafts drawn in accordance with the terms and conditions of the letter of credit."

CONFORMANCE REPORTING The testing and reporting on whether manufactured products meet industry, government, or other organizational standards of performance and quality. The tests are preferably performed by an independent testing body but may also be done by the manufacturer of the product.

CONGLOMERATE A corporation (holding company) which has a controlling interest in many different types of companies that were acquired through past mergers or acquisitions. There need not be any relationship among the componential entities making up the conglomerate. That is, they generally represent a diverse group of companies unrelated in their markets and operations. By uniting different functioning enterprises, the conglomerate takes on a diversified character and becomes less susceptible to business risks associated with the business cycle.

CONSCIOUS PARALLELISM One company engages in an activity or formulates a policy that a competitor has just engaged in. An example is when one company begins its promotional discount for a product that a competitor has just ended.

CONSENSUS RATES Private borrowers in countries that are heavily indebted may arrange for export credits from private insurers (in conjunction with the World Bank) that would otherwise be too risky to be guaranteed by governmental agencies. The borrowing is at consensus rates which result in lower rates of interest due to the cooperation of the international community.

CONSIDERATION In law, that which is given by both parties to a contract in order to make it binding and enforceable. In a contract, both parties promise to do something or abstain from something. In return for the others' promise, each party must give consideration in the form of money, goods, services, etc. (the promisors must give something up). If consideration is not given by both parties, the contract is considered invalid.

CONSIGNMENT Technique of selling inventory in which title to the goods never passes from the consignor (the shipper or seller of the goods) to the consignee. The consignee (the recipient of the goods), in this arrangement is nothing more than a selling agent for the consignor and receives a fee for this function. The consigned goods are included in the inventory of the consignor (and are excluded from the inventory of the consignee) and are insured by him. In a typical consignment arrangement, the consignor delivers goods to the consignee. When they are sold, the consignee remits the sales price of the good less sales commission to the consignor.

CONSOLIDATED REPORT A report that incorporates the activities of all the units being reported. For example, a consolidated balance sheet combines the assets, liabilities and shareholders' equity of the parent company and subsidiaries (investees in which more that 50 percent of the voting common stock are owned by the investor company) as if one combined entity were being reported on. A consolidated income statement reports the results of operations of all the componential entities. A consolidated balance sheet and income statement are prepared by adding the individual statement items of each affiliated company, eliminating all intercompany transactions, and disclosing all related party transactions. *See also* **CONSOLIDATED STATEMENT.**

CONSOLIDATED SHIPMENT The process of combining the freight of different shippers into a large shipment so that any volume discounts being offered by the common carrier could be taken. *See also* **CONSOLIDATION.**

CONSOLIDATED STATEMENT A statement that combines the activities of all the units being reported on. For example consolidated financial statements are statements that combines all the assets, liabilities, and operating activities of a parent company and its subsidiaries. A subsidiary company is an entity in which over 50 percent of its voting common stock is owned by an investor company known as the parent company. A consolidated balance sheet combines the assets, liabilities and shareholders' equity of the parent company and subsidiaries. A consolidated income statement reports the results of operations of all the affiliated entities. A consolidated balance sheet and income statement are prepared by adding the individual statement items of each componential company, eliminating all intercompany transactions, and disclosing all related party transactions. *See also* **CONSOLIDATED REPORT**.

CONSOLIDATION 1. The process of preparing the combined or consolidated financial statements of a parent company and its subsidiaries. *See also* **CONSOLIDATED REPORT** and **CONSOLIDATED STATEMENT.** 2. The process of combining the smaller shipments of different shippers into a larger one for purposes of taking advantage of volume discounts being offered by the common carrier. *See also* **CONSOLIDATED SHIPMENT.** 3. The merger of two or more corporations or commercial interests.

CONSORTIUM Two or more companies band together for some business purpose having a common and beneficial interest to all. The companies may pool or share their assets, talents, and personnel to result in efficiencies, cost control, and productivity. An example is a group formed to promote their similar product lines in a new foreign market. Another example is the Organization of Petroleum Exporting Countries who exercise a lot of influence over the availability and cost of oil.

CONSPIRACY Two or more entities or individuals engage in an illegal activity.

CONSTITUENT COMPANY A company that has been merged, acquired, or consolidated into an affiliated group of companies.

CONSTRUCTED VALUE (CV) The value of a good for customs purposes based on the value of the inputs used to "construct" or produce it. This value is determined when the value of the good cannot be directly determined through a sale or some other independent market valuation technique. The components making up the constructed value of a good consists of: its cost of materials, fabrication, and other expenses incurred in producing the good; general expenses; and profit.

CONSTRUCTIVE DELIVERY The joint acceptance by a buyer and seller that title to the goods being transacted has passed to the buyer although physical delivery has not yet occurred. For example, in a FOB shipping point purchase, title to the goods pass to the buyer when the goods are transferred by the seller to the common carrier. When this event has occurred, the buyer of the goods has experienced "constructive delivery" of the goods and therefore has title to them.

CONSTRUCTIVE LOSS An insurance term indicating that the cost of repairing or recovering an insured item exceeds the value that it is insured for. In this situation, the insurance company would only be liable for the insured value.

CONSUL A government representative who resides in a foreign country to handle the interest of the domestic business including its employees. An example is a United States government official stationed in Italy.

CONSUMER GOODS Products purchased by individuals for the home or personal use such as cleaning supplies. They are consumed for final demand. See also CAPITAL GOODS.

CONSUMPTION EFFECT The effect on the demand for a good as a result of imposing a tariff on it. The effect of a tariff imposition is to raise the purchase price of the imported item in the country imposing it. The increase price results in a reduction of the demand for the good. In general, tariffs are assessed to protect domestic producers. When a tariff is assessed on a product, the price of the domestically produced equivalent becomes more competitive and demand for it increases.

CONTENT APPRAISAL 1. The evaluation of what is in a container or package being shipped. 2. The comparison of the usefulness and effectiveness of advertising messages among competing multinational companies. A determination is made on the best wording and/or graphics to stimulate sales of the product or service.

CONTINENTAL BASIS A way of quoting exchange rates in foreign currency-the foreign currency price of one United States dollar.

CONTINGENT LIABILITY 1. Potential obligation of a guarantor. 2. Potential liability in the present that may materialize into a bona fide liability in the future if certain circumstances come to pass. Generally Accepted Accounting Principles (GAAP) requires that a contingent liability should be currently reported in the financial statements as a liability when: (a) it is probable that a loss will occur and (b) the amount of the loss can be reasonably estimated. For example, let's assume that a company's legal council advises it that its defense in a current legal suit will not prevail and it can be reasonably estimated that the company will be responsible for damages in the amount of $2 million. The company is required therefore to record a loss and liability (although the case has not yet been resolved) in the accounting records and disclose them in the body of the income statement (the loss) and balance sheet (the liability). If the amount of a probable loss cannot be reasonable estimated, footnote disclosure in the financial statements will suffice. If the probability of a potential loss is reasonably possible, i.e., less than probable and more than remote, whether or not the company can reasonably estimate the amount of the loss, GAAP requires that the contingent liability be disclosed in the footnotes. If, on the other hand, the probability of the loss is remote, whether or not the loss can be reasonably estimated, footnote disclosure is not required but is allowed.

CONTINUOUS R&D A research and development (R&D) strategy under which the multinational company develops new technology, building on extensions of its existing technology. This contrasts with R&D in new areas where the company is not well positioned.

CONTRACT A legal agreement between parties to perform for mutual benefit. Each party has a right to demand performance of what was promised. The failure of one party to honor its commitment may result in damages against that party in a court of law. An enforceable contract may be in writing or orally. A multinational company enters into contracts with its employees, suppliers, customers, and other interested parties when conducting **INTERNATIONAL TRADE.**

CONTRACT DEMURRAGE Damages due a shipowner by a charterer because the latter has delayed the vessel beyond the contracted time period. The damages are computed on an hourly, daily or weekly basis.

CONTRACTS IN FOREIGN CURRENCY An agreement between two parties to purchase or sell amounts of a given currency at a specified exchange rate.

CONTROL 1. Internal control in a business entity is a process, established by the board of directors, management, and other personnel in a company, designed to provide reasonable assurance regarding the achievement of objectives in the following categories: (a) reliability of financial reporting, (b) effectiveness and efficiency of operations, (c) compliance with applicable laws and regulations. In an audit of a company's financial statements, **GENERALLY ACCEPTED AUDITING STANDARDS** requires auditors obtain a sufficient understanding of the entity's internal control to plan the audit and to determine the nature, timing, and extent of audit tests to be performed. *See also* **INTERNAL CONTROL. 2.** Internal measures taken by a company in the form of procedures, polices, and standards to insure that its products meet the quality standards that have been established.

CONTROLLED ECONOMY An economy that is not regulated by market forces such as supply and demand but rather by the government in power. An example is communism.

CONTROLLED FACILITY A portion of the territory of a nation which is designated as a free port and is exempt from the payment of duties. Goods purchased in the controlled facility of a country are not assessed duty payments. However, once they leave the controlled facility and are brought into other parts of the country, duties must be paid.

CONTROLLED FOREIGN CORPORATION (CFC) In the United States tax code, a foreign corporation whose voting stock is more than 50 percent owned by United States shareholders, that is United States citizens or corporations, each of whom holds at least 10 percent of the voting power or total value.

CONVERGENCE 1. A coming or bringing together. **2.** A narrowing in the price of the item covered in a futures contract (e.g., commodities) to the cash price of the item. At the expiration date of the contract, the futures price stipulated in the contract will equal the cash price.

CONVERSION 1. Unlawful appropriation of property by another. See also **INVOLUNTARY CONVERSION. 2.** Act of exchanging convertible bonds or convertible preferred shares into **COMMON STOCK. 3.** Change from real property to personal property or vice versa. **4.** Exchange of one type of currency into another at a given exchange rate. **5.** Change from joint ownership to separate ownership or vice versa. **6.** Restrictions placed on the conversion of funds between countries. **7.** Switch in a family of mutual funds. 8. Transferring from a short-term to a long-term insurance policy.

CONVERSION LOSS Lower revenues than expected due to a change in the **FOREIGN EXCHANGE RATE.** It may arise when (1) the foreign-currency receivable is originally worth more of the home-country currency than was ultimately received and (2) an increase in foreign currency payables resulting in realized losses.

CONVERTIBLE CURRENCY A currency that can be readily convertible into any other currency, at least for current account payments, without government restrictions, permission, or interventions.

COORDINATING COMMITTEE ON MULTILATERAL EXPORT CONTROLS (COCOM) A group of NATO countries establishing export restrictions on sensitive goods of previous Soviet bloc countries. Some members of the control group of 17 countries are the United States, United Kingdom, Canada, Germany, France, and Italy. The organization ended in 1994. See also **ADMINISTRATIVE EXCEPTION.**

COPYRIGHT Legal protection afforded writers of published works including books, songs, and art. It is protected for the author's life plus 50 years.

CORNERING THE MARKET The speculative practice of raising the price of a commodity or security (price control) through the acquisition of significantly large amounts of it. The practice of cornering the market is illegal.

CORPORATE CULTURE The set of behavior patterns, values, institutions, and the like that are distinctive to corporations and that condition their operations. It has strong norms of behavior, but these are informal and less explicit than the national culture.

CORPORATE SOCIAL RESPONSIBILITY The notion stating that multinational companies should serve social needs in host countries.

CORPORATE STOCKS All shares, common and preferred, representing owner-ship of a publicly traded corporation. Stock is traded in a stock exchange.

CORPORATION A fictitious entity created under state statute that can act only through human agency: directors, who are elected by the shareholders, and who guide its general policies and elect its officers. The officers, in turn, run the day-to-day operation of the corporation and select and hire employees.

CORRELATION Extent of association between two or more variables. Measures of correlation determine how changes in one or more variables (termed the independent variable[s]) will effect changes in the another variable (termed the dependent variable). Based on computed correlations, predictions can be made regarding how changes in the independent variable(s) will influence changes in the dependent variable. A statistical method for predicting the value of a dependent variable from known values of independent (explanatory) variables is known as regression analysis. Simple regression analysis is utilized when only one independent variable is involved. Multiple regression analysis is used when two or more independent variables are involved. Positive correlation is when variables move in the same direction while negative correlation is when variables move in opposite directions. No correlation may also exist.

CORRESPONDENT BANK A bank located in any other location that holds deposits for and provides a service for another bank on a reciprocal basis.

COST AND FREIGHT (C&F) Exporter's quoted price that includes the freight charges to the destination.

COST DIFFERENTIAL 1. Cost that is considered when a determination must be made regarding whether there should be an increase or decrease of production above a given output. The cost differential allows management to decide what amount incremental output should be priced out at. As long as the additional output and its cost differential sales price does not influence the exiting units and their prices and as long as the minimum sales price for the incremental units exceeds the differential cost, selling incremental output will always add to the company's contribution margin. **2.** Extra compensation paid to a United States employee working in a foreign country.

COST, INSURANCE, AND FREIGHT (CIF) A term used in the delivery of goods from the exporter to the importer. The price includes the costs of the goods, the insurance premium, and the freight charges to the destination. CIF pricing makes it easier to compare the prices of different exporters. It contrasts with **FREE ON BOARD,** where the buyer assumes all costs such as insurance and freight from the seller's point of shipment.

COST MINIMIZATION A competitive strategy in a global economy under which the multinational company strives to compete with the notion of cost reductions and the resulting low prices.

COST OF CAPITAL Also called a hurdle rate, cutoff rate or minimum required rate of return. The rate of return that is necessary to maintain market value (or stock price) of a firm. The firm's cost of capital is calculated as a weighted average of the costs of debt and equity funds. Equity funds include both capital stock (common stock and preferred stock) and retained earnings. These costs are expressed as annual percentage rates. For example, assume the following capital structure and the cost of each source of financing for a multinational company:

| | PERCENT OF TOTAL | | |
Source	Book Value ($)	Weights (%)	Cost (%)
Debt	20,000,000	40	5.14
Preferred stock	5,000,000	10	13.40
Common stock	20,000,000	40	17.11
Retained earnings	5,000,000	10	16.00
Totals	$50,000,000	100	

The overall cost of capital is computed as follows: 5.14 percent (.4) + 13.4 percent (.1) + 17.11 percent (.4) + 16.00 percent (.1) = 11.84 percent. The cost of capital is used for **CAPITAL BUDGETING** purposes. Under the **NET PRESENT VALUE** method, the cost of capital is used as the discount rate to calculate the present value of future cash inflows. Under the **INTERNAL RATE OF RETURN** method, it is used to make an accept-or-reject decision by comparing the cost of capital with the internal rate of return on a given project. A project is accepted when the internal rate exceeds the cost of capital.

COST OF PRODUCTION Costs of factors of production-raw materials, labor, and manufacturing overhead. Sometimes, it covers allocations of general administrative and selling costs.

COST PLUS PROFIT CONTRACT Procedure for valuing a contract. The federal government and its agencies often award cost plus profit contracts. In valuing this agreement, the contractor must determine his costs (generally consisting of direct material, direct labor, and factory overhead). The agreed profit is then added to this amount to get the total value of the contract. The profit that is added may be either a preagreed amount (cost plus contract) or a preagreed percentage markup on cost (cost plus contract percentage). For example, assume that a contract is costed out at $400,000. The agreed profit is $150,000. In this case, the contractor can expect to collect a total of $550,000 from the contractee. If the percentage markup on cost is 35 percent, then the amount of profit is $140,000 ($400,000 X 35 percent) and the total amount to be collected would be $540,000. Cost plus profit contracts are also sometimes used when new products are being developed so as to minimize the uncertainty of the manufacturer of recouping costs.

COUNCIL FOR MUTUAL ECONOMIC ASSISTANCE (CMEA or COMECON) Also called the Soviet Bloc, the now-defunct regional integration group formed in 1949 by the centrally planned economies of the former U.S.S.R. and Eastern Europe to coordinate their trade and other forms of economic relations. It also includes Vietnam, Cuba, and Mongolia. The basic objective of **COME-CON** is not trade liberalization, as in the case of **GENERAL AGREEMENT ON TARIFFS AND TRADE** and the **EUROPEAN COMMUNITY,** but to establish an interbloc division of labor between its member nations in order to achieve specialization in production at low cost.

COUNT CERTIFICATE A certificate indicating that a physical count of inventory took place at a specified time such as at the point of shipment, delivery, etc. The certificate generally notes the type(s) of merchandise counted, the amount, and condition of the goods. In addition, the supervisor in charge usually signs the document providing confirmation that the count took place.

COUNTERCLAIM A defendant initiates a legal action against the plaintiff. It is a counter demand.

COUNTERPURCHASE A **RECIPROCAL BUYING** agreement. It is a form of **COUNTERTRADE** in which a multinational company agrees to buy a certain amount of materials back from a country to which a sale is made.

COUNTERTRADE A type of **POST-TRADE FINANCING** in which the selling firm is required to accept the countervalue of its sale in local goods or services instead of in cash. Payment by a purchaser is entirely or partially in kind instead of hard currencies for products or technology from other countries. It is therefore a whole range of barterlike arrangements. More specifically, contertrade has evolved into a diverse set of activities that can be categorized as five distinct types of trading arrangements: **BARTER, COUNTERPURCHASE,** offset, switch trading, and compensation or buyback.

COUNTERVAILING DUTY An extra amount of tariff levied on an import charged to offset an export subsidy granted by another country. This is permitted by the Code on Subsidies and Countervailing Duties, if the importing country can show that the subsidy would adversely affect domestic industry. United States countervailing tariffs can only be charged after the **INTERNATIONAL TRADE COMMISSION** has determined that the imports are negatively impacting United States companies.

COUNTRY OF DESTINATION The country of final destination for goods being exported for purposes of consumption or additional production. If the final destination of the goods are not known, the country of destination is the last country that the goods were shipped to in the same form as they were exported in.

COUNTRY OF ORIGIN The country in which an item was either fully produced (grown or manufactured) or the last country in which significant production took place if partial production took place in several countries. Import duties are generally assessed according to the country of origin.

COUNTRY RISK. *See also* **POLITICAL RISK.**

COUNTRY SIMILARITY A theory that states that when a commercial entity has created a product that has been in high demand in the markets it serves, it will then search for distribution centers in other countries that are similar to one(s) that the product was developed for in hope that the product may turn out to be highly demanded in these countries as well.

COUPON 1. Detachable certificates attached to a **BEARER BOND** that must be presented to the issuing institution or a bank to receive the payment of semi-annual interest on the principal. **2.** Printed vouchers found in newspapers and magazines that entitle the holder to a discount when purchasing goods or services. **3.** Payment vouchers used when making periodic disbursements such as monthly mortgage payments to a bank. *See also* **CUM COUPON.**

COVENANT Legal term for a promise, commonly found in the form of restrictions in a loan agreement imposed on the borrower to protect the lender's interest. Examples of typical restrictive provisions are a ceiling on dividends and the required maintenance of a minimum working capital. *See also* **INDENTURE.**

COVENANT NOT TO COMPETE An agreement not to perform business activities similar to that of another. An example is a provision in employment contracts not to reveal trade secrets of the employer if the employee ceases employment. Another example is a company agreeing not to compete with a buyer of its business for five years. However, covenants deemed excessively restrictive may not be enforceable.

COVER 1. After a seller breaches its agreement to deliver merchandise to the buyer, the buyer purchases such goods elsewhere. The buyer is legally protected to receive reimbursement from the original seller for the amount the buyer paid in excess of the original contract price. **2.** An investor buying securities to cover a short position. **3.** The adequacy of a company's profitability to pay its obligations. **4.** One company agrees to make good for another company's liability to deliver a product or render a service. *See also* **FORWARD COVER.**

COVERED INTEREST ARBITRAGE A process whereby an investor earns a risk-free profit by (1) borrowing currency, (2) converting it into another currency where it is invested, (3) selling this other currency for future delivery against the initial original currency, and (4) using the proceeds of forward sale to repay the original loan. The profits in this transaction are derived from discrepancies between interest differentials and the percentage discounts or premiums among the currencies involved in the **FORWARD TRANSACTION.**

CRAWLING PEG A system of exchange rate modification in which a country's currency exchange rate changes periodically (in small upward or downward increments) over the months of the year to accommodate significant annual changes in **INFLATION.** The modification of the rate occurs slowly (crawling) over several months rather than occurring as one large change.

CREDIT 1. An agreement between a buyer and seller in which payment for purchase(s) is deferred by the buyer for a predetermined amount of time. A finance charge will be assessed. **2.** In accounting, any entry made on the right side of an account. **3.** Money that is available for borrowing from a **LETTER OF CREDIT** issued by a bank or other open commitment from a financial institution. **4.** An adjustment in favor of a customer's account balance such as in a bank account, credit card, etc.

CREDIT DESIGNATION PERIOD. *See* **END OF THE MONTH.**

CREDIT PROTOCOL Financial aid and **EXPORT CREDIT** arrangements agreed to by various nations that have extended foreign export credit considerations to other nations regarding the use of the credit to finance purchases of goods and services, export credit terms, repayment of the credit, export credit repayment periods, etc.

CREDIT RISK INSURANCE Insurance that covers the risk of loss or nonpayment of goods that have been delivered by a common **CARRIER.** For example, the purchase of marine insurance covers the policy holder for any loss that cannot be recovered from a shipping line.

CREDIT SWAP. *See* **SWAP.**

CROSS-BORDER LEASE A lease agreement in which the two parties to the lease, the lessor and lessee, are located in two different countries. Cross-border leasing is popularly used to finance the acquisition of capital assets in developing **THIRD WORLD** countries.

CROSS CULTURE The differences between the culture of countries that must be adjusted to when employees work overseas. Proper training and experiences are needed to overcome such differences. An example of a culture shock might be United States employees in their first week working in Japan.

CROSS-DEFAULT CLAUSE Clause in a loan agreement specifying that default by a borrower on any other debt owed to the lender will be considered a default on the current loan between the parties.

CROSS-HAULING Trade in similar products in both directions between two nations. An example is the trade of automobiles between the United States and Japan because parts and finished automobiles are exported in both directions.

CROSS INVESTMENT **FOREIGN DIRECT INVESTMENTS** made, as a defense measure, by oligopolistic companies in each other's home country.

CROSS RATE The exchange rate between two currencies derived by dividing each currency's exchange rate with a third currency. For example, if yen/$ is 100 and DM/$ is 1.25, the cross rate between yen and DM is 100 yens/$ divided by 1.25 DM = 80 yens/DM. Because most currencies are quoted against the dollar, it may be necessary to work out the cross rates for currencies other than the dollar. The cross rate is needed to consummate financial transactions between two countries.

KEY CURRENCY CROSS RATES (May 9, 1997)				
	Britain	**Germany**	**Japan**	**United States**
Britain	—	.36519	.00513	.61626
Germany	2.7383	—	.01404	1.6875
Japan	195.02	71.218	—	120.18
United States	1.6227	.59259	.00832	—

CROSS SUBSIDIZATION A marketing methodology utilized by a company to penetrate a **FOREIGN MARKET.** In this process, the profitable export marketing activities in one foreign market is used to subsidize and support the unprofitable export marketing activities in another (where products are sold at less than cost) for the purpose of establishing a reputation and economic foothold in that area. In some countries, like the United States, such a practice, if deemed harmful to an American industry, may result in legal action for the recoupment of damages and injury.

CTA. *See* **CUMULATIVE TRANSLATION ADJUSTMENT.**

CULTURAL ASSIMILATION AND ANALYSIS A program provided to the employees of multinational companies and their families who must work and live abroad. The program consists of familiarizing these individuals to the cultural differences that exist in foreign nations as well as training and acclimating them to what is expected as foreign representatives of the company.

CULTURAL RISK The built-in risk in operating cross culturally. It is the chance of loss because of a multinational company's inaccurate perception of a foreign culture or the manner in which the **CORPORATE CULTURE** and the foreign culture interface.

CULTURE The whole set of social norms, behavior patterns, beliefs, rules, customs, values, techniques, artifacts, institutions, etc., that are distinctive to a population and that condition its behavior. A multinational company must consider the culture of all the foreign countries in which it operates.

CULTURE-BASED PRODUCTS Products whose attributes, configuration, function, etc., are basically in response to culturally determined consumer tastes. An example is chop suey.

CUM COUPON A term used in international bond trading indicating that the purchaser of a bond has the right to collect the next interest payment.

CUMULATIVE TRANSLATION ADJUSTMENT (CTA) ACCOUNT An account entry in a translated balance sheet in which gains and/or losses from currency translation have been accumulated over a period of years.

CURRENCY The medium of exchange in a given country consisting generally of bills (paper) and coins that is issued by the government and designated as legal tender for the payment of all obligations.

CURRENCY ARBITRATE The submission of currency exchange disputes between two companies operating in different countries to arbitration.

CURRENCY BASKET The composite of various currencies separately weighted and valued to generate a unit of account. The currency basket type unit of account for the **EUROPEAN COMMUNITY (EC)** was initially termed the **EURO-PEAN UNIT OF ACCOUNT** but later renamed the **EUROPEAN CURRENCY UNIT (ECU).** The composite currency relationship is subject to review every five years (or upon request) if the weight of any currency changes by 25 percent or more. The ECU is now: the standard for fixing central rates in the EC; the prime unit around which credit is measured in the EC's monetary system; the basis for issuing loan and mortgages; and the unit of measure for traveler's checks, bank accounts, and other monetary uses.

CURRENCY CALL OPTION A purchased right to buy a specific amount of foreign currency at a predetermined exchange rate price for a specified period of time. A holder of a currency call option may choose to exercise the option or let it lapse. There is no obligation to exercise it. *See also* **CURRENCY PUT OPTION.**

CURRENCY CLAUSE In foreign trade, a clause in a contract between two entities which sets a fixed rate of exchange between two currencies. The clause is inserted to avoid any subsequent impact of **CURRENCY DEVALUATION** or **CURRENCY REVALUATION.**

CURRENCY COCKTAIL The composite of a number of currencies making up a unit of account. The unit of account is used to measure monetary transactions. *See also* **CURRENCY BASKET.**

CURRENCY CONTROLS Controls established by a government relating to the amount of foreign currency that residents or visitors of a country may have and how much they must pay to acquire it.

CURRENCY DEVALUATION The official action taken by a government to reduce the rate at which a given currency is exchanged into other foreign currencies. The effect of this action is to reduce the value of the currency relative to other currencies making imports more expensive and exports cheaper. A currency devaluation by a government generally occurs only when the country has fixed the exchange rate relative to other international currencies. When the currency exchange rate is floating, changes are prompted by the supply and demand for the currency and not by government decree.

CURRENCY DIVERSIFICATION The idea of cutting the impact of unforeseen currency fluctuations by engaging activities in a portfolio of different currencies.

CURRENCY FUTURES CONTRACT Contracts in the futures market that call for the delivery of currency in a well known world currency such as the United States dollars, German marks, British pounds, etc. Currency futures contracts are commonly used by multinational companies that sell products around the world to hedge against adverse turns in exchange rates.

CURRENCY INDICES A statistical comparison generally measuring changes from year to year of the value of a foreign currency relative to another, i.e., United States dollars, French francs, British pounds, etc.

CURRENCY OF DENOMINATION The currency that is the legal medium of exchange in a given country. For example, the currency of denomination in the United States is the United States dollar.

CURRENCY OF DETERMINATION The currency used in an international transaction between companies located in different countries. For example, a United States company selling to a French company may elect to state the transaction in terms of Francs.

CURRENCY OPTION CLAUSE An agreement giving the buyer of EUROBONDS issued in a given currency the option to be paid in principal and interest in a different currency.

CURRENCY PUT OPTION A contract that gives the holder the right to sell a specified amount of currency at a given exchange price for a specified period of time. A holder of a currency put option may choose to exercise the option or let it lapse. There is no obligation to exercise it. See also **CURRENCY CALL OPTION.**

CURRENCY REVALUATION A strengthening of the spot value of a currency which has previously been devalued. The value can be increased by raising the supply of foreign currencies via restriction of imports and promotion of exports.

CURRENCY RISK Also called foreign exchange risk or exchange rate uncertainty. For example, when you invest in a **FOREIGN MARKET,** the return on the foreign investment in terms of the United States dollar depends not only on the return on the foreign market in terms of local currency but also on the change in the exchange rate between the local currency and United States dollar. The following example illustrates how a change in the dollar affects the return on a foreign investment.

EXAMPLE:
You purchased bonds of a German firm paying 12 percent interest. You will earn that rate, assuming interest is paid in marks. What if you are paid in dollars? As the exhibit shows, you must then convert marks to dollars before the payout has any value to you. Suppose that the dollar appreciated 10 percent against the mark during the year after purchase. (A currency appreciates when acquiring one of its units requires more units of a foreign currency.) In this example, one mark acquired .616 dollars, and later, one mark acquired only .554 dollars; at the new exchange rate it would take 1.112 (.616/.554) marks to acquire .616 dollars. Thus, the dollar has appreciated while the mark has depreciated. Now, your return realized in dollars is only 10.87 percent. The adverse movement in the **FOREIGN EXCHANGE RATE**-the dollar's appreciation-reduced your actual yield.

EXCHANGE RISK AND FOREIGN INVESTMENT YIELD			
Transaction	**Marks**	**Exchange Rate: No. of Dollars per 1 Mark**	**Dollars**
On 1/1/19A Purchased one German bond with a 12 percent coupon rate	500	$.6051*	$302.55
On 12/31/19A Expected interest received	60	.6051	36.31
Expected yield	12(%)		12(%)
On 12/31/19A Actual interest received	60	.5501**	33.01
Realized yield	12(%)		10.91(%)***

*For illustrative purposes assume that the direct quote is $.6051 per mark.
**$.6051/(1 + .1) = $.6051/1.1 = $.5501
***$33.01/$302.55 = .1091 = 10.91 percent

CURRENCY RISK SHARING A selling and buying company involved in **INTERNATIONAL TRADE** agree in a predetermined ratio to share in any loss due to exchange rate changes.

CURRENCY SWAP. *See* **SWAP.**

CURRENT ACCOUNT BALANCE OF PAYMENTS account keeping track of all the international transactions of goods and services, including payments and receipts for the use of factors of production such as capital and technology. The current account items are analogous to the revenues and expenses of a business firm. When combined, they provide important insights into a nation's international economic performance, just as a firm's income statement conveys vital information about its performance.

CURRENT ACCOUNT BALANCE A **BALANCE OF PAYMENTS** that measures a nation's exports of products and services, minus its imports of goods and services, (which is a merchandise trade balance), plus its net receipts of unilateral transfers during a specified time period.

CURRENT RATE METHOD A method in the translation of the foreign subsidiaries' financial statements into the United States parent's financial statements. Under the current rate method, (1) All balance sheet assets and liabilities are translated at the current rate of exchange in effect on the balance sheet date. (2) Income statement items are usually translated at an average exchange rate for the reporting period. (3) All equity accounts are translated at the historical exchange rates that were in effect at the time the accounts first entered the balance sheet. (4) Any **TRANSLATION GAIN AND LOSS** is reported as a separate item in the stockholders' equity section of the balance sheet. Translation gains and losses are only included in net income when there is a sale or liquidation of the entire investment in a foreign entity.

FOUR CURRENCY TRANSLATION METHODS		
	Current Rate	**Items Translated at Historical Rate**
1. Current rate	All assets and all liabilities and common stock	——
2. Current-noncurrent	Current assets and current liabilities	Fixed assets and long-term liabilities Common stock
3. Monetary-nonmonetary	Financial assets and all liabilities	Physical assets Common stock
4. Temporal	Financial assets and all liabilities and physical assets valued at current prices	Physical assets valued at historical cost Common stock

CURRENT/NONCURRENT METHOD A method of translating the financial statements of foreign affiliates into the parent's reporting currency. Under this method, all current assets and current liabilities are translated at the current rate of foreign exchange, and all noncurrent accounts at their historical exchange rates. See also **CURRENT RATE METHOD.**

CUSTOMERS CLEARING AGENT An individual or firm who, for a fee, will perform all the processing and preparation of documentation needed to "clear" goods imported into a country through customs. The customers clearing agent also insures that the assessment duties and tariffs on the imported goods will be minimized. See also **CUSTOMS BROKER.**

CUSTOMIZED SALES SERVICE A service provided by the **INTERNATIONAL TRADE ADMINISTRATION.** For a fee, American companies are provided with important product information about the goods they are exporting to foreign international markets. Data is accumulated with respect to market potential, competition, sales price, distribution potential, demand, etc. Companies utilize this information to make appropriate modifications to their product, marketing strategy, etc., in order to obtain a larger share of the international sales market.

CUSTOMS 1. The part of a government responsible for examining and valuing goods imported into a country for the purpose of determining the extent of duties that have to be collected. **2.** The taxes and monetary payments that are assessed on imported goods (and less commonly exported goods) before they may be brought into (or sent out of) a country. **3.** Social conventions or practices prevalent in a foreign country.

CUSTOMS BROKER An individual or firm who, for a fee, will perform all the processing and preparation of documentation needed to "clear" goods imported into a country through customs and minimize the payment of duties assessed on them. *See also* **CUSTOMS CLEARING AGENT.**

CUSTOMS CLASSIFICATION The business categories that goods imported into a country are placed into for the purpose of assessing duties. The Customs Cooperation Council was formed in 1950 to study the possibility of developing a global customs classification system. This international group was comprised of members from over 100 countries. The objectives of the council were to appraise and solve problems arising in **INTERNATIONAL TRADE** and establish uniformity and cooperation. As a result of their efforts, the world's first uniform classification system was adopted known as Customs Cooperation Council Nomenclature (CCCN). It was formerly known as the Brussels Tariff Nomenclature (BTN). The categories of this system represented the generally accepted international standard of customs classification until 1987. In that year, the Council of Ministers of the **EURO- PEAN COMMUNITY** established a new international system of customs classification that replaced the Brussels Tariff Nomenclature and improved the standardization of customs procedures and nomenclature used. In place now is a more harmonized system of nomenclature followed by trading countries. *See also* **CUSTOMS COOPERATION COUNCIL; CUSTOMS COOPERATION COUNCIL NOMENCLATURE.**

CUSTOMS COOPERATION COUNCIL (CCC) A council formed in 1950 to study the possibility of developing a uniform global **CUSTOMS CLASSIFICA- TION** system.

CUSTOMS COOPERATION COUNCIL NOMENCLATURE (CCCN) As a result of the efforts of the **CUSTOMS COOPERATION COUNCIL's** study, the world's first uniform classification system was adopted. The CCCN was formerly known as the Brussels Tariff Nomenclature.

CUSTOMS FACILITIES A designated government area utilized to allow goods that have various **INTERNATIONAL TRADE** restrictions to be exchanged, transferred, or otherwise moved.

CUSTOMS IMPORT VALUE The value assessed by the United States **CUSTOMS SERVICE** on goods imported into the United States for purposes of assessing a duty on them. Although this amount is usually based on the value of the goods in the country they were originally exported from, the United States Customs Service retains the right to modify or change their final assessed import value.

CUSTOMS RATE The exchange rate utilized by the United States **CUSTOMS SERVICE** to convert foreign currency invoices into United States dollars for the purposes of assessing duties on goods imported in the country.

CUSTOMS UNION A regional group of countries that abolish tariffs with each other to promote trade.

CUSTOMS VALUATION METHOD The process utilized by customs personnel of countries throughout the world of assigning a value on imported goods for purposes of assessing duty on them. For example, a given country may utilize the transaction value of a good while another may use its cost, insurance, and freight value as a means of computing the tariff of the customs.

CUTOFF RATE. *See* **COST OF CAPITAL.**

CV. *See* **CONSTRUCTED VALUE.**

CWO. *See* **CASH WITH ORDER.**

CYBER INVESTING Investing such as on-line trading on the **INTERNET.**

CYBERSPACE Originally used in Neuromancer, William Gibson's novel of direct brain-to-computer networking, a popular term encompassing all computer networks, including the **INTERNET,** on-line services, and private networks. It refers to the collective realms of computer-aided communication.

D

DANGER PAY Extra compensation paid employees because of either the risk of a position overseas or in the nature of the job. Examples are bonuses paid to those working in a hostile or potentially hostile foreign environment such as in certain parts of the Middle East or employees working with hazardous materials. Danger pay is more common in times of war.

DANGEROUS SHIPMENT The transporting of products or property that may cause physical damage or safety concerns. Examples are flammable goods, nuclear parts, and unsafe chemicals.

DAY LOAN A one day loan for the purchase of stock arranged through a financial institution for the convenience of the stock broker. When the shares are actually delivered, they may be used as collateral for a standard loan.

DAY ORDER Brokerage terminology for an order to buy or sell that will expire if not executed by the end of the trading day on which it was created. A day order is utilized in all types of trades especially commodities.

DAY-TO-DAY MONEY A loan made to another that is to be repaid later the same day. An example is a financial institution lending a company money to buy securities in the morning for which payment is to be made in late afternoon. *See* **CALL MONEY.**

DE FACTO PROTECTIONISM Non-tariff forms of protection to restrict imports. The United States applies **VOLUNTARY QUOTAS** to Japanese autos and has attempted to "jawbone" other nations to cut down their exports to the United States and to extend their imports of United States goods. *See also* **NONTARIFF BARRIERS.**

DEADSPACE Unoccupied or unused premises or space. An example is a multi-national company's warehouse in a foreign country which is currently vacant.

DEALER 1. An entity that is in the business of buying securities, commodities, currencies, etc. for resale. 2. A foreign entity which acts as an **INTERMEDIARY** between a foreign exporter and domestic importer. 3. An entity buying and selling for its own account, e.g., a real estate dealer.

DEBENTURE A long-term debt instrument that is not secured by a mortgage or other lien on particular property. Because it is unsecured debt, it is issued usually by large, financially strong companies with excellent bond ratings. There are two kinds of debentures: a senior issue and a subordinated (junior) issue, which has a subordinate lien. The order of a prior claim is set forth in the bond indenture. Typically, in the event of liquidation, subordinated debentures come after senior debt.

DEBITS 1. Accounting term designating the left side of an account. It may represent either an increase in assets or decrease in liabilities and stockholders' equity . Expenses are debits because they reduce capital. 2. Term designating the left side of a **BALANCE OF PAYMENTS** account.

DEBT 1. The amount of money owed by a country to the public or another country. 2. Legal obligation to pay, the principal and interest on which must be repaid. It may be either short-term (e.g., **ACCOUNTS PAYABLE,** taxes payable,

NOTE), intermediate-term (e.g., bank loans), or long-term (e.g., bonds, mortgages). **3.** Future services due from an advance payment such as a retainer for management consulting services.

DEBT OVERHANG A repayment schedule negotiated between a nation and its creditors (creditors of a nation's external debt) as a result of the country's inability to make debt repayments in accordance with the original borrowing agreement. The debt overhang is a renegotiated agreement based on the nation's current ability to pay, i.e., based on current economic performance of the nation rather than on the original terms of the note.

DEBT RELIEF The forgiveness by a financial institution, in particular a bank, of a large portion of a nation's international debt because of nonpayment. The most common way of providing debt relief is to reduce the amount of principal owed, interest accrued, or some combination of these. A bank may attempt to minimize its losses as a result of nonpayment of debt by selling the debt to a third party at significant discount. In doing so, it may be able to recoup some of the money lost and not have to write off all of the debt as uncollectible.

DEBT RESTRUCTURING A modification of a debt agreement when a creditor grants a concession to a debtor because of financial difficulties and inability of the latter to pay. A troubled debt restructuring may be accomplished in one of the following two ways: Settlement of debt at less than its carrying value and modification of the terms of the debt. In the case of the settlement of debt, the debtor, by virtue of settling the debt at less than its carrying value, must always record an extraordinary gain on the restructuring (Statement of Financial Accounting Standard No. 4). The creditor, on the other hand, will always incur an ordinary loss. In the latter case, the lack of cash flow on the part of the debtor generally results in requesting one or more of the following concessions: (1) extension of the MATURITY DATE of the PRINCIPAL of the loan, (2) reduction of the principal of the loan, (3) reduction of the interest rate of the loan, and (4) deferral or reduction of any interest already accrued on the debt.

DEBT SWAP A financial instrument that requires the replacement of the debt of a nation owed to foreign countries with ownership or rights of value. In general, a SWAP requires an exchange between two entities of assets or payments that is determined to be mutually beneficial for both participants.

DEBT/EQUITY RATIO Total liabilities divided by stockholders' equity. It indicates whether or not a multinational company has a great amount of DEBT in its capital structure. Large debts mean that the borrower has to pay significant periodic interest and PRINCIPAL. Also, a heavily indebted firm takes a greater risk of running out of cash in difficult times. The interpretation of this ratio depends on several variables, including the ratios of other firms in the industry, the degree of access to additional debt financing, and the stability of operations.

DEBT/EQUITY SWAP Financial instrument that requires the replacement of the foreign debt of a debtor nation with a share in the ownership of that nation's businesses and enterprises. In general, a SWAP requires an exchange between two entities of assets or payments that is determined to be mutually beneficial for both participants.

DEBTOR NATION A nation who owes more to foreign nations than foreign nations owe to it.

DECENTRALIZATION A method of structuring the flow of authority and control in a country or business organization in which decision making is relegated to the lower levels of the entity rather than the upper levels. In this type of organization, delegation of authority is maximized and the flow of information is from the bottom up rather than from the top down as would occur in a centralized entity. The greater the amount of entity decentralization, the greater the extent of grass-roots decision making in the organization.

DECEPTIVE ADVERTISING An erroneous, misleading, or even fraudulent representation of the product or service. It may consist of making untrue guarantees, overexaggerated claims of fitness, restrictive qualifications as to use, visual misrepresentations, and made up "testimonials." An example is advertising a 50 percent discount off the purchase price of merchandise when in fact no discount has been given. The United States Federal Trade Commissions looks into any violations.

DECEPTIVE PACKAGING A misleading packaging of goods giving the appearance of more units or weight, or better quality than actually exists.

DECEPTIVE PRACTICES Activities that are designed to fool and/or deceive. For example, deceptive practices regarding a product include: false claims about what it purports to accomplish, false advertising, incomplete disclosures, small-print qualifications and disqualifications, deceptive appearance, visual product distortion, deceptive packaging, etc. A company engaging in such practices may be violating consumer protection laws on both the state and federal levels. The United States Federal Trade Commission investigates deceptive practices.

DECISION SUPPORT SYSTEM. *See* **EXECUTIVE INFORMATION SYSTEM.**

DECLARATION **1.** A statement of goods and properties subject to duty assessment submitted to CUSTOMS agents. **2.** A form completed by an entity that has insured a shipment with a marine INSURANCE company regarding losses under the policy. This coverage is applicable to other forms of insurance coverage as well. **3.** The declared value of goods specified by the owner at time of delivery to a CARRIER. **4.** In a legal proceeding, the statement by a plaintiff regarding the circumstances that gave rise to the current legal action.

DECLARATION FORMS (SINGLE AND MULTIPLE) The forms that must be filed with CUSTOMS when an entity imports goods into a country. The list is scrutinized by the United States **CUSTOMS SERVICE** for the purpose of assessing duties on the inventory.

DEDOMICILING The relocation of a multinational company's headquarters to another country so as to lower operating costs, lower overall taxes, and have less government restrictions on it.

DEEMED-PAID CREDIT A part of taxes paid by a multinational company to a foreign government, allowable as a credit (dollar-for-dollar reduction) in taxes due to its home government.

DEFAULT 1. The failure of an individual, entity, or government to make payments of PRINCIPAL or interest on a bond, NOTE, or other DEBT when they come due. In most instances, creditors make claims against the assets of the defaulter to recover lost payments. Any entity that has defaulted on an obligation risks its credit rating and jeopardizes its ability to raise future funds. 2. The failure to perform on a legal duty or obligation. 3. Action taken by a computer when no alternative has been programmed.

DEFAULT RISK The risk that a debtor may fail to pay principal or interest when due. In that event, the investor will incur losses. The investor may seek a third party guarantee of the debt. If default occurs, the investor may make claims against the debtor's assets.

DEFEASANCE 1. An accounting procedure whereby an entity under specified circumstances was allowed to remove DEBT from its balance sheet without being legally released from the obligation. Under **GENERALLY ACCEPTED ACCOUNTING PRINCIPLES,** the entity was allowed to place cash or low risk government securities into a trust to fund the debt and any accrued interest to maturity with virtually no risk that any further intervention regarding payment on the part of the debtor entity would be necessary. This event generally occurred only when interest rates were very high and the current value of a company's debt was low making such reacquisition desirable. When a company followed such a procedure, it generally would have to record an extraordinary gain on the extinguishment of debt. The objective of doing this is to reduce the debt on the financial statements of an entity as cheaply as possible. This procedure is technically described as an " insubstance defeasance." However, after December 31, 1996, the Financial Accounting Standard Board no longer allows an in-substance defeasance to be accounted for as an extinguishment of debt. 2. To terminate the interest of any entity in a given property (i.e., deed) by virtue of the previously stipulated terms of an agreement. It also refers to the instrument that negates the right of the entity to the property. 3. A contractual provision stipulating that a specified act voids the agreement.

DEFECTIVE 1. Having subnormal function or structure. 2. Manifesting an imperfection or fault causing a shortcoming. 3. Unable to meet normal expectations regarding quality, safety, or performance, e.g., a defective product.

DEFECTIVE TITLE 1. Not having all the composite elements necessary to legally control and dispose of property. 2. Ownership in REAL PROPERTY that is not clear of unrestricted legal encumbrances such as unpaid taxes, ownership by someone else, etc. 3. Title obtained in an other than legal manner.

DEFERRAL OF TAX The postponement of paying taxes to a later year or later years. Examples are delaying the receipt of taxable income to the next year or the acceleration of expenses to the current year.

DEFERRED PAYMENT Payment to be delayed until a later time.

DEFICIT 1. In accounting, a debit or negative balance in the retained earnings account. In most states, a deficit balance in the retained earnings of a corporation precludes it from issuing dividends. 2. Amount to which total debt exceeds total assets. 3. Excess of an actual expenditure over the budgeted amount. 4. The result of spending in excess of that allowed in a given situation. For example, the United States government incurs a deficit when it spends in excess of its revenues. Deficit spending on the part of the government over the years has been, in the opinion of some, the cause of inflationary pressure.

DEFICIT SPENDING. *See* **DEFICIT.**

DEFLATION 1. A general decrease in prices. It is the opposite of **INFLATION** and distinguished from **DISINFLATION,** which is a reduction in the rate of price increases. Deflation is often accompanied by declines in output and employment. Deflation is caused by a deflation policy whose tools include fiscal measures such as tax increases and monetary measures such as high interest rates. 2. Statistical adjustment of a time series data made to compensate for the distorting effects of inflation.

DEGRESSION A decreasing trend such as in the market price and/or quantity of a commodity or product sold over time.

DELEGATE 1. An individual who acts as an agent or representative of another. 2. In a hierarchical organization, the transference of authority and control from one individual to another. In a decentralized organization, delegation of authority is from the bottom up rather than from the top down as would occur in a centralized entity. *See also* **DECENTRALIZATION.**

DELIVERED AT FRONTIER Contractual specification requiring a seller to deliver goods being purchased by a buyer to the border (frontier) of a designated country up to the demarcated customs border. The purchaser then takes title and is required to meet all import requirements and pay any duties or **TARIFFS** that may be assessed.

DELIVERED COST The cost of manufacturing and delivering a product to the target market, including total manufacturing cost, transportation charges, cost of insurance and freight, tariff, and any other cost involved in shipping the product to the market.

DELIVERED PRICING. *See* **ZONE PRICING.**

DELIVERY The act of transferring the ownership or title of property from one entity to another. Delivery does not require that property be physically transferred to the physical premises of the transferee. For example, in the purchase or sale of inventory, **FREIGHT ON BOARD,** shipping point provides for the transfer of title from the seller to the buyer when the goods are delivered to the common **CARRIER.** Delivery may also be constructive if physical conveyance is impossible or very difficult. For example, in the purchase or sale of real estate, the transfer of title requires that the deed be delivered.

DEMAND CHARGE A charge to a user based on the maximum amount of the good or service demanded for a given time period. An example is a utility charge to the consumer of electric based on peak demand not the actual amount consumed.

DEMAND MONEY. *See* **CALL MONEY.**

DEMAND PATTERNS Types and features of goods and services demanded by consumers in different nations. Demand patterns are likely to be similar in nations of the same stage of economic progress.

DEMARKETING The vendor of a product or service attempts to lower sales of the product or service because of problems uncovered such as defects, poor quality, and potential health hazards. For example, the vendor may fail to fill orders, encourage retailers to return it, or cease the advertising campaign.

DEMOGRAPHICS Characteristics associated with a population or part thereof including sex, age, income, number in household, type of work, and schooling. This is a paramount concern in marketing products and services so as to reach the "right" groups.

DEMONETIZATION The withdrawal of a currency from circulation and use.

DENOMINATION **1.** Designated face value of coins, paper money, or other currency units that are assigned as legal tender by a government. **2.** Act of naming someone to conduct some act.

DEPENDENCY **1.** The reliance on the part of a nation of depending on another for aid, imports, and other essentials. **2.** A territorial possession of a governing country. **3.** Statistical correlation between variables. **4.** The act of being able to claim a dependency exemption for another on one's tax return as defined by the Internal Revenue Code.

DEPENDENT NATION A country significantly relying on other countries for something such as foreign aid, imported products or services, or defense.

DEPLETION The physical exhaustion of a natural resource (e.g., oil, coal). The entry to record annual depletion is to debit depletion expense and credit accumulated depletion. Accumulated depletion is a contra account to the natural resource to arrive at book value.

EXAMPLE
A coal mine costs $2,000,000 with a salvage value of $200,000. The expected total tons in the mine is 100,000. In the first year, 15,000 tons are extracted. The depletion expense for the first year is computed below.

Depletion per ton = Cost - salvage value/estimated total tons
Depletion per ton = $2,000,000 - $200,000/100,000 = $18

Total depletion expense for the first year equals:
15,000 tons extracted x $18 = $270,000

DEPLETION EXPENSE *See also* **AMORTIZATION, DEPRECIATION, DEPRECIATION OF THE DOLLAR.**

DEPRECIATION 1. The spreading out of the original cost over the estimated life of the fixed assets such as plant and equipment. Depreciation reduces taxable income. Among the most commonly used depreciation methods are straight-line depreciation and accelerated depreciation such as the sum-of-the-years'-digits and double-declining balance methods. **2.** The decline in economic potential of limited life assets originating from wear and tear, natural deterioration through interaction of the elements, and technical obsolescence. To some extent, maintenance (lubrication, adjustments, parts replacement, and cleaning) may partially arrest or offset wear and deterioration. **3.** The decline in value of a currency. *See also* **AMORTIZATION, DEPLETION EXPENSE, DEPRECIATION OF THE DOLLAR.**

DEPRECIATION OF THE DOLLAR Also called cheap dollar, weak dollar, or devaluation; a drop in the value of the dollar that is pegged to other currencies or gold. *See also* **APPRECIATION OF THE DOLLAR.**

DEPRECIATION TAX SHIELD The process of reducing the amount of taxes that has to be paid as a result of systematically deducting the amount of the cost of property, plant, or equipment (excluding land) held for the production of income in a trade or business. Effectively, the **DEPRECIATION** of the long-lived property provides shelter against taxes until their costs (the costs of the assets) are used up.

DEPRESSION A bottom phase of a **BUSINESS CYCLE** in which the economy is operating with substantial unemployment of its resources (such as labor), a depressed rate of business investment and consumer spending, and the loss of the over-all confidence in the economy. An example is the Great Depression of the 1930s. Depression is a much more serious state of economic decline than recession. The economy is at a virtual standstill. See also **RECESSION.**

DEPTH OF MARKET The magnitude of business that can take place without causing price fluctuations and changes in a market.

DERIVATIVES Financial instruments such as **OPTION(s), FUTURES,** and **SWAP(s)** that are derived from their underlying securities and currencies. Their returns are tied to yields on these securities and currencies. These instruments are used by firms to hedge their risks from swings in securities prices or fluctuations in interest or currency exchange rates. They also can be used for speculative purposes, that is, to make risk bets on market movements.

DESTABILIZATION SPECULATION The instigation of wide swings of currency prices that result in significant foreign currency volatility. Destabilization speculation may occur by selling a currency or selling the currency future short when the exchange rate is low or falling with the expectation that such activity will result in additional slippage. It may also occur as a result of buying a currency or buying the currency future when the exchange rate is high or rising with the expectation that there will be further increases in the exchange rate.

DETERMINATION **1.** Ascertaining for customs purposes the origin of merchandise and the componential materials of goods for determining and assessing customs duties on imports (and less frequently on exports). **2.** Setting forth a ruling or purpose.

DEUTSCHE MARK West Germany's currency.

DEVALUATION. See **DEPRECIATION OF THE DOLLAR.**

DIFFERENTIAL ADVANTAGE The advantage accruing to the economy of a nation as a result of doing what it is best fit to do, i.e., based on its economic structure and level of development. For example, nations that are technologically advanced have a differential advantage in the manufacture of high-tech goods and services. Correspondingly, **THIRD WORLD** nations that are not technologically oriented and are inundated with unskilled labor may have a differential advantage in the production of products and services requiring manual labor.

DIFFERENTIAL PRICING. See **DUMPING.**

DIFFERENTIAL TARIFF A duty that is either higher or lower than usual depending on the type of imported item and/or the country it is from.

DIFFERENTIATION OF PRODUCT OR SERVICE Providing a given product or service with a unique distinctive identity for the purpose of enabling purchasers or users to clearly distinguish it from those of its competition. Product or brand differentiation is an important consideration in attempting to increase one's share of the market.

DIFFERENTIATION STRATEGY A marketing program designed to convince purchasers that a given brand of product or service has a highly positive identity that is both different and superior to those of its competitors. Once a product has a known positive market identification, a manufacturer/distributor will create different varieties of the same product in order to take advantage of the primary product's notoriety.

DIFFUSION PROCESS The process whereby the use of an innovation spreads from company to company and from use to use.

DIMINISHING RETURNS A phenomenon by which all inputs increase by a specified percentage and the resulting output rise is a lesser percentage.

DINAR Monetary unit of Abu Dhabi, Aden, Algeria, Bahrain, Iraq, Jordan, Kuwait, Libya, South Yemen, Tunisia, and Yugoslavia.

DIPLOMACY 1. The practice of negotiating pacts, alliances, and international relationships for the purpose of maintaining cohesion and stability between a host country and other nations of the world. 2. The procedural skill of acting, behaving, and articulating information in a certain manner so as to communicate in a direct forthright manner without creating negativity and ill will among participants.

DIRECT COSTING Also called variable costing. A costing method where the costs to be inventoried include only the variable manufacturing costs. The fixed factory overhead is treated as a period cost—it is deducted along with the selling and administrative expenses in the period incurred. For example:

Direct materials	$xx
Direct labor	xx
Variable factory overhead	xx
Product cost	$xx

Fixed factory overhead is treated as a period expense. In contrast, under **ABSORPTION COSTING,** the cost to be inventoried includes all manufacturing costs, both variable and fixed. Nonmanufacturing (operating) expenses, i.e., selling and administrative expenses, are treated as period expenses and thus are charged against the current revenue.

DIRECT FOREIGN INVESTMENT (DFI). *See* **FOREIGN DIRECT INVESTMENT.**

DIRECT INTERCOMPANY LOAN A loan either between a parent company and one of its subsidiaries, or between two subsidiaries. A third party is not involved in the transaction. The loan may be without interest or with a very low interest rate. The terms of the loan are typically flexible (e.g., repayment period). Such a loan is usually made without restrictions (e.g., collateral requirements).

DIRECT MARKETING The promotion of a product or service directly on an individual or personal basis to a potential customer. It seeks a direct response from the customer. The target audience is usually based on a customer list. Examples of direct marketing are mail order, personal visits, telemarketing, videotext, insertions in magazines, and clip cards. An example is a book publisher who sends out flyers to selected groups.

DIRECT QUOTE The price of a unit of foreign exchange expressed in the home country's currency. For example, the direct quote is $.50 per Deutsche Mark (DM) if the home country is the United States.

DIRECT RESPONSE PROMOTION An **ADVERTISING** program seeking customer response by mailing in a coupon and calling in an order. An example is responding to a mailing. Another example is a television commercial for an album with an "800" number to call to buy it. The only two parties involved are the seller and buyer. Therefore, a distributor is not needed.

DIRECT SELLING A United States company sells directly in a foreign country without third party involvement. Since there is an absence of a "go-between," the exporter transacts either directly with the overseas distributor or customer. The benefit of direct sales are more control and lower cost.

DIRHAM Monetary unit of the United Arab Republic and Morocco.

DIRTY FLOAT Flexible exchange rate system in which central banks intervene directly in foreign exchange markets to manipulate short-term swings in exchange rates in a direction perceived to be in the national interest. *See also* **MANAGED FLOAT.**

DISAFFIRM To disassert or repudiate something such as declaring not to be bound by a fraudulent contract.

DISC. *See* **DOMESTIC INTERNATIONAL SALES CORPORATION.**

DISCHARGE 1. To annul or release from an obligation through payment or forgiveness. 2. To be acquitted or dismissed from court charges. 3. To be released from contractual commitments. 4. To be released or fired from gainful employment. 5. To unload a cargo.

DISCLAIMER 1. A type of opinion issued by a Certified Public Accountant when he or she is unable to gather sufficient evidential matter regarding a material matter during the course of an audit. 2. A contractual clause that denies the liability of an entity in a situation that it would otherwise be fully responsible for. **3.** To renounce one's claim or right to something.

DISCLOSURE **1.** The act of revealing in a company's financial statements all unbiased information of a material nature that might influence an investor's financial decisions. Under generally accepted accounting principles, full disclosure is required of all material financial information. Disclosure may be in the body of the financial statements, separate schedule, or footnotes. **2.** To state publicly previously unknown information.

DISCOUNT **1.** The excess of PAR VALUE of a bond or NOTE over its current selling price. The selling price is below par because the stated interest rate of the instrument is below the going market rate of interest demanded by investors. **2.** The difference between the face value of a financial instrument (its future value) such a Treasury bill and its current selling price. The instrument is said to sell at a discount. **3.** Reducing the price of merchandise for the purpose of effecting a quick sale or cash payment. **4.** Reduction in the invoice price of merchandise or equipment if payment is made within a designated period known as the discount period. It is generally of a short duration, e.g., up to about ten days after the invoice period. **5.** The relationship of the selling price of one national currency to another. For example, the United States dollar may be selling at a discount to the British pound. **6.** Deducting interest from the proceeds of a loan thereby increasing the effective interest rate. **7.** Fee paid when selling a note to a bank based on the MATURITY VALUE of the instrument. **8.** In a forward contract for foreign currency, the amount which the FORWARD RATE is below the spot rate. **9.** Incorporating all public information into a company's stock price.

DISCOUNT PERIOD. *See* **DISCOUNT.**

DISCOUNT RATE **1.** Rate of interest used in discounting future cash flows or payments for the purpose of computing their present value. **2.** The interest rate charged by the Federal Reserve Bank to its member for loans.

DISCOUNTING **1.** Process of computing the present worth of a future cash flow-either a single sum or a series of cash sums to be paid or received. For example, this process is used to evaluate the worth of a **FOREIGN DIRECT INVESTMENTS** project. **2.** Interest deducted in advance from a loan. 3. Reduction in selling price of a product or service to stimulate buyer interest.

DISCREPANCY **1.** A difference between what is and what is expected. For example, because of a large discrepancy between the announced earnings of the corporation and what the market expected for the quarter, the price of the company's stock dropped $10 in one day. **2.** Disagreement or divergence between the facts or claims of two parties. For example, a disparity existed in the documents presented to a bank by an exporter regarding the letter of credit issued by the bank.

DISCRETIONARY POLICY Economic policy that is based on judgment rather than being specifically defined or predetermined. For example, the Federal Reserve Board attempts to control inflationary pressure by modifying discount rates in accordance with its discretionary policy.

DISCRIMINATION 1. Prejudicial tariff treatment of internationally traded goods and services based on the nation that they are exported from or the one that they are imported to. 2. Trade measures that favor one country and restrict another. 3. Adversely treating others because of their ethnic background, religion, sex, etc.

DISECONOMIES Also called diseconomies of scale, the decreases in a firm's long-run average costs as the size of its plant is increased. This may be due to (1) competition among firms in bidding up prices of scarce resources and (2) difficulties of maintaining efficient supervision and coordination.

DISECONOMIES OF SCALE. *See* **DISECONOMIES.**

DISHONOR 1. Refusal on the part of a maker of a **NOTE** to make the required payment when the instrument is presented for payment by the holder. 2. To bring shame or insult. An example is an employee of a multinational company engaging in a disgraceful act.

DISINFLATION A reduction in the rate of **INFLATION.** Fiscal and monetary polices are used by governments and central banks to achieve this. This contrasts with **DEFLATION,** which is the decrease in the general level of price.

DISINVESTMENT 1. Withdrawal of the capital invested in a business or a foreign country. 2. Also called **DIVESTITURE,** the selling-off or closing down all or part of a foreign investment (e.g., foreign subsidiaries) for economic or other reasons.

DISSOLUTION If a large and diversified multinational company has been found to violate **ANTITRUST** rules, it may be forced to separate its business segments.

DISTRIBUTION 1. Movement of merchandise from manufacturers to wholesalers to retailers. 2. Payout of money or property from investments to the owner such as a dividend payout or a share distribution. 3. Cost allocation among departments or responsibility centers.

DIVERSIFIABLE RISK That part of the risk of a security associated with such random events such as lawsuits, strikes, winning or losing a major contract, and other events that are unique to a particular firm. This type of risk can be eliminated by proper **DIVERSIFICATION.**

DIVERSIFICATION 1. Spreading investments among different companies, different industries, or different regions in order to reduce risk. Diversification exists by owning securities of many companies having negative or no correlation.

2. Entry into a different business activity outside of the firm's traditional business. This may be a different product, stage of the production process, or country. Some companies wish to diversify their operations by getting into various industries. It can be a long-term, strategic decision on the part of top management.

DIVERSION **1.** A turning aside of some act such as making an untrue excuse as distinct from the real reason for not doing something. **2.** Modifying the billing rate for transported goods after being shipped but before being delivered.

DIVERSIONARY DUMPING A foreign manufacturer sells to a third country below the product's normal selling price. The good is further manufactured and sent to yet another nation.

DIVESTITURE **1.** Losing or giving up a right such as an interest in property. **2.** Selling assets voluntarily or involuntarily. An example is selling a major division because of an ANTITRUST action.

DIVISION **1.** A segment of a business that is physically and operationally separate from the company that it is a part. Because of the disaggregation of assets and activities, a division may be viewed as a self-sufficient unit of the overall entity. For example, Dodge and Plymouth are separate divisions of the Chrysler Corporation. **2.** A strong difference of opinion among members of a multinational company possibly causing animosity.

DOA. *See* **DOCUMENTS ON ACCEPTANCE**

DOBRA Monetary unit of San Tome and Principe.

DOCK RECEIPT A document evidencing the receipt of a shipment at a particular location. Such receipt is the basis to issue a **BILL OF LADING.**

DOCTRINE OF SOVEREIGN IMMUNITY A defense in litigation by an executive of a multinational company that he or she is immune from an act in violation of the law of the home country because of coercion by a foreign government.

DOCUMENTARY COLLECTION A method of payment for a foreign trade (export and import) transaction that adopts a DRAFT and other informational documents, but not a **LETTER OF CREDIT.**

DOCUMENTARY CREDIT **1.** A financial instrument issued by a bank for an importer on behalf of an exporter for purposes of expediting payment for the sale of goods and services. The bank issuing the documentary credit will authorize payments or agree to pay a DRAFT or drafts to another bank or financial institution. **2.** The financing of foreign trade transactions by a bank by providing the importer with credit and the exporter with immediate cash payment. *See also* **TERM DOCUMENTARY DRAFT.**

DOCUMENTARY DRAFT A **SIGHT DRAFT** or **TIME DRAFT** that is accompanied by instructions and such documents as an **INVOICE,** a **BILL OF LADING,** an **INSPECTION CERTIFICATE,** and an insurance paper.

DOCUMENTARY LETTER OF CREDIT A **LETTER OF CREDIT** for which the issuing bank provides that specified documents must be attached to the **DRAFT.** The documents guarantee the importer that the goods have been sent and that title to the merchandise has been duly transferred to the importer.

DOCUMENTATION 1. Support evidence and informational references to a statement or claim. For example, audit documentation of a client's acquisition of real estate might include a copy of the purchase contract, deed, mortgage note, cash payments on the note, tax statements on the property, etc. 2. The underlying collection of documents and materials that describes the intricacy of how a computer program or system was developed. 3. Reference documents and manuals which fully explain how a transaction or activity should be processed in an organization in accordance with standard operating procedure, e .g., a procedure manual. 4. User-friendly description explaining how a program or computer application works.

DOCUMENTS AGAINST PAYMENT (D/P) Procedure for payment of goods used in **INTERNATIONAL TRADE.** In this scenario, an importer receives the documents for the title of the goods purchased only after full payment has been made against the draft that is presented to him. This form of payment is generally used when other guaranteed forms of financing such as a **LETTER OF CREDIT** have not been arranged between importer and exporter.

DOCUMENTS ON ACCEPTANCE (DOA) Procedure for payment of goods used in **INTERNATIONAL TRADE.** In this scenario, the importer receives the documents for the title of the goods only after acceptance (by signature) is made of the obligation to pay the **TIME DRAFT** (payable at a given future time after acceptance) that is presented to him.

DOLLAR BONDS. *See also* **EURODOLLAR.**

DOLLAR CERTIFICATES OF DEPOSIT. *See* **EURODOLLARS.**

DOLLAR COST AVERAGING A diversified investment approach in which the same dollar amount of stock is purchased at regularly scheduled dates. This strategy is particularly suitable for "blue chip" stocks. Since constant dollar investments are made each period, fewer shares are bought at higher prices and more shares are bought at lower prices. This process usually results in a lower average cost per share. Average cost equals;

$$\frac{\text{Total market price per share}}{\text{Total number of buys}}$$

EXAMPLE

A corporate investment manager invests $1,000,000 each month in XYZ Company as follows:

Date	Investment	Market price per share	Shares bought
1/1	$1,000,000	$25	40,000
2/1	1,000,000	30	33,333
3/1	1,000,000	40	25,000
4/1	1,000,000	35	28,571
The average price equals:$130/4 = $32.50			

DOLLAR DRAIN

The excess of a foreign country's imports from the United States over its exports to the United States.

DOLLAR GLUT A significant decline in the value of the United States dollar as a result of an oversupply in the international monetary markets.

DOLLAR INDICES Various measures of the value of the dollar, provided by the Federal Reserve Board (FRB), Morgan Guaranty Trust Company of New York, and Federal Reserve Bank of Dallas. They show different movements since they include different countries and are based on different concepts and methodologies. The data are provided in nominal values (market exchange rates) and in real values (purchasing power corrected for inflation). The FRB index is published in a press release and in the monthly Federal Reserve Bulletin; the Morgan index is published in the bimonthly World Financial Markets; and the FRB Dallas index is published monthly in Trade-Weighted Value of the Dollar. The FRB and Morgan indexes include 10 and 18 industrial nations, respectively, and the FRB Dallas index includes all of the 131 United States trading partners.

DOMESTIC COMMERCE The commercial area of a given country. Any goods that are admitted into this area are subject to the payment of duties or other taxes that are assessed on imports (as required by the trade laws of that nation). Alternatively, goods that are imported into a nation's foreign trade zone are not subject to import duties as long as they remain there or are directly exported to another country. Once the goods are entered into a nation's domestic commerce, they are assessed the required duties.

DOMESTIC CONTENT A requirement that imported products must include a specified percentage of domestic-related input factors (e.g., capital, labor, etc.). This will have a positive impact on the economy of the domestic nation.

DOMESTIC EXPORTS The exports of a given nation. For example, the domestic exports of the United States represent goods either imported from a foreign country that have been substantially changed from their original form, those that have been enhanced through significant additional manufacturing, or those that have been completely manufactured, produced, or grown in the US.

DOMESTIC INTERNATIONAL SALES CORPORATION (DISC) In taxation, domestic corporations, usually subsidiaries, created by the Revenue Act (1971) to encourage exports and improve the balance of trade. A major benefit is the deferment of 50 percent of a DISC's income for a long period of time.

DOMESTIC VALUE ADDED The value (market price) of a good that has been produced in a country less the value of inputs that were imported and made part of the final product. For example, if a given product has a market price of $120 and the value of its imported components is $50, then its domestic value added is $70.

DOMICILE The residence of a company which is the address of its headquarters. It is often its major place of business. For example, General Motors is headquartered in Detroit, Michigan.

DOMINANT COMPANY A firm having substantial power and control in the marketplace. A change in its pricing or production volume will significantly affect the affairs of other companies in the industry.

DOUBLE-DIGIT INFLATION An annual inflation rate of over 10 percent.

DOUBLE-DIP LEASE A property that is leased to two or more entities at the same time.

DOWNSIDE RISK 1. An amount of investment risk incurred in a worst-case scenario. For example, the downside risk of an option is the initial amount of investment in case the timing and direction is completely missed (i.e., the option expires without an exercise). **2.** A multinational company's loss of earnings in a business downturn.

DOWNSIZING Streamlining the company to reduce costs, improve efficiency, and promote productivity. The objective is to enhance corporate profitability through cost cutting. Downsizing may result in restructuring, reengineering, and layoffs.

DOWNSTREAM DUMPING A situation in which foreign manufacturers sell a product at a loss to a producer in a domestic market. The domestic producer reprocesses the product for resale to another nation.

DOWNSTREAM PRICING A commercial company's control over the price of a commodity because of the volume it buys in producing its own product from it. For example, Dole Foods has a dominant role in deciding what the price of pineapples will be to growers. See also **UPSTREAM PRICING.**

DOWNTURN A downward turn in business, a market, or some other economic activity. For example, a downturn in the stock market signals that a current bull market has turned into a bear market. A downturn in a given business indicates that demand for the products of that business has significantly diminished.

D/P. *See* **DOCUMENTS AGAINST PAYMENT.**

DRACHMA Greece's currency.

DRAFTS Also called a **BILL OF EXCHANGE,** the instrument normally used in foreign trade to effect payment. It is simply an order written by an exporter (seller) requesting an importer (buyer) or its agent to pay a specified amount of money at a specified time. The person or business initiating the draft is known as the **MAKER, DRAWER,** or **ORIGINATOR.** The party to whom the draft is addressed is the DRAWEE. When a time draft is drawn on and accepted by a commercial business, it is called a TRADE ACCEPTANCE. When a **TIME DRAFT** is drawn on and accepted by a bank, it is called a **BANKER'S ACCEPTANCE.** *See also* **BANK DRAFT; DOCUMENTARY DRAFT; SIGHT DRAFT.**

DROP SHIPPING **1.** A customer orders goods from a retailer warehoused and the goods are shipped by the supplier directly to the customer's address. **2.** A foreign company ships goods directly to the domestic buyer in the United States.

DUAL CURRENCY BOND A debt instrument in which **PRINCIPAL** is to be paid in one currency (e.g., British pounds), but interest is to be paid in a different currency (e.g., United States dollars). The objective might be to reduce exchange fluctuation. Interest might be payable at **FIXED EXCHANGE RATES.**

DUAL PRICING SCHEME **1.** The selling of the same goods in different markets for different selling prices. This may indicate **DUMPING.** **2.** An arrangement or agreement that allows a selling division to record the transfer of goods or services at a market or negotiated price, and a buying division to record the transfer at a lower cost-based amount. *See also* **TRANSFER PRICING.**

DUAL SYNDICATE EQUITY OFFERING Two groups of financial entities (e.g., investment brokers) that have jointly undertaken the task of underwriting the issuance of stock or some other equity distribution for a corporation.

DUMPING Also known as differential pricing in the **GENERAL AGREEMENT ON TARIFF AND TRADE (GATT),** the practice of selling a good or service in foreign markets for less than their worth, meaning prices below the cost of production or market price of the same product in domestic or other markets. Since it is generally viewed as an unfair trading practice, this may subject the company to antidumping tariffs or penalties. It is illegal in the United States if the practice harms (or threatens to harm) an industry in the United States. Article VI of the GATT permits levy of antidumping duties equal to the difference between the price sought in the importing country and the normal value of the product in the exporting country.

DURABLE GOODS Products that last a long time regardless of hard wear and continual use such as certain tools. Durable goods are a small but volatile portion of consumer expenditures. Many durable goods are bought on credit.

DUTIABLE Imported merchandise subject to a tariff.

DUTY FREE Products for which no customs tariffs apply.

DUTY PAID Goods that have been imported and have been cleared through customs as a result of having all duties that have been assessed on the goods fully paid. Once the required duties have been paid on such commodities, they may be viewed as the equivalent of domestic produced goods that are available for exportation. After the duties are paid, the goods may also be subject to **DUTY REIMBURSEMENT.**

DUTY RATE. See also **ENTIRETIES DOCTRINE.**

DUTY REIMBURSEMENT The refunding of duties charged to an importer for goods that have been imported into a country and are then exported again. This commonly occurs when a component of a product is imported and utilized in the manufacture of another product that is subsequently exported. *See also* **DUTY PAID.**

E

EAFE Index. *See* **MORGAN STANLEY CAPITAL INTERNATIONAL EUROPE, AUSTRALIA, FAR EAST INDEX.**

EASE 1. A gradual or minor reduction in the level of market prices. **2.** To facilitate something.

EASY MONEY An increase in the amount of money available for business and individual spending as a result of economic conditions.

EC. *See* **EUROPEAN COMMUNITY.**

ECLECTIC VIEW Professor **DUNNING's** theory of international production. The theory argues that the extent, form, and pattern of international production are determined by the configuration of three sets of advantages perceived by companies. It attempts to elucidate multinational company activities based on their **OWNERSHIP ADVANTAGES (O), LOCATIONAL FACTORS (L),** and their use of **INTERNALIZATION (I)-OLI** for short. More specifically, (1) As a necessary condition, there must be the ownership advantage. (2) The host country must offer a locational (L) advantage as a production base. (3) There must be an internalization (I) advantage in order for an multinational company to transfer its ownership advantages across national boundaries within its own rather than sell them or their rights to foreign firms.

ECONOMETRICS A subdiscipline of economics that is concerned with empirical testing of economic theory using various statistical methods such as regression analysis. Econometric analysis involves four basic phases: **1.** Specification of the model, which utilizes economic theory and economic reality. **2.** Estimation of the model, using statistical methods such as regression analysis. **3.** Verification of the model, which involves economic interpretation and statistical tests. **4.** Applications, which include testing economic theorems and forecasting economic variables.

ECONOMIC EXPOSURE. *See* **OPERATING EXPOSURE.**

ECONOMIC INTEGRATION Expansion of financial and trade ties among nations. It involves the establishment of a regional **COMMON MARKET** and **FREE TRADE AREA.** It is argued that greater regional economic integration around the globe will lead to more efficient production and more output, thereby making all countries involved in the integration better off.

ECONOMIC NATIONALISM Conservative attitude and behavior regarding the domestic economy of one's nation. Proponents of economic nationalism generally believe that their nation's markets should be closed to foreign imports, that access to the nation's markets should not be available to foreigners, and that ownership of businesses and property by foreigners should be precluded or highly limited.

ECONOMIC ORDER QUANTITY (EOQ) The order size that minimizes the sum of carrying and ordering costs. At the EOQ amount, total ordering cost equals total carrying cost.

ECONOMIC RISK The chance of loss or uncertain variations in earnings of a business due to economic conditions. Economic risks include foreign exchange risk, inflation risk, and interest rate risk.

ECONOMIC SANCTIONS Prohibition or restrictions imposed by one country on another to punish or penalize it for following certain policies or taking actions that the sanctioning nation disapproves. Economic sanctions may take the form of halting trade, aid programs, military assistance, financial and technical guidance, etc.

ECONOMIC SYSTEM A particular system of organization for the production, distribution, and consumption of products and services people use to achieve a certain standard of living. All societies and nations do not agree on the optimal way to address these economic issues. For example, the United States economy uses a capitalist or free-market system while the former Soviet economy is a socialist or planned economy. There are three basic types of economic systems. They are: traditional, command, and capitalistic economic systems. **1.** A traditional economic system relies upon custom, habit, social mores, and tried-and-true methods for achieving economic goals; technology is primitive; changes are slow and production is undertaken in the same way as last year and the year before. Tradition and the status quo are perpetuated. Examples include the feudal system of the Middle Ages and today's underdeveloped countries. **2.** A command economic system relies on public ownership and centralized control of the basic means of production; service limitations are placed upon individual choice when such choices conflict with government-determined economic priorities. Economic plans and activities are under the control of an economic authority such as a central planning authority. Heavy use is made of governmental directives, the assumption being that the government is in the best position to decide what economic choices and policies are most beneficial for the economy and its component parts. The economic questions are solved by government planning. Individual decision making plays only a small role. Both socialistic and communistic nations are examples of command economies. **3.** A capitalistic or market economic system emphasizes private ownership, individual economic freedom, competition, the profit motive, and the price system in the achievement of economic goals. Each economic unit decides what choices and policies are best for it, the thesis being that in encouraging the drive for individual economic self-interest, the outcome proves also to be in the overall best interests of society because of the strong incentives for efficiency, productivity, and satisfaction of consumers. The "what," "how much," and "for whom" questions are primarily solved by a system of free markets. **4.** The United States economy has a relatively strong capitalistic orientation (although it also has a moderate dose of command and, therefore, is most properly described as a "mixed capitalistic" economic system). There is a mixture of private and public enterprise and decision making. The solutions to the questions above result from government planning and regulation as well as the market system.

ECONOMIC UNION A form of **ECONOMIC INTEGRATION** aiming at (1) removing all trade among integrated group member nations, (2) the adoption of a common currency, (3) the promotion of harmonized monetary and fiscal practices among member countries, (4) the reconciliation of tax rates, and (5) the pursuit of a common trade policy.

ECONOMIC ZONES Areas of a country that are designated by its government as having special economic privileges such as being duty free for all imported goods. For example, manufacturing plants in these economic zones would not be assessed any duties on imported goods that were inputs to products that were then reexported. The term economic zones is commonly used terminology in the independent nations that formerly made up the Union of Soviet Socialist Republics and the People's Republic of China.

ECONOMIES OF SCALE The reductions in unit cost achieved by producing a large volume of a product.. This is a situation in which the average cost of production declines as plant size and output is expanded. Some of the reasons are: (1) increased specialization and division of labor, (2) better use and specialization of labor, and (3) use of more efficient or high-tech machinery and equipment.

ECONOMIES OF SCOPE A situation in which the same investment can support multiple profitable projects or activities less costly together than separately. For example, an airline selling round trips from New York to Los Angeles can produce air transportation less expensively than one selling only one-way routes.

ECU. *See* **EUROPEAN CURRENCY UNIT.**

EDGE ACT CORPORATION. *See* **EDGE ACT AND AGREEMENT CORPORATION.**

EDGE ACT AND AGREEMENT CORPORATION A subsidiary of a United States commercial bank, incorporated under federal law and operating abroad, to engage in various international banking and financing operations. The Edge subsidiary is outside restrictions of United States law and may perform whatever services and functions are legal in the foreign countries on which it is based. Named after Senator Walter Edge of New Jersey, who sponsored the original legislation to permit formation of such organizations. *See also* **AGREEMENT CORPORATION.**

EDR. *See* **EUROPEAN DEPOSITORY RECEIPT.**

EEC. *See* **EUROPEAN ECONOMIC COMMUNITY.**

EFFECTIVE ANNUAL YIELD. *See* **EFFECTIVE INTEREST RATE.**

EFFECTIVE (AVERAGE) EXCHANGE RATE **1.** The actual exchange rate, or **SPOT RATE,** that one receives or pays at a point in time on an exchange transaction. The effective exchange rate incorporates any commission or applicable taxes on the transaction as well. **2.** A country's average currency exchange rate weighed among itself and its trading partners on the basis of degree of trade.

EFFECTIVE (REAL) INTEREST RATE (EFFECTIVE ANNUAL YIELD) **1.** YIELD TO MATURITY. **2.** Real rate of interest on a loan. It is the nominal interest rate divided by the actual proceeds of the loan. For example, assume you took out a $10,000, one year, 10 percent discounted loan. The effective interest rate equals: $1,000/($10,000 - $1,000) = $1,000/$9,000 = 11 percent. In this discount loan, the actual proceeds is only $9,000, which effectively increases the cost of the loan. **3.** The **EFFECTIVE ANNUAL YIELD,** better known as the **ANNUAL PERCENTAGE RATE (APR).** Different types of investments use different compounding periods. For example, most bonds pay interest semiannually. Some banks pay interest quarterly. If an investor wishes to compare investments with different compounding periods, he/she needs to put them on a common basis. The APR is used for this purpose and is computed as follows: APR $= (1 + r/m)^m - 1.0$, where r= the stated, nominal or quoted rate and m= the number of compounding periods per year. For example, assume that a bank offers 6 percent interest, compounded quarterly, then the APR is: APR $= (1 + .06/4)^4 - 1.0 = (1.015)^4 - 1.0 = 1.0614 - 1.0 = .0614 = 6.14$ percent This means that one bank offering 6 percent with quarterly compounding, while another bank offering 6.14 percent with annual compounding, would both be paying the same effective rate of interest.

EFFECTIVE RATE OF PROTECTION The extent that prices of domestically produced goods are protected by government assessed protective tariffs. A **PROTECTIVE TARIFF** raises the price of competitive imported goods, making them more expensive than comparable domestic products. The objective of such an action is to make the latter more economically desirable. The effective rate of protection is an annually computed percentage.

EFFECTIVE TAX RATE. *See* **AVERAGE TAX RATE.** *See also* **MARGINAL TAX RATE.**

EFFICIENT FRONTIER. *See also* **EFFICIENT PORTFOLIO.**

EFFICIENT MARKET Markets that adjust very quickly to new information and it is very difficult for investors to outperform the market. If competition exists and transaction costs are low, prices tend to respond rapidly to new information, and speculation opportunities quickly dissipates. The efficient market hypotheses has been subjected to numerous empirical tests, but with mixed results. For example, the more recent studies seriously challenge the view of an unbiased **FORWARD EXCHANGE RATE.**

EFFICIENT PORTFOLIO The central theme of Markowitz's portfolio theory. Efficient portfolio theory states that rational investors behave in a way reflecting their aversion to taking increased risk without being compensated by an adequate increase in expected return. Also, for any given expected return, most investors will prefer a lower risk and, for any given level of risk, prefer a higher return to a lower return. In **Figure 1,** an efficient set of portfolios that lie along the ABC line, called "efficient frontier" is noted. Along this frontier, the investor can receive a maximum return for a given level of risk or a minimum risk for a given level of return. Specifically, comparing three portfolios A, B, and D, portfolios A and B are clearly more efficient than D, because portfolio A could produce the same expected return but at a lower risk level, while portfolio B would have the same degree of risk as D but would afford a higher return. Investors try to find the optimum portfolio by using the indifference curve, which shows the investor's trade-off between risk and return. By matching the indifference curve showing his risk-return tradeoff with the best investments available in the market as represented by points on the efficient frontier, investors are able to find an optimum portfolio.

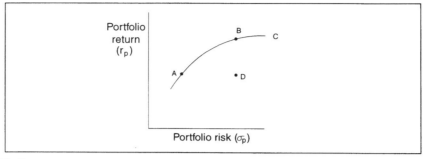

EIS. *See* **EXECUTIVE INFORMATION SYSTEM.**

ELASTIC DEMAND Demand with **PRICE ELASTICITY** of demand greater, in absolute terms, than 1.0 . For example, the demand for luxuries is elastic. If demand is elastic, a price increase(decrease) will induce a decrease (increase) in total revenue. A product that is relatively insensitive to price can have its price substantially increased without a large reduction in demand. The figure below shows the relationships between price elasticity (e_p) and sales revenue (S), which can aid a multinational company in setting its price.

Price	$e_p > 1$	$e_p = 1$	$e_p < 1$
Price rises	S falls	No change	S rises
Price falls	S rises	No change	S falls

ELASTIC SUPPLY Supply which increases (or decreases) more than 1 percent in volume with a 1 percent change in price.

ELECTRIC COMMERCE Conducting sales or other business transactions over the Internet or private networks.

EMBARGO 1. Government restriction on all or some commerce such as for economic reasons or because of some hostility. 2. Government dictates for a company not to do business with a specific country or countries. 3. Government bans as a trade barrier of the transport of specified products. 4. Government prohibition of a commercial ship to enter or leave a particular port.

EMC. *See* **EXPORT MANAGEMENT COMPANY.**

EMERGENCY RATE An ad hoc rate established for the purpose of satisfying an emergency situation requiring special considerations outside of the usual circumstances upon which the standard rate is predicated.

EMOLUMENT To gain from a position or employment such as salaries, bonuses, and stock options awarded to corporate executives.

EMS. *See* **EUROPEAN MONETARY SYSTEM.**

END OF THE MONTH (EOM) A credit period designation that usually means that payment is due at the end of the current month in which a purchase was made. However, convention generally dictates that a purchase made, terms EOM, after the 25th of the current month will not be due until the end of the next month. For example, under EOM terms, any purchase made up to and including March 25 would be due on March 31. However, any purchase made after March 25 would be due by April 30.

ENDORSEMENT **1.** The signature on the reverse side of a check or other negotiable instrument by a payee for the purpose of transferring title to another person or entity. **2.** Written modification of an insurance policy or other type of contract that supersedes the terms of the original agreement. **3.** The act of lending support, approving, sanctioning, or vouching for a product, idea, principle, etc. For example, the endorsement of a product by a highly respected individual significantly improves its marketability. *See also* **ATTACHMENT, RIDER.**

END-USE TARIFF A fee on imported goods based on how they will ultimately be used. For example, an imported product to be used by a charity will be assigned a lower duty than for its commercial use.

ENROUTE EXPENSES A multinational company's reimbursement to its executives for travel expenses between the United States and a foreign country such as for airfare, lodging, limousine, food, and telephone.

ENTERPRISE UNION A union made up of employees at a single firm. It is typically found in Japan.

ENTIRETIES DOCTRINE Applying the duty rate applicable for a finished imported good to imported components thereof.

ENTITY ACCOUNTS. *See* **ACCOUNT.**

ENTITY CENTRALIZATION. *See* **CENTRALIZATION.**

ENTREPOT A temporary warehousing of imported products for sale in the country held or to export again overseas.

ENTRY AND EXIT BARRIERS Types of constraints of new companies entering an industry and/or existing firms from leaving the industry. An example of an entry barrier is the very high-technology nature of the industry and the dominance of a major company in it. An exit barrier might be the substantial cleanup costs from ceasing an operation.

ENTRY DOCUMENTS Documents that must be presented to government agents by an importer in order to clear goods through customs. Examples are customs applications and forms, a **BILL OF LADING**, a **CARRIER'S CERTIFICATE**, seller's invoices, packing slips, etc.

ENTRY STRATEGY A method adopted by a multinational company for entering and penetrating a foreign market. The form has a choice of alternative approaches, including (1) licensing, (2) exporting, (3) local warehousing with direct sales staff, (4) local packaging and/or assembling operations, or (5) full-scale local production and marketing. It may take the form of a direct investment, franchising, **TURNKEY VENTURE,** or other contractual forms.

EOM. *See* **END OF THE MONTH.**

EOQ. *See* **ECONOMIC ORDER QUANTITY.**

EQUITABLE DISTRIBUTION The fair division of assets among affected parties.

EQUITY **1.** That portion of the assets of an entity owned by its owners. For example, in a corporation, equity is represented by stockholders' equity. In a partnership, by partnership equity, and in a sole proprietorship, by owner's equity. **2.** That portion of the value of a real estate holding over and above its mortgage obligation. In order for the owner to receive the cash equivalent of his or her equity, the property would have to be sold (liquidated) and the mortgage obligation paid. The residual cash proceeds would represent the owner's equity in the property. **3.** In a margin brokerage account, the excess of securities owned over the amount borrowed (plus accrued interest) from the broker in order to acquire them. **4.** That which is fair, impartial, and reasonable. **5.** The residual that accrues to the owner in a transaction. **6.** Legal justice. **7.** The remaining value in a futures account if disposed at current market prices.

EQUITY METHOD A method used in preparing a parent company's nonconsolidated financial reports that treats income at the foreign associate's level as being received by the parent when it is earned by the foreign entity. The method requires that the value of the investment in the parent company's balance sheet be increased or decreased to recognize the parent's share of profits or losses since the acquisition. To compute this profit or loss, however, a foreign associate's financial statements must be translated in United States currency, with the translation profit or loss specified.

ERM. *See* **EXCHANGE RATE MECHANISM.**

ESCALATOR CLAUSE A stipulation in an agreement that price may be increased if some uncontrollable eventuality occurs. Examples are rental increases due to either higher property tax rates or fuel prices. Another example is an employment contract in which raises are based on the inflation rate (referred to as the cost of living adjustment).

ESCROW **1.** Property in the form of money, legal documents, other assets, etc., given temporarily to a neutral third party, called the escrow agent, through the mutual agreement of two contracting parties. The escrow agent will deliver the escrow contents to the appropriate party when the conditions of the contract have been met. **2.** Payment of monthly taxes and insurance by a homeowner to the mortgage holder as required by the mortgage note. **3.** Deposits of property to an independent third party for the benefit of another.

ESCROW AGENT. *See* **ESCROW.**

ESCUDO Monetary unit of Azores, Cape Verde Islands, Guinea-Bissau, Madeira, Mozambique, Portugal, Portuguese East Africa, and Timor.

ESPIONAGE The act or practice of spying on another company to obtain key confidential information to obtain a business advantage. Examples are the gathering of secret data on new or existing products, production processes, and current and future company policies.

ESPRIT Sharing among members of a group. *See also* **EUROPEAN STRATEGIC PROGRAM FOR RESEARCH AND DEVELOPMENT IN INFORMATION TECHNOLOGIES.**

ESSENTIAL INDUSTRY An industry whose product is manufactured within its own borders and is economically protected from competition as a result of being considered essential to the security of a country by a government. For example, the United States considers its defense industry to be essential and would never want to be dependent on a foreign nation for defense products during a time of war.

ESTIMATED TIME OF ARRIVAL (DEPARTURE) **1.** The estimated date and time that a shipment of goods is scheduled to arrive at (or depart from) a particular port. **2.** The estimated time that a traveler is expected to arrive at (or depart) from a particular location. **3.** The estimated time that an employee of a multinational company can be expected to arrive at (or depart from) his or her assigned foreign work location.

ETHNOCENTRISM An orientation or style of decision making in the multinational company structure, dictated by the parent company. It is ethnocentric (home-country oriented) in that the parent company's values, knowledge, and interests are reflected in decisions at the subsidiaries. Ethnocentrism is distinguished from **POLYCENTRISM** (host-country oriented); **REGIOCENTRISM** (region-oriented); and **GEOCENTRISM** (world-oriented).

EUROBILL OF EXCHANGE A draft or **BILL OF EXCHANGE** used in **INTERNATIONAL TRADE** calling for an entity (drawer) to pay on demand (sight draft) or at some future specified date (time draft) a designated amount of money to another (drawee) in a foreign currency different from the currency of the country of the current transaction.

EUROBOND MARKET The market for bonds denominated in any currency other than the local one in any country. A bond originally offered outside the country in whose currency it is denominated. Eurobonds are typically dollar-denominated bonds originally offered for sale to investors outside of the United States.

EUROBONDS A bond sold outside the country in whose currency it is denominated. An example is a dollar-denominated bond originally offered for sale to investors outside the United States. It is underwritten by an international syndicate of banks and other securities firms. For example, a bond issued by a United States corporation, denominated in United States dollars, but sold to investors in Europe and Japan (not to investors in the United States), would be a Eurobond. Eurobonds are issued by a **MULTINATIONAL CORPORATION,** large domestic corporations, sovereign governments, governmental enterprises, and international institutions. They are offered simultaneously in a number of different national capital markets, but not in the capital market of the country, nor to residents of the country, in whose currency the bond is denominated. Almost all Eurobonds are in bearer form with a call provision and a **SINKING FUND.** *See also* **EUROBOND MARKET.**

EUROCOMMERICAL PAPER (EURO-CP) **1.** Short-term notes of a multinational company or bank, sold on a discount basis in the eurocurrency market. **2.** Short-term commercial paper issued in **EUROCURRENCY.**

EURO-CP. *See* **EUROCOMMERCIAL PAPER.**

EUROCREDIT **1.** Providing monetary credit in the form of **EUROCURRENCY** by an affiliation of banks. **2.** Any loan of **EUROCURRENCY.**

EUROCURRENCY Any currency deposited in a bank located in a country other than the country issuing the currency. *See also* **EUROCREDIT.**

EUROCURRENCY MARKET (or **EURODOLLAR MARKET**) A market for a currency deposited in a bank outside the country of its origin, say, the United States, which is based primarily in Europe and engaged in the lending and borrowing of United States dollars and other major currencies outside their countries of origin to finance **INTERNATIONAL TRADE** and investment.

EURODEPOSIT Dollar-denominated deposits held in banks outside of the United States. *See* **EURODOLLAR.**

EURODOLLAR MARKET. *See* **EUROCURRENCY MARKET.**

EURODOLLARS Dollar-denominated deposits kept overseas in banks. They represent claims held by Europeans for United States dollars. Typically, these are time deposits ranging from a few days up to one year. These deposit accounts are extensively used abroad for financial transactions such as short-term loans, the purchase of dollar certificates of deposit, or the purchase of dollar bonds (called **EUROBONDS**) often issued by United States firms for the benefit of their overseas operations. In effect, Eurodollars are an international currency.

EUROEQUITY ISSUE A share of equity securities issued on a foreign currency different from the national currency that the securities normally trade in.

EUROMARKET DEPOSITS Dollars deposited outside of the United States. Other important Eurocurrency deposits include the Euro-yen, the Eurodeutsche mark, the Eurofranc, and the Europound.

EUROMARKETS Also called the **EUROCURRENCY MARKET,** the international market that is engaged in the lending and borrowing of United States dollars and other major currencies outside their countries of origin to finance **INTERNATIONAL TRADE** and investment. The main financial instruments used in the Eurocurrency market for long-term investment purposes are the **EUROBONDS.** Despite its name the market is not restricted to European currencies or financial centers. It began as the 'Eurodollar market' in the late 1950s.

EURONOTE A note payable in **EUROCURRENCY** traded in markets outside the jurisdiction of the entity that issued it.

EUROPE 1992 The year targeted by the **EUROPEAN COMMUNITY** as "Europe Without Frontiers" in which all trade and fiscal barriers would be eradicated. The goal was to create a unified, single, powerful economic and political union of European member states. The goal of total unification has not yet been achieved. More time is needed before all planned goals for unity reach fruition.

EUROPEAN COMMON MARKET Also known as the **EUROPEAN COMMUNITY (EC).** The goals of the European Common Market are to reduce trade barriers within the member nations of the European Community and create a strong, unified, cohesive political block. The six founding members of the EC include Belgium, France, Italy, Luxemburg, Germany, and the Netherlands. Subsequent to this, the following European countries also joined: Denmark, Ireland, England, Greece, Portugal, and Spain. Currently, 12 countries constitute the European Community. Other countries that are expected to join in the near future include: Austria, Finland, Sweden, and Norway. The EC is attempting to eliminate custom duties between member states and establish an external tariff that would affect the importation of goods from external countries trading with EC members. In addition, the EC is striving to establish a common agricultural policy and the free movement of labor and capital between its member states.

EUROPEAN COMMUNITY (EC) Also called **COMMON MARKET;** the association of Western European countries formed in 1957 that has eliminated most tariffs among member nations, harmonized some fiscal and monetary policies, and broadly attempted to increase **ECONOMIC INTEGRATION** among them. *See also* **EUROPEAN ECONOMIC COMMUNITY.**

EUROPEAN CURRENCY UNIT (ECU) A composite currency created by the **EUROPEAN MONETARY SYSTEM** to function as a reserve currency numeraire, consisting of fixed amounts of the currencies of the members of the **EUROPEAN ECONOMIC COMMUNITY.** The weighting is based on the foreign currency in the ECU on a percentage relationship to the equivalent United States dollar. The objective is to keep a stable relationship in European currencies among members. It may be used as the numeraire for denomination of a number of financial instruments. For example, **EUROBONDS** may be expressed in ECU terms.

EUROPEAN DEPOSITORY RECEIPT (EDR) A means of trading of foreign investments by Americans in the securities of foreign countries. Purchased foreign securities are deposited in a bank in the country of the securities' origin. A negotiable depository receipt is then issued by an affiliated bank in the country in which the purchaser resides providing proof of ownership of the specific securities purchased. The EDR minimizes the intricacy and expense of security transfer and eliminates the need to ship the stock certificates to the owner.

EUROPEAN ECONOMIC COMMUNITY (EEC) An agreement signed under the treaty of Rome in 1957 that initially joined Belgium, Germany, France, Italy, Luxembourg, and the Netherlands in a **COMMON MARKET** in 1958, was expanded to include Denmark, Ireland, and England in 1973, again in 1981 to include Greece, and finally once again in 1986 to include Portugal and Spain. The objectives of the EEC is to form a common market by eliminating trade barriers among member countries, to work toward the improvement of working and living conditions of its members' people, and to unify Europe overall. The EEC is also known as the **EUROPEAN COMMUNITY, COMMON MARKET,** or the Community.

EUROPEAN MONETARY SYSTEM (EMS) A mini-**INTERNATIONAL MONETARY FUND** system, formed in 1979 by 12 European countries, under which they agreed to maintain their exchange rates within an established range about fixed central rates in relation to one another. These central exchange rates are denominated in currency units per **EUROPEAN CURRENCY UNIT.** The EMS observes exchange rate fluctuations between member-nation currencies, controls inflation, and makes loans to member governments, primarily to serve the goal of **BALANCE OF PAYMENTS** stability.

EUROPEAN STRATEGIC PROGRAM FOR RESEARCH AND DEVELOPMENT IN INFORMATION TECHNOLOGIES (ESPRIT) An organization, formed in 1984, to foster multi-country research in information technology.

EUROPEAN TERMS Foreign exchange quotations for the United States dollar, expressed as the number of non-United States currency units per United States dollar. For example, 1.25 DM/$.

EUROPEAN UNIT OF ACCOUNT A monetary unit composite consisting of a basket of specific **EUROPEAN COMMUNITY** currencies based on the relative economic size of the EC member. The monetary unit was initially termed the European Unit of Account but was later renamed (1979) the **EUROPEAN CUR-RENCY UNIT (ECU)** when the **EUROPEAN MONETARY SYSTEM (EMS)** was established. Under the EMS, the ECU is the exchange rate unit used for fixing central rates, a settlement unit for the central banks, an accounting unit, a reserve unit, and a credit mechanism. The ECU is reviewed every five years (or upon request) if the composite weight of an any currency in the formula changes by 25 percent or more. The ECU is scheduled soon (1999) to become the single used European currency in the EMS.

EVEN-PAR SWAP The simultaneous sale and acquisition **(SWAP)** of a block of bonds of the same nominal par or stated value amount without consideration of any difference in their values. As a result, this block for block exchange is made without any concern for disparity in cash value.

EVERGREEN CLAUSE **1.** A provision in a contract between a multinational company and a distributor permitting the latter to renew the contract as it deems appropriate. **2.** A loan provision giving a financial institution the right each year to convert a **REVOLVING CREDIT** loan to a short-term loan. **3.** A clause in a **LETTER OF CREDIT** allowing for an automatic extension of time.

EVIDENCE OF ORIGIN Data shown in the **CERTIFICATE OF ORIGIN** indicating that imported goods are eligible for a reduced duty assessment due to an exporting nation's preferential trade arrangements with an importing country.

EVIDENCE OF RIGHT TO MAKE ENTRY ENTRY DOCUMENTS that the pur-chaser of imported goods must submit to customs authorities in order to clear goods into a country. Examples are customs applications and forms, a **BILL OF LADING,** a **CARRIER'S CERTIFICATE,** an **AIRWAY BILL** (for goods transported by air), seller's invoices, packing slips, etc.

EX DOCK **1.** Goods shipped are extracted from the receiving dock. **2.** Products are placed by the seller at the shipping point with all duties and import restric-tions satisfied. They are ready and available for the buyer's receipt.

EX SHIP The seller's products will be available for buyer pickup on the ship docked at the receiving port as stipulated in the contractual agreement. The obligation, expense, and risk for transporting the goods over the seas rests with the seller.

EXCEPTIONS **1.** Circumstances which takes a transaction out of the standard processing loop. For example, in **INTERNATIONAL TRADE,** a government may treat a certain country as a special partner and exempt all goods imported from that nation from duty or tariff assessments. **2.** A situation that does not conform to a general rule or procedure. **3.** Any transaction that does not meet an established criteria and therefore requires special attention. An auditor frequently "audits by exception" by looking into only those items that appear to be materially improper or incorrect.

EXCESS CAPACITY The overproduction by a firm or industry of a good or service, causing some of the facilities to remain idle (unused). The possible causes for excess (over) capacity include too many suppliers, overinvestment in plant and equipment, less than expected demand, and inability to sell overseas.

EXCESS FREIGHT Freight exceeding the amount indicated in the **WAY BILL**.

EXCHANGE CONTROLS Restrictions imposed by the government on use of foreign exchange, aiming at limiting outflows of funds from a nation. These restrictions restrained access to foreign currency at the central bank and multiple exchange rates for different users.

EXCHANGE DEPRECIATION The decline in value of a nation's currency due to governmental devaluation, monetary funds, reduction in its underlying support base such as gold, etc.

EXCHANGE EXPOSURE The risk of loss due to unfavorable changes in exchange rates occurring when an entity's assets and liabilities are denominated in a foreign currency.

EXCHANGE PERMIT A permit required by some governments of importing entities that allows an importer to expediently convert the currency of the host nation into foreign currency of the exporter needed for payment of the goods being purchased.

EXCHANGE RATE. *See* **EFFECTIVE EXCHANGE RATE; FIXED EXCHANGE RATES; FOREIGN EXCHANGE RATE.**

EXCHANGE RATE MECHANISM (ERM) The mechanism of the **EUROPEAN MONETARY SYSTEM** in which the countries of the **EUROPEAN ECONOMIC COMMUNITY** control the exchange rates of their respective currencies. Member countries preagree on the limits that their exchange rates may vary. If the exchange rate of two nations exceeds the preagreed limit (when fluctuations exceed plus or minus 2.5 percent of benchmark limits), then their respective central banks intervene and buy or sell the necessary amount of currencies needed to bring the exchange rate back into the range of acceptability.

EXCHANGE RATE UNCERTAINTY. *See* **CURRENCY RISK.**

EXCHANGE RISK. *See* **FOREIGN EXCHANGE RISK.**

EXCHANGE RISK ADAPTATION The strategy of suiting the company's activities to lessen the potential impact of unexpected changes in **FOREIGN EXCHANGE RATE.** This may be accomplished by way of **HEDGING** or other alignments in the foreign currency activities of the firm.

EXCHANGE RISK AVOIDANCE The strategy of eliminating dealings or activities which involve high **CURRENCY RISK,** and/or charging more prices when exchange risk seems to be greater.

EXCHANGE RISK TRANSFER The strategy of avoiding or diminishing **CURRENCY RISK** through the purchase of insurance policies or the use of **HEDGING** to cover possible exchange rate-induced losses.

EXCISE TAX Tax levied on the production and/or consumption of a broad range of goods and services as well as license fees imposed by governments. Examples of excise taxes are federal and local taxes on cigarettes or gasoline. These taxes are typically added to the total sales price.

EXCLUSIVE DEALING AGREEMENT Contractual agreement where a manufacturer or wholesaler grants exclusive concession distribution rights for a product to another party encompassing some specified territorial area. The party signing the exclusive dealing agreement with the manufacturer is promised that it will have an exclusive right to purchase the product from the producer and that it will be its only distributor (retail or otherwise) in a designated geographical area. As part of the agreement, the producer also agrees to prohibit other retailers from selling the product in the designated concession area.

EX-COUPON A **BEARER BOND** that is sold without the latest interest coupon. The person purchasing such a bond would not be entitled to interest until the due date indicated on the next interest coupon generally six months later.

EX-DIVIDEND Purchasing shares of stock of a given corporation which are selling without the right to receive the latest declared dividend. When shares sell "ex-dividend" they are theoretically purchased right after the corporation's date of record. The date of record is the day on which the corporation prepares a list of all the shareholders that are duly entitled to receive the corporation's latest declared dividend. The date of record is about three to four weeks after the date of declaration. However, to allow the stock exchanges to expediently process all transactions, the ex-dividend is set three days before the date of record so that sufficient lead time is available for stock settlement to allow for the preparation of the stockholder list on the date of record. On the date of declaration, the stock selling price increases by the amount of the expected dividend and decreases by that amount on the ex-dividend date when the stock is selling without the right to receive the declared dividend. Thus, the dividend is actually earned on the date of declaration and not on the day of record. Anyone purchasing the company's stock between the date of declaration and the ex-dividend date must pay for the dividend (declared) in the stock purchase price that will be received on the date of payment.

EX-DIVIDEND DATE. *See* **EX-DIVIDEND.**

EXECUTIVE GAMES. *See* **MANAGEMENT GAME.**

EXECUTIVE INFORMATION SYSTEM (EIS) Also called an executive support system **(ESS)**, a decision support system **(DSS)** made specially for top managers and specifically supports strategic decision making. An EIS draws on data not only from systems internal to the organization but also from those outside, such as news services and market research databases. The EIS user interface often uses a mouse or a touch screen to help executives unfamiliar with using a keyboard. One leading system uses a remote control device similar to those used to control a television set. An EIS might allow senior executives to call up predefined reports for their personal computers, whether desktops or laptops. They might, for instance, call up sales figures in many forms by region, by week, by fiscal year, by projected increases. The EIS includes capabilities for analyzing data and doing "what if" scenarios.

EXECUTIVE SUPPORT SYSTEM. *See* **EXECUTIVE INFORMATION SYSTEM.**

EXERCISE PRICE The price at which an option may be used to buy/sell foreign exchange.

EXHIBITION A large scale public display by a manufacturer or producer of goods or services at a convention, fair, profession conference, etc. , for the purposes of stimulating the sale of its products.

EX-IM BANK. *See* **EXPORT-IMPORT BANK.**

EXIT/REENTRY VISA A permit issued by a government enabling a foreign national to leave the country and then reenter at a later time.

EXONERATED CARGO A country's allowance of imported goods customarily subject to **TARIFFS** to enter duty-free on a temporary or permanent basis.

EXPANSION The augmentation of a multinational company's sales capacity for the purpose of taking advantage of new markets or high demand for its products.

EXPANSIONISTIC PRICING A strategy utilized by multinational companies especially in underdeveloped nations to significantly lower the price of goods and services for the express purpose of stimulating demand for its output. The goal of expansionistic pricing is to aggressively reduce prices to obtain a larger market share. *See also* **EXTINCTION PRICING; PENETRATION PRICING.**

EXPATRIATES. *See* **EXPROPRIATION.**

EXPERIENCE CURVE EFFECTS Also called **LEARNING CURVE** effects, the phenomenon in which learning from repetition and experience makes production more efficient or cost-effective includes the labor, management, and resources.

EXPIRATION DATE 1. The date **TARIFFS** will end. 2. Final date specified in a **LETTER OF CREDIT** in which the required documents must be presented to the bank issuing the letter for the purpose of guaranteeing payment to a shipper. The documentation that is presented must be in strict compliance with the letter of credit or payment will not be forthcoming. Upon receipt of the requisite documents prior to the expiration date, payment (to the bank) is directly made by the buyer or the bank takes title to the goods themselves and pays the seller.

EXPORT The process of shipping goods or rendering services outside a country or sovereign domain for sale in another country or sovereign domain.

EXPORT BROKER An entity or individual that acts as an **INTERMEDIARY** or middleman in arranging the sale of goods or services between buyer and seller for a fee. The broker, however, takes no part in the actual sales transaction.

EXPORT BUYER 1. An organization or individual that purchases goods for sale to companies in other countries. *See also* **EXPORT HOUSES.** 2. An entity that purchases closeout inventory, surplus production goods, or discontinued items at significantly reduced prices for resale to companies in other countries around the world. *See also* **EXPORT HOUSES.**

EXPORT COMMISSION AGENT An organization that acts as a commissioned **PURCHASING AGENT** for a foreign buyer. An export commission agent is also known as an export commission house.

EXPORT CONTROLS Controls or restrictions imposed on the export of military, scientific, and other goods deemed by a government as items effecting its national security, competitive selling position, foreign policy, etc.

EXPORT CREDIT 1. Government-sponsored **EXPORT FINANCING** programs to assist domestic producers in the cultivation of new export markets. See also **EXPORT DEPARTMENT,** and **EXPORT-IMPORT BANK.** 2. Extended credit terms or deferred payment programs offered by a producer to stimulate growth in the exportation of goods and services. *See also* **EXPORT FINANCING.**

EXPORT CREDIT GUARANTEE DEPARTMENT. *See* **EXPORT DEPARTMENT.**

EXPORT DECLARATION An exporter's formal export declaration to customs agents at the port of exit providing fundamental data regarding the goods being exported. Governments use this declaration for export control and statistical purposes. For example, the Shipper's Export Declaration is a form required by the United States Treasury Department that requires a shipper to indicate the description, weight, value, destination, etc., of goods being exported. *See also* **RULES OF ORIGIN.**

EXPORT DEPARTMENT An official governmental agency of the United Kingdom which provides British producers with guarantees, insurance against default by importers, and interest rate subsidies so they may easily obtain bank financing for exports to compete worldwide for export markets. Also known as the Export Credit Guarantee Department.

EXPORT DIVERSIFICATION The attempt by a nation to broaden its export items and move away from being a limited number of goods exporter (or a single product exporter) as the source of its foreign trade.

EXPORT DOCUMENTATION SERVICE A service provided for exporters for a fee insuring that all necessary export documentation has been prepared and all regulations have been followed in exporting products from a given host nation. The service insures that all exported goods are properly documented for purposes of **EXPORT DUTY** assessment, **EXPORT CONTROLS,** and general statistical needs. In addition, assurance is provided that all **RULES OF ORIGIN** are followed for ascertaining what duties will be assessed on the goods when they enter the importing nation.

EXPORT DUTY The assessment of a tariff by a government on goods exported from a territory under its domain. *See also* **EXPORT LEVY.**

EXPORT FINANCING **1.** Government-sponsored export financing programs to assist domestic producers in the cultivation of new export markets. *See also* **EXPORT CREDIT, EXPORT DEPARTMENT,** and **EXPORT-IMPORT BANK.** **2.** Extended credit terms or deferred payment programs offered by a producer to stimulate growth in the exportation of goods and services. *See also* **EXPORT CREDIT.**

EXPORT HOUSES An **EXPORT BUYER** or trader that purchases goods for sale to companies in other countries. By purchasing the goods outright, the export house does much more than simply broker a sales transaction for a given purchaser. An export house, for example, promotes the exporter's products, controls all aspects of the sale, and is responsible for purchasers' accounts uncollectibility.

EXPORT INSTABILITY Short-term fluctuations in the prices and earnings of exports due to fluctuating exchange rates, political considerations, etc.

EXPORT INSURANCE Insurance purchased by an exporter for protection against the risk of nonpayment by a foreign importer. It generally covers any financial institution that has extended credit to the foreign importer or has guaranteed the purchase obligation.

EXPORT JOBBER An entity that purchases goods for exportation by reselling them to foreign importers without ever having to take physical possession. Although the export jobber obtains title to the goods, the supplier directly sends them to the new buyer bypassing the need to have them physically transferred to the export jobber.

EXPORT LEVY A tariff charged by a government on merchandise exported from a territory it controls. *See also* **EXPORT DUTY.**

EXPORT MANAGEMENT COMPANY (EMC) An independent firm that acts as the export department for other firms. It provides a full range of services to the manufacturer and handles the entire export function for its customers except supplying the product. The most well-known EMCs are the Japanese "Sogo Shoshas," which handles about half of Japan's total foreign trade and provide global market information, financing, foreign exchange risk bearing and sales negotiating functions as well as physical distribution.

EXPORT MERCHANT An individual business that buys products for its own account and then sells them to foreign buyers.

EXPORT PACKERS Entities that specialize in packing goods for exportation by ship, airline, or railroad. For example, export packers often specialize in the containerization of products that are to be exported.

EXPORT PRICE INDEX Index that measures price changes in agricultural, mineral, and manufactured products for goods sold to foreigners. It represents increases and decreases in prices of exporting goods due to changes in the value of the dollar and changes in the markets for the items of exporting goods. The index is provided monthly by the Bureau of Labor Statistics (BLS) in the United States Department of Labor. The data are published in a press release and the BLS monthly journal, the Monthly Labor Review.

EXPORT PROMOTION A strategy for economic development that focuses on increasing a country's exports to generate foreign exchange and stimulate domestic production. The **LESS DEVELOPED COUNTRY** and less endowed nations in particular feel a dire need to earn foreign exchange through expanding exports. Governmental action to promote exports include sponsoring market research on foreign sales opportunities, arranging trade fairs, establishing trade promotion offices in foreign nations, offering tax incentives in the forms of exemption from certain domestic taxes, special credits for exporters, export insurance programs, and bonus payments or subsidies through administration of **EXCHANGE CONTROLS.**

EXPORT QUOTA Restrictions or quotas imposed by the government of an exporting entity limiting the volume, value, or nature of goods that may be sold to entities in foreign countries around the world. Export quotas may be assessed as part of a policy to protect the consumers or manufacturers of an exporting nation from shortages of certain products, to control prices overseas, or to limit the sale of certain type of high technology goods in certain parts of the world. *See also* **EXPORT CONTROLS.**

EXPORT RATE The cost of transporting goods from a domestic location to a foreign nation via the nearest shipping port. The export rate is usually less expensive than the domestic one.

EXPORT RESTRICTIONS A voluntary restriction arranged between two trading countries in which an exporting nation agrees to limit the amount of exports of certain products to an importing nation at the request of the latter. This usually occurs when the magnitude of importation of a given product is causing competitive hardships for a domestic industry in the importing nation. For example, Japan, in the recent past, agreed to honor an American request to voluntarily cap the number of automobiles exported to the United States in order to protect the auto industry. *See also* **VOLUNTARY QUOTA.**

EXPORT STATISTICS A measure of the total amount of goods (determined through market or quantity valuation) that were exported from the United States to foreign nations. Export statistics generally specify the location from which the exportation took place. For example, merchandise may have been exported from the territories under the auspices of United States Customs, bonded warehouses outside the United States monitored by United States Customs, etc.

EXPORT SUBSIDIES Payments and any other economic benefits (tax credits, price supports, etc.) that are given by a government to a manufacturing entity of that nation if the company sells its output to foreign nations (i.e., the goods are exported). The **GENERAL AGREEMENT ON TARIFFS AND TRADE** has indicated that such governmental interference distorts trade and competition and stymies the accomplishment of the fair trade goals enumerated in the agreement.

EXPORT TARGETING An attempt by the government to stimulate and boost the exportation of products of a given industry (or firm) to foreign countries.

EXPORT TRADING COMPANY A company set up primarily to promote exports of domestic goods and services and help unrelated companies export their products, while being exempt from United States antitrust law. The Export Trading Act of 1982 is a United States initiative aiming at encouraging business firms, particularly small companies, to join together and form export trading companies in order to expand exports. The law permits banks to provide equity capital by taking an ownership interest in these exporting ventures.

EXPORT VALUE The price that exporting foreign manufacturers want for the sale of their goods in the United States. The export value of a good is its net sales price after all applicable discounts.

EXPORTER Any entity (manufacturer, wholesaler, broker, **COMMISSION AGENT,** etc.) that sells or arranges for sales of merchandise and services to a foreign nation.

EXPORTER PARTICIPATION The portion of an export contract that has been organized by one or more exporters as part of a group generally administered by a government-sponsored bank (e.g., **EXPORT-IMPORT BANK**) in which export financing is arranged.

EXPORT-IMPORT BANK (EX-IM BANK) It is the United States agency charged with providing the backbone support for American exports through credit risk protection and funding programs. The programs provided through the EX-IM bank makes international factoring more feasible because they offer credit assurance alternatives that promise funding sources the security they need to agree to a deal. When the EX-IM bank is involved, the payor must be a foreign company buying from a United States company. Just as the EX-IM bank makes international commerce a realistic alternative for wary United States companies, it helps make international factoring as feasible as domestic factoring. The EX-IM bank has nothing to do with imports, in spite of the name, but it plays a key role in determining the competitiveness of the United States among its trading partners because of the buyer credit programs which is often a major component of an overseas customer's ability to finance, and therefore to buy, American products. The EX-IM bank's willingness and ability to insure foreign private or sovereign buyers in any corner of the world often determines whether the United States supplier can offer competitive or acceptable terms to the foreign buyer. The EX-IM bank states that its responsibilities are: to assume most of the risks inherent in financing the production and sale of exports when the private sector is unwilling to assume such risks, to provide funding to foreign buyers of United States goods and services when such funding is not available from the private sector, and to help United States exporters meet officially supported and/or subsidized foreign credit competition. These roles fit into four functional categories: (1) export credit insurance, (2) foreign loan guarantees, (3) supplier credit working capital guarantees, and (4) direct loans to foreign buyers. The EX-IM bank, in addition to other federal support programs for export finance and promotion, can be looked as a competitive weapon provided by the United States to help match export marketing advantages with those extended by foreign governments on behalf of their exporters and United States firms' foreign competition. From 1986 to 1987, the EX-IM bank engaged in a major restructuring to make its programs more accessible to small businesses, easier to use, and more competitive with the export credit agencies of other countries. Approximate overall support through guarantees, loan, or insurance by region is as follows: Latin America, $5.2 billion; Asia, $4.6 billion (the Peoples Republic of China was the biggest recipient in 1994); Europe and Canada, $2.7 billion; Africa and the Middle East, $340 million. Another advantage to factoring brokers is that the EX-IM bank has a wealth of information on foreign buyers as a result of its insurance guarantee and lending activities. Information that has been given in confidence to the EX-IM bank will not be divulged; however, general information about the repayment habits of buyers insured or funded by the EX-IM bank is available. You can call or fax Credit Services at the EX-IM bank for further information. The EX-IM bank's Washington headquarters are at 811 Vermont Avenue NW, Washington, DC 20571, and its toll-free number for general information is 1-800-565-3946, fax (202) 565-3380. There are five regional offices: New York, Miami, Chicago, Houston, and Los Angeles.

EXPORT/IMPORT TRANSACTION Sale of domestic products to foreign countries and purchase of imports. The basic activity of **INTERNATIONAL TRADE** is export-import.

EXPOSURE NETTING An open position in which exposures in one currency are offset with exposures in the same or another currency, where exchange rates are anticipated to move in such a way that losses (gains) on the first exposed position should be balanced with gains (losses) on the second currency exposure.

EXPROPRIATION The action of a country in seizing or modifying the property rights or assets owned by a foreigner or foreign corporation without compensation (or with inadequate compensation).

EXTENDED COVERAGE Insurance coverage that may be purchased that protects against the risk of loss in situations that are not usually covered by typical insurance policies. For example, one may purchase added windstorm and hail coverage to a standard building insurance policy by paying an additional premium.

EXTERNAL BILL A **BILL OF EXCHANGE** or **DRAFTS** that is drawn in one country or state and payable in another. *See also* **FOREIGN BILL.**

EXTERNAL BOND A bond issued in a foreign currency by a corporation, government, or any other entity of a given nation for the purpose of selling outside that country. *See also* **INTERNAL BOND.**

EXTERNALIZATION The practice of contracting with an outside firm (outsourcing) or agent to do the activity instead of doing it in-house. This is in contrast to **INTERNALIZATION,** which is the extension of ownership by a company to cover new markets, new sources of materials, and new stages of the production process.

EXTINCTION PRICING A marketing strategy utilized by multinational companies in which prices for goods are sufficiently reduced in an attempt to undercut the competition and drive them from markets around the world. *See also* **EXPANSIONISTIC PRICING; PENETRATION PRICING.**

EXTRACTIVE FOREIGN DIRECT INVESTMENT (FDI) A form of FDI adopted by the multinational company for the sole purpose of securing raw materials such as oil, copper, agricultural products or other materials.

F

FACILITATING INTERMEDIARY An entity that makes shipping arrangements or actually ships goods to foreign destinations on behalf of others. This may include arranging for or performing all the processing and preparation of documentation needed to "clear" goods successfully imported into a country through customs. *See also* **FREIGHT FORWARDER; CUSTOMS BROKER.**

FACTOR 1. The outright sale of a firm's accounts receivable to another party (the factor) without recourse, which means the factor must bear the risk of collection. Some banks and commercial finance companies factor (buy) accounts receivable. The purchase is made at a discount from the account's value. Customers either remit directly to the factor (notification basis) or indirectly through the seller. 2. The basis or variable on which a shipping charge is based such as a rate per mile the cargo is transported.

FACTORY DOOR COST The cost of manufacturing a product at the factory level. It normally includes, however, marketing and administrative costs and a predetermined markup.

FADE-OUT A government policy toward **FOREIGN DIRECT INVESTMENT** that requires gradual divestment of foreign ownership over time, ending with either complete local ownership or with some maximum foreign percentage ownership. For example, a joint venture may have served the purpose of helping a firm acquire local experience in the initial entry state but no longer serves this need at a later stage.

FAF
"Fly away free," for short.

FAIR MARKET VALUE. *See* **FAIR VALUE.**

FAIR TRADE 1. An arrangement between manufacturer and retailer that required that a manufacturer's goods not be resold by a retailer below a preagreed price. The Consumer Goods Pricing Act of 1975 prohibits this type of arrangement (i.e., fair trade pricing agreements) in interstate commerce. 2. The buying and selling of goods and commodities that have not been acquired unfairly. That is they have been acquired at less than fair market value as a result of government subsidies or artificially low purchase prices. *See also* **UNFAIR COMPETITION; DUMPING.**

FAIR VALUE 1. Price negotiated at **ARM'S LENGTH** between a willing buyer and a willing seller, each acting in his/her best interest. 2. The fair market value of a multinational company's activities that is used as a basis to determine the tax. 3. The appraised amount determined by an independent appraiser.

FALSE ADVERTISING Untrue, incorrect, wrong, or misleading promotion of merchandise, services, or property. Legal liability exposure may exist for fraudulent statements.

FAQ "Frequently asked questions" for short.

FASB. *See* **FINANCIAL ACCOUNTING STANDARDS BOARD.**

FDI. *See* **FOREIGN DIRECT INVESTMENT.**

FEDERAL RESERVE. *See* **FEDERAL RESERVE SYSTEM.**

FEDERAL RESERVE BOARD OF GOVERNORS The seven members of the Federal Reserve Board are nominated by the President and confirmed by the Senate. A full term is 14 years. One term begins every two years, on February 1 of even-numbered years. A member who serves a full term may not be reappointed. A member who completes an unexpired portion of a term may be reappointed. All terms end on their statutory date regardless of the date on which the member is sworn into office. The Chairman and the Vice Chairman of the Board are named by the President from among the members and are confirmed by the Senate. They serve a term of four years. A member's term on the Board is not affected by his or her status as Chairman or Vice Chairman. *See also* **AGREEMENT CORPORATION, EDGE ACT AND AGREEMENT CORPORATION.**

FEDERAL RESERVE SYSTEM The system, created by an act of Congress in 1913, that is made up of twelve Federal Reserve District Banks, their 25 branches, and all national and state banks (about 5,700 member banks) that are part of the system scattered throughout the nation. It is headed by a seven-member Board of Governors. The primary function of the Board is to establish and conduct the nation's monetary policy. The System manages the nation's monetary policy by exercising control over the money stock. It controls the money supply primarily in three ways: (1) by raising or lowering the reserve requirement; (2) by setting the discount rate for loans to commercial banks; and (3) by purchasing and selling government securities, mainly three-month bills and notes issued by the United States Treasury. The System serves as the central bank of the United States. It is a banker's bank that offers banks many of the same services that banks provide their customers. It performs many other functions, such as setting margin requirements, regulating member banks, and acting as Fiscal Agent in the issuance of United States Treasury and United States Government agency securities.

FI "Free in," for short, meaning that all expenses for loading into the hold of a vessel are for the account of the consignee.

FIAT MONEY Money that circulates and is accepted (by law) as legal tender that is not backed by a precious metal e.g., gold, silver, etc.

FIFO *See* **FIRST IN FIRST OUT.**

FINAL GOODS Products that are consumed rather than inputs in manufacturing other products. Final goods are consumed by households.

FINAL SALES Sales of products made to consumers, governments, and foreigners which are not used in the production of other goods. Sales of long-lived equipment and machinery to producers of goods are also considered final sales.

FINANCIAL ACCOUNTING DISCLOSURE **1.** Or simply **DISCLOSURE,** all material and relevant information concerning a firm's financial position and the results of operations, shown usually in the footnotes accompanying the financial statements. Examples are the terms of major loan arrangements and the existence of contingent liabilities. **2.** The Securities and Exchange Commission requirement calling for special disclosures detailing and significant developments in Form 8-K.

FINANCIAL ACCOUNTING STANDARDS BOARD NO. 52 (FASB NO. 52)

The **STATEMENT OF FINANCIAL ACCOUNTING STANDARD (SFAS No. 52)** that requires that business transactions and foreign operations that are denominated and recorded in a foreign currency be restated in terms of US dollars in accordance with Generally Accepted Accounting Principles. The statement sets the accounting and reporting standards for all foreign currency transactions and the translation of foreign currency financial statements. Three of the salient directives of FASB NO. 52 are: (1) Revenues, expenses, gains and losses (Income Statement items) of a foreign entity are to be translated into the reporting entity's currency using the weighted-average exchange rate for the period. (2) Assets and liabilities (Balance Sheet) accounts are to be translated at the current rate of exchange at the Balance Sheet date. (3) Currency translation gains or losses derived from the conversion of foreign currency financial statements should not be recognized in income but should be reported in a separate section of stockholders' equity.

FINANCIAL DERIVATIVE A transaction, or contract, whose value depends on, or, as the name implies, derives from the value of underlying assets such as stocks, bonds, mortgages, market indexes, or foreign currencies. One party with exposure to unwanted risk can pass some or all of that risk to a second party. The first party can assume a different risk from the second party, pay the second party to assume the risk, or, as is often the case, create a combination. The participants in derivatives activity can be divided into two broad types-dealers and end-users. Dealers include investment banks, commercial banks, merchant banks, and independent brokers. In contrast, the number of end users is large and growing as more organizations are involved in international financial transactions. End-users include business, banks, securities firms, insurance companies, governmental units at the local, state, and federal levels, "supernational" organizations such as the World Bank, mutual funds, and both private and public pension funds.The objectives of end users may vary. A common reason to use derivatives is so that the risk of financial operations can be controlled. Derivatives can be used to manage foreign exchange exposure, especially unfavorable exchange rate movements. Speculators and arbitrageurs can seek profits from general price changes or simultaneous price differences in different markets, respectively. Others use derivatives to **HEDGE** their position; that is, to set up two financial assets so that any unfavorable price movement in one asset is offset by favorable price movement in the other asset. T h e r e are five common types of derivatives: options, futures, forward contracts, asset swaps, and hybrid. The general characteristics of each are summarized in the figure below. An important feature of derivatives is that the types of risk are not unique to derivatives and can be found in many other financial activities.

The risks for derivatives are especially difficult to manage for two principal reasons: (1) the derivative products are complex, and (2) there are very real difficulties in measuring the risks associated derivatives. It is imperative for financial officers of a firm to know how to manage the risks from the use of derivatives.

GENERAL CHARACTERISTICS OF MAJOR TYPES OF FINANCIAL DERIVATIVES			
Type	**Market**	**Contract**	**Definition**
Option	OTC or Organized Exchange	Custom* or Standard	Gives the buyer the right but not obligation to buy or sell a specific amount at a specified price within a specified period.
Futures	Organized Exchange	Standard	Obligates the holder to buy or sell at a specified price on a specified date.
Forward	OTC	Custom	Same as futures
Swap	OTC	Custom	Agreement between the parties to make periodic payments to each other during the swap period.
Hybrid	OTC	Custom	Incorporates various provisions of other types of derivatives.

*Custom contracts vary and are negotiated between the parties with respect to their value, period, and other terms.

FINANCIAL DOCUMENTS Certificates, vouchers, and other underlying written support that provides evidence that money is owed by one party to another. Examples of financial documents include: **DRAFTS, BILL OF EXCHANGE, NOTES,** checks, etc.

FINANCIAL FUTURE Futures contracts in which the underlying commodities are financial assets. Examples are debt securities, foreign currencies, or market baskets of common stocks.

FINANCIAL MARKETS The financial markets are composed of **MONEY MAR-KETS** and **CAPITAL MARKETS.** Money markets (credit markets) are the markets for short-term (less than one year) debt securities. Examples of money market securities include United States Treasury bills, federal agency securities, bankers' acceptances, commercial paper, and negotiable certificates of deposit issued by government, business, and financial institutions. The money market securities are characterized by their highly liquid nature and a relatively low default risk. Capital markets are the markets in which long-term securities issued by the government and corporations are traded. Unlike the money market, both debt-instruments (bonds) and equities (common and preferred stocks) are traded. Relative to money market instruments, those of the capital market often carry greater default and market risks but return a relatively high yield in compensation for the higher risks. The **NEW YORK STOCK EXCHANGE,** which handles the stock of many of the larger corporations, is a prime example of a capital market. The **AMERICAN STOCK EXCHANGE** and the regional stock exchanges are still another example. These exchanges are organized markets. In addition, securities are traded through the thousands of brokers and dealers on the over-the-counter (or unlisted) market, a term used to denote an informal system of telephone contacts among brokers and dealers. There are other markets which include (1) the commodity markets which handles various **COMMODITIES FUTURES,** (2) the **FOREIGN EXCHANGE MARKET,** which involves international financial transactions between the United States and other countries, (3) the mortgage market that handles various home loans, and (4) the insurance, shipping, and other markets handling short-term credit accommodations in their operations. A primary market refers to the market for new issues, while a secondary market is a market in which previously issued, "secondhand" securities are exchanged. The New York Stock Exchange is an example of a secondary market.

FINANCIAL TRANSFERS Strategies adopted by multinational companies to move funds across borders, such as loans, profit remittances, and payments for intracompany shipments.

FINDER'S FEE A fee or commission paid to an individual or entity that brokered a given business transaction or "deal". The finder is the party responsible for bringing together the parties to the agreement and insuring its final resolution. Finder's fees generally consist of either a given percentage of the market value of the transaction or a predetermined amount paid for by one, some, or all of the participants in the transaction. For example, a real estate agent is paid a commission or finder's fee by the seller of real property in the form of a percentage of the real estate price paid to the seller of the property at the time of closing the sale.

FIRST IN FIRST OUT (FIFO) A system of inventory valuation under which firms use to compute ending inventory cost from most recent purchases and cost of goods sold from older purchases including beginning inventory. The opposite of **LAST IN FIRST OUT.**

FIRST WORLD In contrast with the **THIRD WORLD,** the industrialized countries. They are primarily members of the **ORGANIZATION FOR ECONOMIC COOPERATION AND DEVELOPMENT.**

FISHER EFFECT A thesis that nominal interest rates (i) in each country equal the required real rate of return (r) plus compensation for the expected amount of **INFLATION** (I) over the period of time for which the funds are to be lent (i.e., $i = r + I$).

FIXATION The establishment of a price for a product or service. An example is setting a price for a commodity or precious metal once a day based on the demand/supply relationship.

FIXED EXCHANGE RATES An international financial arrangement in which governments directly intervene in the foreign exchange market to prevent exchange rates from deviating more than a very small margin from some central or parity value. *See also* **FOREIGN EXCHANGE RATE.**

FIXED FEE CONTRACT A contract requiring that a preagreed compensatory amount be paid to a contractor by a contractee for a given project regardless of the costs that are required for its satisfactory completion.

FIXED INCOME INVESTMENT Any investment that pays a rate of return that is fixed and unchanging over its lifetime. For example, bonds (corporate, government, municipal, etc.) and preferred stock are considered fixed income investments because they generate a constant rate of return for their investors while they are owned.

FIXED PRICE **1.** A meeting of the minds regarding the establishment of a set price. **2.** Contractual price that must be charged regardless of the underlying manufacturing and selling costs. **3.** Price of selling newly issued securities by an investment banker to the public set by contractual mutual agreement. **4.** Price level used in a standard costing pricing system for the valuation of inventory (i.e., pricing raw material, work-in-process, and finished goods). **5.** The sale of a product or service at a set price without any customer negotiation.

FLANKER BRAND A multinational company introduces in the market place a new brand of a product classification when it already has one or more brands in that category. The brand might be differentiated by color, cost, size, taste, or use. An example is a book publisher having a product line of investment books who adds another in the series.

FLAT **1.** The trading price for a bond excluding any accrued interest accumulated since the last interest date. The purchaser of a bond by convention must pay the seller any accrued interest since the last interest date in order to fully complete a bond trade. However, income bonds and bonds in DEFAULT are traded flat. **2.** An apartment on a given floor of a building. **3.** Unchanging fixed lease or mortgage payments. **4.** Earnings of a company that are unchanged compared to the prior year. **5.** A rate that does not manifest change from one period to the next. For example, if interest rates have remained flat they are identical to last year's rates. **6.** An obligation without interest. **7.** Horizontal graph reading indicating lack of change.

FLAT RATE **1.** A price that remains constant regardless of the volume purchased or sold. **2.** Fee that is charged for a given job or project that is fixed irrespective of the amount of labor or time needed for completion. For example, the contractor charged the customer the promised flat rate for the job even though it took him 25 percent more time to complete than he had estimated. **3.** Rate that remains unchanged relative to a prior period.

FLEXIBLE BUDGET Also called a variable budget; a budget based on different levels of activity. It allows for the variation in costs associated with changes in output volume. The costs, for example, at 75 percent of capacity, are different from costs incurred at 90 percent capacity. It is an extremely useful tool in cost control in that the actual cost incurred is compared to the cost allowable for the activity level achieved. The primary use of the flexible budget is for accurate measure of performance by comparing actual costs for a given output with the budgeted costs for the same level of output. For example, flexible budgeting is strongly recommended for performance evaluation and cost control.

FLEXIBLE EXCHANGE RATES Also called **FLOATING EXCHANGE RATES,** an arrangement by which exchange rate levels are allowed to change daily in response to market demand and supply. Arrangements may vary from free float, i.e., absolutely no government intervention to managed float, i.e., limited but sometimes aggressive government intervention in the foreign exchange market.

FLEXIBLE MULTI-ITEM FACTORY A plant that has a high labor/capital ratio and thus the capability to produce more than one diverse product without incurring huge capital costs.

FLEXIBILITY Capable of being flexed or bent. For example, a nation's economy is sometimes viewed as having flexibility if it is sufficiently resilient to absorb an economic downturn or downturns. A company is sometimes thought of as having financial flexibility if even after several loss years, it is still able to take advantage of unexpected opportunities such as financing the acquisition of a company that just became available for sale. An executive is flexible if he can easily adjust to change.

FLEXTIME A multinational company's policy of allowing workers to work eight-hour shifts other than the customary "9 to 5". The advantage to the company is the utilization of facilities for a longer time period, certain cost savings (e.g., utility rates and online data base charges are typically lower during evening hours), and greater employee productivity because the work schedules reflect what employees are comfortable with.

FLOAT **1.** Period of time between the deposit of checks in a depositor's bank and the time of their final collection from the bank(s) upon which they were drawn. Companies sometimes write checks against these funds although the money has fully cleared. **2.** The issuance of securities such as bonds or stocks to the public generally through an investment banker. For example, the company floated a bond issue that was highly in demand. **3.** The amount of funds that have been deposited in one bank awaiting collection from others. These funds represent conditional credits in the account of the depositors.

FLOATER Insurance coverage for property that is moved from one location to another. Frequently such coverage is scheduled; that is, the amount of coverage for each property item is denoted in a schedule appended to the policy.

FLOATING EXCHANGE RATES Also called flexible exchange rates; an arrangement by which exchange rate levels are allowed to change daily in respond to market demand and supply. Arrangements may vary from free float, i.e., absolutely no government intervention to **MANAGED FLOAT,** i.e., limited but sometimes aggressive government intervention in the foreign exchange market. *See also* **FOREIGN EXCHANGE RATE.**

FLOATING INSURANCE Maritime insurance covering all of an entity's shipments exported to foreign countries over a given time period. *See also* **MARINE INSURANCE; OPEN INSURANCE.**

FLUCTUATION Variation and change in the form of increases and decreases in exchange rates, interest rates, stock prices, bond prices, price level indices, Gross National Product, economic conditions, etc. It is the state of continually varying in an irregular way.

FOB. *See* **FREE ON BOARD.**

FOLLOW-ON MARKET The market where a product is introduced following its introduction. This contrasts with the **LEAD MARKET.** Subsidiaries in follow-on markets can learn from the lead market experience, and to the benefit of the total multinational company, has established a durable, competitive presence in a major market capable of giving financial and technical support to activities in other markets.

FOLLOW-THE-LEADER STRATEGY The strategy found in the oligopolistic market, meaning that the follower waits to see how an industry leader operates (e.g., a price hike or introduction of new technology), and then follows a copycat strategy in areas that appear profitable.

FORCE MAJEURE A provision in a marine contract excusing one of the parties for failure to perform because of circumstances beyond their control. Examples include fire, hurricane, earthquake, government seizure, and war.

FORECASTING The process of analyzing available information regarding economic variables and their relationships and then predicting the future values of certain variables of interest (such as costs, a **FOREIGN EXCHANGE RATE,** earnings, sales, revenue, or future general and market conditions) to the firm or to economic policy makers.

FOREIGN AID The policy of a nation of giving financial and technical aid to other countries. Foreign aid may take the form of money in the form of grants, equipment in the form of machinery and tools, short and long-term loans, technical and training assistance programs, etc. Foreign aid may be given as: a general policy of a country (motivated perhaps by self-interest in a given region of the world); emergency assistance in time of disaster such as flood, famine, war, etc.; or military assistance for protection against a common enemy.

FOREIGN BANKING MARKET The market available for services of a foreign bank in a country. An example is a French bank operating in the United States. The market may be for depositors, borrowers, etc.

FOREIGN BILL A bill of exchange or draft drawn in a given state that is payable in another state or foreign country. *See also* **EXTERNAL BILL; BILL OF EXCHANGE; DRAFTS.**

FOREIGN BOND A bond underwritten by a syndicate composed of members from a single country, sold principally within that country, and denominated in the currency of that country. The issuer, however, is from another country. A bond issued by a Swedish corporation, denominated in dollars, and sold in the United States to United States investors by United States investment bankers, would be a foreign bond. Foreign bonds have nicknames: foreign bonds sold in the United States are **YANKEE BONDS;** foreign bonds sold in Japan are **SAMURAI BONDS;** and foreign bonds sold in the United Kingdom are **BULL-DOGS.** The table below specifically reclassifies foreign bonds from a United States investor's perspective.

FOREIGN BONDS TO United States INVESTORS		
	Sales	
Issuer	**In the United States**	**In Foreign Countries**
Domestic	Domestic bonds	Eurodollar bonds
Foreign	Yankee bonds	Foreign currency bonds
		Eurodollar bonds

FOREIGN BOND MARKET That portion of the market for bond issues floated by foreign companies or governments.

FOREIGN BRANCH An exporter's sales or administrative local office situated in a foreign country that goods frequently are exported to. The employees of the foreign branch work for the exporter.

FOREIGN CONTENT The incremental value of a good exported from the United States that is manufactured, added to, or assembled in a foreign country.

FOREIGN CORPORATION 1. Corporation that is chartered under the laws of foreign nation. *See also* **ALIEN CORPORATION.** 2. Corporation that is chartered in a state other than the one in which it does its day to day business in. Relative to the state in which it was formed, the corporation is considered a foreign entity. *See also* **ALIEN CORPORATION.**

FOREIGN CORRUPT PRACTICES ACT A United States law forbidding bribery, kickbacks, and other corrupt practices from being offered or given to foreign officials, directly or indirectly, for the purpose of influencing that individual (or causing that individual to use his or her influence) to obtain or retain business. This law also requires that accounting records be maintained in reasonable detail and accuracy, and that an appropriate system of internal accounting controls be maintained. The title is misleading since the Act's provisions apply to all publicly held companies, even though they conduct no business outside the United States.

FOREIGN CREDIT INSURANCE ASSOCIATION (FCIA) Private United States insurance carrier that insures exporters in conjunction with **EXPORT-IMPORT** bank.

FOREIGN CURRENCY FUTURES A contract to deliver a specified amount of foreign currency by some given future date. *See* **FUTURES.**

FOREIGN CURRENCY OPERATIONS Also called foreign-exchange market intervention, purchase or sale of the currencies of other nations by a central bank for the purpose of influencing foreign exchange rates or maintaining orderly foreign exchange markets.

FOREIGN CURRENCY OPTION An option contract that gives the holder the right (but not the obligation) to exercise it to purchase a given amount of foreign currency at a specified price during a fixed time period. Contract specifications are similar to those of **FUTURES CONTRACTS,** except that the option requires a premium payment to purchase (and it does not have to be exercised).

FOREIGN CURRENCY SWAPS The exchange by an entity of the currency of one nation for another. The exchange is made to protect money from changes in foreign exchange rates. Generally the swap of currencies involves a foreign exchange contract to enable the trader to recover the currency that was swapped.

FOREIGN CURRENCY TRANSACTION Any transaction involving the currency of a foreign nation. For example, foreign currency transactions include the establishment of foreign currency balances with banks in foreign countries, the trading of actual foreign currency, the transacting of foreign currency checks, etc.

FOREIGN CURRENCY TRANSLATION The process of determining the equivalency of an amount of money in one currency in terms of another using the exchange rate that exists between them. In accordance with **FINANCIAL ACCOUNTING STANDARDS BOARD No. 52,** Income Statement items (revenues, expenses, gains, and losses) are translated into the reporting entity's currency using the weighted-average exchange rate for the period. Balance Sheet items (assets and liabilities) are translated at the current rate of exchange at the Balance Sheet date.

FOREIGN DIRECT INVESTMENT (FDI) Investments that involve ownership of a company in a foreign country. In exchange for the ownership, the investing company usually transfers some of its financial, managerial, technical, trademark, and other resources to the foreign country. Types of foreign direct investments include extractive, agricultural, industrial, and service industries. It is distinguished from **PORTFOLIO INVESTMENTS** that are made to earn investment income or capital gains.

FOREIGN EQUITY MARKET The total of offerings of issuers, brokers, and agents that constitute the market involving the purchase and sale of equity securities of entities incorporated outside the United States.

FOREIGN EXCHANGE The financial instruments to pay international trading debts. Such instruments consist not only of currency, but also of checks, drafts, and bills of exchange. A **FOREIGN EXCHANGE MARKET** is available for trading foreign exchanges.

FOREIGN EXCHANGE ARBITRAGE Use of simultaneous contracts to buy and sell foreign exchange at different prices or at different times in such a way that a profit is made and no exchange risk is borne.

FOREIGN EXCHANGE CONTRACT. *See* **FORWARD CONTRACT; FUTURES.**

FOREIGN EXCHANGE HEDGING Protecting against the possible impact of exchange rate changes on the firm's business by balancing foreign currency assets with foreign currency liabilities. *See also* **HEDGING.**

FOREIGN EXCHANGE MARKET A market where foreign exchange transactions take place, that is, where different currencies are bought and sold. In practice this market is not located in any one place, most transactions being conducted by telephone, wire service, or cable. The three functions of the foreign exchange market are to transfer purchasing power, provide credit, and minimize exchange risk. The market is dominated by banks, nonbank foreign exchange dealers, individuals and firms conducting commercial and investment transactions, and exchange brokers who buy and sell foreign currencies and make a profit on the difference between the exchange rates and interest rates among the various world financial centers. In addition to the settlement of obligations incurred through investment, purchases, and other trading, the foreign exchange market involves speculation in exchange futures. New York and London are the major centers for these transactions.

FOREIGN EXCHANGE MARKET INTERVENTION. *See* **FOREIGN CURRENCY OPERATIONS.**

FOREIGN EXCHANGE RATE The price of one country's currency relative to another. The actual exchange rate is determined by the interaction of supply and demand in the **FOREIGN EXCHANGE MARKET.** Such supply and demand conditions are determined by whether the country's basic balance of payments position is in surplus or deficit. Exchange rates can be expressed in **AMERICAN TERMS** or **EUROPEAN TERMS.** Exchange rates can be fixed at a predetermined level (fixed exchange rate), or they can be flexible to reflect changes in demand (floating exchange rate). Foreign exchange is the instruments used for international payments. Foreign exchange rates are determined in various ways: (1) **FIXED EXCHANGE RATES.** It is an international financial arrangement in which governments directly intervene in the foreign exchange market to prevent exchange rates from deviating more than a very small margin from some central or parity value. (2) **FLOATING EXCHANGE RATES.** Also called flexible exchange rates. It is an arrangement by which exchange rate levels are allowed to change daily in response to market demand and supply. Arrangements may vary from free float, i.e., absolutely no government intervention to managed float, i.e., limited but sometimes aggressive government intervention in the foreign exchange market. (3) **FORWARD EXCHANGE RATE.** It is the exchange rate in contract for receipt of and payment for foreign currency at a specified date usually 30 days, 90 days, or 180 days in the future, at a stipulated current or "spot" price. By buying and selling forward exchange, importers and exporters can protect themselves against the risks of fluctuations in the current exchange market.

FOREIGN EXCHANGE RISK. *See* **CURRENCY RISK.**

FOREIGN EXCHANGE TRADING The purchase and sale of foreign currency relative to a host currency such as the United States dollar, British pound, French franc, etc.

FOREIGN FINANCING Form of financing when a foreign company enters into a foreign capital market and borrows money in the local currency. For example, a Japanese company borrows United States dollars in Japan or French francs in Paris.

FOREIGN FUND. *See* **INTERNATIONAL FUND.**

FOREIGN INCOME 1. Income earned by Americans for services performed in a nation outside the United States. **2.** All earnings generated by (an) individual(s) outside their country of citizenship.

FOREIGN INVESTMENT STATUTE Laws passed generally by governments of communist and socialist nations that specify strict operating guidelines for foreign companies doing business in their countries.

FOREIGN LOAN GUARANTEES. *See* **EXPORT-IMPORT BANK.**

FOREIGN MARKET 1. The value of goods and services that a country has sold or has offered for sale in foreign countries. Foreign market sales include the value of all exports that a nation makes to other countries. **2.** The sector of an economy concerned with the importation and exportation of goods, investments, banking transactions, and capital movement with respect to foreign nations.

FOREIGN MARKET BETA The risk of volatility relating to foreign market investments including stocks, bonds, real estate, etc., relative to the overall American stock market. Beta measures give the investor an indication of whether a foreign market investment is less risky, as risky, or more risky than an average stock market investment. This comparison is based on such measures as the Standard and Poor's 500 or the Dow Jones 30 Industrials.

FOREIGN PERSONAL HOLDING COMPANY **1.** A United States company whose objective is to invest or have an interest in foreign companies. **2.** In taxation, a foreign company in which more than 50 percent of voting power or the total value of stock is owned by no more than five United States citizens.

FOREIGN POLICY The direction, course of action, or procedures of a government, or business entity that are intended to influence others (governments, groups, individuals, etc.), determine decisions, affect actions, etc., in its best interests. Foreign policy typically relates to considerations regarding human rights, terrorism, foreign aid, etc.

FOREIGN PORTFOLIO INVESTMENT. *See* **PORTFOLIO INVESTMENTS.**

FOREIGN RISK The risk of loss of investment, other assets, profits, or operational problems of a company in foreign areas. Examples of such risk include changes in the **FOREIGN EXCHANGE RATE,** foreign government expropriation of property, and inhibitive taxes or other restrictions.

FOREIGN SALES AGENT An entity or individual that serves as the sales representative for a domestic based supplier in foreign countries. The primary function of a foreign sales agent is to help increase the sales volume of the domestic supplier abroad.

FOREIGN SALES CORPORATION (FSC) A corporation provided for in the Tax Reform Act of 1984. The FSC replaces the **DOMESTIC INTERNATIONAL SALES CORPORATION** as a tax incentive for exporters. The FSC is a foreign company that exports for a United States firm, which may show its export profits in the FSC and avoid United States taxation on a percentage of the earnings until they are remitted to the parent United States firm. To be eligible for special tax treatment, an FSC must be a foreign corporation, maintain an office outside the United States territory, keep a summary of its permanent books of account at the foreign office, and have at least one director resident outside of the United States. There are some variations: (1) Small FSCs are the same as FSCs, except that small FSCs must file an election with the International Revenue Sales, and have their tax exemption limited to the income generated by $5 million or less in gross export revenues. Small FSCs do not have to meet foreign management or foreign economic process requirements but must fulfill other requirements. (2) Shared FSCs are FSCs which are "shared" by 25 or fewer unrelated exporter "shareholders" for the purpose of reducing costs while obtaining the full tax benefits of an FSC.

FOREIGN SALES CORPORATION (FSC) ACT A United States government act that replaces the **DOMESTIC INTERNATIONAL SALES CORPORATION** legislation. It is a part of the Tax Reform Act of 1984 that is designed to provide a tax incentive for exporting United States-produced goods.

FOREIGN SOURCING Producing or purchasing products or parts from a foreign location, usually to reduce costs. Many electronic firms make their memory chips through contract with local firms in a foreign country such as Taiwan to lower the costs.

FOREIGN SUBSIDIARY An operation within the parent company that is incorporated in a foreign country. It may be wholly or partially owned by the company.

FOREIGN TAX A tax charged by a foreign nation on a United States company for activities within its borders. An example is an income tax on income generated from sales of the company's products in that country. A United States tax credit is allowed for taxes imposed on the same income by a foreign government. *See also* **FOREIGN TAX CREDIT.**

FOREIGN TAX CREDIT If a company pays income taxes to a foreign country, it may be eligible for a United States foreign tax credit. However, the credit cannot be used to reduce the United States tax liability on income from United States sources. It is computed as follows:

Foreign tax credit = Foreign source income x United States tax/Total worldwide income liability

It is economically advantageous for a business to take advantage of all allowable tax credits.

FOREIGN TAX RATE The rate of tax imposed by a nation on an entity doing business within its jurisdiction. It is usually based on the net income earned within such territory or jurisdiction.

FOREIGN TRADE ORGANIZATION (FTO) A government trading company run by a communist country.

FOREIGN TRADERS INDEX (FTI) A statistical index compiled by the United States and Foreign Commercial Service. It is overseas contact files covering information about foreign entities, addresses, contact persons, revenue, company size, and products sold or services rendered.

FOREIGN-BASE COMPANY A foreign corporation that derives a substantial portion of its income from sales, services, or shipping. *See also* **ALIEN CORPORATION; FOREIGN CORPORATION.**

FORFAITING A means of export financing similar to **FACTORING,** which is the sale of receivables by an exporter for cash. Forfaiting is the discounting-at a fixed rate without recourse-of medium-term export receivables denominated in fully convertible currencies (United States dollar, Swiss franc, Deutsche mark). This technique is typically used in the case of capital-goods exports with a five-year maturity and repayments in semiannual installments. The discount is set at a fixed rate-about 1.25 percent above the local cost of funds or above the **LONDON INTERBANK OFFERED RATE.** Forfaiting differs from factoring in two ways: (1) forfaiting may be for years, while factoring may not exceed 180 days; (2) forfaiting typically involves political and transfer uncertainties but factoring does not. This method of financing was used most frequently to finance imports into Eastern Europe. A third party, usually a specialized financial institution, guarantees the financing. Many forfaiting houses are subsidiaries of major international banks, such as Credit Suisse. These houses also provide help with administrative and collection problems.

FORFEITURE **1.** The punitive loss of tangible or intangible property (or anything else of value) as a result of not complying with the law. **2.** The loss of escrow assets as a result of a default on a contract.

FORMER BUYER Customers who have not made any new purchases of merchandise from a supplier for a relative long period, generally a year or more. Mailing lists of former buyers are frequently in demand because such individuals or entities represent excellent prospects for return business.

FORWARD CONTRACT A mutual written agreement between two parties for the actual purchase or sale of a stipulated amount of a commodity, currency, financial instrument, or other item at a price determined at the present time with delivery and settlement to be made at a future date, usually 30, 90, or 180 days.

FORWARD COVER The utilization of foreign forward exchange contracts to protect an entity from fluctuations in the exchange rate as a result of its involvement in a current **FOREIGN CURRENCY TRANSACTION.**

FORWARD DIFFERENTIAL. *See* **FORWARD DISCOUNT; PREMIUM.**

FORWARD DISCOUNT Also called forward differential, the difference between a **SPOT RATE** and **FORWARD RATE,** expressed as an annual percentage. *See also* **PREMIUM.**

FORWARD EXCHANGE RATE The contracted exchange rate for receipt of and payment for foreign currency at a specified date usually 30 days, 90 days, or 180 days in the future, at a stipulated current or "spot" price. By buying and selling forward exchange contracts, importers and exporters can protect themselves against the risks of fluctuations in the current exchange market.

FORWARD FOREIGN EXCHANGE MARKET Simply called forward market. The market where foreign exchange dealers can enter into a contract to buy or sell any amount of a currency at any date in the future. It differs from the **FUTURES MARKET.**

FORWARD INTEGRATION The expansion by a manufacturer into more of the operation and marketing cycle of a product especially getting closer to the good's final user. For example, the opening of a Nike retail store by Nike Corporation is an example of forward integration in the sneaker industry.

FORWARD MARGIN The spread between the price of currency today and its price at some future date.

FORWARD MARKET. *See* **FORWARD FOREIGN EXCHANGE MARKET.**

FORWARD POSITION The current net status of an individual or entity with respect to the difference between its forward purchases and sales obligations of foreign currency at a given point in time.

FORWARD RATE The exchange rate to buy or sell currencies for future delivery at a specified later date. The more distant the contract date, usually the lower the exchange rate. *See* **FORWARD EXCHANGE RATE.**

FORWARD TRANSACTION Transactions in the foreign exchange market. In the forward market, unlike in the spot market where currencies are traded for immediate delivery, trades are made for future dates, usually less than one year away. The forward market and the **FUTURES MARKET** perform similar functions, but with a difference. In the forward market foreign exchange dealers can enter into a contract to buy or sell any amount of a currency at any date in the future. In contrast, futures contracts are for a given month (March, June, September, or December), with the third Wednesday of the month as delivery date.

FORWARD-FORWARD The simultaneous purchase and sale of a given currency through forward foreign exchange contracts having a different **MATURITY DATE.**

FOUL BILL OF LADING A receipt issued by a common carrier to the transportation company that has contracted it to move freight between two destinations indicating that the goods it received for transportation were damaged or insufficient in quantity when received. *See also* **BILL OF LADING.**

FOUR Ps Four basic elements in the **MARKETING MIX-PRODUCT,** place, price, and **PROMOTION.**

FOUR TIGERS Taiwan, Hong Kong, South Korea, and Singapore.

FRANC Monetary unit of the following nations: Belgium, Benin, Burundi, Cameroons, Central Africa, Chad, Comoros, Congo, Dahomey, Djibouti, France, French Somalialand, Gabon, Guadeloupe, Ivory Coast, Liechtenstein, Luxembourg, Madagascar, Malagasy, Mali, Martinique, Monaco, New Caledonia, New Hebrides Islands, Niger, Oceania, Reunion Island, Rwanda, Senegal, Switzerland, Tahiti, Togo, and Upper Volta.

FRANC AREA The group of former French colony nations that keep on using the French franc as a satisfactory currency and/or link their currency values to the franc.

FRANCHISING 1. A franchiser granting to franchisee for a fee (fixed percentage based on sales) the right (license) to use the franchiser's name. Typically, the franchisee must use the franchiser's products or services. The franchisee enjoys other benefits bestowed by the franchiser such as advertising, displays, and service contracts. Examples are Burger King and Baskin Robbins. A franchising agreement is often entered into in international trade between a United States manufacturer and a foreign company to engage in production or distribution of goods. 2. A license to market a company's merchandise in a particular territory, region, or outlet. 3. A government right, sometimes exclusively, given to an entity such as to provide utility or cable television services.

FREE ALONGSIDE SHIP (FAS) Shipping terms where the seller maintains ownership and responsibility of risk of the goods until they are delivered alongside the ship that has been chartered by the purchaser. When the goods are placed "alongside the ship," title is transferred to the purchaser. The sales price for goods sold "free alongside ship" generally includes the cost of delivery to the purchaser's ship, unloading costs, and insurance coverage up to the point of delivery.

FREE AND OPEN MARKET Market structure where the prices of goods and services are determined by the unrestricted supply and demand for the goods being sold. In a **CONTROLLED MARKET,** supply, demand and/or price for these items are regulated and externally determined (i.e. artificially set by a government).

FREE ASTRAY A misrouted shipment to the wrong place. To make good, the shipper must correctly transport it to the correct location and absorb the additional cost itself.

FREE FLOAT To arrange for financing (e.g., loan) without a service charge (e.g., points).

FREE FLOATING EXCHANGE RATES Exchange rates among countries determined solely by market forces rather than reserve holdings. Alternatively, the exchange rate may be determined through a managed float where the central bank of a government sets the exchange rate but varies it frequently. In a single currency peg, the exchange rate of a given country is pegged to the currency of a major country such as the United States dollar. *See also* **MANAGED FLOAT.**

FREE IN (OUT) Shipping term indicating that the entity chartering a ship (seller or purchaser of goods) must absorb either the cost of loading the goods on board (free in) or unloading them onto the dock (free out).

FREE LIST A list of products prepared by the customs administration of a nation enumerating those items that are exempt from the assessment of customs duties on a county's imports and exports. For example, imported goods from a "friendly" or "preferred" country may be duty free.

FREE MARKET 1. Unimpeded movement of goods into and out of a market without the assessment of customs duties or other government TARIFFS. 2. A market that operates without the interference of a government or any other economic force.

FREE OF CAPTURE A provision in an export insurance contract between the carrier and insurance company exempting from coverage any losses arising from stipulated **FOREIGN RISK** or **POLITICAL RISK** such as civil strife, seizure, and government confiscation.

FREE ON BOARD (FOB) Free on board some location (e.g., shipping point or destination). It indicates that the invoice price includes delivery at seller's expense and seller's risk to the specified location. For example, "FOB our warehouse in Duluth, Minnesota," means, to a buyer requesting New York City delivery, that the seller who might have its headquarters and billing office in Chicago, will pay shipping costs from Duluth to New York. Title usually passes from seller to buyer at the FOB point.

FREE OVERSIDE The seller is responsible for all shipping costs to deliver merchandise to the place of importation. After being unloaded, the buyer takes responsibility including that for any **TARIFFS.**

FREE PORT A port having no duties assessed on ships docking or undocking from it. It is a free-trade zone such as Hong Kong.

FREE TRADE A governmental policy by which no intervention or restrictive devices are exercised in trading between nations-by **TARIFFS, QUOTAS,** or other measures. **NORTH AMERICAN FREE TRADE AGREEMENT** is an example of such an attempt.

FREE TRADE AREA. *See* **FREE TRADE ZONE.**

FREE TRADE ZONE Also called a free trade area. Area that is physically on United States soil, but considered to be outside United States commerce. Products imported into this zone are duty free and without trade restriction until they leave the zone.

FREE TRADE ASSOCIATION Association of trading countries whose members agree to promote free trade (impose no restrictive measures), such as the European Free Trade Association.

FREEZE 1. Governmental intervention to fix prices or wages at a given or current level. In a democratic country, price or wage freezes only occur during wartime or some other national emergency. For example, during World War II, price freezes were in effect to insure price stabilization and insure that wartime shortages didn't cause massive **INFLATION. 2.** To prohibit the continued manufacture or use of a product. For example, when the manufacturer found that the product that it was selling was defective, it froze further manufacture of the good and warned others who had already purchased it from refraining from using it until the cause of the defect could be determined and rectified. **3.** Preventing the withdrawal of assets of an individual or foreign government from a country as a result of government edict. For example, during the late 1970s the United States government froze Iranian assets that were deposited in American banks when Iran overran the American Embassy in Tehran and held the Americans working in the embassy hostages. **4.** Stopping the purchase or sale of a multinational company's products or services for probable cause.

FREEZED ACCOUNT The legal act of making funds unavailable to the owner of the account such as when a government or judge freezes a company's account for some wrong doing or in case of eminent bankruptcy.

FREIGHT **1.** Goods, merchandise, products, etc., generally transported by a commercial carrier from one destination to another. Freight may be carried overland, by sea, air, or rail. **2.** The cost of transporting goods or merchandise by a commercial common carrier.

FREIGHT FORWARDER An entity that provides a full line of exportation services (commonly to overseas destinations) for compensation. For example, freight forwarders commonly provide shippers with the following export related services: preparing all required export documentation, arranging for the common carrier, purchasing insurance, advising the appropriate parties of the forthcoming export, providing the domestic manufacturer/ dealer/ wholesaler with guidance related to any product requirements of the importer or quality standards of the country into which the good will be imported, etc.

FREIGHT INSURANCE Insurance coverage for goods that are shipped on a common carrier. There are generally two kinds of freight insurance policies that may be purchased: (1) a Single Risk Cargo Policy which covers a single shipment of goods and (2) an Open Cargo Policy which provide automatic insurance coverage for all shipments of goods that may be made by a shipper over a period of time. *See also* **CARGO INSURANCE.**

FREIGHT INWARD (OUTWARD) Freight charges that are paid by the purchaser of goods received (or paid by the seller for outgoing shipments).

FRONT-END LOADING Sales fees or other charges that must be initially paid in addition to the cost of the investment itself when making certain investments such as acquiring shares of certain mutual funds. Back-end loading requires that such charges be paid when one sells shares in the mutual fund.

FRONTING LOANS. *See* **BACK-TO-BACK LOANS.**

FROZEN ACCOUNT A bank account seized or attached by judicial lien obtained by the actions of an administrative agency, government, or other authorized entity to enforce payment of a judgment or claim, or to prevent the withdrawal of funds pending the determination of an issue under advisement.

FSC. *See* **FOREIGN SALES CORPORATION.**

FTI. *See* **FOREIGN TRADERS INDEX.**

FTO. *See* **FOREIGN TRADE ORGANIZATION.**

FULFILLMENT 1. An entity's system of satisfying its direct marketing sales. Fulfillment functions include: (a) expediently delivering the product that was ordered; (b) billing customers and recording their payments; (c) accounting for customer transactions including being able to retrieve all customers sales and payment information; and (d) providing any other customer service when necessary. **2.** To carry out a promise or duty to do something. **3.** To satisfy a requirement.

FULL COSTING. *See* **ABSORPTION COSTING.**

FULL COVERAGE The payment in full by an insurance company of all insured losses.

FULL COSTING. *See* **ABSORPTION COSTING.**

FUNCTIONAL CURRENCY As defined in **FINANCIAL ACCOUNTING STANDARDS BOARD NO. 52,** in the context of translating financial statements, the currency of the primary economic environment in which a foreign affiliate operates and in which it generates and expends cash.

FUNCTIONAL DISCOUNTS Special reductions in price given to wholesalers and middlemen on a new product when it is initially introduced into the market. The purpose of such allowances is to compensate these individuals for their efforts in selling and promoting the good and stimulate them to continue to take whatever steps are necessary to successfully market it.

FUNCTIONAL GAMES. *See* **MANAGEMENT GAME.**

FUNCTIONAL INTERMEDIARY An entity that receives a good subsequent to its production such as an **EXPORT PACKER** or common carrier making modifications or changes to it to successfully insure that it will be shipped to the satisfaction of the customer.

FUNCTIONAL ORGANIZATION Organizational structure predicated on performance achievement. A functional organization generally consists of line and staff personnel and contains such departments as sales or marketing, manufacturing, personnel, accounting, purchasing, etc.

FUNCTIONAL STRUCTURE The structure of multinational companies organized by managerial functions such as marketing, manufacturing, human resources, and finance; and the heads of these responsible divisions have worldwide responsibilities as line executives. This structure was the traditional form used by European companies. It has the advantage of concentrating management attention on the internal functions. On the other hand, it suffers from some disadvantages with multiple product lines. That is, the functional specialists either would need to have expertise in each product line and sales and production tend to become separated in their objectives.

FUNDAMENTAL ANALYSIS 1. An analysis based on economic theory drawn to construct sophisticated econometric models for predicting exchange rate movements. The variables contained in these models include a relative money supply **GROWTH RATE, INFLATION** rate, interest rate, and other variables related to countries' **BALANCE OF PAYMENTS** positions. **2.** Also called fundamental investment analysis, the evaluation of a company's financial statements. Fundamental analysis is used primarily to select what to invest in, while technical analysis is used to help decide when to invest in it. Fundamental analysis concentrates on the future outlook of growth and earnings. The analysis studies such elements as earnings, sales, management and assets. It looks at three things: the overall economy, the industry, and the company itself. Through the study of these elements, an analyst is trying to determine whether the stock is undervalued or overvalued compared to the current market price.

FUNGIBLES Products or financial bearer instruments that are interchangeable or may be substituted for each other. Examples are equivalent commodities (e.g., corn) and bonds in the same company.

FUTURES A contract to deliver a specified amount of an item by some given future date.

FUTURES CONTRACT. *See* **FUTURES.**

FUTURES FOREIGN EXCHANGE CONTRACT. *See* **FUTURES CONTRACT.**

FUTURES MARKET A financial market allowing buyers and sellers of contracts for future delivery of financial instruments, commodities, and currencies to transact. Such contracts may be used to reduce risk by a multinational company. For example, if a multinational company wants to buy a commodity 6 months from now and wants to lock in the current price it protects itself against the risk of having to pay a higher price in the future if commodity prices substantially increase.

G

G-7. *See* GROUP OF SEVEN.

GAAP. *See* GENERALLY ACCEPTED ACCOUNTING PRINCIPLES.

GAAS. *See* GENERALLY ACCEPTED AUDITING STANDARDS.

GAIN-SHARING AGREEMENT An english agreement between management and labor to share economic gains from new equipment being installed.

GALLOPING INFLATION An extremely high rate of inflation. Also called HYPERINFLATION.

GAP ANALYSIS 1. The difference between budgeted and actual sales levels for a business entity for a specific period of time. The discrepancy may be due to increased competition, changes in consumption patterns of the product's users, breakdowns in the company's distribution mechanism, unrealistic projected sales goals, etc. 2. An interest rate sensitivity procedure.

GAP ANALYSIS 1. The difference between budgeted and actual sales levels for a business entity for a specific period of time. The discrepancy may be due to increased competition, changes in consumption patterns of the product's users, breakdowns in the company's distribution mechanism, unrealistic projected sales goals, etc. 2. An interest rate sensitivity procedure.

GATEWAY 1. A means of access or entry such as an airport or seaport. Customs clearance may be at this location. 2. A locality where a shipment is transferred from one vehicle (e.g., railroad) to another vehicle (e.g., truck).

GATT. *See* GENERAL AGREEMENT ON TARIFFS AND TRADE.

GENDER ANALYSIS Examining a mailing list for the purpose of dichotomizing the names into male and female categories. Each list would then be used to promote products that would be of interest to either one gender or the other.

GENERAL AGREEMENT ON TARIFFS AND TRADE (GATT) An agreement signed at the Geneva Conference in 1947 which became effective on January 1, 1948. It set a framework of policies and guidelines for international trade, including a negotiation of lower international trade barriers, and settling trade disputes. GATT also acts as international arbitrator with respect to trade agreement abrogation. More specifically, GATT has four basic long-run objectives: (1) reduction of tariffs by negotiation, (2) elimination of import quotas (with some exceptions), (3) nondiscrimination in trade through adherence to unconditional most-favored-nation treatment, and (4) resolution of differences through arbitration and consultation.

GENERAL TARIFF A duty on a product or commodity which is universally applied irrespective of the country from which it is imported. All countries are treated the same.

GENERALLY ACCEPTED ACCOUNTING PRINCIPLES (GAAP) The rules, standards, conventions, and guidelines that accountants must follow in the preparation of external financial statements. Generally Accepted Accounting Principles are those principles that have "substantial authoritative support". Statement of Auditing Standards No. 69, The Meaning of 'Present Fairly in Conformity With Generally Accepted Accounting Principles' in the Independent Auditor's Report, notes that the current most authoritative level of GAAP, designated as Category (a) (the first level), consists of the **FINANCIAL ACCOUNTING STANDARDS BOARD**'s Statements of Financial Accounting Standards (SFAS) and Interpretations, the Accounting Principles Board's (APB) Opinions, and the Committee on Accounting Procedure's (CAP) Accounting Research Bulletins.

GENERALLY ACCEPTED AUDITING STANDARDS (GAAS) The general rules and guidelines that an auditor must follow in fulfilling his professional responsibilities in the audit of an entity's financial statements. GAAS includes considerations of the auditor's professional qualities such as technical training, independence and competence as well as standards of reporting and fieldwork. The broadest guidelines that auditors must follow in the performance of an audit are the ten generally accepted auditing standards (GAAS) that were developed by the **AMERICAN INSTITUTE OF CERTIFIED PUBLIC ACCOUNTANTS (AICPA)** in 1947 and have remained fundamentally the same over the years. The most authoritative guidance currently available to auditors are the Statement on Auditing Standards (SAS) issued by the Auditing Standards Board of the AICPA. SASs are viewed as interpretations of the ten GAAS previously noted. Together, GAAS and SAS represent the current collective authoritative guidance that auditors must follow in the performance of an audit.

GENERIC **1.** An item applying to an entire group, class, or kind. **2.** A broad grouping of consumers for a product or service. **3.** A description of a whole product classification. **4.** An advertising of a general product category rather than by brand name such as orange juice. **5.** An unlabeled brand in the stores usually selling at a much lower price than the brand name goods. **6.** A conceptual knowledge as a basis for practical technological application.

GEOCENTRIC ORGANIZATION A world-oriented organization that involves collaboration between subsidiaries and headquarters to establish universal standards and permissible local variations on the basis of which key decisions are made. This has costs, largely related to communication and travel expense, time spent on decision making due to the desire to educate personnel about global objectives and to secure consensus, and the expense of a relatively large headquarters bureaucracy.

GEOCENTRISM. *See* **ETHNOCENTRISM.**

GLASNOST A Russian term popularized for the political reform policies (openness of information) of President Mikhail S. Gorbachev in the Soviet Union.

GLOBAL ALLIANCE An agreement among multinational firms for the purpose of establishing an international marketing association so that certain common fixed costs such as sales office space, machinery, equipment, etc., located around the world may be shared so as to reduce expenditures and increase the overall profitability of the alliance.

GLOBAL FOCUS A program developed by a multinational firm enabling it to achieve its international marketing objectives and strategies.

GLOBAL FUND A mutual fund that invests in both United States and foreign securities. Unlike an **INTERNATIONAL FUND,** it invests anywhere in the world, including the United States. However, most global funds keep the majority of their assets in foreign markets.

GLOBAL INTERNATIONAL An association of trade unions from nations around the globe.

GLOBAL LOGISTIC NETWORK An integrated network of plants, each specializing in one or more products or components and each serving a world or a regional market. This is used by multinational companies with a global strategy pursuing to strengthen its competitive position by considering all markets simultaneously and by designing a least-cost supply strategy for the system as a whole.

GLOBAL MARKETING 1. Promoting a standard product in the domestic and overseas markets. It is international marketing so there is no distinction for local differences. **2.** A strategy to reach all market segments. It is a long-term objective. Increasing volume will result in declining cost per unit and manufacturing efficiencies.

GLOBAL POLICY A company whose marketing strategy is to produce goods that are utilizable worldwide requiring only minimal modifications for use in specific countries. The rest of the company's functional operations, i.e., advertising, accounting, financial, purchasing, etc., are also designed for general global adaptability.

GLOBAL QUOTA Specific limits set by a nation regarding the total dollar value or quantity of goods that may exported to or imported from other countries around the world.

GLUT A very significant oversupply of a product or service. This situation may be due to overproduction or favorable weather condition in the case of agricultural products. Glut may lead to a drop in the price of the item since supply exceeds demand.

GOAL CONGRUENCE 1. The structuring of mutual goals and objectives between employees and the employing organization so that the satisfaction of one group's purpose and plan will also result in the satisfaction of the other's. For example, rewarding employees for efficiency improvement also results in increased income for the organization. 2. The objectives of the subunits (e.g., departments) are the same as that of the company as a whole. Goal congruence may be achieved through budgets and organization charts.

GOAL PROGRAMMING A form of linear programming which allows for consideration of multiple goals that are often in conflict with each other. With multiple goals, all goals usually cannot be realized exactly. For example, consider an investor who desires investments that will have a maximum return and minimum risk. These goals are generally incompatible and therefore unachievable. Other examples of multiple conflicting objectives can be found in organizations that want to: (1) maximize profits and increase wages; (2) upgrade product quality and reduce product cost; (3) pay larger dividends to stockholders and retain earnings for growth; and (4) reduce credit losses and increase sales. Goal programming does not attempt to maximize or minimize a single objective function as does the linear programming model. Rather, it seeks to minimize the deviations among the desired goals and the actual results according to the priorities assigned. The objective function of a goal programming model is expressed in terms of the deviations from the target goals.

GOAL SETTING Methodology or procedure for establishing the goals of an individual, organization, or group. A fundamental tenet of organizational behavior regarding goal setting is that it should be participative and agreed to consensually. That is, employees will be most committed to satisfying the goals of an organization if they had input in establishing the objectives that they would be responsible for accomplishing.

GO-BETWEEN An individual or group that acts as an **INTERMEDIARY** or broker (i.e., arranging a contract, compromise, or other such agreement between two or more entities or groups), relationship maintainer, or simply a communicator so that participants are able to indirectly confer with each other. The go-between is generally paid a fee or commission for his or her effort. For example, in labor negotiations, a mediator often acts as a go-between for labor and management when they refuse to sit down together at the negotiating table.

GOLD STANDARD A country's currency expressed on its equivalent value to gold such as one United States dollar equating to 23.22 grains of fine gold. It displays how much of the units of a currency are exchangeable into a certain amount of gold. If a significant outflow of gold occurs, a deficit in the **BALANCE OF PAYMENTS** may arise. A gold standard may aid stability in exchange rates. The gold standard worked acceptably for a period of more than 40 years up to World War I. The United States dropped this standard in the early 1930s.

GOLDEN PARACHUTE Highly attractive termination benefits awarded to current management in the event of a takeover of the company. Examples of benefits include stock options, bonus, severance pay, and extra amounts given to the retirement plan.

GOOD DELIVERY Designation of the securities industry indicating that a given security certificate has met all the requirements needed to properly and legally affect a title transfer from seller to buyer. For example, some of the requisites that must be satisfied is seller endorsement, signature guarantee, correct denomination, etc.

GOOD FAITH Good faith consists of an honest intention to abstain from taking any unconscionable advantage of another.

GOOD TILL CANCELED (GTC) ORDER A customer's order to his or her broker to buy or sell a security at a given price. The order remains in effect until it is executed or canceled by the customer.

GOOD TITLE An ownership interest in real or personal property that is clear and free, without words of limitation, and without defect or encumbrance from any current or future lawsuit. The title is valid and merchantable. An example is buying real property that has no lien against it or cannot legally be claimed by another.

GOODS IN FREE CIRCULATION Goods that may not be assessed with customs duties and restrictions.

GOODS OF THE SAME KIND Goods that are categorized similarly. They generally fall into a range of identicalness. Such goods are generally produced by a given industry or industry group. For example, in the automobile manufacturing industry, cars are categorized as being either sub-compacts, compacts, mid-size, full-size, and luxury autos.

GOODWILL In theory, the discounted value of future additional profits of a business over other businesses in the industry. It relates to the reputation of a business. The business is viewed in a more favorable light than others because of such factors as perception of quality, reliability, and good customer relationships. Goodwill can only be recorded in a business combination accounted for under the purchase method where the cost to the acquirer exceeds the fair market value of the net assets acquired. For example, if company X pays $10 million for company Y which has a fair market value of net assets (assets less liabilities) of $9 million, the extra amount paid for company Y's goodwill is $1 million. (Negative goodwill is the opposite case). Goodwill is an intangible asset to be amortized using the straight line method over the period benefited not exceeding 40 years.

GOVERNMENT PROTECTION **1.** Government policy to protect a domestic industry from foreign competition. **2.** Government program designed to protect the identity of those individuals whose testimony enabled prosecutors to successfully convict individuals who have committed crimes. These individuals may now be physically threatened and in jeopardy because of the assistance they rendered and seek government protection.

GOVERNMENT RELATIONS The division of the government dealing with public relations and its interaction with nongovernmental entities.

GOVERNMENT SUBSIDY Payments, tax rebates, or other such benefits extended by the government to certain individuals, groups, business entities, or industries that require special protection and support. For example, government domestic subsidies are given to the agricultural industry to encourage food production and support the incomes of farmers. It is also given to families living at or under the poverty level who need of assistance in the form of money (welfare payments), food stamps, health care services, etc. Export subsidies are given to companies that export specific goods to encourage them to compete in foreign markets. *See also* **EXPORT SUBSIDIES.**

GRACE PERIOD A period of time (e.g., 30 days) that is allowed after payment is due in most insurance policies, mortgage agreements, and loan contracts before cancellation or default is declared.

GRADUATION The graduation or removal of a country from preferential tariff listings (Generalized or Unilateral System of Preferences) due to increased production, export earnings, and an overall improvement in its standard of living. As a result of reaching economic independence and increased competitiveness, the nation's graduation provides that it now undertake the obligations and responsibilities of a developed nation.

GRAFT The improper use of an individual's position (e.g., business executive, politician) to gain money such as in a payoff.

GRANDFATHER CLAUSE A stipulation covered in a new policy or regulation that exempts from the rule an individual or business already engaged in the activity coming under regulation. This provision allows those already partaking in an activity about to be restricted to continue their present activities.

GRANT A contribution or donation by a governmental entity or private source for a specified purpose (e.g., research). Grants for specified categories are termed categorical grants; grants for general purposes are termed block grants.

GREEN CONSUMER Consumers who are very concerned about the environment and will refrain from buying and using products that cause or result from environmental problems. An example are people who will not buy fur coats because of cruelty to animals or those who will not purchase pollution causing goods.

GREEN REVOLUTION Reference to a significant increase in the agricultural production in developing countries in the 1960s due to the use of disease resistant, high yielding seeds especially for wheat, rice, and corn. As a result of the use of these seeds, artificial fertilizers, and plentiful watering, output doubled and even tripled in some instances. Hindsight analysis, however, indicates that the "Green Revolution" benefitted only the large landowners who could afford to buy the high-tech seeds and other products necessary for the increased output.

GREENMAIL A "legal bribe" paid by a company taken over or to be taken over to the acquiring group via paying a much higher selling price than prevailing in the market to reacquire the shares. Sometimes management does this to protect their jobs.

GRETHAM'S LAW A law that is popularly phrased as "bad money drives good money out of circulation." More accurately, the law asserts that when an item has a use as both a commodity and money, it will be used where its value is greater. The rapid disappearance of silver certificates is an example of Gretham's law. If a one dollar silver certificate entitles the holder to more than a dollar's worth of silver, the certificate will be hoarded, melted down, exported or exchanged for silver bullion, thereby disappearing from circulation. The law is named after Sir Thomas Gresham, Master of the Mint under Queen Elizabeth I during the sixteen century.

GROSS BILLING 1. The gross amount billed to clients for goods sold or services rendered without any deductions for returns, credits, adjustments, etc. 2. The cost of advertising that is billed to a client including applicable advertising agency commissions.

GROSS TON Constituting 2,240 pounds.

GROSS UP. *See* DEMAND PAID CREDIT.

GROSSED-UP DIVIDEND The sum of the dividend received by the parent, the withholding tax on the dividend, and the income taxes paid by the subsidiary on the income that produced the dividend.

GROUP DYNAMICS The processes, changes and activities that occur in a group of individuals as a result of their interpersonal interaction. Committees and other types of groups are established in businesses and other environments to accomplish specific goals and objectives and to derive creative contributions and participative consensus from their members.

GROUP IDENTIFICATION The association or affiliation of an individual to a nation, religion, group of people, organization, department, committee, etc. based on his or her nationality, beliefs, political leanings, work associations, education, and other lifetime experiences.

GROUP OF FIVE (G-5) A group of five countries, that is, France, Japan, United Kingdom, United States, and West Germany. Finance ministers and central bankers of these countries met in the mid-1980s to discuss coordinating global economic policies.

GROUP OF SEVEN (G-7) A group of seven countries-Canada, France, Germany, Italy, Japan, United Kingdom, and the United States. Political leaders from theses countries met in 1990 and 1991 to discuss common issues including economic aid to the Soviet Union and whether to intervene in the foreign exchange markets to attempt to stop the rising value of the United States dollar.

GROUP OF TEN (G-10) A group of ten non-Communist countries, meeting in the mid-1980s to establish the Basle Accord as well as deal with other common global economic issues such as providing a more flexible international system of monetary reserves and urged internal financial discipline upon member countries. The group may lend their currencies when needed to the **INTERNATIONAL MONETARY FUND.** Nine of this group were responsible at the Stockholm Monetary Conference, March 30, 1968, for recommending the creation of the so-called special drawing rights.

GROUP OF THIRTEEN (G-13) A group of thirteen countries formed in 1984 to compete with the **ORGANIZATION FOR ECONOMIC COOPERATION AND DEVELOPMENT** by the **GROUP OF SEVEN.** This group includes Algeria, Argentina, Egypt, India, Indonesia, Jamaica, Malaysia, Nigeria, Peru, Senegal, Venezuela, Yugoslavia, and Zimbabwe.

GROUP OF FIFTEEN (G-15) A group of fifteen countries formed in 1990, being made up of financially strong or large developing nations. The G-15 attempts mutual understanding and cooperation in enhancing their global economic policies. Members include: Algeria, Argentina, Brazil, Egypt, India, Indonesia, Jamaica, Malaysia (a very active member), Mexico, Nigeria, Peru, Senegal, Venezuela, Yugoslavia, and Zimbabwe.

GROUP OF SEVENTY-SEVEN (G-77) A group of 77 developing countries whose main objective is to express the members' goals mostly in areas of improving mutual economic cooperation and dealing with relevant issues. There are 125 member countries.

GROWTH OPTIONS Those alternatives available to an investor interested in purchasing investments which provide for maximum capital appreciation over the long term such as growth mutual funds, growth stocks, certain appreciating real estate, and other assets. Growth investments are generally viewed as being more risky and volatile than more conservative, slowly appreciating investments but also hold the greatest promise for value enhancement.

GROWTH PATH A measure of change of a nation's development based on indicators such as per capita income or consumption. The growth path is shown by the actual or predicted change in these variables over a period of time. Different investment strategies produce different growth patterns. For example, if large amounts of capital are invested in capital assets then there will only be modest increases in the growth path until the consumer goods industries of the country sufficiently matures and develops from the investment. When this occurs, the nation's growth path will rise appreciably.

GROWTH RATE The degree of percentage change in some measured variable. For example, if we are discussing the productivity of a nation, the growth rate might be measured by the percentage change of the Gross National Product adjusted for price inflation. If we are discussing the growth rate of a business entity, we might discuss percentage changes in the entity's net income, earnings per share, dividends per share, market price of stock, etc.

GUARANTY 1. An agreement in which one individual assumes the responsibility for paying the debt of another. **2.** Something given as security for the performance or execution of an outcome in some specified way. **3.** A guarantee given to an individual or entity regarding a product or service.

GUILDER Monetary unit of the Netherlands, Antilles, and Surinam.

GULF RIYAL Monetary unit of Dubai and Qatar.

H

HAIRCUT FINANCE Borrowing money using one's securities as collateral.

HAMMERING THE MARKET Aggressive selling of security positions in anticipation of a large sell-off in the market. Speculators who believe that such an event is imminent will hammer the market by selling short. These individuals sell securities, commodities, foreign currency, or other assets that they do not actually own hoping to buy them back at a lower price than they sold them at. *See also* **SELLING SHORT.**

HARD DOLLARS Actual payment made by a client firm for certain services.

HARD GOODS Durable products such as ovens, refrigerators, televisions, and furniture.

HARDSHIP ALLOWANCE A bonus paid to employees working in a risky, dangerous, or unpleasant environment such as United States employees in certain Middle Eastern countries where the population generally resents outsiders.

HARMONIZE **1.** The process of unifying the member states of the European Community by abolishing all trade impediments (i.e., customs assessments and tariffs) and passing new national laws and administrative regulations affecting the unification of the common market. Pursuant to the augmentation of these objectives, the **GENERAL AGREEMENT OF TARIFFS AND TRADE** on Technical Barriers to Trade (1979) attempts to block, at the international level, any standards or regulations that attempt to create trade disharmony among member nations. **2.** The attempt by nations, through mutual agreement, to establish equivalency among each other's laws and statutes. **3.** The process of bringing into uniformity and agreement that which was previously divergent.

HECKSCHER-OLIN THEORY. *See* **COMPARATIVE COST THEORY; LEONTIEFF PARADOX.**

HEDGE **1.** The process of protecting oneself against unfavorable changes in prices. One may enter into an offsetting purchase or sale agreement for the express purpose of balancing out any unfavorable changes in an already consummated agreement due to price fluctuations. Hedge transactions are commonly used to protect positions in (a) foreign currency, (b) commodities, and (c) securities. **2.** The financing of an asset with a liability of similar maturity.

HEDGE CLAUSE **1.** A clause written into a contract or agreement that repudiates one's assumed responsibility for the accuracy of information derived from other sources affecting the accord. **2.** A contractual provision requiring a multinational company to engage in hedging transactions to reduce the risk from foreign currency exposure.

HEDGING. *See* **BALANCE SHEET HEDGING.**

HETARCHY A management structure in which all participants are deemed equal. No one is over someone else. Such a situation may exist when there is a joint venture between companies.

HETEROGENOUS PRODUCTS/SERVICES Relating to differing or dissimilar products or services. For example, a department store sells heterogenous products because it sells a variety of different goods and services. A butcher shop, on the other hand, sells one homogenous product i.e., meat. *See also* **HOMOGENEOUS PRODUCTS/SERVICES.**

HIDDEN ASSET Asset value that is unrealistically understated because of intent or as a result of the nature of the accounting principle under which it was valued. For example, the value of an entity's ending inventory using **LAST IN FIRST OUT** is very low and understated on the balance sheet (when inventory prices are increasing and stocks are not decreasing) because **GENERALLY ACCEPTED ACCOUNTING PRINCIPLES** requires that such an inventory be valued using the earliest, oldest costs that was purchased by the entity since its inception that hasn't yet been sold. Because it is so unrealistically low, most firms choose to disclose the inventory's current replacement cost in the notes to the financial statements so that the reader can appreciate its true value.

HIDDEN DAMAGE Damage to goods that has been incurred during transit that is not readily identified by examining them. Claims for hidden damage to merchandise are frequently difficult to substantiate with insurance companies.

HIDDEN INFLATION. *See* **DISGUISED INFLATION.**

HIERARCHICAL RELATIONSHIPS Vertically defined relationships in a system in which there are several layers of authority between the lowest rank to the highest rank.

HIGH FLYER An equity security whose price has been ascending rapidly compared to other stocks during the recent past.

HIGH TECH Reference to cutting-edge technology. For example, "high tech" generally relates to advanced computer systems, communications, information technologies, sophisticated network systems, etc.

HIJO(S) Spanish word for son(s).

HIT THE BRICKS A strike by employees for some reason such as low wages and/or poor working conditions.

HOLDER IN DUE COURSE A good faith (bona fide) party who has received a negotiable instrument for consideration. He has no knowledge that the instrument has a problem such as having been dishonored, overdue, or other valid claim against it.

HOLDER OF RECORD Owner of the securities of a corporation determined by the corporation's transfer agent at a given point in time. When an entity's securities are sold, the transfer agent records the new holder of record. Holder of record status is important because corporate dividends are allocated only to the holders of record of the company's stock at the date of record.

HOLDING COMPANY An entity that has established, through its acquisition of the requisite amount of voting stock, the ownership of many other corporations in a myriad of different industries and areas. Control of another company requires the ownership of at least 51 percent of that entity's stock. However, effective control can be achieved through a lesser percentage if ownership in that entity is widely dispersed and there is no cohesion among existing stockholders. Although holding companies give its subsidiaries some degree of independence, its objective is to manage and maintain overall control by monitoring the subsidiaries' activities. Pyramiding of control by holding companies is subject to legislative limitations. *See also* **CONGLOMERATE.**

HOME COUNTRY **1.** The country in which the headquarters of a company that is actively engaged in international investment and trade resides. *See also* **HOST COUNTRY.** **2.** The nation of birth of an expatriate. *See also* **EXPATRIATES.**

HOME LEAVE A stipend that is given to employees of multinational companies that require their personnel to work abroad year round. The stipend covers the expense of returning back to the employees' **HOME COUNTRY** to see family, friends, and business associates. The frequency of such trips is a function of the individual's job and location overseas. Home leave is generally granted to maintain the employee's long-term well being and stability.

HOMOGENOUS PRODUCTS/SERVICES Products and services that are greatly similar. Homogeneous products generally are manufactured using the same (interchangeable) input components and parts. Companies producing such products can produce them more cheaply than an entity that produces non-homogenous goods. *See also* **HETEROGENOUS PRODUCTS/SERVICES.**

HORIZONTAL INTEGRATION The combining of businesses manufacturing and/or distributing similar products. Main goals of horizontal integration are to expand market share and hurt competition. It may be in violation of antitrust law in certain cases. *See also* **VERTICAL INTEGRATION.**

HORIZONTAL TRADING COMPANY **1.** Entity that exports a wide variety of identical or similar goods provided by a number of different manufacturers or suppliers. **2.** Organization formed by producers of similar products for the purpose of exporting their goods to other nations, e.g., association of dairy producers, cattle producers, agricultural producers, etc.

HOST COUNTRY The target or recipient country of direct foreign investment and in which a multinational company is based and operates externally to its domestic jurisdiction.

HOT CARGO **1.** A shipment of goods to a company engaged in a labor strike with the union. **2.** Products produced or transported by non-union employees. Union members may refuse involvement with such goods.

HOT MONEY Money that moves internationally from one currency to another either for speculation or because of interest rate differentials, and swings away immediately when the interest difference evaporates. A multinational company is likely to withdraw funds from a foreign country having currency problems.

HRM. *See* Human Resource Management.

HUCKSTER The peddling of a product or service through erroneous and misleading assertions and statements.

HUMAN RESOURCE MANAGEMENT (HRM) The part of the organization that is concerned with the "people" dimension. It involves staffing, training, management development, motivation, performance evaluation, compensation activities, and maintenance of employees so as to achieve organizational goals. HRM is complicated in an international business by the profound differences between countries in labor markets, culture, legal systems, economic systems, and so on.

HUSH MONEY Bribe paid to buy the silence of the recipient. For example, a politician caught doing something illegal might pay the discoverer hush money to conceal the transgression from the public.

HYBRID FOREIGN CURRENCY OPTIONS Purchase of a put option and the simultaneous sale of a call-or vice versa- so that the overall cost is less than the cost of a straight option.

HYPERINFLATION COUNTRIES Nations with extremely high rates of inflation such as some South American countries.

HYPOTHECATION A multinational company's pledging of property as collateral for a loan or other business reason but still holding it. If sold, the multinational company is obligated to use the proceeds from the property to pay off its obligations.

I

IAPC. *See* INTERNATIONAL AUDITING PRACTICES COMMITTEE.

IASC. *See* INTERNATIONAL ACCOUNTING STANDARDS COMMITTEE.

IAU. *See* INTERNATIONAL ACCOUNTING UNIT.

IBF. *See* INTERNATIONAL BANKING FACILITY.

IBRD. *See* INTERNATIONAL BANK FOR RECONSTRUCTION AND DEVELOPMENT.

ICA. *See* INTERNATIONAL CONGRESS OF ACCOUNTANTS.

ICC. *See* INTERNATIONAL CHAMBER OF COMMERCE; INTERSTATE COMMERCE COMMISSION.

ICS. *See* INDUSTRIALIZED COUNTRIES.

ILLIQUID 1. Lacking the ability to pay current debts as they come due. 2. Not having sufficient cash or assets that may be converted to cash to pay obligations that are currently maturing. 3. Not easily convertible into cash. For example, because the company owned many land sites and buildings, its assets were generally viewed as being illiquid.

ILO. *See* INTERNATIONAL LABOR OFFICE (ILO).

IMF. *See* INTERNATIONAL MONETARY FUND.

IMIS. *See* INTERNATIONAL MANAGEMENT INFORMATION SYSTEM.

IMM. *See* INTERNATIONAL MONEY MANAGEMENT.

IMPAIRMENT **1.** To damage or reduce the quality of something. An entity may purchase insurance in order to protect itself against the impairment of the value of its assets. **2.** In financial accounting, impairment occurs when the carrying value of an asset is not recoverable. This results in the writedown or complete write-off of the asset. **3.** Adversely affecting the trade interests of a nation by the action or lack of action taken by another nation.

IMPERFECT MARKET Market where imperfect competition exists. Imperfect competition includes monopoly and oligopoly where one or more sellers can control the market price. *See also* **PERFECT MARKET.**

IMPLIED CONTRACT A contract inferred from the actions of the parties but not necessarily in written or oral form. Such signs may be inferred by a reasonable person. An example is where A renders services that are accepted by B without compensation being mentioned.

IMPLIED WARRANTY A warranty that is based on implication and inference of law rather than being expressly designated. For example, when goods are sold they carry an implied warranty of merchantability. That is, the seller warrants, without expressly saying so, that the goods that were sold are of sufficient quality to be used for the purposes they were purchased for.

IMPORT **1.** To bring in goods and services from a nation outside the one in which they will be consumed or sold. **2.** A good that was produced in a foreign country.

IMPORT CERTIFICATE A document that is required to be completed by all importers of a nation so that the government may maintain control over what is being imported (i.e., be cognizant of what is being imported, its quantity, destination, etc.).

IMPORT DEPOSITS The amount of money (a percentage of the value of the import) that must be deposited by an importer before the government allows the required foreign currency to be released for payment to an exporter. Import deposits must be made before goods are allowed into a country. It represents a means of controlling imports by the government.

IMPORT DUTIES Taxes assessed on goods imported into a country.

IMPORT MERCHANT A merchant that purchases large amounts of a limited number of goods in a foreign nation for resale domestically. The import merchant prepares all requisite import documentation and pays for all transportation costs on the acquisition.

IMPORT PRICE INDEX Index that measures price changes in agricultural, mineral, and manufactured products for goods bought from foreigners. It represents increases and decreases in prices of imported goods due to changes in the value of the dollar and changes in the markets for the items. The index is provided monthly by the Bureau of Labor Statistics (BLS) in the United States Department of Labor. The data are published in a press release and the BLS monthly journal, the Monthly Labor Review.

IMPORT QUOTAS Method of restricting the amount and value of goods that may be acquired abroad and brought into a nation by an importer. Import quotas may be imposed by the producer of the goods (to control supply in an area), the government of the importer (achieved through the issuance of licenses), or a foreign government from the nation in which the goods are produced and from which they are exported.

IMPORT RESTRICTIONS The use of restrictive measures by a government to control the importation of foreign goods into a country. For example, import restrictions might consist of: **TARIFFS, IMPORT QUOTAS, IMPORT DEPOSITS,** surcharges (payments over and above regular tariff fee), boycott of goods, etc.

IMPORT SUBSTITUTION An industrialization strategy used by many Latin American countries and other developing nations that encourages the domestic production of substitutes for imported goods and services. Stiff import duties are levied to protect domestic industries from competition from imports.

IMPORT SUBSTITUTION DEVELOPMENT STRATEGY A policy of developing and expanding the domestic industry of a nation for the purpose of replacing imported goods with domestically produced ones. This is a commonplace goal for young, developing nations where a majority of consumer products are imported.

IMPORTER An individual or entity that acquires goods or services that were produced in a foreign country for consumption or resale domestically. The importer is responsible for the payment of any tariffs, duties, or other fees that may be assessed by the government on the imported products.

IMPORTER DISTRIBUTOR An importer who acquires foreign produced goods for his or her own account and resells them at a profit to domestic retailers. Frequently, import distributorships are maintained on a exclusive territory basis to minimize competition in the sale of a given product or service.

INC. "Incorporated." American English word for a business formed as a corporation. *See also* **LIMITED.**

INCENTIVE FEE The payment of a fee to someone to encourage them to do something. For example, incentive fees or other remuneration are frequently given to sales individuals to encourage them to sell more of a given product.

INCOME GROUP The organization of individuals, consumers, users, etc. into categories with the same range of income.

INCOME STATEMENT Most analyzed financial statement issued by an enterprise. The income statement, also known as the statement of earnings, measures the past performance of the entity for a specified period of time, generally a year. Based on past performance, investors, creditors, and other users of the financial information of the enterprise use this data to predict the amount and timing of the entity's future cash flows and resulting future success. The two most popular presentations of the income statements in use today is the multiple-step format and single-step format. In a recent sampling of companies by the **AMERICAN INSTITUTE OF CERTIFIED PUBLIC ACCOUNTANTS,** two thirds used the multiple-step format (detailed and highly captioned format) and one third used the single step format (less detailed and captioned format). An illustration of the captions used in a condensed multiple step format follows:

Levita Corporation Income Statement For the Year Ended December 31, 2002		
Net Sales		$ XXX
Cost of Goods Sold		XXX
Gross Profit		$XXX
Operating Expenses		
Selling Expenses	$XXX	
General and Administrative Expenses	XXX	XXX
Income from Operations		$XXX
Other Revenues and Gains		XXX
Other Expenses and Losses		XXX
Income from Continuing Operations before Income Taxes		$XXX
Income Taxes		XXX
Income from Continuing Operations		$XXX
Discontinued Operations		XXX
Income before Extraordinary Item and Cumulative Effect of a Change in Accounting Principle		$XXX
Extraordinary Item- Net of Taxes		XXX
Cumulative Effect of Change in Accounting Principle -Net of Taxes		XXX
Net Income		$XXX

As per **FINANCIAL ACCOUNTING STANDARDS BOARD** Statement Number 128, an earnings per share disclosure must also be made on the face of the income statement.

INCOME-BASED PRODUCTS Products whose attributes, features, configuration and function are reacting to consumer tastes and income. Examples are automobiles and television sets.

IN-COUNTRY DISTRIBUTION Flows and patterns of logistics within a single nation.

INCREMENTAL IMPACT A project's impact on the company measured in terms of increased benefits and costs and the spillover effects on other activities of the company.

INCREMENTAL SPENDING The spending differential between two separate spending levels indicated in a budget. In evaluating the efficacy of incremental spending, the incremental spending (costs) must be analyzed against the incremental benefits (e.g., revenues) derived from that spending.

INDEMNIFY To agree to compensate for a loss or damage incurred by an individual or a firm.

INDENT A request by an individual or entity to an importer to have certain goods imported at a given price. The importer either agrees to the terms through his acceptance or refuses them by communicating this fact to the purchaser.

INDENTURE The contract between the company issuing a bond and its bondholders spelling out such considerations as: the type of bond being issued, its face amount, the term of the debt, its interest rate, the property collateralizing the debt, any requirements that the issuer must satisfy during the term of the bond such as maintenance levels of working capital, amounts of retained earnings that must be periodically appropriated, etc.

INDEX LINKING Correlating wages, interest rates, capital spending, etc., to a price index or some other relevant linkage.

INDEXED CURRENCY OPTION NOTE Liability in the form of a note whose repayment is predicated on the exchange rate between the currency of the country incurring the debt and its most important trading partners. For example, interest payments made in one currency would be either increased or decreased based on the relationship between the current rate of exchange and some predetermined level.

INDICATOR Data that is used to describe, analyze, and predict business and economic conditions. The indicators currently issued by the United States Government are classified according to their timing in relationship to the ups and downs of the business cycle. For example, they may anticipate (lead), coincide with, or lag behind general business conditions. Some of the leading indicators that are regularly published are: average weekly claims for state unemployment insurance benefits, new orders for consumer goods and materials adjusted for inflation, contracts and orders for plant and equipment adjusted for inflation, new building permits, changes in manufacturers' unfilled orders for durable goods, and the index of consumer expectations.

INDIFFERENCE CURVE. *See* **EFFICIENT PORTFOLIO.**

INDIRECT EXPORTING Any method for exporting through various types of home-based exporters and export agents. It is easier than direct exporting since it requires neither special expertise and skills nor large cash outlays. Indirect exporting use (1) manufacturer's export agents, who sell for the maker; (2) export commission agents, who purchase for their foreign customers; and (3) export merchants, who buy and sell for their own accounts and at their own risk.

INDIRECT QUOTE The price of a unit of a home country's currency, expressed in terms of a foreign country's currency. For example, in the case of United States, 125 yens per dollar. Banks in the United Kingdom quote the value of the pound sterling in terms of the foreign currency (e.g., 1 pound sterling = $1.65). This method of indirect quote is also used in the United States for domestic purposes and for the Canadian dollar. In their foreign exchange activities, however, United States banks follow the European method of **DIRECT QUOTE.**

INDIRECT TAX 1. A tax levied on an individual with the expectation that he will indemnify himself by shifting the burden to someone else. For example, a tax is levied on a company who, in turn, adds the cost of the tax to its product. Ultimately the consumer pays the tax. **2.** A tax assessed on expenditures such as **EXCISE TAX,** sales tax, or **VALUE-ADDED TAX.**

INDUSTRIAL ADVERTISING The promotion of products or services to business entities. Examples are ads in industry journals for raw materials and machinery in the manufacturing process.

INDUSTRIAL CONSUMER A business entity that buys and uses industrial goods for business purposes. An example is a company that buys cleaning equipment for use in the office.

INDUSTRIAL ESPIONAGE The attempt by an outsider to steal or illegally obtain protected trade, process, or technology secrets from a business. The attempt is made by, for instance, eavesdropping, hacking into the target firm's computer database, or bribing a key company employee or scientist.

INDUSTRIAL FATIGUE The exhaustion and weariness of employees from physical or emotional factors on the job. It typically causes less interest, motivation, job satisfaction, productivity, and performance. Management must determine the reasons for this negative condition so that corrective action may be implemented. Some possible causes are abusive boss, poor working environment, hostile and uncooperative coworkers, undue stress, tight work schedules, and understaffing.

INDUSTRIAL GOODS Production or services bought to use in the manufacturing of other products or services, or in the normal activities of the business, or to resell. Examples are manufacturing equipment and raw materials.

INDUSTRIAL INTERNATIONAL An agency of a **GLOBAL INTERNATIONAL** that represents union workers' interests within a specific industry.

INDUSTRIAL POLICY The collective measures taken by a government to enhance technological progress, employment opportunities, and job growth. Operationally, industrial policy is accomplished through government programs that involve a favorable across-the-board attitude towards business as a means promoting growth (e.g., tax reduction to business), financial sponsorship and support to business, low cost loans to fledgling industries, programs to aid companies in industries that have been in a severe slump, etc.

INDUSTRIAL PROPERTY The property owned by a business necessary for it to operate and generate net income. Industrial property consists of the business' current and long-term assets including property, plant, and equipment, natural resources, intangibles, and other assets.

INDUSTRIAL PSYCHOLOGY Segment of psychology involving the study and analysis of such work and work environment considerations as job satisfaction, employee motivation, commitment to the employing organization, turnover, job performance, entrance and exit interviews, employee selection techniques, training, etc.

INDUSTRIAL RELATIONS The employment rules, policies, and conventions adopted and maintained by an entity with regard to its employees. For example, industrial relations encompasses all aspects of the employment relationship (all interactions between the employer, its representatives, and the employees of the organization). *See also* **INDUSTRIAL RELATIONS STAFF; INDUSTRIAL RELATIONS SYSTEM.**

INDUSTRIAL RELATIONS STAFF The group of administrators, staff, and employees responsible for establishing and maintaining quality industrial relations between the company and its employees. For example, an entity's industrial relations staff may consist of its Human Resource Department, the Office of Personnel, the industrial psychologist, the Office of Labor Relations, etc. *See also* **INDUSTRIAL RELATIONS; INDUSTRIAL RELATIONS SYSTEM.**

INDUSTRIAL RELATIONS SYSTEM The procedures and practices that an entity follows to create, maintain and regulate positive employer and employee relationships. *See also* **INDUSTRIAL RELATIONS; INDUSTRIAL RELATIONS STAFF.**

INDUSTRIALIZED COUNTRIES (ICS) Countries with a high level of industrial production rather than agriculture or raw materials, high per capita incomes relative to the rest of the world, and with market-economy orientation.

INDUSTRY A group of companies manufacturing substitutable goods or rendering similar services.

INDUSTRY STANDARD The norm or benchmark set and accepted by the industry in technical specifications, production procedures, labor time required, materials used, etc.

INDUSTRY SUBSECTOR ANALYSIS An analysis of the specific part of an industry assessing, for example, the supply, demand, price level, marketing considerations, etc., relevant to the product(s) or services produced by it.

INELASTIC DEMAND Demand with **PRICE ELASTICITY** of demand less, in absolute value, than 1.0 . For example, the demand for necessities is inelastic. If demand is inelastic, a price increase (decrease) will induce an increase (decrease) in total revenue. In effect, a firm would be able to get away with a price increase.

INELASTIC SUPPLY Supply which increases (or decreases) less than 1 percent in volume with a 1 percent change in price.

INFANT INDUSTRY An underdeveloped industry. In the face of competition abroad, it may not be able to survive the early years of struggle before reaching maturity. The infant industry argument for protection goes that a new industry, if given temporary protection in the form of protective tariffs, will be able to reduce costs by experience and become competitive with foreign makers. It is in support of the imposition or retention of a protective import tariff.

INFERIOR GOOD Any product or service whose demand decreases with increasing income levels.

INFLATION A general rise in the price level determined over a specified period of time (annually, quarterly, monthly). When inflation is present, a dollar today can buy more than a dollar in the future. Although the causes of inflation are diverse, a frequent source of inflationary pressures is the excess demand for goods and services which pulls product prices upward-**DEMAND-PULL INFLATION.** Rising wages and material costs may lead to the upward pressure on prices-**COST-PUSH INFLATION.** Furthermore, excessive spending and/or heavy borrowing due to a **BUDGET DEFICIT** by the federal government can be inflationary. All of these sources may be intermingled at a particular point in time, making it difficult to pinpoint the cause for inflation. Measures of inflation include the Consumer Price Index and the Producer Price Index. *See also* **DOUBLE-DIGIT INFLATION.**

INFORMATION DISCLOSURE The process of revealing information about something through a given medium e.g., hardcopy (written), electronic, telephonic, etc.

INFORMATION TRANSFER The transference of information from one nation to another within a multinational company. This sometimes develops into a political issue in relations among the governments because some types of information being transmitted are viewed as sensitive by the governments.

INFORMATION SUPERHIGHWAY A buzzword referring to the Clinton/Gore administration plan to deregulate communication services allowing for the integration of all aspects of the **INTERNET,** cable TV, telephone, business, entertainment, information providers, education, etc.

INFRASTRUCTURE Also called **SOCIAL OVERHEAD;** roads, airports, sewage and water systems, housing, schools, railways, the telephone and other public utilities through expenditures made usually by governments. It is regarded as a prerequisite for economic development and improvements in the standard of living.

INHERENT VICE Insurance jargon for a manufacturing weakness or defect in a given product that could result in damage to the product without obvious external cause. Claims for damages due to inherent vices are generally excluded by insurance policies.

INJUNCTION A judicial order prohibiting the occurrence of some act such as the court directing a union not to strike the multinational company.

INJURY 1. Violation of the rights of another individual or entity where legal recourse is available. 2. The legal determination by the United States **INTERNATIONAL TRADE COMMISSION** that damage has occurred to a particular industry due to imports from foreign nations (under Section 201 of the Trade Act of 1974). If such an injury is determined to have occurred, trade restrictions may be implemented.

INLAND CARRIER (1) A carrier who transports products from the point of entry of the country to a destination within it or (2) transports goods from within the country to the exporting point.

INNOVATION A technology creation or breakthrough that is successfully introduced into the marketplace. It may involve a substantial cash outlay of money and developmental time.

INSOLVENT The inability of a business to pay debt when due. An evaluation of insolvency is directed at the financing mix, cost structure, and the **DEBT/EQUITY RATIO.**

INSPECTION CERTIFICATE A document indicating that an inspection of goods was made and it was determined that they conform to requisite quality standards. Inspection certificates are required by certain purchasers or countries that import goods.

INSTALLMENT CONTRACT Contractual commitment in which the debtor has agreed to make payments or perform some service or function in a series of sequential installments. For example, in an installment purchase, a customer may agree to make partial payment to a department store for goods or services acquired the first day of each month for the next 12 months.

INSTITUTE OF CHARTERED ACCOUNTANTS IN ENGLAND National organization of Chartered Accountants in Britain. The Chartered Accountant (CA) license designation in England is equivalent to the Certified Public Accountant (CPA) license designation in the United States. The Institute of Chartered Accountants in England, like its American counterpart, the American Institute of Certified Public Accountants in the US, supports research and professional projects and publishes the monthly prestigious journal, Accountancy, for its readership. Topics commonly covered in the journal include: all areas of accounting, information systems, professional ethics, law, and general management. *See also* **AMERICAN INSTITUTE OF CERTIFIED PUBLIC ACCOUNTANTS; CERTIFIED PUBLIC ACCOUNTANT; CANADIAN INSTITUTE OF CHARTERED ACCOUNTANTS.**

INSTRUMENT 1. A formal, legal document providing evidence of an event or agreement. An example is a note payable. 2. A measuring device.

INSUBSTANCE DEFEASANCE. *See* **DEFEASANCE.**

INSURANCE A contractual agreement between an insured (an individual or entity) and an insurance company where the latter, in consideration for a periodic premium payment, agrees to reimburse the former for damage or loss to property as a result of flood, fire, acts of g-d, theft, etc. The concept of insurance is based on transferring the risk of loss from the insured to the insurer, i.e., the insurance company, in consideration for the payment of a **PREMIUM.** Some typical types of insurance include life insurance, auto insurance, liability insurance, homeowner's insurance, business risk insurance, etc. Insurance may not be purchased by an insured unless an insurable interest exists between the insured and the insured item. An insurable interest exists when the insured can derive some financial benefit from the existence of the insured item or would incur material loss if it were destroyed.

INSURANCE CERTIFICATE Evidence of insurance held for specified risks such as a marine insurance policy covering transit for merchandise shipped, naming the exporter and the insurer.

INSURED VALUE The value that goods are insured for. The insured value is generally the invoice price of the product plus the freight costs of delivering it to the purchaser's place of business. In addition, insurance and an additional percentage (generally 10 percent) are added in as well.

INTEGRATION 1. Achieving coordination between subunits within an organization. 2. An establishment of regional common markets. *See* **HORIZONTAL INTEGRATION; VERTICAL INTEGRATION.** *See also* **REGIONAL ECONOMIC INTEGRATION.**

157

INTELLECTUAL PROPERTY RIGHTS (IPRS) The ownership of the right to possess or otherwise use or dispose of products created by human ingenuity. Examples are trademarks, patents, trade names, trade secrets, and copyrights. There are international organizations which deal solely with intellectual property, such as **INTERNATIONAL AND TERRITORIAL OPERATIONS.** A generic phrase for legal protection afforded in foreign countries to United States granted patents, tradenames, trademarks, and copyrights as well as to a United States company's owned software, semiconductors, sound recordings, trade secrets, biotechnology, and industrial designs. Without such foreign protection theft of United States company's property and rights thereto may occur. International trade is fostered when a violation of property rights leads to criminal prosecution by a foreign government against its citizens for violating intellectual property rights. Some international agreements are clearly worded to protect intellectual rights such as the **NORTH AMERICAN FREE TRADE AGREEMENT.** A description of some intellectual property rights follows. A copyright is an exclusive right to print or otherwise multiply copies of an intellectual or artistic production, to publish and sell it, and to prevent others from doing so. A patent protects an invention that is novel, useful and obvious. Patentable subject matter includes processes, their improvements, and manufactured designs. A trademark is a sign, symbol, or device attached to goods offered for sale, to distinguish them from similar goods and to identify them as being produced by a particular manufacturer.

INTERBANK FINANCIAL TELECOMMUNICATIONS Financial communications between banks including foreign exchange transactions, Eurodeposits, bank transfers, domestic fund transactions, financial messages, etc. compared to those that occur between banks and nonbank customers.

INTERBANK MARKET The market for exchange of financial instruments between commercial banks. Most foreign exchange in the United States is traded in this market.

INTERCOMPANY LOAN Loan that is made between affiliated entities of a consolidated group (where consolidated financial statements or tax returns are prepared). The loan is not considered a liability of the consolidated entity because the obligation is not owed to an individual or entity outside the group. Because of this, intercompany loans are reversed out in the preparation of consolidated financial statements. *See also* **INTERCOMPANY TRANSACTION.**

INTERCOMPANY TRANSACTION Transaction that is made between affiliated entities of a consolidated group (where consolidated financial statements or tax returns are prepared). Intercompany transactions are not considered transactions of the consolidated entity because they occurred between units of the group and did not occur between the consolidated group and an outside individual or entity. As a result, intercompany transactions are reversed out (eliminated) in the preparation of consolidated financial statements. *See also* **INTERCOMPANY LOAN.**

INTEREST ARBITRAGE Arbitrage in foreign exchange that involves buying foreign exchange in the spot market, investing in a foreign currency asset, and converting back to the initial currency through a **FORWARD CONTRACT**. It is similar to two-way or three-way arbitrage, in that it requires starting and ending with the same currency and incurring no exchange rate risk. In this case, profits are made by exploiting the **INTEREST RATE DIFFERENTIAL** as well as exchange rate differentials. In other words, this works when the **INTEREST PARITY THEORY** is not valid.

INTEREST PARITY. *See* **INTEREST RATE PARITY.**

INTEREST RATE DIFFERENTIAL The variance in interest rates between two nations. The **INTERNATIONAL FISHER EFFECT** proposes that the spot exchange rate should change by the same amount as the interest rate differential between two countries.

INTEREST RATE PARITY (IRP) A condition where the differences between national interest rates for securities of similar risk and maturity should be equal to but opposite in sign to the forward exchange rate differential between two currencies. Specifically, the premium or discount should be:

$$P \text{ (or D)} = \frac{r_f - r_d}{1 + r_f}$$

where r_f and r_d = foreign and domestic interest rates.

(When interest rates are relatively low, this equation can be approximated by: P (or D) = $- (r_f - r_d)$).

The IRP implies that the P (or D) calculated by the equation should be the same as the P (or D) calculated by:

$$P \text{ (or D)} = \frac{F - S}{S} \times \frac{12 \text{ months}}{n} \times 100$$

EXAMPLE

On May 3, 1995, a 30-day forward contract in Japanese yens was selling at a 4.82 percent premium:

$$\frac{.012003 - .011955}{.011955} \times \frac{12 \text{ months}}{1 \text{ month}} \times 100 = 4.82 \text{ percent}$$

The 30-day United States T-bill rate is 8 percent annualized. What is the 30-day Japanese rate. Using the equation:

$$P \text{ (or D)} = \frac{r_f - r_d}{1 + r_f}$$

$$.0482 = \frac{.08 - r_f}{1 + r_f}$$

$-0.0318 = - 1.0482 \, r_f$

$r_f = 0.0303 = 3.03$ percent

The 30-day Japanese rate should be 3.03 percent

INTEREST RATE RISK The variability in the value of a security as the interest rates and conditions of the money and **CAPITAL MARKETS** change. Interest rate risk relates to fixed-income securities such as bonds. For example, if interest rates rise (fall), bond prices fall (rise). Price changes induced by interest-rate changes are greater for long-term than for short-term bonds.

INTEREST RATE SWAPS A financial arrangement where two entities agree to pay the interest payments of the other's debt (different interest payment streams) based on some principal amount. The arrangement is based on congruent benefits accruing to both parties to the arrangement. That is, by exchanging interest payments, both parties benefit based on their relative needs. There are different types of interest rate swaps based on the nature and character of the interest payments that need to be made.

INTEREST TAX SHIELD Legislative provision allowing certain interest payments to be free from income taxes. For example, interest revenue payments on state and local obligations are free from federal taxation. This represents an interest tax shield for taxpayers.

INTEREST YIELD The interest rate that an investor actually receives on an investment. For example, for a long-term bond, the interest yield is really a combination of the stated rate of the bond and the amortization of any discount or premium that was derived when the security was purchased. The interest yield on a bond is also known as its long-term yield to maturity.

INTERLINE Relating to two or more transportation lines. For example, interline freight refers to shipping goods over two or more transportation lines during the course of reaching its destination.

INTERLOCKING DIRECTORATE A management relationship between two or more companies without any financial aspects. This relationship is legally prohibited among competitors.

INTERMEDIARY One who serves as a "dealmaker" between two independent parties. For example, a stockbroker acts as an intermediary between the seller and purchaser in the trading of financial securities. A real estate agent acts as an intermediary in the purchase and sale of real estate. *See* **FACILITATING INTERMEDIARY.**

INTERMEDIARY LOAN A program run through the **EXPORT-IMPORT BANK** of the United States designed to help American firms against competition from those foreign nations that are financially subsidized by their government. Through the program, fixed rate low cost loans are provided to those institutions that lend money to overseas buyers of United States exports.

INTERMEDIATE CONSIGNEE An entity that acts as a "middleman" or agent in a foreign nation for an exporter, purchaser, or consignee to insure that exported goods are delivered to their final destination (final consignee). The intermediate consignee may be a bank, or any other designated entity.

INTERMEDIATE GOODS Goods that receive further processing and are transformed into as a result or become part of a different product. For example, wood and steel girders are intermediate goods in the construction industry.

INTERMITTENT PRODUCTION Generating several different products on the same production line for the purpose of maximizing line productivity. Production runs generally take place sequentially. After the first production run is completed, the second is run, and so forth.

INTERMODAL Transporting freight using different modes of travel such as air, sea, rail, truck, etc.

INTERNAL AUDIT The testing and verification of financial information performed by the internal auditors of a company. Assurance is needed that organization procedures are being carried out, proper internal controls are in place, and no fraudulent activities is taking place. The records of the business must be properly maintained. The auditor undertakes his/her examination in accordance with proper audit techniques and procedures.

INTERNAL BOND A bond issued by a nation representing debt that will be satisfied (by the government) in its own currency.

INTERNAL CONTROL The practices and procedures employed by a company to ensure that their financial statements are prepared in conformity with **GENERALLY ACCEPTED ACCOUNTING PRINCIPLES.** During an audit engagement, the independent auditor evaluates the client company's internal control system to determine the nature, timing, and extent of audit of auditing procedures that need to be performed for the purpose of expressing an opinion on the client's financial statements.

INTERNAL EXPANSION Entity expansion such as the building of an additional plant, factory, or building that is financed through internally derived funds.

INTERNAL FINANCING As opposed to **EXTERNAL FINANCING** such as equity and debt financing, a source of financing raised internally within the firm, such as retained earnings.

INTERNAL RATE OF RETURN (IRR) The rate of interest that equates the initial investment (I) with the present value (PV) of future cash inflows.

That is, at IRR, I=PV, or NET PRESENT VALUE (NPV) =0. Under the internal rate of return method, the decision rule is: accept the project if IRR exceeds the cost of capital; otherwise, reject the proposal.

EXAMPLE
Consider the following data:
Initial investment $12,950
Estimated life   10 years
Annual cash inflows $ 3,000
Cost of capital (minimum required return)   12(%)

We will set up the following equality (I=PV): $12,950 = $3,000 x T4

Then T4 = $12,950/$3,000 = 4.317, which stands somewhere between 18 percent and 20 percent in the 10-year line of Table 4 in the Appendix.

INTERNAL REVENUE SERVICE (IRS) Federal tax laws are administered by the Treasury Department. The IRS is part of the Treasury Department and is responsible for the enforcement of federal tax laws. Supervision of the IRS and organizational policy is determined by the Service's Commissioner who is appointed by the President. Overall, the IRS is responsible for the collection and administration of a myriad of tax categories including: personal income taxes, corporate income taxes, estate taxes, gift taxes and excise taxes. Organizationally, the IRS includes 10 service center across the United States that are primarily responsible for processing tax returns and for selecting returns for audit. Taxpayers are required to file their returns to the service center that has jurisdiction over them (generally determined by the location of the taxpayer's residence). In addition, there are 33 District Directors across the country who are responsible for the performance of audits and the collection of delinquent taxes. *See also* **ADVANCE DETERMINATION RULING.**

INTERNALIZATION As opposed to **EXTERNALIZATION,** extension of ownership by a firm to obtain new sources of materials, new stages of the production process, and new markets. By growing internally, a business attains greater control, efficiency, and productivity. It is usually less costly than growing through acquiring other businesses. It is the business strategy opposite to **VERTICAL INTEGRATION** and **HORIZONTAL INTEGRATION.**

INTERNATIONAL   1. Any interaction (economic, political, humanitarian, etc.) that occurs between a country and any other foreign nation or solely among foreign nations. **2.** Transcendence across national boundaries.

INTERNATIONAL ACCOUNTING STANDARDS COMMITTEE (IASC) A multinational association founded by the leading professional accounting organizations of many nations whose goal it is to improve and harmonize regulations, accounting standards, and procedures relating to financial statement presentation worldwide. The elimination of accounting principles and financial statement presentation variability is a very difficult task because the objectives of financial reporting in the United States, for example, is very different from the objectives in other countries. There is, however, continued interest in establishing uniform international accounting standards throughout the world. For example, The Financial Accounting Standards Board recently passed Statement of Financial Accounting Standards (SFAS)128 on Earnings Per Share in which the board strived to achieve international harmonization of accounting standards in computing earnings per share. The IASC issued International Accounting Standard (IAS) 33 on earning per share concurrently with SFAS 128. The provisions of IAS 33 are substantially the same as those in SFAS 128.

INTERNATIONAL ACCOUNTING UNIT (IAU) A unit of measure used in NATO projects. It is based on the exchange rate of the 16 member NATO nations and is reevaluated each half year.

INTERNATIONAL AND TERRITORIAL OPERATIONS An international organization which deals solely with intellectual property. It covers operations external to the United States, including activities between United States points separated by foreign localities or international waters.

INTERNATIONAL ACQUISITION (TAKEOVER) The acquisition and managerial takeover of the controlling share of a foreign entity by a purchasing entity.

INTERNATIONAL AGREEMENT A formal agreement between two or more nations, international organizations, or multinational companies in which a meeting of the minds or understanding that has been reached is reduced to a written document and signed by the participants.

INTERNATIONAL AUDITING PRACTICES COMMITTEE (IAPC) The IAPC is a committee of the International Federation of Accountants (IFA) set up with the responsibility and authority to issue exposure drafts and guidelines on **GENERALLY ACCEPTED AUDITING STANDARDS** and the content and form of audit reports. The IAPC attempts, through the issuance of such guidelines, to establish uniformity in auditing standards throughout the world. As a committee of the IFA, the IAPC attempts to meet the goals of the IFA whose primary objective is the "development and enhancement of a coordinated worldwide accountancy profession with harmonized standards."

INTERNATIONAL BANK FOR RECONSTRUCTION AND DEVELOPMENT (IBRD) The bank that was initiated to assist less developed countries in developing their economies; also called the World Bank. It attempts to promote economic and social progress through the creation of modern economic and social infrastructures. It makes loans to countries or firms for such purposes as roads, irrigation projects, and electric generating plants.

INTERNATIONAL BANKING FACILITY (IBF) A separate banking operation within a domestic United States bank, created to allow that bank to accept

EUROCURRENCY DEPOSITS from foreign residents without the need for domestic reserve requirements, interest rate ceilings, or deposit insurance premiums.

INTERNATIONAL CHAMBER OF COMMERCE (ICC) A world business organization that promotes international trade, investment and the market economy system worldwide; makes rules that govern the conduct of business across borders; provides essential services, foremost among them the ICC International Court of Arbitration, the world's leading institution of its kind. Members from 63 national committees and over 7000 member companies and associations from over 130 countries throughout the world present ICC views to their governments and coordinate with their membership to address the concerns of the business community. The ICC's address is: 38 Cours Albert 1er, 75008 Paris, France.

INTERNATIONAL CHANNEL LAG COEFFICIENT A measure of the effectiveness of an international marketing distribution channel used by an entity. It is used to assess whether a distribution system is meeting its objectives in supplying distributors and retailers and meeting marketing projections worldwide. Technically, the international channel lag coefficient is the ratio of controllable to uncontrollable marketing costs. The greater the ratio, the more expensive it is to internationally distribute products.

INTERNATIONAL COMMODITY AGREEMENT A formal accord among the countries that produce and export significant amounts of a given commodity worldwide. The written agreement generally includes a negotiated price range for the sale of the good as well as export limits. Other general inclusions in a commodity agreement are: methods of cooperative communication between exporters and importers, research and development commitments, export marketing and promotion, etc.

INTERNATIONAL CONGRESS OF ACCOUNTANTS (ICA) An organization of the major professional organization of accountants from countries across the globe whose purpose it is to deal with the problems associated with diversity of accounting principles and practice from country to country. The first major conference of the ICA was held in St. Louis in 1904 to discuss and exchange accounting information relating to the diversity of accounting practice from county to country. However, no real effort was made to establish accounting principle uniformity at this conference. At the Tenth International Congress of Accountants, held in Sydney Australia (1972), two new organizations were established to deal more effectively with the problem of accounting principle divergence. These two new organizations were the **INTERNATIONAL ACCOUNTING STANDARDS COMMITTEE (IASC)** and the International Federation of Accountants both of which are in existence today. The primary goal of both of these groups is the development and enhancement of a worldwide harmonized set of accounting standards.

INTERNATIONAL CONTRACTOR A company with subsidiaries, branches, or other controlled affiliates engaged in international business in at least two countries. Examples are multinational companies and companies involved in exports, joint venture, direct investment, foreign licensing, or any other form of business that crosses national boundaries.

INTERNATIONAL CORPORATION A corporation that does business in many different foreign countries throughout the world through the exporting and importing of goods and services.

INTERNATIONAL DATABASE A database of social, economic and demographic information relating to all the nations of the world created and maintained by the Center For International Research. The database provides information on a myriad of diverse topics including: population demographics, health information, income, employment opportunities, labor force characteristics, gross national product, price indices, educational levels of the population, religion demographics, etc.

INTERNATIONAL DEBT ISSUE A debt obligation that is underwritten or sold outside of the issuing country. For example, a **FOREIGN BOND** or **EUROBOND** is an example of an international debt issue.

INTERNATIONAL DEBT RATING Debt rating given to large borrowers such as states, municipalities, banks, companies, etc., based on their prior repayment track record and degree of credit risk that the entity has taken on by virtue of loans it has made to other entities. This evaluation is important because the interest that an entity must pay on new borrowed funds is significantly effected by its international debt rating.

INTERNATIONAL DEPOSITORY RECEIPT A negotiable receipt representing the ownership of stock (by an investor) of equity securities outside the country of origin. An international depository receipt is issued by the bank in which the securities reside. The bank acts as the custodian for the securities and will turn them over to the owner when the depository receipt is presented for redemption.

INTERNATIONAL DIVERSIFICATION 1. An ability to reduce the multinational company's risk by operating facilities in more than one country, thus lowering the **COUNTRY RISK. 2.** The effort to reduce risk by investing in more than one nation. By diversifying across nations whose **BUSINESS CYCLES** do not move in tandem, investors can typically reduce the variability of their returns.

INTERNATIONAL DIVISION A division in the organization responsible for a firm's international activities such as exports, foreign-based production, and so on.

INTERNATIONAL FEDERATION OF ACCOUNTANTS. *See* **INTERNATIONAL AUDITING PRACTICES COMMITTEE.**

INTERNATIONAL FINANCE SUBSIDIARY A subsidiary (of a company) involved in such functions as foreign lending, international banking operations, foreign investment, etc.

INTERNATIONAL FINANCING 1. Also called **FOREIGN FINANCING,** raising capital in the **EUROCURRENCY MARKET** or **EUROBOND MARKET.** **2.** A strategy used by multinational companies for financing direct foreign investment, international banking activities, and foreign business operations.

INTERNATIONAL FISHER EFFECT A theory that states that the spot exchange rate should change by the same amount as the interest differential between two countries.

INTERNATIONAL FUND Also called a foreign fund, a mutual fund that invests only in foreign stocks. Because these funds focus only on foreign markets, they allow investors to control what portion of their personal portfolio they want to allocate to non-United States stocks.

INTERNATIONAL IMPORT CERTIFICATE A certificate required by the United States Department of Commerce of importers of certain goods from the United States indicating that the imported goods will be disposed of responsibly. An international import certificate must be obtained from the government of the country importing the good.

INTERNATIONAL INVESTMENT An investment by an entity or individual in equity or debt securities in a foreign based company, government, trust, etc. A long term investment in a foreign company for the purpose of exerting influence in its management (besides investment purposes) is called a direct investment. A **FOREIGN DIRECT INVESTMENT** in the United States is defined as owning 10 percent or more of the voting stock of a United States business enterprise.

INTERNATIONAL LABOR OFFICE (ILO) A United Nations affiliate with representation from employers, unions, and governments dealing with trade union rights, employment terms and conditions, and the protection of the right of workers to organize and bargain collectively.

INTERNATIONAL LEASE A lease agreement where the lessor and lessee of the contract are in a country other than the United States.

INTERNATIONAL MANAGEMENT INFORMATION SYSTEM (IMIS) A computer-based or manual system which gathers, stores, processes, disseminates, and transforms data into information useful in the support of decision making in international business environments. Data come from the two main sources: (1) Internal sources: market analysis, special reports, data from Macs' sales, accounting, manufacturing, financial records as reported by foreign subsidiaries or affiliates, agents, representatives, and customers. (2) External sources: Reports and financial statistics from central and commercial banks, multinational trade organizations, trade associations, international business and finance periodicals, industry representatives, and home and host countries.

INTERNATIONAL MARKETING CHANNEL The process and procedures taken by a firm to internationally market and deliver a firm's exports to the final users of the products. The international marketing channel includes the sum of all efforts of entities and individuals who follow procedures designed to insure that the company's exports successfully reach their import destinations (i.e. the worldwide customers of the producer).

INTERNATIONAL MONETARY FUND (IMF) A fund created at the close of World War II to supervise the international financial system, to lend official reserves to nations with temporary payments deficits, and to decide when exchange rate adjustments are needed to correct chronic payments deficits. It aims at promoting international trade, encourage monetary cooperation between nations, and making funds available to nations needing it. The IMF has an international paper currency called **SPECIAL DRAWING RIGHTS** to increase international liquidity. The IMF is affiliated with the United Nations and funded by member contributions.

INTERNATIONAL MONETARY FUND (IMF) BAILOUT Financial Assistance by the IMF. The IMF lends money only to member countries with payments problems, that is, to countries that do not take in enough foreign currency to pay for what they buy from other countries. The money a country takes in comes from what it earns from exports, from providing services (such as banking and insurance), and from what tourists spend there. Money also comes from overseas investment and, in the case of poorer countries, in the form of aid from better-off countries. Countries, like people, however, can spend more than they take in, making up the difference for a time by borrowing until their credit is exhausted, as eventually it will be. When this happens, the country must face a number of unpleasant realities, not the least of which are commonly a loss in the buying power of its currency and a forced reduction in its imports from other countries. A country in that situation can turn for assistance to the IMF, which will for a time supply it with sufficient foreign exchange to allow it to put right what has gone wrong in its economic life, with a view to stabilizing its currency and strengthening its trade. A member country with a payments problem can immediately withdraw from the IMF the 25 percent of its quota that it paid in gold or a convertible currency. If the 25 percent of quota is insufficient for its needs, a member in greater difficulty may request more money from the IMF and can over a period of years borrow cumulatively three times what it paid in as a quota subscription. In lending to a member more than the initial 25 percent of quota, the IMF is guided by two principles. First, the pool of currencies at the IMF's disposal exists for the benefit of the entire membership. Each member borrowing another's currency from the pool is therefore expected to return it as soon as its payments problem has been solved. In this way, the funds can revolve through the membership and are available whenever the need arises. Second, before the IMF releases any money from the pool, the member must demonstrate how it intends to solve its payments problem so that it can repay the IMF within its normal repayment period of three to five years (which in certain cases can be extended up to ten years). The logic behind these requirements is simple. A country with a payments problem is spending more than it is taking in. Since the IMF has an obligation to the whole membership to preserve the financial integrity of its transactions, it lends only on condition that the member use the borrowed money effectively. The borrowing country therefore undertakes to initiate a series of reforms that will eradicate the source of the payments difficulty and prepare the ground for economic growth. Along with its request for a loan, the potential borrower presents to the IMF a plan of reform, typically undertaking to lower the value of its money in terms of other currencies (if its money has been overvalued), encourage exports, and reduce government expenditure. The specifics of the program are selected by the member, and hence the program of reform is the member's, not the IMF's. The IMF's only concern is that the policy changes are sufficient to overcome the member's payments problem and do not cause avoidable harm to other members. Depending on the seriousness of the payments problem and the amount the member wishes to borrow, the Executive Directors, representing the entire membership, judge whether the reform measures are in fact sufficient and whether the IMF can reasonably expect payment. If the Executive Directors are satisfied that the reforms will solve the problem, the loan is disbursed in installments (usually over one to three years) tied to the member's progress in putting the reforms into effect. If all goes well, the loan will be repaid on time, and the member, with necessary reforms now in place, will come out of the experience economically stronger. The IMF lends to member countries with payments problems under a variety of mechanisms that differ according to the specific problems they address. Two frequently used mechanisms are stand-by arrangements and extended arrangements. These provide a line of credit to a member having trouble in staying current in its foreign obligations to support a program of one to two years (in the case of stand-by arrangements) or three to four years (in the case of extended arrangements) to allow it time to reorganize its finances, restructure its economy, and take measures to restore growth. During the period of the program, the member can borrow from the IMF in installments up to the maximum value of the credit to make its foreign payment, on condition that it stays with its program of policy adjustments. Over the past 25 years, the IMF has lent to its members through a mechanism designed to address a temporary decline in the member's export earnings for reasons substantially beyond the member's control. For example, if frost destroys most of the coffee beans that a member exports in order to earn the foreign exchange (United States dollars, for example) that goes to pay for the member's day-to-day financial obligations to other members. The member then applies to the IMF for a loan-known as compensatory and contingency financing-related to its loss of export revenue, that will supply it with the necessary dollars to stay current in its obligations until the next coffee harvest is exported and the normal flow of revenues resumes. Another mechanism makes money available at low interest rates to poor nations while they radically restructure their economies to rid themselves of long-standing inefficiencies. A novel feature of this method of lending-known as structural adjustment lending-requires close coordination with the World Bank, the IMF's sister institution that works exclusively for the economic development of the world's poorer nations, in putting in place reforms that will eradicate the source of the payments difficulty and prepare the ground for economic growth. This mechanism is funded by voluntary contributions from member countries that, in a spirit of cooperation, forgo the market rate of interest they could otherwise have obtained on those funds. The IMF's better-off members have made available nearly $20 billion to finance this mechanism. If a member borrows money from the IMF, it pays various charges to cover the IMF's operational expenses and to recompense the member whose currency it is borrowing. Presently, the borrower pays in service charges and commitment fees about 1/2 of 1 percent of the amount borrowed and in interest charges about 4 percent (except for the structural adjustment mechanism described above, for which interest charges are much less). An IMF member earns interest on its quota contributions only if other members borrow its currency from the pool. How much the member earns varies but lately has been slightly less than 4 percent of the amount of its currency that other members have borrowed from the IMF. Both the interest charges a borrower pays to the IMF and the recompense a creditor receives from the IMF are slightly below market rates in keeping with the cooperative spirit of the institution.

INTERNATIONAL MONETARY SYSTEM 1. A financial market for transactions between countries that belong to the **INTERNATIONAL MONETARY FUND (IMF),** or between one of these countries and the IMF itself. **2.** The set of policies, arrangements, mechanisms, legal aspects, customs, and institutions dealing with money (investments, obligations, and payments) that determine the rate at which one currency is exchanged for another.

INTERNATIONAL MONEY MANAGEMENT (IMM) Financial policies used by multinational companies aiming at optimizing profitability from currency and interest rate fluctuation while controlling risk exposure.

INTERNATIONAL PRODUCT CYCLE A theory of trade advanced by Vernon explaining why a product that begins as a country's export eventually becomes its import. The theory illustrates both trade flows and foreign investments based on product position in the following stages: (1) exports of an industrialized nation, (2) initiating foreign manufacture, (3) overseas competition in export markets, and (4) import competition in the country where the product was introduced originally. See the following figure:

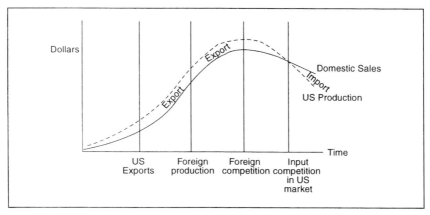

169

INTERNATIONAL RESERVES The total reserves of a country in the form of United States dollars, British pounds, gold, etc., that may be used to pay off obligations owed to other countries.

INTERNATIONAL STANDARD INDUSTRIAL CLASSIFICATION An economic categorization system used by the United Nations for summarizing and presenting official statistical data.

INTERNATIONAL TRADE A trading relationship between two or more nations.

INTERNATIONAL TRADE ADMINISTRATION (ITA) Previously known as the United States Tariff Commission, the United States Trade Act of 1974 augmented the organization's responsibilities to regulate and protect American trading interests and insure that all of the country's trading activities are in accordance with US law and treaties. A primary function of the International Trade Administration is to oversee imports, import duties, and assess the effect of the foreign imports structure on the United States economy. Some other responsibilities of the ITA includes: determining the necessity of import duty relief for domestic industries, providing counsel concerning trade negotiations, investigating unfairly traded, subsidized, or dumped manufactured or agricultural imports entering the country, monitoring the trading activities of America's trading partners, etc. *See also* **AGENCY/DISTRIBUTOR SERVICE.**

INTERNATIONAL TRADE ASSOCIATION (ITA) A division of the United States Dept. of Commerce who offers to help United States exporters and businesses compete in the global marketplace. It has information about export opportunities for specific industries, as well as information about specific nations. The ITA's home page on the **INTERNET** is http://www.ita.doc.gov/.

INTERNATIONAL TRADE COMMISSION (ITC) A United States government agency concerned with protecting American interests in international trade. The agency has the authority to assess duties and tariffs in response to unfair trade practices perpetrated against American companies. Some of the salient functions of the International Trade Commission is to monitor international trade, provide guidance in the area of trade negotiations, review unfair importation practices, and investigate allegations on the part of American companies regarding unfair governmental subsidization of foreign competitors.

INTERNATIONAL TRADING COMPANY An export agent that trades in global markets for its parent company.

INTERNATIONAL TRANSACTION A foreign trade that involves an exporter and an importer in different countries.

INTERNATIONAL TRANSFER PRICE The price at which a multinational company sells goods and services to its foreign affiliates or, alternatively, the price at which an affiliate sells to the parent. For example, a parent that wishes to transfer funds from an affiliate in a depreciating-currency country may charge a higher price on the goods and services sold to this affiliate by the parent or by affiliates from strong-currency countries. Transfer pricing affects not only transfer of funds from one entity to another but also the income taxes paid by both entities. It is therefore determined on the basis of tax liabilities, royalties, and other payments because of different laws in different countries. Since tax laws are different in different nations, **MULTINATIONAL CORPORATIONS (MNCs)** have different incentives to set transfer prices that will increase revenues (and profits) in low-tax nations and increase costs (thereby reducing profits) in high-tax nations. International tax authorities look closely at transfer prices when examining the tax returns of MNCs engaged in related-party transactions that cross national borders. *See also* **TRANSFER PRICING.**

INTERNATIONAL UNION Also called a multinational union, a union with regionals or locals in more than one nation. It is affiliated with the International Trade Secretariats (ITSs), most of which are headquartered in Geneva and structured along trade and industry lines. The most important are the International Conference of Free Trade Unions (ICFTU) and the European Trade Union Federation (ETUF). Membership of unions is still limited to the employees within a particular country.

INTERNATIONALIST Developed by The Center for International Business Information, the source for books, directories, publications, reports and maps on international business, import/export, international relations and world communications. Its home page on the **INTERNET** is http://www. internationalist.com/.

INTERNET The world's largest computer network. It is in fact a global network of networks that allows people and businesses to send e-mail, participate in discussions, and access information. The Internet may become the ultimate information source to a multinational business for both the competition and the market. It already provides access to information provided by government (.gov), for-profit business (.com), nonprofits (.org), universities (.edu), and individuals.

INTERSTATE COMMERCE COMMISSION (ICC) Federal agency that regulates the rates and service of common carriers and transportation companies that provide interstate service in the United States. The Interstate Commerce Commission attempts to make sure that the public gets fair and equitable treatment from the firms providing service relating to interstate commerce.

INTERTEMPORAL ARBITRAGE. *See* **INTEREST ARBITRAGE.**

INTI Peru's currency.

INTRANET A private network within a company or organization that may allow users to connect to the **INTERNET** but limits access from the Internet.

INTRINSIC VALUE **1.** Commodity value of a piece of money (e.g., the market value of the weight of silver in a silver coin). **2.** Theoretical value of a **CALL** or **PUT** option. **3.** Worth of something.

INVENTION The generation of new knowledge or technology that may have application to a multinational company.

INVENTORY MANAGEMENT Planning and control of inventory of raw materials, work-in-process, and/ or finished products involving a decision as to how much of some item to order (or produce) and when to place an order (or commence production).

INVESTMENT BANKERS A financial organization (employees thereof) that specializes in selling primary offerings of securities. Investment bankers buy new securities from issuers and resell them publicly, that is they underwrite the risk of distributing the securities at a satisfactory price. They can also perform other financial functions, such as (1) advising clients about the types of securities to be sold, the number of shares or units of distribution, and the timing of the sale; (2) negotiating mergers and acquisitions; and (3) selling secondary offerings. Most function as broker-dealers and offer a growing variety of financial products and services to their wholesale and retail clients.

INVESTMENT CLIMATE Laws, conditions, and constraints that exist in a country that affect the opportunity for investment in a foreign nation.

INVESTMENT COMPANY. *See* **INVESTMENT TRUST.**

INVESTMENT LIFECYCLE The period of time from the initial acquisition of an investment to its ultimate sale. Hindsight analysis of the investment life cycle enables an investor to compute the degree of success or failure of an investment (i.e., total return on investment over its life span).

INVESTMENT PERFORMANCE REQUIREMENTS Constraints imposed by a foreign government on investors who want to make direct investments in its country.

INVESTMENT STRATEGY Investment program designed to maximize return while considering such investor parameters as aversion to risk, amount available to invest, term of investment, projections regarding inflation, interest rates, economic growth, etc. An investment strategy provides for an allocation plan (choices of investment in equity securities, bonds, commodities, real estate, etc.) designed to satisfy these criteria.

INVESTMENT TRUST A company that invests in other companies after which it sells its own shares to the public. If it is a closed-end company, it sells its shares only. If it is an open-end company, or a mutual fund, it repeatedly buys and sells its shares.

INVISIBLE IMPORTS Financial and personal services trade (noninventory items, i.e., invisible services) rendered to the natives of a country by foreigners. The following services are examples of invisible imports: investment, consulting, management advice, insurance, freight, banking, etc. *See also* **INVISIBLE ITEMS OF TRADE**.

INVISIBLE ITEMS OF TRADE Exportation and importation of financial and personal services (noninventory items i.e., invisible services). These are added to a country's exported and imported goods in determining its balance of payments with respect to other nations. Invisible items of trade, i.e., imported and exported financial guidance, consulting services, insurance, etc., are, however, distinct from the export and import of goods. *See also* **INVISIBLE IMPORTS**.

INVOICE A detailed bill submitted to a purchaser indicating the price of goods acquired (shipped) and services utilized. An invoice enumerates the quantity of items purchased along with their respective unit price. The sum of the extensions on an invoice represents the total owed by the purchaser to the seller.

INVOLUNTARY CONVERSION A disposition of property that is beyond the control of its owner. Involuntary conversions occur when property is destroyed by: a casualty or theft, foreign government seizure or nationalization of property, government condemnation of property under the power of eminent domain, and other situations. Involuntary conversion losses are always recognized in full. However, involuntary conversions gains may be deferred if qualified replacement property is purchased.

IRP. *See* **INTEREST RATE PARITY**.

IRR. *See* **INTERNAL RATE OF RETURN**.

IRREVOCABLE LETTER OF CREDIT A noncancellable **LETTER OF CREDIT** in which the designated payment is guaranteed by the issuing bank if all terms and conditions are met by the drawee. It is as good as the issuing bank.

IRS. *See* **INTERNAL REVENUE SERVICE**.

ISSUE 1. The sale of a designated amount of financial securities i.e., stocks or bonds, by an entity (corporation, governmental body, etc.) through a broker (on a commission basis), underwriter, or private placement. 2. A point of discussion or disagreement with another. 3. The act of circulating, distributing, or publishing something. 4. Proceeds from an estate or fines. 5. A particular copy of a periodical.

ISSUING BANK A bank which opens a straight or a negotiable **LETTER OF CREDIT**. This bank assumes the obligation to pay the beneficiary or a **CORRESPONDENT BANK** if the documents presented are in accordance with the terms of the letter of credit.

ITA. *See* INTERNATIONAL TRADE ADMINISTRATION.

ITEMS OF TRADE Goods and services that a nation buys and sells in the world market. Examples are high tech products, heavy machinery and equipment, commodities, credit, and services.

J

JAWBONE. *See* DE FACTO PROTECTIONISM.

J-CURVE THEORY A graph that describes the influence of foreign currency fluctuations on a country's trade balance. If the country's currency appreciates sufficiently relative to other currencies, its exports decrease (due to raising export prices) and its imports increase (due to reducing import prices). Therefore, its trade balance worsens. If its currency subsequently depreciates, the reverse situation occurs. Over a period, the graph of the country's trade balance will look like a J shape. The J-shape curve traces the initial declining in trade followed by a recovery.

JOB CLASSIFICATION The allocation of jobs into categories for purposes of analysis and compensatory (salary) comparisons.

JOB DESCRIPTIONS AND SPECIFICATIONS Job description refers to a written statement enumerating the specific functions and responsibilities that must be followed in satisfactorily fulfilling a given job function. Job specification relates to the minimum requisite education, experience, expertise, and proficiency that an individual must have to perform a particular job. It identifies the qualifications required of the jobholder. Job descriptions and specifications provide useful information in **JOB EVALUATIONS.**

JOB EVALUATIONS A systematic analysis of a job in a business organization for the purpose of ascertaining its relative worth and importance compared to other job functions. Based on this evaluation and determination of its value, compensatory guidelines for the job may be established. **JOB DESCRIPTIONS AND SPECIFICATIONS** provide useful information in performing a job evaluation.

JOB LOT 1. The production run for a given job order. 2. Designation by number of the production of a particular order of goods or services.

JOB ROTATION The process of upgrading the skills, work interests, motivation, and promotibility of workers by moving them from one job to another without changing the basic tasks that constitute a given job function. By broadening the worker's skills, the employer also achieves greater flexibility in scheduling. Examples of job rotation include: an assembly worker working at two or three work stations in the course of a given day; a management trainee working in two or three different departments during his or her apprenticeship; and an office worker changing between typing and filing functions during a given period of time.

JOB SHARING A system of allocating the responsibilities and time of a given job between two people as an alternative to laying off one of them altogether. Both of the workers then become part-time employees compared to full-time ones. When economic conditions stabilize and improve, it is expected that both employees will be re-hired as full-timers.

JOBBER A "middleman" who actually purchases goods from a wholesaler and attempts to resell them to a retailer at a profit. Because the goods are actually acquired and owned by the jobber until they are sold, it is clear that the jobber does not function as a broker.

JOINT COSTS The costs of simultaneously manufacturing or buying two or more items in the same process.

JOINT PRODUCTS Two or more major products manufactured and processed at the same time. An example is gas and fuel oil derived from crude oil. Joint product costs are allocated to the specific products based on either volume or sales value.

JOINT VENTURE A joining together of two or more business entities or persons in order to undertake a specific business venture. A joint venture is not a continuing relationship such as a partnership, but may be treated as a partnership for income tax purposes. Two firms from different countries form some type of partnership. Either firm may be the dominant partner, depending on local legal restrictions. Two firms from different countries might also join to operate in a third country, in which case the operation would resemble a wholly-owned foreign operation. Many combinations are possible, with mutual trust the critical variable in a venture's success. Joint ventures can facilitate a marketer's international involvement at a faster pace than sole **FOREIGN DIRECT INVESTMENT.** Many countries have restricted sole direct investment in recent years.

JOURNAL OF COMMERCE An international business magazine, published by Two World Trade Center, 27th Floor, New York City, NY 10048, that covers information on domestic and foreign economic developments plus export opportunities, agricultural trade leads, shipyards, export ABCs and trade fair information. There are feature articles on **TARIFFS** and non-tariff barriers, licensing controls, joint ventures and trade legislation in foreign countries.

JUDGMENT LIEN 1. A court ordered lien on property until payment is made by the company to satisfy the judicial decree. An example is a creditor's lien against secured property of the borrower for nonpayment. 2. A federal or state tax lien on property for unpaid taxes. **3.** A landlord's lien on a tenant's property for failure to pay rent or damages to the leased premises. **4.** A mechanic's lien for work done but never paid for such as on the company's fleet of delivery trucks.

JUDICIAL REVIEW A higher court reevaluates a lower court decision for possible mistakes. A judicial review generally results in the confirmation of a decision or set of facts, a reversal of a lower court's decision, or sending back the case for further review based on newly discovered facts. The United States Court of International Trade has jurisdiction in actions involving imports such as the dumping of products, categorization of goods, duties, and unfair trade practices.

JUMBO LOANS Loans that differ from conforming loans in that they are above the maximum conforming amount and reflect each lender's own guidelines. Jumbo loans are purchased on the secondary market by **FREDDIE MAC.**

K

KABUSHIKI-KAIVHI A Japanese term for stock company.

KANGAROO BONDS Australian dollar-denominated bonds issued within Australia by a foreign firm.

KEIRETSU Groups of large numbers of suppliers, banks, intermediaries, trading firms, and other related firms into industrial power centers in post-War Japan.

KEY INDUSTRY An industry that is very important to a country's economy because of its large size and manufacturing capacity, employment of a large number of citizenry, interdependency of other industries on it, general influence, etc. A nation must be very careful to insure (through legislation) that foreign investment does not gain control of its key industries. For example, the defense industry of a country must never fall into the hands of foreign ownership.

KEY-AREA APPRAISAL Managerial concept developed by Peter Drucker that advocates planning objectives with follow-up appraisals in the following key areas: productivity, profitability, market standing, innovation, managerial development and performance, employee attitudes and performance, financial and physical resources, and public and social responsibilities.

KICKER A feature offered in a debt security to improve its attractiveness to potential investors such as a conversion privilege and stock rights. The sweetener may also result in a lower interest rate.

KIDNAP INSURANCE Insurance protection to a business if a key executive or employee is kidnapped on office premises. It may also cover any related criminal act such as the employee's providing access to company documents, files, assets, or premises to the criminals.

KK. *See* **KABUSHIKI-KAIVHI.**

KNOW-HOW LICENSING The licensing of technical information by one firm to another allowing the latter to use this technology in the production of goods and services. Licensing of information in this manner oftentimes increases competition by allowing for the irreversible transfer of "high-tech know-how" to trading partners. Companies licensing know-how technology attempt to control the transfer of information (like a patent) by limiting the locations by contract in which the technology may be used.

KNOWLEDGE INTENSIVE Activity requiring a significant amount of education and training. For example, performing a surgical operation is a very knowledge intensive function requiring years of medical education, training, and experience. Directing the Federal Reserve is a knowledge intensive activity requiring years of study and training in the area of economics and business.

KNOWN LOSS Damage to a shipment of goods that becomes known to the purchaser and seller before they are delivered. That is, the loss becomes known either during shipment or at the time of delivery.

KORUNA Monetary unit of Czechoslovakia.

KRONA Monetary unit of Iceland and Sweden.

KRONE Monetary unit of Denmark and Norway.

KRUGERRAND A bullion coin from South Africa which contains one troy ounce of gold.

KWACHA Monetary unit of Angola.

KYAT Monetary unit of Burma.

L

LABOR AGREEMENT Meeting of the minds between management and labor regarding future terms of employment including compensation, working conditions, resolutions of disputes, etc. A labor agreement is generally the precursor to a formal labor contract which spells out the binding, legal responsibilities of both management and labor for a preagreed specified period.

LABOR AUGMENTING TECHNICAL CHANGE Using up-to-date technology to make existing labor more productive. As a result, production volume will increase and cost per unit will decrease.

LABOR CONTRACT Also called a **LABOR AGREEMENT,** an agreement specifying the terms and conditions of employment as negotiated between organized labor and management.

LABOR INTENSIVE An industry or company with mostly labor rather than fixed assets. It has a high ratio of variable costs to total costs. If revenue decreases, layoffs of employees may take place to lower overall costs. Labor unrest (e.g., strikes, slowdowns) is always a concern. An example of labor intensive are service-oriented businesses. *See also* **CAPITAL INTENSIVE.**

LABOR PRODUCTIVITY The average number of units produced per worker.

LADING Cargo or freight that is transported by rail, truck, ship, etc. *See also* **BILL OF LADING.**

LAG **1.** As a way of reducing foreign exchange exposure, delaying the collection of receivables in foreign currency if that currency is expected to appreciate, and delaying conversion when payables are to be made in another currency in the belief the other currency will cost less when needed. **2.** A lagging economic indicator meaning it turns subsequent to the business cycle turns. An example is the prime interest rate.

LAGGING. *See* **LEADING AND LAGGING.**

LANDED VALUE A maritime insurance term referring to the wholesale value of goods that have arrived at their final shipping destination and are ready to be released to the purchaser, its agent, or its respective assignee.

LAST IN FIRST OUT (LIFO) A system of inventory valuation under which the cost of goods sold equals the cost of the latest inventory purchases and a firm computes the ending inventory cost from the costs of the older units. In periods of rising prices and increasing inventories, LIFO leads to higher reported expenses and therefore lower reported income and lower balance sheet inventories than does **FIRST IN FIRST OUT.**

LATENT DEFECT A known defect in a product that either has yet not surfaced or cannot be detected through a careful and reasonable physical examination of the good.

LAW OF AGENCY The legal requirements and responsibilities surrounding a relationship in which one entity or individual (the agent) acts on behalf of another entity or individual (the principal). The principal has given authority to the agent to enter into contractual agreements for the principal. *See also* **AGENT.**

LAW OF ONE PRICE. *See* **PURCHASING POWER PARITY.**

LAY DAYS The specified period of time (in terms of days) in which a ship is supposed to be loaded or unloaded.

L/C. *See* **LETTER OF CREDIT.**

LDC. *See* **LESS DEVELOPED COUNTRY.**

LDC DEBT SWAP. *See* **LESS DEVELOPED COUNTRY DEBT SWAP.**

LEAD As a way of reducing foreign exchange exposure, accelerating (leading), rather than delaying (lagging), international payments by modifying credit terms, normally on trade between affiliates. Accelerating the collection of receivables in foreign currency if that currency is expected to appreciate, and accelerating conversion when payables are to be made in another currency in the belief the other currency will cost less when needed. This contrasts with a **LAG.**

LEAD MARKET The market where new products are first introduced. To a multinational company, lead markets are typically the higher income markets which tend to encourage innovation (i.e., bringing new products to market) and reward successful innovation (e.g., with substantial profits).

LEADER PRICING A lowering of selling price on a consumer demanded product so as to encourage traffic in the store to stimulate the buying of other products at their regular selling price. An example is offering a significant discount on a computer that will bring in customers who will also need to buy fully priced peripherals such as modems, printers, and monitors.

LEADING AND LAGGING **1.** Timing of indicators in relationship to the ups and downs of the **BUSINESS CYCLE.** For example, if an indicator anticipates general business conditions, it is considered a leading indicator. If, on the other hand, it lags, it is considered a lagging indicator. **2.** Modifications by importers/exporters in paying their international debts or converting export receipts into foreign currency based on anticipated devaluations. For example, if a currency devaluation is feared and an importer has foreign currency obligations, he will make lead payments (i.e., he will attempt to make the payments as soon as possible so that he will not have to pay more as a result of the devaluation of his national currency). On the other hand, an exporter in such a situation stands to gain by lagging the conversion of export receipts of foreign currency.

LEARNING CURVE The relationship between units manufactured and direct labor hours per unit. As employees gain more experience, the time it takes to perform a task and its cost should decrease.

LEASE GUARANTEE PROGRAM **EXPORT-IMPORT BANK** of the United

States' program of loan guarantees to foreign buyers of American manufactured goods and services. The loan guarantee fully covers both principal and interest payments. The program was established to help American manufacturers compete against foreign competitors who are frequently subsidized by their governments.

LEASING The act of granting the use of property (e.g., real property, equipment, machinery, etc.) by a lessor (the party doing the granting) to a lessee (the party to whom the use of the property is granted) for a specified period of time. The lessee, in turn, compensates the lessor for the use of the property by making cash payments to him each month called rents. Terms of a lease include rental payment, lease time period, restrictions on use, and renewal options (if any).

LEAST COST METHOD OF PRODUCTION The combination of inputs and selection of technology that minimizes total manufacturing cost.

LEONTIEF PARADOX Contrary to the predictions of the Heckscher-Ohlin Theory, the empirical finding by United States Nobel Laureate Economist Wassily Leontief that the United States in 1947 had a lower capital/labor ratio in production of export products than in imports. That is, the United States was exporting labor-intensive goods to the rest of the world in exchange for capital-intensive imports. Professor Leontief suggested that perhaps the United States was really labor abundant relative to the rest of the world in the sense that United States workers were so much more efficient than foreign workers that they contributed three times as much labor per person-year as did foreign workers. This might be due, according to him, to superior United States entreprenuership and organization of industry, which somehow coaxed much more efficiency out of United States workers.

LESS DEVELOPED COUNTRY (LDC) Countries, most of whose trade involves the export of raw materials, fuels, minerals and some food products to the industrialized, rich and developed countries, in exchange mostly for manufactured goods, more often called developing countries. More and more less developed countries, however, are striving to industrialize their nations by concentrating on manufacturing labor-intensive products and exporting them at prices lower than the ones offered by developed nations.

LESS DEVELOPED COUNTRY (LDC) DEBT SWAP A debt swap by an **LDC**. The LDC is a third world country with low industrial development, low per capita income, high illiteracy, etc. In the LDC debt swap, the LDC benefits by exchanging existing foreign debt for new debt commitments.

LETTER OF CREDIT (L/C) A credit letter normally issued by the buyer's bank in which the bank promises to pay money up to a stated amount for a specified period for merchandise when delivered. It substitutes the bank's credit for the buyer's and eliminates the seller's risk. It is used in **INTERNATIONAL**

TRADE. The letter of credit can be revocable or irrevocable. A **REVOCABLE LETTER OF CREDIT** is a means of arranging payment, but it does not carry a guarantee. It can be revoked, without notice, at any time up to the time a draft is presented to the issuing bank. An **IRREVOCABLE LETTER OF CREDIT,** on the other hand, cannot be revoked without the special permission of all parties concerned, including the exporter. A letter of credit can also be confirmed or unconfirmed. A **CONFIRMED LETTER OF CREDIT** is an L/C issued by one bank and confirmed by another, obligating both banks to honor any drafts drawn in compliance. An **UNCONFIRMED LETTER OF CREDIT** is the obligation of only the issuing bank. The three main types of letter of credit, in order of safety for the exporter, are (1) the irrevocable, confirmed L/C; (2) the irrevocable, unconfirmed L/C; and (3) the revocable L/C. A summary of the terms and arrangements concerning theses three types of L/Cs is shown below.

	Irrevocable	Irrevocable confirmed L/C	Revocable L/C unconfirmed L/C
Who applies for	Importer	Importer	Importer
Who is obligated to pay	Issuing bank and confirming bank	Issuing bank	None
Who applies for amendment	Importer	Importer	Importer
Who approves amendment	Issuing bank, exporter, and confirming bank	Issuing bank and exporter	Issuing bank
Who reimburses paying bank	Issuing bank	Issuing bank	Issuing bank
Who reimburses issuing bank	Importer	Importer	Importer

See also **BACK-TO-BACK LETTER OF CREDIT; DOCUMENTARY LETTER OF CREDIT; NONDOCUMENTARY LETTER OF CREDIT; REVOLVING LETTER OF CREDIT; TRANSFERABLE LETTER OF CREDIT.**

LETTER OF INTENT **1.** A written statement articulating the actions to be taken by another in the near future. **2.** Communication to interested parties regarding the intent of two or more entities to merge.

LEVEL OUT A level of production, achievement, or volume that has been determined to be desirable for a particular entity (based on analysis and prior experience) given its resources and capacity. For example, if a company levels out production at X units, it knows, based on projected demand and constraints of materials and capacity, that it will not have material shortages, end the period carrying too much inventory, or be faced with other adverse occurrences.

LEVEL OF PLAYING FIELD The circumstances where all parties who are participants to a negotiated agreement start out on an equal footing. Companies that start out on a level playing field are assumed to not have any unfair advantages over their contractual opponents at the outset of the talks.

LEVEL PREMIUM A **PREMIUM** that remains the same (equal) during the entire payment period of an insurance policy.

LEVERAGE The use of debt to achieve increased profitability of an entity by obtaining a greater return on the use of the funds than the required interest payments. It this occurs, then the firm is said to achieve positive leverage. Negative leverage occurs when the opposite situation takes place. Positive leverage benefits shareholders by causing equity share price to increase. Negative leverage produces a decrease in share price.

LEVERAGED BUYOUT A takeover by a company of another company by the use of borrowed money. The borrowing group borrows the necessary funds, using the assets of the acquired company as collateral and expect to retire the debt over time with the cash flow from operations or the sale of corporate assets.

LEVIES Different tariff assessments applied to the imports of a foreign county.

LIABILITY 1. An obligation on the part of an entity that must be repaid, e.g., a debt, money owed, etc. 2. An obligation to perform. For example, if an entity receives money in advance to perform some function (e.g., landscaping) it has an obligation (i.e., liability) to perform that function. 3. To have a responsibility to do something.

LIBOR. *See* **LONDON INTERBANK OFFERED RATE.**

LICENSING The granting for a fee of the right to another (licensee) to use the licensor's patent, copyright, etc. The payment may be a lump sum or a percentage of sales, or a combination.

LIEN A creditor's right to retain possession or control of a debtor's property until full payment of the obligation is made. A lien may be general (on all property of a party) or specific (on some specified property). An example is a mortgage on a company's building held by the bank. Another example is the government's judgment on property of a delinquent corporate taxpayer.

LIFE CYCLE 1. The change in consumption habits of consumers over their life time. 2. A movement of a firm or its product through stages of development, growth, expansion, maturity, saturation, and decline. Not all products go through such a life cycle. See Figure 1. For example, paper clips, nails, knives, drinking glasses, and wooden pencils do not seem to exhibit such a life cycle. Most new products seem to, however. Some current examples include high-tech items such as computers, VCRs, and black and white TVs. See also **PRODUCT LIFE CYCLE**.

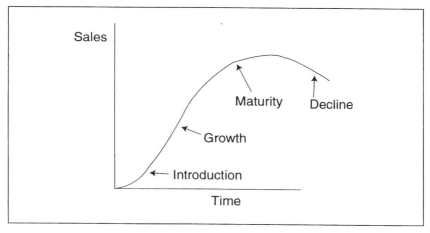

LICENSING The granting for a fee of the right to another (licensee) to use the licensor's patent, copyright, etc. The payment may be a lump sum or a percentage of sales, or a combination.

LIEN A creditor's right to retain possession or control of a debtor's property until full payment of the obligation is made. A lien may be general (on all property of a party) or specific (on some specified property). An example is a mortgage on a company's building held by the bank. Another example is the government's judgment on property of a delinquent corporate taxpayer.

LIFO. *See* **LAST IN FIRST OUT.**

LIKE PRODUCT A product that is the same functional type as another. A like product may be directly substituted for another. In financial accounting, when a like product is exchanged for another, **GENERALLY ACCEPTED ACCOUNTING PRINCIPLES** usually precludes the recognition of a gain on the transaction unless boot (monetary consideration transferred to equalize the value of the assets exchange) is received. If boot is received, then the portion of total gain that is recognized should be in proportion to the amount of boot received relative to the total amount received.

LIMIT PRICING Oligopolists attempt at restricting companies from entering the industry by establishing low prices. *See also* **OLIGOPOLY.**

LIMITED (LTD) British English word for a business formed as a corporation. It is the same as **INC.**

LIMITED DISTRIBUTION The distribution (by design) of a company's products to only a limited geographical location or to specific number of retailers for sale.

LIMITED LIABILITY Confining one's personal responsibilities for losses to the amount invested. Stockholders of a corporation enjoy limited liability. That is, they are not personally responsible for losses incurred by the corporate entity over and above the amount they contributed when they invested in the corporation's stock. Limited liability may be achieved in other legal forms. For example, personal liability may also be restricted to the amount invested if one is a limited partner in a limited partnership. In a limited liability partnership **(LLP)**, partners are also protected against the fraudulent actions and liabilities incurred by other partners of the organization.

LIMITED LIABILITY PARTNERSHIP. *See* **LIMITED LIABILITY.**

LINE 1. Functions relating to the direct production of goods or service outputs. Staff functions provide support, advice, and service to line positions. *See also* **LINE AND STAFF ORGANIZATION.** 2. Relating to one's profession, trade, or area of interest. 3. Category of inventory produced by a manufacturer.

LINE AND STAFF ORGANIZATION Line functions in a business organization are its production or operating departments. Their primary purpose is to produce goods or services outputs. Line managers are expected to achieve their objectives effectively and efficiently. In order to accomplish this, they frequently need the assistance of specialists. The group of departments that provide advice and counsel to the line departments is the staff organization. Staff functions include: purchasing, production planning and control, inventory stores, maintenance of plant and equipment, etc.

LINE EXTENSION A change or modification to an established product line resulting in a new variation of the brand. For example, a manufacturer of hot oatmeal breakfast cereals may decide to extend the product line to a family of cold cereal oatmeal products. *See also* **LINE ORGANIZATION.**

LINE OF CREDIT A loan agreement whereby a bank or other financial institution agrees to loan up to a preagreed amount to a borrower for a specified period generally not exceeding a year. The borrower may decide to borrow only a portion of the credit line at a particular time. If additional funds are needed from the unused line, a new loan application need not be filled out nor additional fees paid. A bank sometimes requires that a borrower satisfy compensating balance requirements in order to have a line of credit.

LINE ORGANIZATION The part of an entity's organization relating to the production of goods and service outputs. The line organization of a manufacturing entity, for example, is made up of its production departments. The line organization of a service entity are its operations and sales departments. *See also* **LINE AND STAFF ORGANIZATION.**

LINK FINANCING. *See* **BACK-TO-BACK LOANS.**

LIQUIDATE 1. To convert totally into cash. 2. To settle the affairs of an entity by converting all of its assets into cash and using it to satisfy all outstanding debts with any residual going to the stockholders or owners, e.g., to liquidate a business. 3. To settle an obligation or claim.

LIQUIDATED DAMAGES Preagreed damages that the victim of a breach in a contractual agreement is paid by the perpetrator.

LIQUIDATED VALUE Price for an asset that an entity accepts in a forced sale of its property when it is going out of business. The liquidated value of an asset is usually much lower than what would have been realized from selling the property in the normal course of business.

LIQUIDATION 1. The determination process that occurs when a business entity ceases to operate as a going concern. All the assets of the business are converted into cash by virtue of a sale or disposal, all debts are paid, and any residual funds that remain are allocated to the stockholders or owners. 2. Point at which customs agents assess the duty that will have to be paid on a good.

LIQUIDITY 1. The ease at which a company may convert its assets into cash to pay its debts as they come due. 2. The ability of a business to utilize its current assets to pay its current liabilities. Liquidity sensitivity relates to the period of time it takes to convert an asset into cash for the purpose of current debt satisfaction. The more liquid a company, the less its risk of debt default. 3. Reference to the ability of an asset to be converted into cash without an expected loss of value. The more illiquid an asset is, the greater the loss in value is expected if it must be sold. For example, if an entity's plant and equipment (illiquid assets) is sold in a liquidation sale, a much greater loss in value is expected compared to the sale of its trading securities (liquid assets) which can easily be sold in the stock market.

LIQUIDITY RISK The risk that a company will be unable to pay its current debts out of current assets. An illiquid company has a deficient cash position which may lead to bankruptcy. Liquidity risk may be appraised by computing a multinational company's current ratio (current assets/current liabilities), quick (acid-test) ratio (cash plus trading securities plus accounts receivable/current liabilities), working capital (current assets less current liabilities), accounts receivable turnover (credit sales/average accounts receivable), and inventory turnover (cost of goods sold/average inventory).

LIRA Monetary unit of Italy, Turkey, San Marino, and Vatican City.

LLOYD'S REGISTRY An organization that categorizes shipping vessels into different types. The classification of a ship is important because it influences carrier shipping rates, insurance premiums, ability to attract sailors, safety, and requests for use. The classification of a ship considers such factors as condition, age, quality, and make.

LOAD   1. A unit of freight in a given shipment. For example, a shipment consisting of two loads of computers. **2.** A sales charge assessed by a mutual fund for the privilege of purchasing fund shares (front load) or selling shares (back-end load). For example, Fidelity's Magellan Fund, the largest in the world, charges a 3 percent front load fee. Those mutual funds that do not charge sales fees to either purchase or sell shares are called no-load funds.

LOAD FACTOR The factor used to determine the amount of a sales charge that a customer will be assessed when buying or selling shares in a load mutual fund. For example, if a fund has a front load factor of 5 percent, customers are charged an incremental sales fee of 5 percent to buy into the mutual fund. *See also* **LOAD.**

LOAN SYNDICATION A group of banks or financial institutions who have associated together for the purpose of loaning a material amount of money to another entity for a given project. The syndication was formed because no lender would have wanted to incur the risk of singularly loaning the funds to the borrower.

LOBBYIST A paid entity or individual that is hired by a company for the purpose of trying to influence the vote of legislators or other public officials for a specific cause or policy.

LOCAL AREA NETWORK (LAN) A network connecting computer systems and devices within a close geographic area such as a single building.

LOCAL COSTS Costs of goods and services from suppliers that must be incurred by an exporter in the importer's country as a part of the execution or completion of a sales contract or project with the importer.

LOCK BOX A controlled-oriented system of cash collections by an entity. Customers of a company to whom money is owed send their cash payments to a locked post office box not far from the company's bank. Bank employees empty the box each day and deposit all checks to the account of the entity. The bank apprises the entity of the deposits collected on an ongoing basis. The purpose of a lock box arrangement is to hasten cash collections so a greater rate of return may be earned by the multinational company.

LOCKED IN   1. Reference to a guarantee of a fixed rate of return on a bank certificate of deposit (CD), bond, or other investment for a period of time or a given rate of interest on a loan, mortgage, etc. **2.** The delaying of the recognition of a profit on a stock sale or redemption of certain bonds due to a desire to defer the income tax liability that would result from the transaction.

LOCKOUT A situation in labor-management negotiations whereby management prevents union members from returning to work.

LOMBARD RATE An official interest rate established in a country (e.g., Germany) to influence the supply and demand for money in that country. A change in the interest rate by the banking authority in the country can have a significant affect on money market conditions. For example, a lowering of the interest rate makes money available at lower interest rates to multinational corporate borrowers.

LONDON INTERBANK OFFERED RATE (LIBOR) The deposit rate on interbank transactions in the **EUROCURRENCY MARKET.** It is used as a base rate for many international interest rate transactions. The rate, however, varies according to circumstances - at which funds can be borrowed in particular currencies, amounts, and maturities in the market. This rate is used as the base for determining the lending rate charged by banks engaged in medium-term (rarely exceeding two years) lending of Eurocurrencies for a variety of purposes. The development of North Sea oil fields being a prime example. The rate charged on a loan is a margin plus LIBOR.

LONG POSITION A position taken when a party buys something for future delivery. This may be done in the expectation that the item bought will increase in value. It may also be done to hedge a **CURRENCY RISK.**

LONG-RANGE PLANNING Future planning for periods of five years or more. Long-range planning attempts to anticipate how future projected trends and events will influence some of the following variables affecting a company: overall operations, product demand, competitive position, market share, etc.

LONG-TERM DEBT An obligation payable in money, goods, or services for a period in excess of one year. It is listed under noncurrent liabilities in the balance sheet. Examples are bonds payable, mortgage payable, and long-term notes payable.

LONG-TERM NATIONAL FINANCIAL MARKETS FINANCIAL MARKETS in different countries. That is, markets for long-term **CAPITAL MARKETS** trading stocks and bonds in different nations.

LOOK-THRU To search or examine a situation for decision making purposes.

LOOSE REIN A management style promoting a relaxed atmosphere so employees are less stressed, more imaginative, and teamwork fostered.

LOSS LEADER A product promoted or sold at a loss by a retail business so as to draw clientele into the store to buy other profitable items.

LOUVRE ACCORD An agreement in 1987 for certain countries to help stabilize the declining United States dollar. Acceptable limits were established for currency values.

LOW COST UNIT FACTORY The manufacturing facility with lowest costs, either because of low labor costs, large capital investment, or **ECONOMIES OF SCALE.**

LOWER INVOLVEMENT MODEL A mode of advertising in which there is a minimal interaction with consumers. An example is a promotion of a product over the radio.

LTD. *See* **LIMITED.**

LUXURY GOOD Consumers buy more of the product as their income level increases. Examples of luxury goods are fur coats and a Mercedes Benz.

M

MACHINE LOADING Capability of some machines to automatically load and set themselves up for use without any external human involvement. For example, in booting up a computer, the system automatically runs a small program in read only memory that loads its operating system from disk into memory in order to make applications use possible; many cameras automatically load themselves when the film is placed into the camera.

MACRO POLITICAL RISK. *See* **MACRO RISK.**

MACRO RISK More exactly macro political risk, the political risk facing all **MULTINATIONAL CORPORATIONS** in a particular country. It occurs when all foreign firms are affected in much the same way by politically motivated discontinuities in the business environment.

MAJOR MULTINATIONALS Also called **SEVEN SISTERS,** the world's giant oil companies, including Chevron, Royal Dutch Shell, Exxon, Mobil, British Petroleum (BP), Texaco, and Amoco.

MAKE BULK The process of consolidating exporters' shipments for the purpose of sharing freight costs. By consolidating shipments, money is saved by exporters by taking advantage of the large volume discounts frequently offered by common carriers. *See also* **CONSOLIDATED SHIPMENT.**

MAKE-OR-BUY (OUTSOURCE) DECISION The decision whether to produce a component part in-house or to buy it externally (or, outsource or subcontract) from an outside supplier. Examples are: (1) Develop a training program in-house or send employees outside for training. (2) Provide data processing and network services internally or buy them (Benefits: access to technology and cost savings). This decision involves both quantitative and qualitative factors. The qualitative considerations include ensuring product quality and the necessity for long-run business relationships with the subcontractors. The quantitative factors deal with cost. Make-or-buy decisions of international businesses are complicated by the volatile nature of countries' political economies, exchange rate fluctuations, temporal changes in relative factor costs, and the like. The make-or-buy decision must be investigated in the broader perspective of available facilities. The alternatives are: (1) leaving facilities idle; (2) buying the parts and renting out idle facilities; or (3) buying the parts and using unused facilities for other products.

MALINGERER A worker faking illness to avoid certain work tasks and duties.

MALINGERING Fabricating an illness or some other excuse for the purpose of avoiding work responsibilities or duties.

MANAGED CURRENCY Currency which is managed by the central bank or government of a country. The central bank or government of a nation may increase or decrease the money supply, buy or sell its currency for the purpose of affecting changes in its exchange rate (relative to other countries), and take other actions to achieve the political, economic, and other objectives that are in its best interests. *See* **MANAGED FLOATING EXCHANGE RATE.**

MANAGED FLOAT Also called **DIRTY FLOAT,** a country's attempt to control their currency exchange rates to add stability by regulating the supply of its currency.

MANAGED FLOATING EXCHANGE RATE A policy of intervention by the central bank or government of buying and selling a nation's currency for the purpose of affecting changes in its exchange rate. This managed intervention is an alternative to allowing market forces determine the value of a nation's currency relative to other international currencies. *See* **MANAGED CURRENCY.**

MANAGEMENT 1. The function of controlling an entity (especially a business) and insuring that it is operating in accordance with the objectives and goals set by the entity's Board of Directors. Controlling consists of planning, organizing, administering, and supervising to insure profitability, stability and organizational growth. 2. The individuals in an organization (managers, supervisors, executives, etc.) who are actively engaged in the management function as described in the previous definition. The larger the organization, the more managerial personnel necessary. Small organizations are frequently run by a single owner/manager.

MANAGEMENT AGREEMENT Agreement among managers providing for the allocation of administrative and supervisory responsibilities of the business entity for a given period of time. It frequently establishes managerial accountability for the projects of the organization.

MANAGEMENT AUDIT An evaluation of the effectiveness and efficiency of a given manager in an entity. The review is usually in depth and attempts to determine whether the manager has expediently accomplished the goals and objectives that have been set out for him or her. The review also assesses the manager's ability to work with his subordinates and superordinates. In short, the management audit is an examination of the quality of the manager. A management audit may be used to evaluate the success of the management of an entire department, division, or company.

MANAGEMENT BY CRISIS A **MANAGEMENT STYLE** where policies, rules, and guidelines are established in response to the adversity that results from a crisis. The strategy in this scenario is to set up a mechanism that will prevent a recurrence of the circumstances that caused the crisis. This is a reactive rather than proactive style and generally results in management without direction or goals.

MANAGEMENT BY EXCEPTION A management concept or policy by which management devotes its time to investigating only those situations in which actual results differ significantly from planned results. The idea is that management should spend its valuable time concentrating on the more important items (such as the shaping of the company's future strategic course). Attention is only given to material deviations requiring investigation. The tools that facilitate this use of this concept include Decision Support Systems **(DSS)**; Expert Systems; and Performance Reporting.

MANAGEMENT BY OBJECTIVE (MBO) A system of performance appraisal having the following characteristics: (1) It is a formal system in that each manager is required to take certain prescribed actions and to complete certain written documents; and (2) The manager and subordinates discuss the subordinate's job description, agree to short-term performance targets, discuss the progress made towards meeting these targets, and periodically evaluate the performance and provide the feedback.

MANAGEMENT CONTRACTS Contracts that a firm make with a foreign-owned firm, involving sending management personnel to aid in certain management functions for a specified period of time. The third world countries, lacking managerial knowledge, generally exert pressure for management contracts. A disadvantage to consider is the risk of developing future competitors.

MANAGEMENT CYCLE Period of time it takes for a recurring managerial project to be completed. For example, it may take a manager a full working day to supervise and oversee the yearly physical count of a retail entity's merchandise inventory.

MANAGEMENT FEE **1.** Annual fee (delineated by the fund's expense ratio) charged to holders of shares of a mutual fund for its management and administration. **2.** Fee charged by a real estate management company to manage real estate property. **3.** Fee charged to an investor by a stockbroker or financial advisor for managing an investor's portfolio for a given period of time.

MANAGEMENT GAME A form of simulation. Both simulation and management games are mathematical models, but they differ in purpose and mode of use. Simulation models are designed to simulate a system and to generate a series of financial and operating results regarding system operations. Games do the same thing except that in games human beings play a significant part. That is, participants make decisions at various stages. Thus, the games are distinguished by the idea of play. The major goals of the game are: (1) To improve decision making and analytical skills; (2) To develop awareness of the need to make decisions lacking complete information; (3) To develop an understanding of the interrelationships of the various functions of business (accounting, finance, marketing, production, etc.) within the firm and how these interactions affect overall performance; (4) To develop ability to function cooperatively and effectively in a small group situation. Management games offer a unique means of training accountants and have been used successfully as an executive training device. Management games generally fall into two categories: executive games and functional games. Executive games are general management games and cover all functional areas of business and their interactions and dynamics. Executive games are designed to train general executives. Functional games, on the other hand, focus on middle management decisions and emphasize particular functional areas of the firm. Examples of executive games in wide use include "XGAME", "COGITATE", and "IMAG-INIT." Examples of functional games include "MARKSIM," "FINSIM," and "PERT-SIM".

MANAGEMENT INFORMATION SYSTEM (MIS) A computer-based or manual system which transforms data into information useful in the support of decision making. MIS can be classified as performing three functions: (1) MIS that generates reports. These reports can be financial statements, inventory status reports or performance reports that are needed for routine and nonroutine purposes. (2) MIS that answer "what-if" kinds of questions asked by management. For example, questions such as "what would happen to cash flow if the company changes its credit term for its customers" can be answered by MIS. This type of MIS can be called **SIMULATION** or **WHAT-IF MODEL.** (3) MIS that support decision making. This type of MIS is appropriately called Decision Support System **(DSS).** DSS attempt to integrate the decision maker, the data base, and the quantitative models being used.

MANAGEMENT SCIENCE A collection of mathematical and statistical methods used in the solution of managerial and decision-making problems, also called operations research. There are numerous tools available under these headings such as linear programming, **ECONOMIC ORDER QUANTITY, LEARNING CURVE** theory, **PROGRAM EVALUATION AND REVIEW TECHNIQUE,** and regression analysis.

MANAGEMENT STYLE The leadership behavioral style utilized by a manager. Blake and Mouton postulated two basic assumptions about managerial behavior in an attempt to help supervisors understand their managerial style with the ultimate goal of improvement. They are: (1) concern for production - with the emphasis on getting the job done and (2) concern for people. Using these two variables as a theoretical underpinning, they developed a description of several styles based on how much each of them were applied by managers in their jobs. For example, they postulated that the "team manager"style would be the best since such a manger was rated high in both variables. That is, he or she showed high concern for the organization's production needs as well as for his or her subordinates. Such a manager believes that both the organization and its employees can be integrated by fully involving people in making decisions about the strategies and conditions of work. Such a manager attempts to develop work teams that can achieve both high productivity and high employee morale.

MANAGEMENT TECHNOLOGY The know-how used to run a business. It is the managerial skills that enable a multinational company to compete in the global market by using its limited resources optimally and profitably.

MANAGERIAL ACCOUNTING The process of identification, measurement, accumulation, analysis, preparation, interpretation, and communication of financial information, which is used by management to plan, evaluate, and control within an organization. It is the accounting used for the planning, control, and decision-making activities of an organization. Managerial accounting is concerned with providing information to internal managers who are charged with directing, planning and controlling operations and making a variety of management decisions. Managerial accounting can be contrasted with financial accounting, which is concerned with providing information, via financial statements, to stockholders, creditors, and others who are outside the organization.

MANAGING AGENTS A foreign based individual or entity hired to represent the interests of a company in a foreign nation (especially in dealing with the government). Managing agents generally have the authority to legally bind the company in negotiating contracts, agreements, and commitments.

MANUFACTURER'S EXPORT AGENT **1.** An exporting company that purchases products from a domestic manufacturer and attempts to resell them abroad at a profit. Since the exporter purchases the goods outright from the domestic manufacturer, all risks of resale are assumed. *See also* **EXPORT MANAGEMENT COMPANY.** **2.** An entity that serves as an agent of a domestic manufacturer in a foreign country and who seeks to sell the manufacturer's products abroad for a sales commission. Since the inventory is not purchased outright from the manufacturer, the agent assumes no risk of resale. Frequently, noncompeting manufacturers are represented by the same manufacturer's export agent.

MANUFACTURER'S OUTPUT INSURANCE LIABILITY insurance purchased by a manufacturer/provider to protect it against lawsuits relating to the goods that it manufactures or services it performs.

MANUFACTURING COST Those costs associated with the manufacturing activities of the company. They consist of three categories: direct materials, direct labor, and factory overhead.

MARGIN **1.** The ratio of profit to sales. **2.** Downpayment given for buying a security or **FUTURES CONTRACT** with the balance being on credit. To buy a stock, at least 50 percent of cash must be paid. **3.** The forward versus spot rate for a foreign currency.

MARGIN CALL A demand made by a broker of a client to pay in additional funds or put up additional collateral in the form of stocks or bonds to cover a loan in the purchase of securities. A margin call is made when the equity in a customer's margin account falls below a predetermined minimum amount. This occurs when the market value of assets collateralizing the customer's account unexpectedly falls. It is risky buying on margin.

MARGINAL COST (MC) The change in total cost associated with a unit change in quantity. For example, the marginal cost of the 500th unit of output can be calculated by finding the difference in total cost at 499 units of output and total cost at 500 units of output. MC is thus the additional cost of one more unit of output. It is calculated as: MC = change in total cost/change in quantity
MC is also the change in total variable cost associated with a unit change in output. This is because total cost changes, whereas total fixed cost remains unchanged. MC may also be thought of as the rate of change in total cost as the quantity (Q) of output changes and is simply the first derivative of the total cost (TC) function. Thus, MC = dTC/dQ. Economists normally assume firms to be producing at a point at which marginal costs are positive and rising. In managerial applications of this concept, MC is viewed as being equivalent to incremental cost which is the increment in cost between the two alternatives or two discrete volumes of output. *See also* **MARGINAL REVENUE.**

MARGINAL PRODUCT The additional output of a product produced from an additional unit of input, e.g., labor, materials.

MARGINAL REVENUE The rate of change of total revenue with respect to quantity sold. Marginal revenue indicates to a firm how total sale revenues will change if there is a change in the quantity sold of a firm's product. In economics, marginal revenue must equal marginal cost in order for profit to be maximized. Under perfect competition, price is fixed and thus marginal revenue is constant and equal to the price. In a discrete range of activity, marginal revenue is equivalent to incremental revenue. *See also* **MARGINAL COST.**

MARGINAL PROPENSITY TO IMPORT That portion of each additional dollar of national income paid for imported products and services.

MARGINAL REVENUE The additional income generated from selling one more unit of a good.

MARGINAL TAX RATE The highest tax rate used in computing a company's total tax obligation which is the tax rate applicable to the next dollar of income. The federal income tax rate is graduated, meaning that as additional profits are earned, the tax rate on the incremental earnings increases. The federal corporate tax rates are as follows:

Taxable Income	Marginal Tax Rates (%)
$0 - $50,000	15
$50,001 - $75,000	25
$75,000 to $10 million	34
Over $10 million	35

There is an additional 5 percent surtax on taxable income between $100,000 and $335,000. *See also* **AVERAGE TAX RATE.**

MARINE BILL OF LADING A receipt for freight prepared by the shipper for the transportation of goods by sea. A marine bill of lading represents a contract for the transportation of goods from one point to another between shipper and marine carrier. It can also be used as a document of title assuming it is negotiable. That is, a marine bill of lading can be used to sell the goods while in ocean transit.

MARINE CARGO INSURANCE Marine insurance purchased by the owners of goods being shipped by sea. It provides for reimbursement by the insurer for losses or damage to the goods being transported in excess of the amount that is recoverable from the marine carrier while in transit. *See also* **CARGO INSURANCE.**

MARINE INSURANCE An insurance policy on merchandise being transported over air, land, or sea as well as coverage of the shipping vehicles, e.g., airplane, truck, ship. Loss reimbursement may arise from various causes depending on the policy such as accident, theft, and fire. The amount of coverage and terms a vendor should decide on depends on such factors as carrier responsibility and coverage, risk, cost, time period, and restrictions.

MARINE SURVEYOR A specialist working for a marine insurance company who attempts to ascertain the cause and extent of loss or damage to property occurring on a seafaring vessel.

MARITIME Commerce activity over the water including ports. It relates to navigation as a shipping mechanism.

MARITIME LAW Legal aspects surrounding business transactions involving the seas and harbors. An example is the legal issues surrounding a cargo being transported by ship.

MARKDOWN A reduction in the original retail selling price of an item in an attempt to make it more attractive to buyers and accelerate its sale. If the good should suddenly become popular with buyers again, management may decide to cancel the markdown or part of it (called a markdown cancellation) and attempt to sell the good at a higher price. Markdowns less markdown cancellations are called net markdowns. See also MARKUP.

MARKET ABSORPTION CURVE A graph portraying the percentage of the market that has purchased (absorbed) a product (on the Y-axis) since the product was first introduced in the market (on the X-axis).

MARKET ACCESS A measure of the ease of accessibility of a foreign market to an exporting producer. Market access is a function of an importing nation's potential willingness to open its doors to foreign made products and assess **TARIFFS** on imported goods.

MARKET ALLOCATION The strategy used by **MULTINATIONAL CORPORATIONS** to limit activities of each affiliate to specified markets to eliminate competition among these units.

MARKET ANALYSIS Research done to ascertain an exporter's strength relating to current and future international market accessibility. Market research is performed so that an exporter can: determine which new markets to pursue, whether to expand in current markets, which markets will the demand for its products wane, etc.

MARKET AREA The region of the world or country from which a company derives the greatest demand for its products or services.

MARKET CONCENTRATION (POWER) The influence a seller has in the market for its product ranging from little influence (perfect competition) to control (monopoly).

MARKET DISRUPTION The dumping of foreign made goods in a domestic market causing the price of the goods to crash. The effect of such an action produces chaos and disruption in the market for those products.

MARKET ECONOMIC SYSTEM. *See* **ECONOMIC SYSTEM.**

MARKET ECONOMY. *See* **MARKET-BASED ECONOMY.**

MARKET PENETRATION **1.** Amount of a specific good bought in its market. **2.** The use of assertive selling techniques to increase orders of a product or service.

MARKET RISK The exposure to the possibility of financial loss resulting from any unfavorable movement in interest rates, currency rates, equity prices, or commodity prices. Prices of all securities are correlated to some degree with broad swings in the stock market. Market risk refers to changes in a firm's security's price resulting from changes in the stock or bond market as a whole, regardless of the fundamental change in the firm's earning power.

MARKET SECTOR That portion of a dual economy that is marked-based and is connected to global business with the industrial countries.

MARKET SEGMENTATION A multinational company strategy under which the firm tries to identify and compete based on defining and pursuing a niche or segment of the total market, such as the highest quality segment or the smallest size segment. In this approach, the multinational company identifies segments of national markets that could profitably be given separate treatment across national boundaries.

MARKET SHARE A ratio of a firm's sales to total industry sales, either actual or estimated. An increased market share is often a measure of business success, but by no means a guarantee of increased earnings.

MARKET TEST The sampling of a small portion of a given market by a company as a means of testing the strength and success of its products and marketing strategies. Manufacturers often utilize market tests as indicators of how the whole country will react to a given product, strategy, etc.

MARKET TIMING 1. Decision on the part of a manufacturer as to when to market its products. Market timing is very important to the success of a marketing strategy. Recently, for example, a movie company decided not to release James Cameron's early summer extravaganza, entitled "Titanic". Because of a delay in the production of the movie, its new release date was projected to be very late in the summer. That is, it would have to be released after all the other summer blockbusters had already saturated the market. To insure maximum marketing popularity and not to be outdone by its competitors, the movie company decided to make the movie a Christmas release. Clearly market timing is very important to the financial success of a project. **2.** Decision as to when to buy or sell securities by an investor based on such factors as the economy, interest rates, the level of stock prices as indicated by the Dow Jones Industrials average, inflationary expectations, etc.

MARKET VALUE METHOD (FOR INVESTMENTS) United States multinational companies must record investments in trading securities (intent is to hold for short-term profits) and available-for-sale securities (intent is to hold for a long-term time period) at their market values in the balance sheet. The securities may be stocks or bonds in other companies. Unrealized (holding) losses or gains arise from differences between the initial cost and market value. Unrealized losses or gains on trading securities are presented as a separate item in the income statement. Unrealized losses or gains on available-for-sale securities are presented separately in the stockholder's equity section of the balance sheet.

MARKETABILITY The degree to which inventory, products, investments, etc. are demanded by buyers and are therefore saleable.

MARKET-BASED ECONOMY Also called **MARKET ECONOMY,** a system of efficient allocation of resources involving the interaction of buyers and sellers for goods and services. In this system, most factors of producing is privately owned. Further, market forces, prices, and earnings determine how much of which products or services will be provided. The degree of competition and efficiency is typically characterized by several variables such as the number and size of the buyers and sellers involved, ease of entry, and the extent of **PRODUCT DIFFERENTIATION.**

MARKET-IF-TOUCHED ORDER (MIT) A contingent buy or sell order of securities at market price if execution of another order takes place at a given price.

MARKETING **1.** The process of carefully planning the pricing, promotion, and distribution of goods and services in accordance with the producing entity's objectives and goals. International marketing is an extension of marketing activities performed in foreign countries. To successfully market a product internationally, a company must be cognizant of the following considerations relating to the nation in which the goods will be marketed: economic conditions of the country; cultural, political, environmental, and legal factors relating to the product; its advertising media; its distribution channels; etc. **2.** The total of all commercial functions in transferring a product from producer to final consumer.

MARKETING MIX The **FOUR Ps** in marketing decisions - product attributes, distribution strategy, communication strategy, and pricing strategy. The marketing mix is the set of choices that determine a multinational company's offer to its target market(s). **MULTINATIONAL CORPORATIONS** often vary their marketing mix from country to country in light of differences in national culture, economic development, product standards, distribution channels, and the like.

MARKETING PLAN Marketing strategy consisting of pricing, promotion, and distribution activities performed by a company to maximize the sale of a given product, family of products or entire line.

MARKETING RESEARCH A systematic, objective, bias-free inquiry of the market and customer preferences. Marketing research is essentially a twofold activity. It involves (1) collecting current data describing all phases of the marketing operations, and (2) presenting the findings to marketing managers in a form suitable for decision making. The focus is on the timeliness of the information. A variety of tools such as surveys, questionnaires, pilot studies, and in-depth interviews are used for marketing research. Marketing research can identify the features that customers really want in a product or from a service. Important attributes of products or services-style, color, size, appearance, and general fit-can be investigated through the use of marketing research. Marketing research broadly encompasses advertising research and consumer behavior research. Advertising research is research on such advertising issues as ad and copy effectiveness, recall, and media choice. Consumer behavior research answers questions about consumers and their brand selection behaviors and preferences in the marketplace. Research results are used to make **MARKETING MIX** decisions and for pricing, distribution channels, guarantees and warranties, and customer service.

MARKET-SERVING FOREIGN DIRECT INVESTMENT (FDI) An FDI by the multinational company aiming at targeting the host country.

MARKING The placing of letters, numbers, and other information on freight so that it is properly identified to all interested parties.

MARKING DUTIES Extra duties assessed on goods that are improperly marked. Improper marking results when one cannot determine the country of origin of the goods. Custom regulations of most countries require that goods have **MARKS OF ORIGIN.**

MARKKA Finland's currency.

MARKOWITZ'S PORTFOLIO THEORY. *See* **EFFICIENT PORTFOLIO.**

MARKS The letters, numbers, and other information on freight enabling it to be properly identified to all interested parties. *See also* **MARKING.**

MARKS OF ORIGIN The marking on a good indicating where it was produced. The custom regulations of most countries require that all imported goods have marks of origin.

MARKUP 1. An increase in the original retail selling price of an item as a result of increased demand and limited supply. If the increased demand for the good suddenly dissipates (or supply increases), management may decide to cancel the markup or part of it (called a markup cancellation) and attempt to sell the good at a lower price. Markups less markup cancellations are called net markups. *See also* **MARKDOWN. 2.** The difference between the cost of a good and its original selling price is called the original markup.

MASS APPEAL Broad-based marketing approach that attempts to appeal to all segments of the population rather than being directed to one or more special sub-groups.

MASS MEDIA Communication pathways to the general public. The mass media includes television, radio, the **INTERNET,** newspapers, magazines, and all other broad-based communication sources that disseminates current information and data to the public.

MASS PRODUCTION The manufacturing of standard products in significant volume with production equipment and parts that are interchangeable. It is a continually recurring process that may be automated.

MASTER STRATEGY A formalization of the basic approaches to be used in achieving a strategic objective, for example, locating a plant in Germany to be close to the market.

MATCHING Generally accepted accounting principle that provides the underpinning upon which the income statement is based. The matching principle requires that the accounting entity (business) cumulatively aggregate all the revenue earned from the first day of the period to the last and subtract from it (net) all the costs that were incurred in the process of generating the revenue. The difference between the aggregated revenues and related aggregated expenses is either net income (if revenues exceed expenses), net loss (if expenses exceed revenues) or break even (if revenues equal expenses).

MATERIALS MANAGEMENT The total of all activities related to managing the raw materials that are utilized in a manufacturing operation. This includes monitoring their requisition, ordering, purchasing, storage, and movement in the production area.

MATRIX STRUCTURE An organizational structure as a grid with intersecting responsibilities. This is a dual rather than a single chain of command and some managers report to two bosses rather than one. For example, marketing in Asia may report to both a functional manager (marketing) and a geographical manager (Asia) in terms of hierarchical relationships.

MATURE MULTINATIONAL COMPANY The multinational company that has the following characteristics: (1) It has a global perspective on operations. (2) It has well geographically distributed product markets and resource markets. (3) It serves customers well and operates at lowest cost.

MATURING PRODUCT A product on the mature end of the **PRODUCT LIFE CYCLE** before the decline stage. The product is losing steam since it faces competition, its **PROPRIETARY TECHNOLOGY** is no longer monopolized, and it faces increasing **PRICE ELASTICITY** of demand.

MATURITY The time when a **NOTE,** bond, **TIME DRAFT,** or other negotiable instrument becomes due and payment may be demanded from the debtor. *See also* **MATURITY DATE.**

MATURITY DATE **1.** The specific date when a note, bond, time draft, or other negotiable instrument becomes due and payment may be demanded. At the maturity date, the negotiable instrument is presented to the debtor and redemption is requested. *See also* **MATURITY.** **2.** The date on which an insurer of a life insurance policy becomes fully liable to the **BENEFICIARY,** or beneficiaries, of the insured for the proceeds of the policy. This generally occurs on the date in which the insured dies.

MATURITY GAP The amount of monetary exposure that occurs when a company has asset and liability positions in the same monetary currency that mature at different times.

MBO. *See* **MANAGEMENT BY OBJECTIVE.**

MC. *See* **MARGINAL COST.**

MECHANIZATION To accomplish functions or tasks through the use of machines or with mechanical assistance.

MEDIATION The settling of disputes between companies by a neutral third party who can recommend but not impose a settlement. Since it is undertaken out-of-court costly litigation is avoided. *See also* **ARBITRATION.**

MERCANTILISM The premise that a country is economically better off exporting more than importing.

MERCHANDISE CONTROL Activities insuring proper execution, recording, and safeguarding of an entity's inventories. Some of the areas relating to merchandise control include: maintenance of proper inventory levels to minimize carrying costs and avoid stockouts; physical protection of inventories; proper accounting of inventory balances and related cost of goods sold, etc.

MERCHANDISE TRADE **1.** The act of reselling or trading merchandise that has been acquired by a wholesaler or retailer. **2.** Goods that have been acquired and marketed for resale.

MERCHANDISE TRADE ACCOUNT Account used in an entity's accounting system that contains the dollar value of the inventory that is available for sale. If the entity utilizes a perpetual system of accounting, the balance of the merchandise trade account reflects the inventory balance updated for current purchases and sales of inventory. If the entity utilizes a periodic inventory system, then the inventory balances reflects the opening balance of the inventory at the beginning of the period. It is subsequently adjusted at the end of the period to reflect the amount determined by a physical count.

MERCHANDISING **1.** Systematic marketing of goods for the purpose of maximizing sales volume. **2.** Sum of all activities, e.g., promotion, advertising, special sales, etc., performed by a wholesaler, retailer, or dealer for the purpose of selling its inventory.

MERCHANTABLE A salable product suiting the purpose and quality for which it was designed.

MERCHANTING The sale of merchandise involving the following scenario: A vendor in one country purchases goods in another for sale in a third country. The goods are directly shipped from the second country to the third without ever having to pass through the nation in which the sale was initiated.

MERGERS AND ACQUISITIONS 1. Business combination of two or more entities. In a merger of Company A and Company B, Company B merges into Company A leaving only Company A left after the combination. That is, Company B's assets and liabilities are absorbed by Company A with Company B ceasing to exist. In an acquisition of Company B by Company A, both companies retain their identities after the combination. However, Company A, functions as the parent company and maintains control over Company B, the subsidiary. **2.** The department of a consulting or management services entity that provides advice to other companies on potential business combinations.

METHOD OF ENTRY The means utilized by an entity to establish a base of operations in a foreign country. The following are examples of methods of entry: by investment in another entity already operating in that country; through exportation of its products and ultimate expansion into the foreign country; by government solicitation and licensing, etc.

MFN. *See* **MOST-FAVORED NATION.**

M-FORM COMPANY A business structured around decentralized units.

MICRO POLITICAL RISK. *See* **MICRO RISK.**

MICRO RISK More exactly micro political risk, the political risk facing all **MULTINATIONAL CORPORATIONS** in a particular country. It involves abrupt and politically motivated changes in the business environment that are selectively directed toward specific industries, firms, or projects. In technical jargon, macro risk is industry, firm, or project specific. **MACRO RISK** is dramatic, while micro risk is prevalent.

MIDDLE MANAGEMENT Managerial personnel holding leadership positions such as department heads, division supervisors, section managers, and group leaders. These individuals have extensive supervisory responsibilities and are directly accountable to upper management.

MINIMUM REQUIRED RATE OF RETURN. *See* **COST OF CAPITAL.**

MINISTRY OF INTERNATIONAL TRADE AND INDUSTRY (MITI) The Japanese government agency in charge of monitoring Japan's trading policy and overseeing export industries. It funds many Japanese export programs. It keeps track of the export financing activities of Japan's Export-Import Bank, has export insurance programs, develops foreign-related training programs, and engages in research support for new technology. To achieve specific national goals, the MITI has been known to control overseas investment by Japanese firms and restrict free imports by foreign firms.

MIS. *See* **MANAGEMENT INFORMATION SYSTEM.**

MISMATCH An inequality in an entity's foreign currency assets and liabilities as a result of differing magnitude or **MATURITY.**

MISSION STATEMENT A broad statement defining the multinational company's scope and purpose, usually including profit orientation, consumer needs, community responsibilities, and the like.

MISSIONARY RATE A very low freight rate offered by a carrier such as to obtain new clients or to help out a financially troubled company in time of need which has been a loyal client over the years.

MIT. *See* **MARKET-IF-TOUCHED ORDER.**

MITI. *See* **MINISTRY OF INTERNATIONAL TRADE AND INDUSTRY.**

MITIGATING CIRCUMSTANCES The conditions present that should act to reduce the damages from a breach of contract or offense. An example is a party failing to meet a contractual deadline date because of a serious illness in the immediate family. Another example is a company failing to meet a contractual delivery date for goods because of a fire or strike at the plant.

MITIGATION OF DAMAGES An injured party in a contract arising from the breach or tort of another must exercise reasonable care not to make the ensuing injury and monetary damages worse. The injured party is obligated to act in good faith in controlling the situation. For example, if X is hired for a year and is discharged at the end of six months, he must mitigate damages by trying to find another position (though not a different type of position, nor a position in a different locality).

MIX (PRODUCT AND SERVICES) The relative proportions of the product sold. For example, a company has three products and their respective sales are as follows:

	A	B	C	Total
Sales	$30,000	$60,000	$10,000	$100,000

Then the sale mix ratio for A, B, and C are 30 percent, 60 percent, and 10 percent, respectively. Since products sometimes tend to follow a typical **PRODUCT LIFE CYCLE,** it is imperative to maintain a proper mix of newly launched products, growth products, and mature lines. The product mix must be considered in the context of its broader **MARKETING MIX,** price, promotion, and advertising.

MIXING RATES The use of differing rates of exchange by a nation for specially designated types of foreign traded goods.

MNCs. *See* **MULTINATIONAL CORPORATIONS.**

MOBILE RESOURCES A company can move its resources (e.g., labor, equipment) freely geographically so as to be most productive, efficient, and profitable.

MODELING The process of converting a real-life system into a mathematical abstract. Financial modeling for **BUDGETING** and "what-if" analysis is an example.

MOMENTUM The impetus or acceleration of movement. For example, an economy or business that has momentum is rapidly growing.

MONETARY UNION An agreement between nations that are economically associated to also: share a common currency; maintain fixed currency exchange rates; allow for the unimpeded movement of capital; etc. For example, the **EUROPEAN COMMUNITY** of nations is currently attempting to establish a monetary association among its members.

MONETARY/NONMONETARY METHOD A foreign exchange translation method that applies the current exchange rate to all financial assets and liabilities, both current and long term. Physical, or nonmonetary, assets are translated at historical rates. In contrast with the **CURRENT-NONCURRENT METHOD,** this method rewards holding of physical assets under devaluation.

MONEY BROKER An entity or individual who operates as an **INTERMEDIARY** between a lender and borrower.

MONEY MARKET HEDGE A **HEDGE** in which a multinational company borrows in one currency and converts the proceeds into another currency. Funds to repay the loan may be generated from business operations, in which case the hedge is **COVERED.** Or, funds to repay the loan may be purchased in the **FOREIGN EXCHANGE MARKET** at the **SPOT RATE** when the loan matures, which is called an uncovered or open edge. The cost of the money market hedge is determined by differential interest rates. For example: XYZ, an American importer enters into a contract with a British supplier to buy merchandise for 4,000 pounds. The amount is payable on the delivery of the good, 30 days from today. The company knows the exact amount of its pound liability in 30 days. However, it does not know the payable in dollars. Assume that the 30-day money-market rates for both lending and borrowing in the United States and U.K. are .5 percent and 1 percent, respectively. Assume further that today's foreign exchange rate is $1.50 per pound. In a money-market hedge, XYZ can take the following steps:

Step 1. Buy a one-month U.K. money market security, worth of 4,000/(1+.005) = 3,980 pounds. This investment will compound to exactly 4,000 pounds in one month.

Step 2. Exchange dollars on today's spot (cash) market to obtain the 3,980 pounds. The dollar amount needed today is 3,980 pounds x $1.7350 per pound = $6,905.30.

Step 3. If XYZ does not have this amount, it can borrow it from the United States money market at the going rate of 1 percent. In 30 days XYZ will need to repay $6,905.30 x (1+.1) = $7,595.83.

Note that XYZ need not wait for the future exchange rate to be available. On today's date, the future dollar amount of the contract is known with certainty. The British supplier will receive 4,000 pounds, and the cost of XYZ to make the payment is $7,595.83.

MONEY MARKETS The markets for short-term (less than one year) debt securities influenced by the demand/supply relationship. Examples of money market securities include United States Treasury bills, federal agency securities, a **BANKERS' ACCEPTANCE, COMMERCIAL PAPER,** and negotiable certificates of deposit issued by government, business, and financial institutions.

MONITORING 1. The stockholders' ability to oversee management actions. **2.** An executive's ability to keep tabs on its workers. **3.** Watching the actions of competitors. **4.** Keeping abreast with economic and political factors affecting the business.

MONOPOLY. *See* **BILATERAL MONOPOLY.**

MONOPOLY POWER The power a monopolist enjoys such as pricing and **MARKET SHARE.**

MONOPSONY There exists just one buyer for a company's product or service. In such a case, the buyer has much influence and can demand a lower price.

MORAL HAZARD A company overuses a resource due to a loophole in the insurance policy.

MORALE The status of an individual or group's general attitude and spirit as indicated by their state of cheerfulness, confidence, motivation to work hard, commitment, etc. Many organizational behavioral procedures are structured to insure that the employees have high morale and are motivated to do their utmost to accomplish the goals of the organization.

MORATORIUM 1. The authorization by a lender to temporarily suspend the repayment of a loan by a debtor. **2.** A period of time in which some defined activity is temporarily suspended. **3.** The temporary suspension of any given activity.

MORGAN GUARANTY DOLLAR INDEX The index that measures the value of foreign currency units versus dollars. It is a weighted-average of 15 currencies including that of France, Italy, United Kingdom, Germany, Canada, and Japan. The weighting is based on the relative significance of the currencies in world markets. The base of 100 was established for the period 1980-1982.

MORGAN STANLEY CAPITAL INTERNATIONAL EUROPE AUSTRALIA FAR EAST (MSCI EAFE) INDEX Reflects the performance of all major stock markets outside North America. It is a market-weighted index composed of 1,041 companies representing the stock markets of Europe, New Zealand, and the Far East. It is considered the key "rest-of-the-world" index for United States investors, much as the Dow Jones Industrial Average is for the American market. It is used as a guide to see how United States shares are faring against other markets around the globe. It also serves as a performance benchmark for international mutual funds that hold non-United States assets. Morgan Stanley has created its own indices for 18 major foreign markets. To make the MSCI-EAFE Index, those country indices are weighted to reflect the total market capitalization of each country's markets as a share in the world.

MOST-FAVORED-NATION (MFN) A country that qualifies for the best trade terms with another country.

MOTION STUDY The analysis of the detailed activities making up a given task for the purpose of determining how they may be restructured so that the task is performed in the most cost effective way. Time and motion studies (as they are sometimes called) were frequently performed on automobile assembly lines to maximize the efficiency and effectiveness of auto workers.

MOVEMENT **1.** The oscillation or change of the price of a stock, bond, or commodity. **2.** An organized effort to achieve some goal by a group of individuals. **3.** A series of events that collectively precipitate a new law or policy.

MSCI EAFE INDEX. *See* **MORGAN STANLEY CAPITAL INTERNATIONAL EUROPE AUSTRALIA FAR EAST INDEX**

MULTICURRENCY CLAUSE A clause in a bond or loan agreement that the debt may be repaid in several different currencies. The proceeds of the debt may be issued in more than one currency as well. *See also* **MULTICURRENCY LOAN.**

MULTICURRENCY LOAN A bond or loan in which the debtor is permitted to make payments in one or more different currencies. *See also* **MULTICURRENCY CLAUSE.**

MULTILATERAL AGREEMENT An accord reached by more than two nations in which all agree to abide by the provisions of the pact.

MULTILATERAL NETTING The strategy used by some **MULTINATIONAL CORPORATIONS (MNCs)** to reduce the number of transactions between subsidiaries of the firm, thereby reducing the total transaction costs arising from foreign exchange dealings with transfer fees. It attempts to maintain balance between receivables and payables denominated in a foreign currency. MNCs typically set up "multilateral netting centers" as a special department to settle the outstanding balances of affiliates of a multinational company with each other on a net basis. It is the development of a "clearing house" for payments by the firm's affiliates. If there are amounts due among affiliates they are offset insofar as possible. The net amount would be paid in the currency of the transaction. The total amounts owed need not be paid in the currency of the transaction; thus, a much lower quantity of the currency must be acquired. Note that the major advantage of the system is a reduction of the costs associated with a large number of separate foreign exchange transactions.

MULTILATERAL TRADE Trade transactions occurring among more than two nations (three or more).

MULTINATIONAL CORPORATIONS (MNCs) A company operating in two or more countries. Its ownership is in only one country. Special features of an MNC are as follows: (1) Multiple-currency problem. Sales revenues may be collected in one currency, assets denominated in another, and profits measured in a third. (2) Various legal, institutional, and economic constraints. There are variations in such things as tax laws, labor practices, **BALANCE OF PAYMENTS** policies, and government controls with respect to the types and sizes of investments, types and amount of capital raised, and repatriation of profits. (3) Internal control problem. When the parent office of a multinational company and its affiliates are widely located, internal organizational difficulties arise.

MULTINATIONAL MARKETING Also called **GLOBAL MARKETING,** selling the product in several different foreign markets.

MULTINATIONAL SOURCING A capability enjoyed by some **MULTINATION-AL CORPORATIONS** to find or establish manufacturing sources in more than one country, thus enabling them to lower their costs relative to companies that make or outsource in only one nation.

MULTINATIONAL TRANSFER PRICE. *See* **INTERNATIONAL TRANSFER PRICE.**

MULTINATIONALITY The whole point of the multinational company. By operating simultaneously in several nations, the multinational company can transfer information about prices and demand conditions, move funds and products to preferred locations, and generally free the restrictions imposed by the environment in a single country. *See also* **MULTINATIONAL CORPORATIONS.**

MULTIPLE EXCHANGE RATE The use of different exchange rates for different types of transactions. For example, a country's central bank may grant a more generous exchange rate for foreign investment transactions within its borders than allowed for certain import transactions which it would like to discourage.

MULTIPLE MANAGEMENT PLAN A management training strategy where middle and lower management work with upper management in planning and establishing the future goals, objectives, and administration of a corporate entity. The multiple management plan allows upper management to work alongside and interact with the up and coming managers of the company and provides them with a means of assessing which individuals should be groomed for future leadership positions.

N

NAFTA. *See* **NORTH AMERICAN FREE TRADE AGREEMENT.**

NATIONAL FOCUS The competitive strategy used by some **MULTINATIONAL CORPORATIONS** that hints tailoring of products to each country market in which they are based and operate.

NATIONALIZATION **1.** Public takeover of private property. **2.** The forced takeover of a multinational company's assets by the host government with remuneration. Often this is accomplished by forcing sale of controlling ownership to local investors. The multinational company may end up with some partial ownership.

NATIONALIZED EXPORTS Flow through merchandise that is imported by a nation and subsequently exported without any substantive changes being made to the product.

NATURAL ADVANTAGE The advantage that a nation has in the production of a given good as a result of its location, natural resources and accessibility, climate, etc. *See also* **COMPARATIVE ADVANTAGE; ABSOLUTE ADVANTAGE.**

NAV. *See* **NET ASSET VALUE.**

NEAR MONEY Liquid assets readily convertible into money as needed such as marketable securities, money market funds, and time deposits.

NEGATIVE DIFFERENTIAL Computational cost associated with an alternative that indicates that a given option is more economical than comparative alternatives. For example, in analyzing the viability of international locations where a given product could be manufactured compared to the United States, it may be determined that there is a negative cost differential in manufacturing the product in country A. That is, it is less expensive to have the product manufactured in country A than in America.

NEGATIVE PLEDGE CLAUSE A clause in a bond agreement saying that a corporation does not have to pledge assets to newly issued debt unless previously issued debt under the agreement is equally secured.

NEGOTIABLE INSTRUMENT Any instrument that can readily be converted into cash. It is a written **DRAFT** or **PROMISSORY NOTE,** signed by the maker or drawer, have an unconditional promise, and be an order to make payment of a certain sum of money on demand by the bearer or to the order of a named party at a determinable future date. A **HOLDER IN DUE COURSE** of a negotiable instrument is entitled to payment despite any personal disagreements between drawee and drawer.

NEGOTIABLE LETTER OF CREDIT A **LETTER OF CREDIT** issued in such form that it allows any bank to negotiate the documents. Negotiable credits incorporate the opening bank's engagement, stating that the **DRAFT** will be duly honored on presentation, provided they comply with all terms of the credit.

NEGOTIATED TRADE Trade orchestrated by government agreement rather than by the **FREE MARKET.**

NEGOTIATION **1.** To confer, arrange, or settle by discussion and consensus. **2.** The bargaining that occurs among parties in pursuance of reaching an agreement or contract e.g., management of a company and representatives of the workers union generally have protracted negotiations in attempting to hammer out an agreement that meets the needs of both sides in a contract.

NET **1.** To subtract one or more numbers from another. For example, net sales is computed by subtracting sales discounts, sales returns, and sales allowances from gross sales. **2.** The residual that remains after all pertinent expenses have been subtracted. For example, net income is the residual that remains after all expenses have been deducted from revenues earned. **3.** A short version for the **INTERNET.** For example, you might be asked if you surfed the net recently.

NET ASSET VALUE (NAV) It is a measure of the value of a mutual fund share, which shows what each share of the mutual fund is worth. NAV equals:

$$\frac{\text{Fund's total assets - liabilities}}{\text{Number of shares outstanding in the fund}}$$

EXAMPLE:
Assume that a fund owns 100 shares each of General Motors (GM), Xerox, and International Business Machines (IBM). Assume also that on a particular day, the market values below existed. Then NAV of the fund is calculated as follows (assume the fund has no liabilities):

(a) GM-$90 per share x 100 shares	= $9,000
(b) Xerox-$100 per share x 100 shares	= 10,000
(c) IBM-$160 per share x 100 shares	= 16,000
(d) Value of the fund's portfolio	$35,000
(e) Number of shares outstanding in the fund	1,000
(f) Net asset value (NAV) per share =(d)/(e)	$35

If an investor owns 5 percent of the fund's outstanding shares, or 50 shares (5 percent x 1,000 shares), then the value of the investment is $1,750 ($35 x 50). NAV represents one component of the return on mutual fund investments. An investor also receives capital gains and dividends. Therefore, the performance of a mutual fund must be judged on the basis of these three returns.

NET PRESENT VALUE (NPV) The difference between the present value (PV) of cash inflows generated by the project and the amount of the initial investment (I). The present value of future cash flows is computed using the **COST OF CAPITAL** (minimum desired rate of return, or hurdle rate) as the discount rate.

NETTING A process of efficient cash transference between foreign subsidiaries of **MULTINATIONAL CORPORATIONS** for the purpose of generating savings on commissions, transfer costs, and conversion fees of foreign currency. In addition, it enables the subsidiaries to have quick and easy access to needed funds. The netting process consists of having foreign subsidiaries that are in a net payable position forward funds to the clearing manager of the company who in turn forwards them to subsidiaries having a net receivable position.

NETWORK 1. A system of interconnection between computers at different locations that provide for the sharing of information, hardware (e.g., printers, scanners, etc.), e-mail communications, etc. A **LOCAL AREA NETWORK** refers to the linkage of computers in close proximity i.e., the same or adjacent buildings. A **WIDE AREA NETWORK** refers to the hookup of computers over a wide, diverse area such as an international connection. Network security such as access controls is very important. 2. The business contacts that a person has to accomplish his or her goals.

NEW INTERNATIONAL ECONOMIC ORDER A concept established in the United Nations in the early 1970s whose idea is to develop mechanisms for redistribution of income between rich and poor nations. The attempt was basically abandoned after the oil crisis of 1973-74.

NEW ISSUE A new issue of stock or bonds offered to the public for sale. The issue may be sold by the existing entity or it may be an initial public offering by a previously private company. An investment banker may act as the selling agent. In this situation, it may be purchased outright by an investment broker or the broker may choose to sell the new issue for a commission to be deducted from the proceeds of the sale (best efforts underwriting). In the former situation, the investment broker underwrites (purchases) the entire issue outright by guaranteeing the issuer a certain sum and then attempts to resell the securities at the highest possible price. The issuer of the securities may also decide to sell the new issue to a large private financial institution or group of individuals without the help of an underwriter (private placement). Under most circumstances, the issuer is required to register the new issue with the **SECURITIES AND EXCHANGE COMMISSION.**

NEW MONEY 1. Additional amount of money currently being financed by an entity (e.g. corporation, government, governmental agency, etc.) in excess of the amount that is maturing or being redeemed. 2. Incremental funds privately raised by an importer or exporter for a business endeavor.

NEW PRODUCT **1.** A product that has just been released by a manufacturer that either has no marketing track record or a very limited one. New products are usually test marketed in various parts of the country before they are distributed nationally and internationally. **2.** A new financial product sold by a **BROKER,** bank, **INVESTMENT BANKERS,** etc. designed to meet the specific needs of certain investors. For example, derivative financial products such as **INTEREST RATE SWAPS** are relatively new financial products issued by companies.

NEW YORK STOCK EXCHANGE (NYSE) The NYSE , or "Big Board" as it is sometimes called, is the largest and undoubtedly most well-known stock exchange in the United States. Located in the heart of Wall Street, it is essentially an auction market where stockbrokers execute buy and sell orders of stock and other securities on behalf of their clients. In order for a company's stock to be traded on the NYSE, the company must meet very stringent listing requirements. Among the financial instruments traded on the NYSE are: common stock; preferred stock, bonds, notes; warrants; options; rights; etc.

NEWLY INDUSTRIALIZING COUNTRY (NIC) Among the **LESS DEVELOPED COUNTRIES,** a group of developing countries which have reached a relatively advanced stage of economic growth and have experienced high growth rates in recent years. Some of the NICs are Brazil, Hong Kong, Korea, Mexico, Singapore, and Taiwan. Occasionally its use encompasses other countries as well, such as Indonesia and Thailand.

NEXT BEST ALTERNATIVE The investment project that would be undertaken using the available resources if the one under evaluation were rejected. The cost of forsaking this alternative is the **OPPORTUNITY COST** of the project.

NIC. *See* **NEWLY INDUSTRIALIZING COUNTRY.**

NICHE **1.** That particular area in which a company specializes and is successful. An example is a specialty food store catering to wealthy customers. **2.** Company policy concentrating efforts in a specific new or established market segment. Competitive factors may be a consideration. **3.** A suitable position or place.

NIF. *See* **NOTE ISSUANCE FACILITY.**

NIGERIAN TRUST FUND (NTF) A fund provided by the **AFRICAN DEVELOP-MENT BANK** for lending for approved programs and projects in Nigeria to promote that country's economic or social condition. The loans are made on attractive terms including lower interest rates and extended time periods.

NOMINAL **1.** The rate of interest shown on the face of a financial instrument such a bond or note without considering the effects of compounding, e.g., the stated rate. The nominal rate of interest of a bond adjusted for the effects of compounding is its effective rate. The nominal yield of a bond adjusted for the effects of compounding is its effective yield. **2.** In accounting, the nominal accounts refer to the revenue, expenses, and dividend (drawing in a sole proprietorship or **PARTNERSHIP**) accounts of an entity which are closed out to retained earnings (or capital) at the end for the period. **3.** Insignificant amounts of money. **4.** The amount of earned wages without considering the effects of **INFLATION,** i.e., their purchasing power.

NOMINAL EXCHANGE RATE Actual **SPOT RATE** of foreign exchange, in contrast to **REAL EXCHANGE RATE,** which is adjusted for changes in inflation.

NOMINAL RATE OF PROTECTION The assessment of tariff duties on low priced foreign goods for the purpose of enabling domestic producers to successfully compete with foreign manufacturers who export cheaply made goods. *See also* **EFFECTIVE RATE OF PROTECTION.**

NONCONTESTABILITY CLAUSE Standard clause on an insurance policy that prevents an insurer from contesting the validity of a policy ostensibly on the basis of fraud, mistake, etc., after the policy has been in force for some minimum period (one or two years in most states). For example, if an insured dies within the noncontestability period of a life insurance policy and the insurer determines that the cause of death was a predetermined condition that was not indicated on the insurance application, it can refuse payment on the basis of nondisclosure (fraud).

NONCURRENT METHOD. *See* **CURRENT/NONCURRENT METHOD.**

NONDIVERSIFIABLE RISK That part of a security's risk that cannot be eliminated by diversification. It covers **MARKET RISK** that comes from factors systematically affecting most firms (such as war, **INFLATION,** recessions, and high interest rates).

NONDOCUMENTARY LETTER OF CREDIT Also called a **CLEAN LETTER OF CREDIT,** a letter of credit for which no documents need to be attached to the draft. Most L/Cs issued in connection with commercial transactions are documentary. *See also* **DOCUMENTARY LETTER OF CREDIT.**

NONDUMPING CERTIFICATE A certificate provided by an exporter indicating that price of the goods being sold are equal to what would have been charged had the goods been sold in the country in which they were manufactured. This certificate is provided to prevent the depression of domestic market prices of a **COMMODITY** due to dumping of underpriced foreign made goods.

NONDURABLE GOODS Products having a shorter life because of faster use or replacement. An example is poultry and meats.

NONFEASANCE The failure to perform a legally contractual obligation without reasonable excuse such as an agent not conducting for the principal a specific duty.

NONTARIFF BARRIERS (NTBs) Less visible restraints on trade than **TARIFFS.** NTBs are divided into five categories: (1) Government intervention in trade.

Discrimination in government procurement, state trading, subsidies, counter-vailing duties, etc. (2) **CUSTOMS** and entry procedures. Regulations covering valuation methods, classification, documentation, health, and safety. (3) **STANDARDS.** Standards for products, packaging, labeling, marking, etc. (4) Specific limitations. **QUOTAS,** import restraints, licensing, foreign exchange controls. etc. (5) Import charges. Prior **IMPORT DEPOSITS,** credit restrictions for imports, special duties, variable levies, etc.

NORM 1. Conforming to a standard or level that is considered typical. 2. A model or standard for comparison. 3. The average (mean, mode, etc.).

NORMAL GOOD OR SERVICE A product which has greater demand as the income of consumers increase.

NORMAL PRICE 1. Price that is expected to exist in a market over a relevant time period. 2. Price at which the production rate equals the consumption rate in the long haul. 3. Assessment basis for an imported product subject to a duty.

NORTH AMERICAN FREE TRADE AGREEMENT (NAFTA) The agreement among the United States, Canada, and Mexico, approved in 1993. It eliminates all trade restrictions over 10 years. A goal is for the three countries to improve employment from increased trade. Provisions of the NAFTA agreement are to progressively eliminate tariffs, eliminate other trade barriers (e.g., import licensing mandates, customs user fees), treat NAFTA-origin products similarly to domestic products, and provide equal access (e.g., investment, sale of products and services). In the **FREE TRADE ZONE** there should be equal treatment, free transfer of funds, arbitration of disputes, and following international law.

NOT SUFFICIENT FUNDS (NSF) A term used by a bank when a check is drawn on an account not having sufficient fund balance.

NOTE A negotiable financial instrument such as a **PROMISSORY NOTE** that provides evidence of indebtedness. A note signed by a borrower is a formal written promise to pay a certain sum in a specific period of time at a given rate of interest. It is viewed as a note payable to the debtor and a note receivable to the lender.

NOTE ISSUANCE FACILITY (NIF) A facility provided by a syndicate of banks that allows borrowers to issue short-term notes, which are then placed by the syndicate in the **EUROCURRENCY MARKETS.** This syndicate of underwriting banks guarantees the availability of funds to the borrower by purchasing any unsold notes or by providing standby credit. The discount rate is often tied to the **LONDON INTERBANK OFFERED RATE.**

NOTICE OF CANCELLATION CLAUSE A contractual clause requiring that a party to a contract be formally notified in writing of the intent of another party to cancel an agreement. Cancellation is not deemed to have legally occurred under this circumstance until due notice has been received.

NOTICE OF DEFAULT Written notice sent to a debtor indicating that default of a loan has occurred. Many states require that a lender must formally notify a debtor of his default before any action can be taken to satisfy the obligation. That is, a lender may not liquidate **COLLATERAL** that is being held without first giving the debtor a chance to make payments.

NOVATION An original party to a contract substitutes another with the permission of the other original party. This approved substitution ends the original contract and generates a new one. An example is when a creditor agrees to allow an original debtor to substitute another financially sound party to payoff the debt. Another example is where an individual contracts to build a house with certain material, and then because of the scarcity of the material, has the old contract cancelled and a new one substituted which calls for construction of a different type of house using different material.

NPV. *See* **NET PRESENT VALUE.**

NSF. *See* **NOT SUFFICIENT FUNDS.**

NTBs. *See* **NONTARIFF BARRIERS.**

NTF. *See* **NIGERIAN TRUST FUND.**

NYSE. *See* **NEW YORK STOCK EXCHANGE.**

OBSOLESCING BARGAIN The bargaining power diminished as a result of the commitment by a multinational company of its capital and human resources to an investment project in a host country. The company's bargaining position relative to the host government obsolesces, because it has critical resources at risk in the host country. Over the long haul, the host government tends to increase even greater ability to compel the company to adopt its intended goals as the company becomes more integrated into the local economy.

OCCUPANCY LEVEL A measure of the extent of apartments in a building, commercial office property, etc., that is currently being rented or leased. Occupancy levels have been calculated for these properties for the purpose of ascertaining break-even levels. For example, office buildings and shopping centers have break-even occupancy levels of around 80 percent to 85 percent.

OCCUPATIONAL HAZARD The characteristics of the work environment of a given occupation which causes individuals who work in it to have an increased probability of sickness, disease, or even death. Occupational hazard classifications are given different job classifications for purposes of assessing a **PREMIUM** or premiums for life, health, and workman's compensation insurance as well as other underwriting considerations.

ODD-NUMBER PRICING A pricing practice, noticeable in retailing, that sets prices in such a way that they end in an odd number. The assumption is made that it is possible to sell a great number of items priced at 31 cents rather than 30 cents, or at 99 cents rather than $1.00. The idea applies to higher-priced merchandise as well.

OECD. *See* **ORGANIZATION FOR ECONOMIC COOPERATION AND DEVELOPMENT.**

OFF PRICE Retail price of an item that is being offered for substantially less than that offered by other retail establishments. Off price stores, for example, offer a whole contingent of items at price levels substantially lower than elsewhere. The lower prices are possible because the off price stores purchase their inventory at **LIQUIDATION** sales, bankruptcies, partially damaged goods, etc.

OFFER LIST A list of items that a country in the process of negotiating a **MULTILATERAL TRADE** agreement is willing to offer in working towards an agreement.

OFFER PRICE **1.** Also called the **ASK PRICE.** The price at which a trader is willing to sell foreign exchange or other securities. **2.** The price per share that a new or existing security is offered for sale to investors. An example is an initial public offering for XYZ Company (a fictitious new company) stock being priced offered to the public at $10 per share. **3.** The price at which an owner of a stock or bond offers to sell it to another.

OFFICIAL EXCHANGE RATE The monetary exchange rate that is used in exchanging one nation's currency for another.

OFFICIAL RESERVES The total reserves that a nation has in the form of gold, international convertible currencies, and reserves on deposit in the **INTERNATIONAL MONETARY FUND** called **SPECIAL DRAWING RIGHTS (SDRs).** SDRs are used to settle debts with other nations or with the International Monetary Fund.

OFFICIAL SETTLEMENTS BALANCE The bottom line **BALANCE OF PAYMENTS** when all private sector transactions have been accounted for and all that remain are official exchanges between central banks and the **INTERNATIONAL MONETARY FUND (IMF).** This balance measures the country's net inflows of official holdings of **FOREIGN EXCHANGE, SPECIAL DRAWING RIGHTS,** gold, and the country's borrowing position at the IMF.

OFFICIAL VALUE The value assigned to specific imported goods. In assessing duties on imports of foreign goods, the official value of the good (assigned by a nation) is determined by comparing it to the invoice price of the commodity. The higher of the two amounts is used in assessing **IMPORT DUTIES.**

OFFSET **1.** The purchase or sale of a security or option having the same features as one currently held. An example is buying a put option on a stock owned to protect a capital gain. *See also* **PUT. 2.** A short sale (selling a stock you do not own by borrowing it) to protect a capital gain on the stock you do own. **3.** A bank's right to seize deposit funds to cover the default on a loan. **4.** An account that reduces the gross amount of another account to derive a net balance. For example, accumulated depreciation is a contra-account to fixed assets to obtain book value. **5.** An entity or person balances or compensates for something. For example, a company that is owed a specified sum of money may agree to forgive the debt for services rendered.

OFFSET DEALS Compensatory arrangements between importers and exporters established as a precondition of trade transactions in international industrial and commercial sales among domestic companies, multinational companies and governments. Offset deals may be indirect or direct. For example, in a direct offset deal, the nation of the company making a large defense equipment sale may agree to incorporate into the final manufactured products certain parts produced by the importing country. In an indirect sale, the exporter may agree to purchase other unrelated products from the importing nation as a precondition for the sale. A large industrial exporter nation (like the United States, England or France) may either have to agree to an offset deal or risk jeopardizing the deal. An importer nation, on the other hand, may require such an arrangement in order to reduce its overall net cost, increase its domestic employment, or promote technological growth at home.

OFFSHORE ASSEMBLY The overseas production of goods whose inputs are constructed or processed in one country and then the final products are shipped to the target market for sale.

OFFSHORE FINANCE SUBSIDIARY A subsidiary of a company located outside the United States established for the purpose of performing banking, financing, or some other financial related activity. The subsidiary may have been established offshore rather than in the United States because the activities it is associated with are either heavily regulated, taxed, or illegal under American law.

OFFSHORE PRODUCTION Either offshore sourcing or **OFFSHORE ASSEMBLY.**

OLI. *See* **ECLECTIC VIEW.**

OLIGOPOLY A few sellers control the market for a product and service. Therefore, they are able to substantially impact price and quantity. A member of the selling group may act by itself or in cooperation with others. An example is steel manufacturers who dominate the market. Although in an oligopoly there is less competition among companies, it is not as in control of the market as a monopoly.

OMA. *See* **ORDERLY MARKETING AGREEMENT.**

ON-LINE DATABASE A collection of information transmitted via telephone wire and accessed with a modem generally on a computer for display on a monitor or for printing. Privately owned on-line databases generally contain a wealth of information on a myriad of topics and are available for a fee to computer users.

ONSPECULATION Work performed for a client by a firm for which they will be compensated only if the work is used. That is, the entity and firm have no contract and preagree that there will be no compensation without acceptance. For example, a team of independent freelance writers produce a television script. for a nationally syndicated weekly situation comedy series. They send the script to the television producer and realize that the only way that they will be compensated is if the producer likes the script and agree to utilize it on the television series.

OPEC. *See* **ORGANIZATION OF PETROLEUM EXPORTING COUNTRIES.**

OPEN 1. BROKER and **DEALER** terminology for an unexecuted order to buy or sell securities. **2.** Reference to opening an account in a bank or a **LETTER OF CREDIT. 3.** In **INTERNATIONAL TRADE,** an agreement between an exporter and importer in which the exporter agrees to send goods to an importer without any written promise of payment. *See also* **OPEN ACCOUNT. 4.** Any unpaid balance.

OPEN ACCOUNT 1. In **INTERNATIONAL TRADE,** an agreement between an exporter and importer in which the exporter agrees to send goods to the importer without any assurance or guarantee of payment. Because of the obvious risk on the part of the exporter, it is imperative that this relationship be undertaken only with importers that the exporter knows will pay for the goods. **2.** Credit agreement between a buyer and seller. **3.** Unpaid credit balance.

OPEN DISTRIBUTION Unrestricted distribution of a product in a given area of a sales sector by an unlimited number of dealers. In open distribution, no one distributor gets the exclusive right to sell a given product. In addition, there are no restrictions regarding the number of products that the dealer may sell.

OPEN ECONOMY The economy in which an **INTERNATIONAL TRADE** in the form of imports and exports occupies a substantial portion of the national income.

OPEN INSURANCE POLICY 1. An insurance policy option allowing automatic open-ended coverage to all freight that an insured may desire to be protected in the course of doing business. **2.** A type of policy that covers all of an exporter's shipments during a specific time frame rather than just one specific shipment.

OPEN MARKET OPERATIONS The activity of the Federal Reserve Bank in buying and selling of government securities so as to influence bank reserves, the interest rates, the volume of credit, and the money supply. It is an instrument of monetary policy. If securities are bought, the money paid out by the Fed increases commercial bank reserves and the money supply increases. If securities are sold, the money supply contracts. The following diagram summarizes the impact of open market operations on the money supply, level of interest rates, and loan demand.

Fed buys (sells) securities —> Bank reserve up (down) —> Bank lending up (down) —> Money supply up (down) —> Interest rates down (up) —> Loan demand up (down)

OPEN POSITION A state in which an entity has an open foreign currency position (a net asset or net liability position) which has not yet been settled. As a result, the entity is open to risk of loss due to fluctuations in the exchange rate until settlement occurs.

OPEN SHOP A company having both union and non-union employees.

OPEN STOCK Stock that can be purchased from a retailer unrestrictedly. As long as demand for a given product continues, a retailer will continue to replenish it from its supplier/manufacturer until it is no longer available.

OPEN-DOOR POLICY 1. A policy of treating the citizens and products manufactured in foreign countries no different than a nation treats its own citizens and domestically produced goods. **2.** A willingness on the part of an employer to allow his or her subordinates to speak their mind about any job related issue without fear of repercussions and punitive actions.

OPEN-TO-BUY The amount of money that is available to a retail buyer to make new purchases in the current period. The open-to-buy amount fluctuates during the year as demand changes and markdowns and markups affect inventory sales. A buyer must monitor his or her open-to-buy available before he can commit his purchase dollars for inventory acquisition.

OPERATING EXPOSURE Also called **ECONOMIC EXPOSURE,** the possibility that an unexpected change in exchange rates will cause a change in the future cash flows of a firm and its market value. It differs from translation and transaction exposures in that it is subjective and thus not easily quantified. The best strategy to control operation exposure is to diversify operations and financing internationally.

OPERATING PLAN A explicit plan on how the subunits of the multinational company will function together in accomplishing strategic goals and objectives.

OPERATING STRATEGY The day-to-day procedure of conducting business that a multinational company must adapt to business situations and conditions in each host country. Operating strategy hinges to a great extent on the environments in which the firm is operating, such as government regulation, competitive conditions, and other factors.

OPERATIONAL AUDIT An appraisal of actual operating activities and functions to determine if they conform to corporate objectives and policies. A determination is made of the adequacy of controls and procedures. Is a responsibility unit or center effective and efficient? Are goals being met? When warranted, corrective action is implemented. A written report with conclusions and recommendations is prepared.

OPM. *See* **BLACK-SCHOLES OPTION PRICING MODEL.**

OPERATIONAL CONTROL The control over the operating activities of a business. In a large business entity, control over activities is vested in the chief operating officer, usually the president of the organization. In a small business, operational control is usually vested in the owner/manager.

OPPORTUNITY COST The income foregone by refusing an alternative option. For example, if credit is extended to more risky customers the opportunity cost is the return foregone on the incremental investment tied up in the accounts receivable for a longer time period. Assuming the money tied up in the receivables is $600,000 for an extra 4 months and the annual return rate is 8 percent the opportunity cost is $16,000 ($600,000 x 8% x 4/12).

OPTIMAL CAPACITY The maximizing output level for a business to produce, which corresponds to the minimum point of the average total cost schedule.

OPTIMUM CURRENCY AREA An area where the currency exchange rate of two or more nations remains fixed as well as variable. For example, the exchange rate of Canada and the United States has over the years been somewhat fixed due to their close proximity to each other. Yet both currencies are allowed to fluctuate on world markets on a daily basis. The same is true of other areas and nations of the world as well such as the European Community (with certain exceptions).

OPTION **1.** The ability or right to choose a certain alternative. **2.** The right to buy or sell something (e.g., securities, property, foreign exchange) at a specified price within a specified period of time. If the right is not exercised after a specified time, the option expires. **3. PUT** or **CALL** options on a security (such as stock, **COMMODITY,** or stock index). A put is an option to sell 100 shares of the underlying security at a specified price for a given period of time for which the option buyer pays the seller (writer) a price, termed a **PREMIUM.** A call is the opposite of a put and allows the owner the right to buy 100 shares of the underlying security from the option writer. **4.** An employee stock option. It is the option granted to key employees of buying company stock at a below-market price.

ORANGE GOODS Lower-priced consumer products that will be replaced after a while due to use, style or taste changes, or weather changes. Examples are shirts, blouses, pants, and coats.

ORDER BILL OF LADING A **BILL OF LADING** certifying that the cargo has been placed aboard the named vessel and is signed by the master of the vessel or his representative. With this shipping document, possession and title to the shipment reside with the owner of the order bill of lading.

ORDERLY MARKETING AGREEMENT (OMA) Sometimes called **VOLUNTARY EXPORT AGREEMENTS,** bilateral agreements restricting imports from one nation to another. OMAs are often engaged in to avoid unilateral import constraints. Contracts negotiated between two or more governments, in which the exporter wants to be assured that international trade in certain "key" products will not inhibit or hurt the importing country's industries or employees.

ORDINARY ANNUITY A series of equal periodic payments or receipts due or receivable at the end of a period (e.g., year-end). for example, a multinational company is to receive $1,000,000 per year (at the end) for each of 10 years. Although the total to be received is $10,000, 000, the present (discounted) value of those cash receipts are less taking into account the time value of the money. Assuming an interest rate of 10 percent, the present value factor obtained from a present value of an ordinary annuity table for 10 years at 10 percent is 6.145. Therefore, the present value of the future receipts is $6,145,000 ($1,000,000 x 6.145). In other words, the stream of cash inflows is worth today (in today's dollars) $6,145,000. *See also* **ANNUITY.**

ORDINARY COURSE OF TRADE Following the normal course of business. Performing those activities and transactions that are considered reasonable and necessary in ordinary commercial practice.

ORGANIZATION BEHAVIOR The academic study and professional practice concerned with the interaction of people in business organizations. The study of organizational behavior encompasses such areas as conflict resolution, motivation, leadership, achieving goal congruency, participative decision making, organizational building, etc.

ORGANIZATION FOR ECONOMIC COOPERATION AND DEVELOPMENT (OECD) Countries including the United States, England, France, Germany, Canada, Japan, Greece, and Australia. Economic issues of mutual concern are addressed with a view of expanding foreign trade, economic growth, and employment. Financial aid is provided to poorer nations so as to improve living standards. Research is undertaken to alleviate economic problems. Statistical information is issued to members.

ORGANIZATION FOR EUROPEAN COOPERATION An international group started in the late 1940s to provide assistance to 18 West European countries. The program arose in conformity with the Marshall Plan. It fostered greater trade among countries. *See also* **ORGANIZATION FOR ECONOMIC COOPERATION AND DEVELOPMENT.**

ORGANIZATION OF PETROLEUM EXPORTING COUNTRIES (OPEC) 1. A producer's cartel formed in 1960 by 13 oil producing countries in order to control the quantity and price at which crude oil is sold to foreign countries. However, fighting between members has restricted its influence in world oil markets. An example was in November 1993 when the price of oil took a sharp decline to about $15 a barrel. Further, there are now cheaper oil substitutes and demand for oil has declined world-wide. OPEC at times over the years has restricted supply of oil to drive up oil prices. Production quotas were agreed to by the members. In 1973, for example, the cartel's power was used to stop selling oil to some countries and quadruple prices to others. This created a world recession. Some members of OPEC include Saudi Arabia, Kuwait, and Iran. **2.** The group of countries in the world that are the major producers and suppliers of oil. The association sets policies regarding the availability, terms, and price of petroleum. For example, an oil embargo can drastically result in higher oil prices. Some of the members of this organization are Saudi Arabia, Venezuela, Kuwait, Iran, United Arab Emirates, and Ecuador. The organization is based in Austria.

ORGANIZATIONAL CHART A chart that enumerates the way that authority, responsibilities, and accountability is set up in an organization. An important objective of an organizational chart is to specify areas of control for upper, middle, and lower management. An important objective of the organizational chart is to provide in clear, written, succinct terms managerial personnel's interrelationship with each other within the organization. This minimizes any conflict and confusion that may result when transactions and events overlap areas of jurisdiction.

ORGANIZATIONAL STRUCTURE The different ways that authority and personnel accountability are allocated in an organization. For example, several different types of organizational structures are utilized in business today. These are structured so that they can specialize task performance (creating an appropriate division of labor) and coordinate different jobs into a unified workable group. Structural designs include the functional organization (standard pyramid) in which senior management is at the top, middle and lower management below, and workers at the bottom differentiated by task-specialized departments. In the product organization, activities are based on the differentiation of goods and services according to similarities in their manufacture or end use. For example, General Motors allocates its product grouping into Cadillac, Buick, Oldsmobile, Pontiac and Chevrolet divisions. In a matrix organization, managers can make lateral or vertical moves to establish the necessary relationships so that adaptable and flexible systems of procedures and resources can be achieved in satisfying the entity's project objectives.

ORIGINATION FEE A charge by a bank or other lender to a borrower for the cost of establishing and executing a loan, especially a mortgage. It generally covers administrative costs, and sales commission. Some lending institutions may include the appraisal cost and credit check in the origination fee charged to the borrower.

OTC. *See* **OVER-THE COUNTER MARKET.**

OUTCRY MARKET A market in which the prices for the purchase and sale of the product is determined by constant and continuous verbal negotiations between buyers and sellers. The most common and well known outcry market is the commodities exchange.

OUTLET STORE A retail store owned and operated by a manufacturer for its irregular products (e.g., slightly damaged, out-of-season, older). The goods are offered at discounted prices.

OUTRIGHT QUOTATION The full price, in one currency, per unit of another currency.

OUTRIGHT RATE Actual forward rate expressed in dollars per unit of a currency, or vice versa.

OUTSOURCING Contracting with another firm to manufacture, service, or supply part of the business so as to result in cost savings and operating efficiencies. In some cases, entire functions and departments might be subcontracted out.

OVER KILL 1. Over excessiveness in an endeavor. 2. An attempt to convince that is excessive to the extent of causing negative adverse reactions rather than positive ones.

OVERAGE The determination that an amount is greater than it should be. For example, an importer upon receiving his goods ordered from a foreign exporter may discover upon counting them that there is an overage relative to the amount indicated on the **BILL OF LADING.** That is, more goods were received than indicated. In another situation, a clerk may find that he or she has an overage of stock upon counting the inventory as part of the annual physical inventory count.

OVERBASE SALARY Salary level that is over the starting or minimum level established for a particular job function. If an individual joins an entity with special talents, experience, or reputation desired by an employer, he may command an overbase salary.

OVERBOOKED A practice adopted by airlines, cruise lines, hotels, and others in which reservations are accepted for more seats, rooms, etc. than are physically available. The rationale for this practice is that since it is expected that many individuals who made reservations will not show up, overbookings are needed to fill up those units that have not been filled. On occasion, most everyone who has booked a reservation shows up. This causes a deficiency of inventory resulting in passengers being left without seats or rooms. In this situation, the airline or hotel will often give the customer a free airline ticket or room at a later time to compensate them for their inconvenience. This goodwill gesture usually appeases the customer and allows for the perpetuation of the overbooking practice.

OVERBOUGHT The result of excessive buying of a product or security causing downward market pressure on its price due to the resulting deficiency of remaining buyers. As a result, the price of the item becomes unstable and susceptible to a price decrease. Because of the tremendous growth of the stock market in past years, financial analysts believe that it is overbought and therefore highly sensitive to a crash comparable to the ones that occurred in 1929 and 1987.

OVERCHARGE Charging an individual more than the actual price of an item either intentionally or as the result of an error. For example, a common carrier might overcharge a seller for transporting his goods overseas. Customers may be willing to accept such a practice (assuming they realize what happened) once or twice but undoubtedly would change carriers, vendors or retailers, etc., if it persisted beyond that.

OVERHANG The existence of an unusually large amount of inventory of an item in the hands of a potential seller such as currency, stock, bonds, commodities, real estate, etc., that has the ability to significantly reduce the price of such item if it were sold on the open market.

OVERHEATING A economy in which demand has outpaced supply causing upward pressure on prices and inflation.

OVERPRODUCTION The condition of producing more than can be sold. The effect of overproduction is a downward pressure on the price of the good. In the past, oil and gas inventories in the United States were plentiful and prices were very low due to overproduction of crude oil by the oil producing states of the Middle East.

OVERRIDE **1.** To ignore the constraints or limits of an agreement or contract in a given situation. **2.** An attempt on the part of Congress to reverse a veto cast by the President. **3.** A sales commission collected by an executive in addition to that received by a sales subordinate. **4.** A procedure used to automatically supersede an automatic default control.

OVERRUN Production beyond maximum capacity. Overruns occur, for example, because of errors in orders (i.e., accepting an order in excess of production capacity) or attempting to take advantage of excess materials.

OVERSHOOTING The failure of a currency exchange rate to adjust to its true level reaching instead a level beyond it as a result of temporary external pressures. The outcome of overshooting is eradicated when its effect becomes known and appropriate adjustments are made.

OVER-THE-COUNTER **1.** Securities market that is conducted through a computer and telephone network rather than being traded on the floor of an organized stock exchange like the **NEW YORK STOCK EXCHANGE.** Price quotations for securities that are traded over-the counter are commonly provided by the National Association of Securities Dealers Automated Quotations (NASDAQ). **2.** Non-prescription medicine that is sold in a drug store.

OVERTRADING **1.** Abusive, excessive trading on the part of a broker for a client's discretionary fund. **2.** The inability of a firm to pay for many of its positions at settlement due to a liquidity deficiency as a result of overextended trading.

OWNERSHIP LOCATIONAL INTERNALIZATION. *See* **ECLECTIC VIEW.**

P

PACKAGE **1.** A group of items sold as a single unit. The sum of the items sold separately frequently exceeds the cost of the total package. That is, the seller gives the buyer a discount because an entire package of items was purchased. **2.** An offer composed of several items each of which must be accepted before the contract is binding. **3.** A boxed object into which items are placed.

PACKAGE DESIGN The blueprint of the plan and structure of the packaging of a product. In developing a package design, variables such as the following should be considered: appearance, size, shape, color, weight, costs, protection of the product, convenience in opening and closing, labeling, effect of package discardment on the environment, i.e, recyclable, etc.

PACKAGED GOODS Consumer merchandise packaged by the producers and sold in retail outlets. Examples are household goods, drinks, and food.

PACKING LIST An enumeration of the contents of a package placed on top when it is sealed closed so that it may be easily retrieved by the individual opening the package. It is used to physically compare the contents of a package for the purpose of insuring that the contents are all that one was suppose to receive.

PALLET A low movable platform to stack goods or materials. A pallet may be used to rest goods on temporarily including for assembling purposes. It facilitates handling and diminishes damage. It is often used in a warehouse facility.

PAR VALUE **1.** For a stock, the dollar amount assigned each share of stock in the company's charter. For preferred issues and bonds, the value on which the issuer promises to pay dividends. **2.** For a country's currency, the value established by the government for it relative to other currencies.

PARALLEL EXPORTING The exporting of goods by an independent operator that is not part of the producer's regular distribution network. The parallel exporter is the wholesaler who exports products independently of manufacturer authorized export agents or buys goods for export and diverts them to the domestic market. He/she may compete with the authorized exporter or with a subsidiary of the foreign maker that produces the product in the domestic market.

PARALLEL LOAN. *See* **BACK-TO-BACK LOAN.**

PARALLEL MARKET An unofficial **FOREIGN EXCHANGE MARKET** condoned by a government but not officially backed. The exact distinction between a parallel market and a **BLACK MARKET** is not very clear.

PARCEL SHIPMENT In overseas trade, a small parcel consisting of a sample or advertisement material relating to a product. Generally, these types of parcels are restricted as to their weight and value.

PARENT COMPANY 1. In consolidation, a company that owns more than 50 percent of the voting common stock of other companies (subsidiaries). **2.** A holding company investing in the stock of other companies but is not engaged in a trade or business. *See* **ETHNOCENTRISM.**

PARITY 1. The exchange rate at which an official **CURRENCY** may be fixed. When exchange rates are fixed, currencies must be frequently traded in the open market in order to preserve parity stability. **2.** When data is transferred in a electronic medium such as a computer, a parity check bit is appended to make sure that the data was transferred properly. The computer periodically adds up the number of one (on) bits to insure that their sum is always odd or even.

PARITY PRICE A price for a product or service considered fair by an independent party.

PARTIAL BREACH A slight breach of a contract such that the injured party does not have a legal basis to cancel it in its entirety. However, damages for the part breach may be seeked.

PARTIAL SHIPMENT The goods being delivered represent a part rather than the entire order. Contractual provisions should allow for such depending upon the circumstances (e.g., strike, unavailability of raw materials).

PARTICIPATION CERTIFICATE 1. A certificate indicating that an entity has an interest in a credit instrument that carries a given rate of interest for a specified amount of principal. For example, an entity may have a certificate that indicates an interest in a mortgage pool or other such funds. **2.** A certificate showing participation in a lending agreement using **EUROCURRENCY.**

PARTICIPATIVE LEADERSHIP A style of leadership in which interactive decision making among the management team is the rule rather than the exception. The rule of thumb in a participative leadership environment is to involve all those who are either part of the problem or part of the solution. Participative leaders expand the problem-solving process to all those directly effected by empowering individuals by giving them the ability to participate and have an influence in the decision-making process.

PARTICULAR AVERAGE. *See* **AVERAGE.**

PARTNERSHIP An association of two or more individuals to enter into a business for a profit.

PASS-THROUGH **1.** Means of bypassing trade restrictions or a trade bloc through the shipment of goods through another country which does not have such restrictions and enjoys preferential trade status. **2.** The process of transferring income or loss to the owners of such entities as a sole proprietorship, **PARTNERSHIP, S Corporation,** etc. These entities are not considered as legal entities from the perspective of the taxing authorities and as a result pass the income or losses of the period through to their underlying owners who declare them on their income tax returns. **3.** The process of passing income and cash flow from debtors to investors through an **INTERMEDIARY** such as a bank by virtue of a security agreement. For example, in mortgage backed securities, debtors principal payments and interest passes through the lending institution to the investors of the securities.

PASSIVE INCOME Income derived from activities in which an investor does not participate, i.e., not derived from "sweat of brow" activities. For example, income derived from rental properties or other non-participative activities produce passive income. From a tax perspective, passive income or loss is computed separately for each passive activity in which a taxpayer has invested in. Generally, the loss from one passive activity may be used to offset income from other passive activities but may not offset active or portfolio activities.

PATENT An exclusive right conferred on an inventor for the use of an invention, for a limited time (usually 17 years). It creates a temporary monopolistic power and is intended as a device for promoting invention.

PATTERN BARGAINING An industry-wide bargaining strategy featured by a contract resolution with one firm that forms a basis for other companies in the industry to follow.

PAYBACK PERIOD The length of time required to recover the initial amount of a capital investment. If the cash inflows occur at a uniform rate, it is the ratio of the amount of initial investment over expected annual cash inflows, or Payback period = initial investment/annual cash inflows.

EXAMPLE:

Assume projected annual cash inflows are expected to be $4,500 a year for five years from an investment of $18,000. The payback period on this proposal is 4 years, which is calculated as follows:

$$\text{Payback period} = \$18,000/\$4,500 = 4 \text{ years.}$$

If annual cash inflows are not even, the payback period would have to be determined by trial and error. The method is very effective in dealing with risky investment projects.

PAYLOAD Terminology used by a common carrier referring to the transportation of freight for which compensation is being received. The actual goods being transported are referred to as the payload. A payload may also be considered goods being returned to a vendor in the course of a carrier making another delivery to that vendor so as to not make the return unprofitable.

PAYMENT DOCUMENTS The documents that must be completed and submitted by an exporter to insure that payment will be received for goods sold. For example, an export **LETTER OF CREDIT** is a payment document issued by the bank of an importer purchasing goods. The letter of credit states the importer's bank promises to make payment to the exporter upon receipt of certain documents delineated in the letter indicating that the sale and delivery of goods to the importer has been consummated. *See also* **BILL OF LADING.**

PAYMENTS NETTING Settling transactions between trading countries in a manner that does not create serious balance of payments deficits or exhaust their foreign exchange reserves. A bilateral payment agreement, for example, resulting in payments netting between two nations, has the disadvantage of restricting trade. On the other hand, multilateral agreements, such as the European Monetary Agreement where all participating nations agree to net and settle their payments through a single clearing house are less trade restrictive.

PEAK 1. The highest point in the **BUSINESS CYCLE** of an entity. **2.** The graphical high point of a given activity. For example, summertime is generally the peak of customer demand for electricity.

PECUNIARY EXCHANGE Any trade transaction that involves money.

PEFCO. *See* **PRIVATE EXPORT FUNDING CORPORATION (PEFCO).**

PEGGED EXCHANGE RATE An exchange rate fixed within a preestablished minimum-maximum range.

PEGGING The stabilization or fixing of a **CURRENCY,** security, **COMMODITY,** or other items at a given price. Manipulating a **FREE MARKET** for such purposes is illegal in the United States and is constantly monitored by the **SECURITIES AND EXCHANGE COMMISSION.** Pegging is generally accomplished by controlled heavy buying and selling of an item at specific prices.

PENDENTE LITE A contingency related to a pending lawsuit. For example, a company leasing office space may withhold and deposit into a bank account the monthly rent payable to the landlord while the matter of dispute (e.g., lack of heat) is in litigation.

PENETRATION PRICING A pricing policy that involves establishing low initial prices in order to gain quick acceptance in a broad portion of the market. It calls for the sacrifice of some short-term profits in order to gain a better long-term **MARKET SHARE.** The lower price is then often raised as the product moves into its growth stage. One objective is to obtain a committed customer. This policy is also used by a firm when consumer demand is price-elastic. *See also* **SKIMMING PRICING.**

PERESTROIKA Russian term for the economic reform policies of President Mikhail S. Gorbachev of the Soviet Union, implying modernizing of facilities and economic structure, as well as decentralizing decision power to local levels of government.

PERFORMANCE **1.** The satisfaction of one's obligation in a contract. **2.** The fulfillment of an economic promise or requirement. **3.** An accomplishment. **4.** The act of performing a role or demonstrating a skill before an audience.

PERIPHERY That section of a country's population that is economically most disadvantaged.

PER-SHARE COMMISSION **1.** A fee paid for services rendered such as to a broker to execute a trade in the form of shares of stock. An example is a multinational company giving an investment banker 10,000 shares of stock for its efforts. **2.** A multinational company giving another entity an ownership share to undertake some activity, function, or investment.

PERSISTENT DUMPING The recurring sale of a United States company's goods in a foreign country at below normal prices charged domestically. It may be an attempt to hurt in some manner the foreign manufacturer such as by eliminating or curtailing competition. Alternatively, the policy may be for the United States manufacturer to gain a foothold in the foreign country.

PERSONAL SELLING The salesperson deals with the potential customer person-to-person whether in physical form, in writing, or on the telephone. An advantage is the salesperson getting to know what is or is not important to the particular prospect. Further, the salesperson can obtain feedback from the facial, voice, and body movement of the potential buyer. The salesperson can change his approach to make the sale based on his perception of the customer's reaction.

PERT. *See* **PROGRAM EVALUATION AND REVIEW TECHNIQUE.**

PESETA Monetary unit of Spain, Andorra, Balearic Island, and Canary Islands.

PESO The currency of the following countries: Argentina, Chile, Columbia, Cuba, Dominican Republic, Mexico, Republic of Philippines, and Uruguay.

PETRODOLLARS Money paid to an oil exporting nation and deposited in Western banks. It is a Eurodollar deposit of the oil producing country.

PHYSICAL DISTRIBUTION The sum of all activities involved in transporting a good from the place it was manufactured to its final sales destination.

PHYSICAL PRODUCTIVITY A technological efficiency of the manufacturing operation. It is evaluated through the input-output relationship.

PIECE WORK A compensation plan to workers tied to the units they finish such as $.50 per shirt.

PIGGYBACK EXPORTING The exportation by a manufacturer of related complementary products (manufactured by the selling company or perhaps by one of its subsidiaries) with the sale of its primary products in international markets.

PIGGYBACKING A producer of a product contracts with another company to market and distribute its goods. An example is a United States company delegating the exporting function to another company specializing in the European marketplace.

PILOT PLAN The testing and evaluation on a limited basis of an activity or operation before full implementation is undertaken. The objective is to gain experience and reduce risk before full scale operations begin. An example is producing a small number of a new product to determine any manufacturing problems (e.g., quality, scheduling).

PLACE One element in the **FOUR Ps** in the marketing mix. Place is the means of physically distributing the product to the customer. It includes production, transportation, storage, and distribution on both the wholesale and retail levels. Where to deliver the product to the customer, and how to get the product to this location, are the principal concerns of place analysis subsystems. Typically, a distribution chain starts at the manufacturing plant and ends at the final consumer. In the middle is a network of wholesale and retail outlets employed to efficiently and effectively bring goods and services to the final consumer. But where are the best places to locate manufacturing facilities, wholesale outlets, and retail distribution points. Factors such as manufacturing costs, transportation costs, labor costs, and localized demand levels become factors that are critical to answering this issue.

PLANNING To derive a course of action or direction for the future. In private enterprise, the planning function is an important control function to insure that the economic entity is following a profitable course of action in accordance with the goals and objectives set out by its Board of Directors. Examples of planning include the preparation of the myriad of budgets that an entity must generate in the course of a given period. Along with their preparation, comparisons must ultimately be made by the entity of actual results to planned budgeted outcomes so that any material deviations can be analyzed and explained.

PLAZA AGREEMENT In 1985, a meeting of representatives of industrial countries who decided to intervene to decrease the value of the dollar quickly because it was too strong at the time. With the declining value of the dollar resulting from the central banks intervention the value of the German mark, British pound, and Japances yen, among others, increased.

PLOW BACK The reinvestment by the multinational company of its profits into the business instead of making dividend distributions. Growth companies typically reinvest all or most of their net incomes.

POINTS QUOTATION A **FORWARD CONTRACT** quotation expressed only as the number of decimal points.

POISON PILL A company about to be acquired by another attempts to block the acquisition through some action such as borrowing heavily to be less attractive financially or by issuing excessive preferred stock.

POLITICAL RISK Also called sovereign risk. Risk associated with political or sovereign uncertainty. Clearly, political factors are a major determinant of the attractiveness for investment in any country. Examples of political risk are government expropriation of property, currency conversion restrictions and import barriers. Countries viewed as likely candidates for internal political upheaval or with a pronounced trend toward elimination of the private sector will be unattractive to all investors, foreign and domestic alike. There is no reason to believe that local investors will be systematically optimistic regarding their country's future. When political risks increase significantly, such investors will attempt to diversify from the home market as rapidly as will foreigners. As a result, prices will fall until someone will be satisfied to hold the securities of a risky country. Political instability, limited track records, poor statistics-they all make gauging risk a risky business. Several companies try to evaluate the risk in some of the countries that are receiving the most attention from foreign investors:

EUROMONEY Magazine's annual **COUNTRY RISK RATING,** which is based on a measure of different countries' access to international credit, trade finance, political risk and a country's payment record. The rankings are generally confirmed by political risk insurers and top syndicate managers in the **EURO-MARKETS.** Rating by **ECONOMIST INTELLIGENCE UNIT,** a New York-based subsidiary of the **ECONOMIST GROUP,** London, which is based on such factors as external debt and trends in the current account, the consistency of the government policy, foreign-exchange reserves, and the quality of economic management. **INTERNATIONAL COUNTRY RISK GUIDE,** published by a United States division of **INTERNATIONAL BUSINESS COMMUNICATIONS, LTD.,** London, which offers a composite risk rating, as well as individual ratings for political, financial and **ECONOMIC RISK.** The political variable - which makes up half of the composite index - includes factors such as government corruption and how economic expectations diverge from reality. The financial rating looks at such things as the likelihood of losses from exchange controls and loan defaults. Finally, economic ratings consider such factors as inflation and debt-service costs. **DATA BOOK** (quarterly), published by Thompson BankWatch, Inc., 61 Broadway, New York, NY 10006, provides a Thompson country rating assessing overall political and economic stability of a country in which a bank is domiciled.

POLITICAL UNION A form of economic regional integration that requires full political integration between nations (i.e., birth of a single political jurisdiction).

POLYCENTRIC ORGANIZATION A host-country oriented multinational company that assumes that local people always know what is best for them and that the unit of the multinational company located in a host country should be as local in identity and behavior as possible. This type of a multinational company has the advantage of making intensive use of local resources and personnel but at the cost of global growth and efficiency and the synergistic benefits of multinational operations.

POLYCENTRISM A business views a key ingredient to decision making as the differences existing within the organization and among its managers and employees.

POOL 1. Combining money, resources, supplies, financing, talent, etc. 2. Contributing to a common fund. 3. Investment group combining their funds to buy a diversified portfolio. 4. **JOINT VENTURE** or arrangement among businesses.

POOLING 1. Accounting method used in a business combination in which the net assets of the acquired company are bought forth at book value. Net income of the acquired company is included in earnings for the entire year irrespective of the date of acquisition. Costs of the pooling are immediately expensed. 2. Insurance company sharing premiums and losses among themselves to spread their risks.

PORT OF ENTRY The port location accepting imported goods into the country. An example is San Diego as a port of entry for products received from some Asian countries.

PORT SHOPPING The selection of a port to use by importers or exporters using as the prime criteria the quality of the customs function.

PORTFOLIO INVESTMENTS **1.** Investments that are undertaken for the sake of obtaining investment income or capital gains rather than entrepreneurial income which is the case with **FOREIGN DIRECT INVESTMENT.** It typically involves the ownership of stocks and/or bonds issued by public or private agencies of a foreign country. **2.** Investing in a variety of assets to reduce risk by diversification. An example of a portfolio is a mutual fund, which is a popular investment vehicle which consists of a variety of securities or assets which are professionally managed. A major advantage of investing in mutual funds is diversification. Investors can own a variety of securities with a minimal capital investment. Since mutual funds are professionally managed, they tend to involve less risk. To reduce risk, securities in a portfolio should have negative or no correlations to each other.

PORTFOLIO THEORY Theory advanced by H. Markowitz in attempting a well diversified portfolio. The central theme of the theory is that rational investors behave in a way that reflects their aversion to taking increased risk without being compensated by an adequate increase in expected return. Also, for any given expected return, most investors will prefer a lower risk, and for any given level of risk, they will prefer a higher return to a lower return. Markowitz showed how quadratic programming could be used to calculate a set of a **EFFICIENT PORTFOLIO.** An investor then will choose among a set of efficient portfolios the best that is consistent with the risk profile of the investor.

POSITION **1.** The net balance in an account or foreign currency. **2.** The financial condition of a business. **3.** The amount invested in a security. **4.** The attitude or opinion. **5.** The strategic market location. **6.** The placement of something or someone. **7.** The rank in the organization.

POSITION TRADER A trader in a security or **COMMODITY** buying it with the intent of holding for a long-term period of one year or more. The goal is long-term gains without undue risk.

POSSESSIONS CORPORATION Under the United States tax code, a corporation operating in United States possessions. Such companies are entitled to certain tax benefits.

POST-TRADE FINANCING Credit extended to the exporter or importer after shipment. The exporter has various options. It can seek another bank loan to cover the period until payment by the importer. The importer may generally use a **LETTER OF CREDIT** plus a **TIME DRAFT** for post-trade financing.

POUND Monetary unit of Great Britain, Cyprus, Egypt, Gibraltar, Republic of Ireland, Lebanon, Malta, Sudan, and Syria.

POWER OF ATTORNEY A written document in which an individual (principal) appoints another to act on his behalf. The agent has legal authority to deal with other parties and bind the principal. An example is when a very ill person designates someone else to handle business and financial matters. Another example is giving an agent the power to sign legal documents or to settle tax disputes with the **INTERNAL REVENUE SERVICE** on behalf of a principal. There are two types of powers; general and special. A general power gives the agent broad powers on any matters pertaining to the principal. A special power limits the agent's authority to act to a limited number of matters.

PREDATORY DUMPING The setting of selling prices for exports temporarily so low in the foreign market so as to discourage competition. The selling prices of the exporter are usually less than the typical selling prices for the goods produced in that foreign country or that available from other foreign countries. When competition is driven out, the exporter will be able to raise its selling prices to a normal, representative level.

PREDATORY RATE A shipping fee set by a carrier so low as to discourage competition.

PRE-EMPTION 1. Evaluation or looking at an action before it occurs. An example is a multinational company anticipating what a competing company might do in the future in a particular market. **2.** The right of custom agents to seize and sell imported goods that were fraudulently undervalued so as to pay less of a tariff.

PREEMPTIVE PRICING The setting of a selling price for a good or service low enough so as to either prevent competitors from stepping into the market or if in the market to withdraw. For example, the selling price may be barely above the total manufacturing cost per unit. **ECONOMIES OF SCALE** may result in even lower per unit prices due to the increased quantity. If enough units are sold and no competition exists, the business will still be successful in the long-term. Further, the company name will be exclusively associated with the product and may in fact benefit other products because of name association.

PREFERENCES 1. The advantage afforded a company or individual. **2.** The selection of one alternative over another. An example is consumers preferring bright color summer clothing. **3.** The advantages offered by a country to its trading partners such as lower **TARIFFS**.

PREFERENTIAL TARIFF A lower duty on imported products from selected countries to favor them relative to other countries. Such as policy might be implemented to give "preferred" treatment to politically friendly nations (e.g., the United States and England).

PREFERRED STOCK A class of securities that have certain "preferences" or "restrictions" that common stock does not have. Preferred stock is generally issued at its par (face) value and pays a fixed dividend return that is expressed as percentage of its par value. Even though the stock carries a fixed dividend return, that dividend is not guaranteed to stockholders. It only becomes guaranteed and irrevocable when it is declared by the board of directors. If the preferred stock is cumulative, however, then the fixed dividend is never lost. If the board of directors of the company chooses not to declare the preferred stock dividend in a given year, then it becomes a dividend "arrearage" of the entity and must be disclosed in the notes or financial statements. The common stockholders of the company may not receive any current or future dividends until the preferred stockholders not only receive any dividends in "arrears" but also receive their current year's dividend as well. The following preferences are characteristic of most preferred stock issues:

1. Dividend Preferences - Dividends that are declared to preferred stockholders in a given year must be paid in full before common stockholders are entitled to any dividends.
2. Preferences to Assets in the Event of Liquidation - In the event of a liquidation, preferred stockholders will receive their stated liquidation value before common stockholders can receive any liquidation proceeds.
3. Callable at the Option of the Issuing Corporation - Most preferred stock that is issued in recent years is callable at the option of the issuing corporation. This means that if the issuing corporation chooses to redeem the preferred stock at any time that the shares are outstanding (or any contractual designated period indicated) the investor is required to turn his or her shares into the corporation for the shares' indicated call price.
4. Nonvoting - Preferred stockholders generally do not have voting rights which means they have absolutely no control in setting company policy or directing the operations of the business.
5. Conversion Provision - Some preferred stock provide the stockholder with the option of converting into common stock at some designated rate at the holder's option during a specified period that the shares are outstanding. Of course, the holder may choose not to exercise this right and not convert into common stock.

Because of the aforementioned characteristics, many individuals believe that preferred stock is more of a debt security than an equity security. However, currently **GAAP** does not make any distinctions between preferred stock and other classes of capital stock for balance sheet presentation purposes.

PREMIUM **1.** The inducement given to stimulate a consumer to buy a product or service such as giving a "free" promotion item. **2.** The additional amount paid for something. **3.** The fee such as an insurance payment. **4.** Something selling for a higher value. **5.** The amount paid for a call or put option on a stock. **6.** The excess amount received over the par or face value of a security. **7.** The price paid for a contract. **8.** The extra payment made to employees or outside service provider as an incentive such as giving a salesperson a bonus if he exceeds the sales quota, or giving a factory worker a bonus to work a late shift or holiday. **9.** The amount in excess of market value paid in a tender offer. **10.** The excess of call price over face value of a bond extinguished early. **11.** The excess of the forward rate over the spot rate for a foreign currency.

PRESHIPMENT FINANCE An exporter's borrowing to cover its costs before shipping the merchandise overseas.

PRESTIGE ADVERTISING A sales promotion undertaken to improve a company's image as well as its product and service lines. The appearance of a quality business will stimulate consumer interest and respect.

PRETRADE FINANCING Credit extended to an exporter or an importer before shipment. For example, the importer uses a **LETTER OF CREDIT,** allowing payment to be postponed for some period of time, such as 180 days. For the exporter, this is a form of working capital loan.

PRICE CONTROLS Limits or ceilings on upward movements of prices set by a government with a view toward combating inflation. This policy measure is frequently used when the government has been unable to control **INFLATION** by monetary or fiscal policies.

PRICE DISCRIMINATION An illegal practice of charging two similar groups different prices for the identical goods or services even though the cost of each unit is the same for both.

PRICE ELASTICITY The responsiveness of the quantity demanded of a good to its own price. It is measured as the percentage change in demand that occurs in response to a percentage change in price.

PRICE INDEX A means to measure changes in the general price level over time by comparing the cost of specified items. Price indexes are used to measure inflation and costs of living. Two popular ones are: the Consumer Price Index (CPI) and Producer Price Index (PPI). The CPI measures the cost of buying a fixed bundle of goods (some 400 consumer goods and services), representative of the purchase of the typical working-class urban family, while the PPI is a measure of the cost of a given basket of goods priced in wholesale markets, including raw materials, semifinished goods, and finished goods.

PRICE FIXING An illegal practice in violation of antitrust laws to increase, decrease, or stabilize the price of a product or service. It is horizontal if the price fixing is among competitors. It is vertical if the price fixing is among the manufacturer, wholesaler, or retailer.

PRICE LEADERSHIP A dominant company in an industry increases the selling price with the others following suit.

PRICE LEVEL **1.** The market price of products or services relative to other time periods. **2.** The measure of **INFLATION** such as the Gross National Product Price Deflator, Consumer Price Index (CPI), or Purchasing Power Index (PPI).

PRICE LINING The formulation of a selling price for a product or service based on points reflecting attributes to stimulate consumer interest such as price, quality, size, and color. For example, an appliance store may carry different brands of air conditioners segregating them as to price (e.g., $200-$299, $300-$399).

PRICE STABILIZATION To give stability to prices of goods, services, and supplies. For example, the United States Federal Reserve Bank may undertake monetary policy measures to slow down the **INFLATION** rate.

PRICE SUPPRESSION 1. To restrain, repress, or inhibit price increases. 2. To keep prices of goods produced domestically lower so as to compete with cheap imports.

PRICE TAKER The selling price for a product depends upon market conditions. Companies in the industry do not have the power to individually control the price.

PRICE WAR A situation in which competing companies are reducing their prices cutting into their profitability. Examples are winter discounts offered by airlines to the public, and retailers underpricing each other to attract buyers. In extreme cases, companies may go bankrupt from selling products below their cost.

PRICE-SPECIE-FLOW As the prices of imported product components increase so does the prices of the finished products.

PRICING STRATEGY An important component of the overall international marketing mix. The strategy includes such considerations as (1) price discrimination, charging different prices for the same product in different countries, (2) demand elasticity, and (3) some of the regulatory factors such as government-mandated price controls and **ANTIDUMPING RESTRICTIONS** that limit a firm's ability to charge the prices it would prefer in a country.

PRIMARY COMMODITY 1. The most important item or good. 2. The **COMMODITY** with no or little processing involved.

PRIMARY DISTRIBUTION A new issuance of securities (e.g, stocks, bonds) to the public. It differs from a secondary distribution which refers to securities which have previously been sold.

PRIMARY PRODUCT 1. The major good manufactured or sold. 2. The product in its natural form such as fruits or fish.

PRINCIPAL 1. The major individual to a transaction such as the buyer or seller. 2. The owner or user of property. 3. The owner of a private business. 4. In agency law, the individual who acts on behalf of another. 5. The face value of an obligation or debt upon which interest is based. 6. The payment made on a debt less the interest portion. 7. The first in importance or ranking.

PRIORITIZATION The establishment of a priority order or preference by importance.

PRIVATE EXPORT FUNDING CORPORATION (PEFCO) A private United States corporation, established with government support, that helps finance United States exports. It raises private capital for funding the export of big-ticket items by American firms by purchasing the medium- to long-term debt obligations of importers of United States goods at fixed interest rates.

PRIVATIZATION The process of making a publicly held business a privately held one.

PRO FORMA 1. The presentation of forecasted transactions or events such as in the forecasted financial statements. When amounts are projected, there should be disclosure of the hypothetical assumptions and possibly minimum-maximum ranges. A pro forma financial statement may be prepared in such cases as in a loan application or in valuing a possible acquisition target. 2. An informal document specifying preliminary information before it is finalized.

PRO FORMA INVOICE A vendor invoice to the buyer before goods are shipped so the buyer knows what, how much, specifications, characteristics, and cost of the items.

PRO RATA A proportionate amount such as allocating the cost of buying two or more assets based on their appraised values. Assume $100,000 is paid for land and building having fair market values of $60,000 and $50,000, respectively. The pro rata allocation cost amounts assigned to land would be $54,545 ($60,000/$110,000 x $100,000) and to building would be $45,455 ($50,000/$110,000 x $100,000).

PROCESS TECHNOLOGY The methods and techniques used in production to organize and process the inputs. Process technology pertains to the process by which a given product or service is processed into the finished product.

PRODUCER COMMODITY LEVEL The group of suppliers of a major raw material used throughout the world.

PRODUCER GOODS The capital resources (inputs) used by a company in manufacturing its products.

PRODUCT DIFFERENTIATION A strategy used by a multinational company or **STRATEGIC BUSINESS UNIT** that help the firm compete based on factors other than price differentials. Quality differentials, packaging, credit terms, or superior maintenance service can all differentiate products, as can advertising that leads to brand-name identification.

PRODUCT LIFE CYCLE Time span between initial concept (typically starting with research and development) of a product or service and time when the firm ceases to support customers who have bought the product or service. This is the concept that is particularly useful in forecasting and analyzing historical data of new products. It presumes that demand for a product follows an S-shaped curve growing slowly in the early stages, achieving rapid and sustained growth in the middle stages, and slowing again in the mature stage.

PRODUCT LINE A group of products produced by a company having similarities in manufacturing and use. The company may market the entire product line to consumers. An example is household appliances.

PRODUCT MODIFICATION A strategy adopted by some **MULTINATIONAL CORPORATIONS** that implies adjusting a product to meet local conditions without changing the core concept of the product (e.g., focusing on smaller, energy efficient cars in Europe since roads may be tinier and fuel more costly than in the United States).

PRODUCT PAYBACK **1.** The trade financing of an import with exports produced by it. **2.** The amount of time it takes to recover the cost or initial investment in producing a product.

PRODUCT SHIFTING **1.** A retailers' replacing the sale of one product with another or a manufacturer switching the production of one product to another. **2.** The switching of the export of one good to another. **3.** The rearrangement of the order or visibility of products. **4.** The movement of a good from one location, position, or market to another.

PRODUCT STRUCTURE Organizational structure defined by products.

PRODUCT TECHNOLOGY The methods or know-hows used to make any product.

PRODUCT TESTING **1.** The examination of a product such as for quality, usefulness, reliability, or feasibility. **2.** The marketing of a new product in a test (trial) market before a full-scale selling program is undertaken. **3.** Product certification so that it may be sold in another country.

PRODUCTION The manufacture of a product.

PRODUCTION AGREEMENT **1.** An understanding among members of an organization or among countries as to how much of a product should be manufactured. **2.** A contractual provision as to the amount to be produced. **3.** A business contract with another to manufacture its product for a fee.

PRODUCTION ALLOCATION Allocating production that is needed internationally to various affiliates or subsidiaries in order to save transportation costs and allocate scarce resources more profitably.

PRODUCTION EFFECT The increase in volume of a product by a domestic producer caused by higher import prices due to protective tariffs.

PRODUCTION SHARING **1.** Two or more companies share on some basis the amount to be manufactured for a product. **2.** Two or more companies agree to produce parts of a final product.

PRODUCTION SMOOTHING As a means of **PRODUCTION ALLOCATION,** assigning production to various affiliates or subsidiaries for the purpose of keeping relatively steady output levels at all locations.

PRODUCTION SWITCHING The shifting, changing, or transferring of manufacturing to a different process or location such as to lower manufacturing costs.

PRODUCTIVITY **1.** Abundant production or service activity. **2.** An input-output relationship. An example is evaluating the cost and quantity of raw materials relative to the quantity and quality of the resulting finished products. **3.** Efficiencies such as an increase in units produced per worker or per hour. **4.** A very active person.

PROGRAM BUDGETING A budget of revenue and costs by program such as a computer network training program offered to update executives.

PROGRAM EVALUATION AND REVIEW TECHNIQUE (PERT) A management tool for planning, coordinating, and controlling large complex projects such as construction of buildings and installation of computers. The development and initial application of PERT was done in connection with the development of the Polaris submarine by the United States Navy in the late 1950s. The PERT technique involves the diagrammatic representation of the sequence of activities comprising a project by means of a network consisting of arrows and circles (nodes). Arrows represent "tasks" or "activities," which are distinct segments of the project requiring time and resources. Nodes (circles) symbolizes "events," or milestone points in the project representing the completion of one or more activities and/or the initiation of one or more subsequent activities. An event is a point in time and does not consume any time in itself as does an activity. An important aspect of PERT is the Critical Path Method (CPM). A path is a sequence of connected activities.

PROHIBITIVE TARIFF **1.** An excessive fee on selected imported items to discourage their importation into the United States It may also be an attempt to restrict trade with a certain foreign country. Such a strategy may either be designed to reduce or eliminate trade in the selected good(s). **2.** An additional duty on an imported item on the amount in excess of a predetermined level.

PROJECT LINE A bank line of credit to a multinational company to finance a particular project.

PROJECTION To forecast or estimate future financial results or performance. A corporate planner may use financial models in doing so.

PROMISSORY NOTE A formal written note to pay a specific amount of money at some future date at a specified interest rate. From the prospective of the maker or payer (entity promising to make payment) the promissory note is called a note payable. From the prospective of the payee (entity to whom payment will be made) the promissory note is called a note receivable. *See also* **ACCEPTANCE.**

PROMOTION All the means of marketing the sale of the product, including advertising and personal selling. Product success is a direct function of the types of advertising and sales promotion done. The size of the promotions budget and the allocation of this budget to various promotional mixes are important factors in deciding the type of campaigns that will be launched. Television coverage, newspaper ads and coverage, promotional brochures and literature, samples, public appearances, and training programs for salespeople are all components of these promotional and advertising mixes.

PROPERTY RIGHT An ownership or other interest in possessing or using scarce resources such as land, capital, and other goods. An example is the ownership of a building and the resulting right to use it.

PROPRIETARY ASSET Assets unique to a firm that can enjoy competitive advantage, such as technology, human resources, and trade secrets, so as to bring about lower costs, higher revenues, or less risk than its competitors.

PROPRIETARY LIMITED (PTY.LTD.) Term used in Australia, Singapore, and other countries for an owned corporation.

PROPRIETARY TECHNOLOGY Technology that is unique and owned or controlled by particular individuals or organizations. It may be held as a trade secret, or it may be published as a patent.

PROSPERITY A prosperous financial condition of a business, individuals, or economy. In economic terms, prosperity is indicated in part by economic expansion and high employment levels.

PROTECTED MARKETS A geographic area, region, or marketplace for products or services shielded or defended in some way. An example is a country having very high import tariffs on a particular product to protect domestic producers of that item.

PROTECTED NICHE The competitive strategy aimed at obtaining government protection for the multinational company's activities in the nations where it operates.

PROTECTIONISM Polices limiting foreign competition to protect domestic industries. Protectionism may be used for infant industries. It may include import restrictions such as quotas and tariffs. It may be used to correct an imbalance of payments between nations.

PROTECTIVE TARIFF A tax on imports structured so as to shield domestic industries from foreign competition.

PROTESTANT WORK ETHIC As one of the driving forces in the development of the United States economy, the duty of Christians to glorify God by hard, physical work and the practice of thrift. The philosophy finds its origin in the middle ages when Protestantism sought to distance itself from other forms of Christianity with its belief that "work is prayer."

PROTOCOL OF ACCESSION A legal document specifying rights and duties of a multinational company involved in international trade.

PROVISO A clause in an agreement providing for some condition or stipulation such as exempting one party from a provision restricting property use for some designated purpose.

PROXY The authority given another to act on one's behalf. An example is a power of attorney by which a stockholder transfers his voting rights to another party.

PTY. LTD. See PROPRIETARY LIMITED.

PUBLIC GOODS Goods that are nonrival and nonexclusionary in consumption and therefore benefit persons other than those who buy the goods. A good is nonrival in consumption if the consumption of the good by one person does not preclude other people from also consuming the good. A good is nonexclusionary if, once provided, no one can be excluded from consuming it. Examples of public goods are radio signals, lighthouses, national defense, and clean air.

PUNT Ireland's currency.

PUFFING A salesperson's overexaggeration of the benefits of a particular property, product, or service to stimulate a buyer's order. The salesperson must be cognizant, however, of possible legal exposure if the statements made are very misleading or lack any basis in fact. An example is stating that a particular medicine will cure a disease which in fact has no medical basis.

PUNITIVE DAMAGES A court award of extra damages above the actual (nominal, compensatory) amount designed to punish the wrongdoer for its grossly improper conduct or tortious acts (e.g., fraud, maliciousness, mean-spirited). Punitive damages are designed to deter the defendant from similar conduct in the future, and to set an example for others. An example might be an award against a pharmaceutical company for its willful disregard for human life by releasing a new drug it knows is unsafe just to profit from it. Another example is treble (triple) damages awarded because of antitrust violations.

PURCHASING AGENT **1.** An agent authorized to buy merchandise on behalf of his company or other business entity. **2.** An agent who buys products in his country as a representative of a foreign buyer.

PURCHASING POWER PARITY The notion that the price of internationally traded commodities should be the same in every country, and therefore the exchange rate between the two currencies should be the ratio of price levels in the two countries:

$$\frac{F}{S} = \frac{1 + P_d}{1 + P_f}$$

where F = forward exchange rate (e.g., $/foreign currency)
S = spot exchange rate (e.g., $/foreign currency)
P_d = domestic inflation rate
P_f = foreign inflation rate

EXAMPLE:
Assume the following data for United States and France:
Expected United States inflation rate = 5 percent
Expected French inflation rate = 10 percent
S = $0.220/FR
Then,

$$\frac{F}{0.220} = \frac{1.05}{1.10}$$

So F = $0.210/FR

If France has the higher inflation rate, then the purchasing power of the franc is declining faster than that of the dollar. This will lead to a forward discount on the franc relative to the dollar.

PURCHASING POWER RISK Also called **INFLATION RISK,** the failure of assets to earn a return to keep up with increasing price levels. Bonds are exposed to this risk because the issuer will be paying back in cheaper dollars in inflationary times.

PUSH INCENTIVES A bonus in dollars or other compensation paid to salespeople to strongly encourage a consumer order of certain merchandise or services. It may be offered to promote a new or slagging product.

PUT **1.** An option to sell a specific security at a specified price within a designated period for which the option buyer pays the seller (writer) a **PREMIUM** or option price. Contracts on listed puts (and calls) have been standardized at date of issue for periods of three, six, and nine months, although as these contracts approach expiration, they may be purchased with a much shorter life. **2.** Bondholder's right to redeem a bond prior to **MATURITY.**

PUT OPTION. *See* **PUT.**

PYRAMIDING **1.** The acquisition of other companies mostly through debt financing. **2.** Using holding gains from a securities position as security (collateral) to invest in additional positions on margin with brokers. **3.** Growth in a company by expanding distributors and dealerships.

Q

QUALITATIVE RESEARCH AND ANALYSIS A multinational company's engaging in research aimed at improving its quality and image among consumers. The research may be in the form of personal or mail interviews. An analysis of the findings are made to determine the quality level and factors bearing thereon.

QUALITY CONTROL The maintenance of quality standards in manufacturing goods or rendering services.

QUALITY ENGINEERING The planning, designing, or constructing of high quality products. Any quality problems are identified and corrected.

QUANTITATIVE RESEARCH A multinational company engages in studying the quantity (amount) produced relative to what consumers want. Production levels should be in line with consumer demand.

QUANTITATIVE RESTRICTIONS **1.** Limits placed on the quantity of goods to be produced or sold, or on the amount of service hours to be rendered. **2.** A ceiling placed on the amount or value of products that may be exported or imported over a given time period. Such restrictions may arise from an **INTERNATIONAL TRADE** agreement among countries.

QUANTITY Units or volume of a product or service.

QUANTITY CONTROLS **1.** The regulating, restraining, or limiting the amount of a product or service produced or sold. **2.** Government restriction on the amount of foreign currency to be paid on a particular purchase of goods or services.

QUEUING THEORY Also known as waiting line theory, analysis concerned with trade offs (in time, dollars, etc.) between customers waiting for service and the number of service facilities of the firm. Typical applications have involved cargo traffic at shipyards or airports and the number of cash registers at a supermarket.

QUORUM The minimum number of members that must be present before the group may act in the business.

QUOTA CARTEL An understanding among companies in an industry in which each one is allocated a part of the market for the product or service.

QUOTAS **1.** Maximum number of imports allowed so the government can protect domestic industries from foreign competition. *See also* **PROTECTIONISM.** **2.** Maximum number of exports allowed (e.g., government restrictions on military equipment to be sold overseas). **3.** Sales or production targets established by a multinational company for its salespersons or factory workers.

QUOTATION **1.** Or, quote. The highest bid to buy and the lowest offer to sell a security in a particular market at a given time. If you ask your **BROKER** for a quotation on a stock, he/she may say, for example, "30 1/4 to 30 3/4." This means that $30.25 was the highest price any buyer wished to pay (bid) at the time the quotation was given on the exchange and that $30.75 was the lowest price at which any holder of the stock offered to sell. **2.** The selling price offered to a potential buyer.

QUOTE. *See* **QUOTATION.**

R

RAIDER An unfriendly company threatens or actually attempts to acquire another company. After acquisition, new management is instituted. When a company buys a 5 percent or more interest in another business, it must file its intentions with the **SECURITIES AND EXCHANGE COMMISSION.**

RALLY **1.** A significant increase in the market price of a particular stock, bond, or commodity or in the overall securities or commodities market. **2.** To come together for a common cause.

RAND Monetary unit of Lesotho, South Africa, and South West Africa.

RATE **1.** Schedule of charges for **TARIFFS.** **2.** Fee charged based on some predetermined arrangement such as service charge per hour for accessing the **INTERNET** or freight charge per pound on a shipment. **3.** Exchange rate between currencies of different countries. **4.** Amount of something relative to something else such as the degree of change in the **INFLATION** rate. **5.** Selling price per unit. **6.** Return rate on assets. **7.** To score an item such as establishing a priority order of a multinational company's business priorities. **8.** A rate basis for a utility established by its regulatory commission. **9.** To have value or status.

RATE CARD A written record of the promotion cost and other relevant details for each advertising unit including hours, space, advertising fees, and media statistics.

RATE SCALE A graduated listing of rates based on some predetermined factor such as weight, size, distance, or geographic zone.

RATING 1. Ranking products or services based on some predetermined criteria. 2. Evaluating the investment quality of a stock. 3. Putting something into a particular class or ranking such as a Standard and Poor's or Moody's bond rating or Best's rating of insurance companies. 4. Risk rating assigned to an insuree by the insurer. The rating influences the premium cost and terms of coverage. 5. A media measure such as audience.

RATIO ANALYSIS The evaluation performed by financial statement preparers and users to appraise the financial strength or weakness of a multinational company and its operating trend. Various ratios are computed, depending upon the user's purpose in analyzing the financial statements. Short-term creditors are most interested in a company's ability to pay its short-term debt from current assets, so they emphasize liquidity and cash flow. Long-term creditors want to be paid back in the long term, so they concentrate on solvency ratios such as total debt to total stockholders' equity. Investors are interested in dividends and appreciation in market price of stock, so they concentrate on profitability ratios (e.g, profit margin) and market measures (e.g., price-earnings ratio, dividend payout, dividend yield). Management is interested in creating shareholder worth so they are interested in ratios dealing with earnings, market price of securities, and risk. Management computes ratios by division and department to determine areas of strength and vulnerability. When a ratio indicates a problem, management will attempt corrective action.

RATIONAL EXPECTATIONS The belief of some economists that companies and individuals take into account all available economic information in formulating their decisions such as to buy or sell. Other information is either unimportant or not considered.

RATIONALIZED PRODUCTION The manufacturing of various product components or parts at different domestic and/or international geographic areas so as to obtain certain advantages such as greater productivity and efficiency, cost reduction, availability of labor and/or materials, less government regulation, tax advantages, etc.

RATIONING The control of the right to purchase essential commodities when there exist extreme scarcity so that everyone will have a minimum share. Examples are gasoline rationing or food rationing in Russia.

RAW DATA The initial information someone (such as a manager) works with in starting the evaluative process and making business decisions.

RAW MATERIAL Items placed into production to make a product. An example is steel used in the manufacture of cars or wood to make furniture.

REAL EXCHANGE RATE In contrast to **NOMINAL EXCHANGE RATE,** the rate adjusted for **INFLATION.**

REAL PROPERTY Land and whatever is on or affixed to it such as a building and landscaping. It applies to the benefits, rights, and interests in the ownership of real estate.

REBATE **1.** Refund arising from a purchase or tax. **2.** Refund for an overcollection. **3.** Return of part of a payment such as for service charges or assessments. **4.** Payment to a customer who buys a product or service as an inducement or sales tactic. **5.** Full or part refund of the United States government to a multinational company for duties paid on imported goods that are later exported overseas. **6.** Refunding unearned interest to a borrower for paying off the loan early.

RECALL **1.** To take back products such as due to defect, safety, or health hazard. A multinational company's recall of a product has adverse financial consequences (e.g., lost sales, shipping costs) and damages the company's reputation and image (e.g., for quality and reliability). **2.** A country's permanent or temporary removal of an official from another country.

RECAPITALIZATION Recasting the capital structure of a multinational company such as by exchanging bonds or preferred stock for common stock. While the mix of debt and equity financing changes the total amount of capital it is still the same. This process may occur in connection with a corporate reorganization in conformity with the bankruptcy laws.

RECAPTURE **1.** To retake something such as property. **2.** Contractual provision in which one party gets a predetermined interest percentage such as the owner of a mall receiving a percentage of a store's sales in addition to a fixed monthly rental. **3.** Taxpayer repays tax savings received in a prior year due to some event or transaction. An example is treating part of the gain on the sale of a capital asset as ordinary income rather than capital gain due to previous excess **DEPRECIATION** taken by the company. Note that ordinary income is taxed at a higher rate than capital gain.

RECESSION An extended time period of deteriorating economic conditions possibly resulting in a trough in the **BUSINESS CYCLE.** Many economists define recession as the decline in Gross National Product for two consecutive quarters.

RECIPROCAL BUYING An agreement in which two companies agree to buy each others merchandise or services.

RECIPROCAL TRADE AGREEMENT OF 1934 An act giving the President of the United States the power to undertake trade negotiations with foreign nations to promote the United States trade position. In 1962, the act expired.

RECIPROCITY 1. A country grants relief in its tariff structure or other trade barriers in return for similar trade relaxation of another nation. 2. A foreign government allowing a United States multinational company to operate in its country on the same terms as its own domestic companies. 3. Mutual exchange of something such as rights or privileges. An example is one multinational company returning a favor to another multinational company. An example is an airline accepting the plane tickets of another airline on strike which did the same for it in a prior year.

RECOGNITION 1. Recording a business occurrence in the accounting records. 2. The taxability of an item or transaction. 3. Determining the attributes of an item (e.g., amount, quality) before accepting it. 4. Identifying a person, thing, or product such as through media coverage or advertising.

RECONCILIATION 1. Adjusting for the difference between two items (e.g., amounts, balances, accounts, or statements) so that the figures agree. The manager often has to evaluate the deviation between two items, such as in preparing a bank reconciliation. For example, a reconciliation occurs when comparing the home office books account related to branch transactions with the corresponding account on the branch office books related to home office transactions. These two accounts are adjusted for the reconciling items causing the difference. 2. To reestablish good relations after some sort of strained relationship. An example is the management of two multinational companies coming together after a dispute.

RECONSIGN 1. To change the destination or routing of a shipment before or during transit. 2. To change the consignee for a shipment.

RECOURSE 1. Loan arrangement in which the cosigner is responsible if the borrower fails to pay. 2. Lender has **COLLATERAL** securing a loan in the event of nonpayment by debtor. The debtor is still responsible for the excess of the loan balance relative to the collateral value of the property. 3. To ask for assistance such as a United States company complaining to the United States government about the actions of a foreign competitor.

RECOVERY 1. An increase in stock or bond prices after a period of declining prices. 2. The receipt of net cash inflow from a project or asset that covers its initial cost. 3. The collection of a customer's balance which was written- off as uncollectible. 4. An improvement in the economy after a downturn. 5. An improvement in business conditions for a multinational company after deteriorating.

RECYCLING The reprocessing of discarded or used items to form new products. It involves passing through a cycle again. Examples are paper and bottles.

RED GOODS The products bought by individuals that are consumed quickly and are typically low-priced. They have lower profitability per unit. Examples are perishable goods such as fruits and vegetables.

REENGINEERING A multidisciplinary approach to making fundamental changes in how operations, activities, functions, and procedures are conducted within a multinational business. The objective of such change is to improve performance, productivity, and profitability. Reengineering should be undertaken if the benefit exceeds the cost of doing so considering money and time. Reengineering may be for the company as a whole, one or more business units, or particular geographic locations. There is a risk in reengineering of not enough or too much change. For reengineering to succeed the following should be present: employee understanding and cooperation, sound project planning and management, timely assessment, benchmarks, and realistic expectations.

RE-EXPORT **1.** Shipment of goods originally produced in the United States between different foreign countries (e.g., France to Italy). **2.** Exportation of imported products without significant or no processing.

REFINANCE (REFUNDING) **1.** Using the proceeds of a new bond issue to pay-off the principal of a maturing bond issue. **2.** Issuing stock in substitution for debt. **3.** A borrower's increasing the amount of current debt or extending the **MATURITY DATE.** **4.** Modifying a loan payment schedule such as to lower the monthly payments.

REFORMATION A judicial modification of contractual terms which the court finds did not reflect the actual intent of both parties.

REGIOCENTRISM The modification of regional markets depending upon market potential for a company's products or services. An example is a multinational company diversifying its sales base overseas such as in Europe.

REGIONAL ECONOMIC INTEGRATION An establishment of a regional **COMMON MARKET** and **FREE TRADE ZONE.** There are various forms of degrees of regional economic integration. They are: (1) the free trade zone, (2) **CUSTOMS UNION,** and (3) common market.

REGIONAL FUND A mutual fund that solely invests in a particular region in the world such as in Asia.

REGIONAL INTERNATIONAL An association of trade unions from a specific region of the world, for example, Western Europe.

REGIONAL TRADING ARRANGEMENTS A mutually beneficial trade agreement between two or more countries relaxing either their trade restrictions, TARIFFS, or employee movement. An example is the **EUROPEAN ECONOMIC COMMUNITY.**

REGISTERED BOND A bond registered in the owner's name and listed on the records of the issuer or jurisdiction as well as with the registrar. A **BEARER BOND** is an example of unregistered bonds.

REGRESSION ANALYSIS A statistical procedure for estimating mathematically the average relationship between the dependent variable and the independent variable(s). Simple regression involves only one independent variable, such as price or advertising in a demand function. Multiple regression involves two or more variables, such as both price and advertising in the prediction of sales. Regression analysis is used to do the following: (1) To find the overall association between the dependent variable and a host of explanatory variables. For example, foreign exchange rates are explained by inflation rates, interest rates, balance of payment, etc. (2) To attempt to identify the factors that influence the dependent variable. For example, factors critical in affecting sales include price, advertising, taste, and competition. (3) To use it as a basis for providing sound forecasts of the dependent variable. For example, sometimes cash collections from receivables are forecasted from credit sales of prior months since cash collections lag behind sales.

REGULATION United States authoritative body's control over the activities of multinational companies such as over pricing, manufacturing, hiring, environmental control (e.g., pollution), etc.

REINSTATEMENT **1.** To restore to a prior state or position. Examples are restoring a former business policy or practice, or dismissed employee. **2.** Restoring a terminated insurance policy because of the insured's nonpayment of a **PREMIUM**.

REINTEGRATION **1.** The process by which a company initiates automated production techniques into the manufacturing process. **2.** The process by which a company manufactures items that were previously purchased.

REINVOICING CENTER A financial subsidiary used by a multinational company that takes title to all goods sold by one corporate unit to another affiliate or to a third-party customer. The center pays the seller and in turn is paid by the buyer. The main objective of this facility is to reduce **TRANSACTION EXPOSURE** by having all home country exports billed in the home currency and then reinvoiced to each operating affiliate in that affiliate's local currency.

RELATIVE PRICE A price of a good or service compared to the price of another.

RELATIVE PRODUCTIVITIES Productivity of one country compared to the one of another country due to differences in available resources and technology. The output produced by production factors in one country may differ from the output produced by the same amount of production factors in another country.

RELEASE The relinquishment or giving up of a known right or claim by the person who claims to have ownership and given to the person against whom the claim may have been demanded or enforced.

RELOCATION ALLOWANCE A bonus paid to a worker who moves from the United States to a foreign country. It includes coverage for moving and travel costs. After the worker completes his overseas assignment, he is reimbursed as well for his return back to the United States

REMBRANDT BONDS Dutch guilder-denominated bonds issued within the Netherlands by a foreign issuer (borrower).

REMITTING BANK A bank sending a **DRAFT** to a foreign bank for collection.

REMONETIZATION 1. Reinstating an exchange medium as allowable **CURRENCY**. **2.** Supporting a currency's backing by a valuable precious metal (e.g., gold).

RENEGOTIATE The modification of the oral or written provisions of a legally binding contract or agreement.

REOPENER CLAUSE A contractual provision allowing for the reopening of an agreement before it expires provided predetermined conditions have occurred. An example is a union contract granting salary increments if the Consumer Price Index (CPI) exceeds a predetermined amount.

REORDER POINT The inventory level at which it is appropriate to replenish stock. Reorder point is calculated as follows: Reorder point = average usage per unit of lead time x lead time + safety stock First, multiply average daily (or weekly) usage by the lead time in days (or weeks) yielding the lead time demand. Then add safety stock to this to provide for the variation in lead time demand to determine the reorder point. If average usage and lead time are both certain, no safety stock is necessary and should be dropped from the formula. For example, assume that annual demand is 35,000 dozen baseballs, lead time is constant at two weeks, and there are 50 working weeks in a year. Then reorder point is 1,400 dozen = (35,000 dozen/50 weeks) x 2 weeks. Therefore, when the inventory level drops to 1,400 dozen, the new order should be placed. Suppose, however, that the store is faced with variable usage for its baseballs and requires a safety stock of 300 additional dozens to carry. Then the reorder point will be 1,400 dozen plus 300 dozen, or 1,700 dozen. *See also* **ECONOMIC ORDER QUANTITY.**

REORGANIZATION 1. To organize anew a company such as that arising from an attempt to make the business leaner and more efficient or that due to bankruptcy. The purpose is to improve the company's financial position. **2.** Changing the management structure of a business such as making organizational changes, and changes in responsibility among executives. **3.** Exchange of stock or property of one company for that of another.

REPATRIATION The transfer of assets, profits, or personnel held abroad to a home country.

REPORTING CURRENCY The currency in which the parent firm translates its own financial statements (e.g., United States dollars for a United States firm). Usually this is the parent's home currency.

REPOSSESSION The foreclosure of property by the creditor because of debtor default. Such property may then be resold.

REPUDIATION **1.** A refusal of a multinational company to conduct agreed upon activities or operations. Such refusal may or may not result in legal damages depending on the legitimacy of the action. **2.** A foreign government agency which refuses to honor an agreement with or without cause. The multinational company may carry expropriation insurance as protection for such eventuality. **3.** The disowning or disavowal of an agreement between two or more parties.

REQUISITION An order for materials, merchandise, service, or equipment. It may be ordered from another company, between departments of the same company, or ordered within the department. An example of the latter is a written request for office supplies from the supply room.

RESALE PRICE MAINTENANCE A vendor's enforcement by some action of insuring that its stated selling price of the good or service is kept by a retailer.

RESCHEDULING **1.** To schedule a function, activity, or operation for a different time than initially provided. An example is changing the date for a sales presentation because of inclement weather. **2.** Changing the due dates of debt payments such as because of a debtor's deteriorating financial condition.

RESCISSION The legal revocation, suspension, or cancellation of an agreement. An example is a clause in a contract giving a multinational company the right to cancel its relationship with a distributor who fails to sell at least 10,000 units of a product in the first year.

RESISTANCE LEVEL The upper limit of a stock or bond price within a trading range. For example, ABC stock trades within a range of $100 to $150 per share. Therefore, the resistance level is $150 per share. If the stock price goes above $150, technical investment analysts view that positively because it may mean the stock will go to even new higher prices.

RESOLUTION **1.** The resolving of something such as a problem situation facing a multinational company. An example is offering customers a discount for a minor quality defect in a product. Another example is solving a trade dispute such as by a resolution panel. **2.** A formal document evidencing some action on the part of management or the Board of Directors of a multinational company.

RESOURCE The inputs into the manufacture of products or services comprising of money, materials, time, machinery, equipment, land, etc. The manager of a multinational company must allocate resources in the most efficient and productive way.

RESOURCE-ORIENTATION PRODUCTION The manufacture of product components or elements in a foreign nation for shipment to the multinational company's country.

RESTITUTION **1.** Giving back something lost or taken away. An example is a foreign country returning to a multinational company improperly confiscated property or goods. It is returning to the status quo. **2.** Reimbursement for a loss such as an insurance company paying the insured for damage to its property. **3.** In law, a contract remedy limited to the value of performance rendered by the injured party.

RESTRAINED EXPORTERS Nations having a policy of voluntary limitations on exports of specified goods and services to particular markets.

RESTRAINT OF TRADE **1.** Attempt by either a multinational company itself or in combination with other companies to inhibit trade. An example are policies enacted to interfere with free competition in commercial transactions such as in the form of restricting production or selling price changes. This practice might be illegal because of its adverse effect on consumers. **2.** Attempt by one country or a group of countries to restrict trade with others.

RESWITCHING A company's ability to use one manufacturing technique when earnings are poor and another one when earnings are good.

RETAINAGE The funds due another for partial work already performed but still unpaid until a specific future date or until further work is completed. In fact, some contracts call for payment only after full performance. The objective is to make sure the work meets all specifications and standards before payment is made.

RETALIATION The act of returning in kind as a form of punishment for some injury caused. An example is country X increasing its tariff on imported goods from country B for a similar prior act of country B. Another example is one company making a counterclaim on another business for some unacceptable act. The retaliatory step should be in like measure or intensity.

RETALIATORY DUTY A penalty tariff charged those foreign countries deemed behaving improperly in **INTERNATIONAL TRADE.** Alternatively, trade concessions may be demanded.

RETROACTIVE **1.** An act of reverting the rule or policy to an earlier date. An example is giving back pay to employees as a result of a new contract. **2.** The restatement of prior years' financial statements to present financial information on a comparable basis. This may be required for certain accounting errors and a change in reporting entity (e.g., merger).

RETURN ON INVESTMENT (ROI) **1.** Net profit as a percentage of average capital employed in a business. It is a major financial ratio used to measure the profitability of business as a whole, a segment thereof, or of particular investment projects. **2.** For the company as a whole, net income divided by invested capital. Invested capital may be total assets or stockholders' equity.

Depending upon which is used as a measure of invested capital, there are the rate of Return On Assets (ROA) and Return On Equity (ROE). For example, assume that net income is $18,000 and total assets are $100,000. The ROA is then $18,000/$100,000=18 percent. If the stockholder's equity is $90,000, the ROE would be $18,000/$90,000=20 percent. **3.** For a segment of an organization, net operating income divided by operating assets. **4.** For **CAPITAL BUDGETING** purposes, also called simple, accounting, or unadjusted rate of return, expected future net income divided by initial (or average) investment.

RETURNED WITHOUT ACTION (RWA) An application for an export license in international trade is returned because something is missing, incorrect, or omitted. Upon correction, the application can be resubmitted.

REVALUATION A rise in the foreign exchange value of a currency that is pegged to other currencies or gold. *See also* **APPRECIATION OF THE DOLLAR**.

REVENUE WAYBILL A document listing the fee and contents associated with a shipment.

REVERSE (NEGATIVE) LEVERAGE When a multinational company earns a rate of return less than the interest cost to borrow resulting in lower profitability.

REVERSE PREFERENCES A developing country's relaxing of trade restrictions and lower import duties to selected industrialized countries to promote trade with them. In so doing, the developing country hopes to obtain economic and/or technological advantages.

REVERSION The providing of an interest or right in something at a later date. It is going back to a former state or practice.

REVOCATION **1.** The cancellation of a contract, agreement, or instrument. **2.** The termination of an offer. **3.** The withdrawing or repealing an act.

REVOCABLE LETTER OF CREDIT A **LETTER OF CREDIT** subject to possible recall or amendment at the option of the applicant, without the approval of the **BENEFICIARY**. Neither the issuing bank nor the advising and paying bank guarantees payment.

REVOLVING CREDIT A credit line with a financial institution that a multinational company may use repeatedly up to a maximum amount over a specified time period. As part of the loan is paid, the amount of repayment may be borrowed again under the contractual understanding. A bank commitment fee will typically be required.

REVOLVING LETTER OF CREDIT A **LETTER OF CREDIT** which includes a provision for reinstating its face value after being drawn under within a stated period of time. This kind of credit facilitates the financing of ongoing regular purchases.

RIDER **1.** An addition or amendment to a document such as to an insurance policy stipulating changes in coverage. **2.** A multinational company, typically a relatively unknown one in the international market, that sells its product along with the product of a well known established multinational company, overseas. By so doing, the small multinational company is able to improve its foreign sales and obtain some recognition in foreign markets. *See also* **ATTACHMENT; ENDORSEMENT.**

RIGHT OF REDEMPTION The right to recover property that was transferred because of a lien or foreclosed mortgage by paying the delinquent debt.

RINGGIT Malaysia's currency.

RISK ANALYSIS AND MANAGEMENT An appraisal and measurement of the risks to which a multinational company is subject. There exists risk in basic operations such as overdependence on a few key employees, unreliable suppliers, and militant union. **POLITICAL RISK** applies to foreign operations and governmental regulation. Multinational companies have risk exposure related to repatriation of funds, currency fluctuations, and local customs and regulations. Operations in politically and economically unstable foreign regions can cause major problems. Multinational companies reliant on government contracts and subsidies have less stability and vulnerability to changing political whims of legislators. An unfriendly regulatory government body may also result in difficulties. Social risk such as discrimination cases may result in significant losses. Multinational companies have greater operating risk when their product lines or services are susceptible to changes in the weather. Inadequate insurance coverage will result in huge losses. A multinational company's risk exposure can be reduced through **DIVERSIFICATION** and insurance protection.

RISK PREMIUM **1.** The amount by which the required return on an asset or security exceeds the risk-free rate, r_f. In terms of the **CAPITAL ASSET PRICING MODEL,** it can be expressed as $b(r_m - r_f)$, where b is the security's **BETA COEFFICIENT,** a measure of **SYSTEMATIC RISK,** and r_m is the required return on the market portfolio. The risk premium is the additional return required to compensate investors for assuming a given level of risk. The higher this **PREMIUM,** the more risky the security and vice versa. **2.** The difference in the expected future spot rate versus forward rate for a currency.

RISK-FREE RATE The interest rate that would exist on a riskless security if no inflation were expected, and it may be thought of as a rate of interest on short-term United States Treasury securities in an inflation free world.

ROI. *See* **RETURN ON INVESTMENT.**

ROLE PLAYING An exercise in which managers or employees of a multinational company set out different scenarios of an event or situation as a basis to predict real life. It is a simulated environment for instructional purposes.

ROLLOVER 1. A bank's permission to a borrower (e.g., multinational company, foreign country) to postpone a principal payment on the loan. A refinancing arrangement is often involved. Footnote disclosure should be made of such an occurrence by both lender and borrower. 2. Putting matured funds (e.g., bond, certificate of deposit) into a new bond or certificate of deposit.

ROS. *See* **RUN OF SCHEDULE.**

RUBLE Soviet Union's currency.

RULES OF ORIGIN Guidelines in determining the initiating country in which imported products come from such as to set appropriate tariffs or barriers to entry. For example, raw materials from a hostile foreign country may have significant import restrictions by the receiving country.

RUN OF SCHEDULE (ROS) Media advertisement for a product or service when the television or radio station deems suitable to its schedule. Rates are usually lower under this arrangement.

RUPEE Monetary unit of India, Maldives, Mauritius, Nepal, Pakistan, Seychelles, and Sri Lanka.

RUPIAH Indonesia's currency.

RWA. *See* **RETURNED WITHOUT ACTION.**

S

SA. *See* **SOCIEDAD ATINITTIA; SOCIETE ANONYME.**

SACI. *See* **SOCIEDAD ANONIMA DE CAPITAL E INDUSTRIA**

SAFETY MARGIN The amount to which actual sales exceed break-even sales. If break-even units are 10,000 and actual units are 12,000, there is a safety margin of 2,000 units. This means sales may go down by 2,000 units before the multinational company experiences a loss.

SALE 1. The transfer with compensation of products, services, real property, securities, etc. from a seller to a buyer. Consideration may be in the form of cash, cash equivalent, or other property. Revenue is recognized at the time of sale. A conditional sale depends on the performance of some condition before the final sale may be consummated. Some sales are subject to approval by the buyer of the merchandise otherwise the goods are to be returned. **2.** A retailer's discounting of the selling price to promote sales of inventory especially if cash is needed.

SALE AND LEASEBACK The sale of property to another (usually a finance or leasing company) and then leasing it back. It may be done when the initial owner is in need of cash. Any gain or loss on the sale is deferred and amortized in proportion to the amortization expense of the leased asset.

SALES COMMISSION The fee paid to a salesperson or broker for a purchase of merchandise, services, securities, or property. The **COMMISSION** may be a percentage of the purchase price or a flat fee. The percentage sales charge may decrease as the amount paid increases.

SALES EFFECTIVENESS TEST A measurement method and study to determine a multinational company's ability to successfully promote the sale of a specific or group of products and services. A common measure is market share by geographic area and type of customer (e.g., class, size, age).

SALES INCENTIVE A bonus in the form of cash or other benefit (e.g., property) given to a salesperson for the actual sale of goods or services beyond the quota established. It is designed to stimulate business either for all products or specific ones such as slow moving items.

SALES PORTFOLIO A pamphlet containing sales information such as selling prices, discount rates, and warranties used by salespeople.

SALES REPRESENTATIVE An agent authorized to act to sell a product or service on behalf of a multinational company.

SAMPLING 1. The extracting of a representative statistical number of items or units from a population for testing purposes. Examples are randomly selecting units of a product to evaluate its quality, and appraising a small group of consumers representative of a larger group to test the demand for a new product. **2.** The promotion of a new product by offering samples for free or at a minimal price.

SAMURAI BONDS Yen-denominated bonds issued within Japan by a foreign borrower. This contrasts with **SHOGUN BONDS.**

SANCTION 1. To approve or confirm some act. **2.** To punish an individual or business for some infraction such as a multinational company's violation of an **INTERNATIONAL TRADE AGREEMENT. 3.** To boycott.

SARL. *See* **SOCIETA A RESPONSABILITA LIMITADA; SOCIETE A RESPONS-ABILITE LIMITEE.**

SBU. *See* **STRATEGIC BUSINESS UNIT.**

SCALAGE An allowance in percentage terms of weight for merchandise having some problem (e.g., shrinkage, defect). For example, a leaky product may call for a 10 percent reduction in weight.

SCALE ECONOMIES IN ADVERTISING The situation in which the incremental costs of each unit of advertising expenditure are falling. This occurs where fixed costs of advertising can be spread over an increasingly large total market.

SCALE ECONOMIES IN DISTRIBUTION Cost reductions attained by delivering large quantities of goods, thereby lowering the unit shipping costs relative to the competition that distribute less quantities.

SCALE ECONOMIES IN FINANCING The reduction in unit cost achieved by borrowing large amounts of money at lower financing cost than charged to borrowers of smaller amounts.

SCALE ECONOMIES IN PRODUCTION Simply called economies of scale, cost reductions gained by a large size of production. When large-scale output is achieved, per unit cost usually declines. The major component of this phenomenon is the ability to spread fixed costs over a large volume.

SCALE ECONOMIES IN PURCHASING Cost reductions resulting from volume buying. The per unit cost goes down due to price breaks or quantity discounts.

SCARCE RESOURCES Resources in limited supply such as oil during an oil embargo.

SCHEDULE **1.** A list of items, events, activities, details, and times for planning purposes. **2.** A priority or ranking of items. **3.** An accounting or financial workpaper. **4.** A supporting documentation or analysis for a number presented in a multinational company's financial statements.

SCHILLING Austria's currency.

SCIENTIFIC TARIFF The imposition of a protective fee on imported goods so as to make them more expensive to help the sales of the domestic industry. The objective is to put the domestic companies at a competitive advantage.

S&D TREATMENT. *See* **SPECIAL AND DIFFERENTIAL TREATMENT.**

S/D-B/L. *See* **SIGHT DRAFT AND BILL OF LADING ATTACHED.**

SDRs. *See* **SPECIAL DRAWING RIGHTS.**

SEASONAL ADJUSTMENT **1.** The adjustment made by a businessperson in evaluating or forecasting a multinational company's operational or financial performance or activities. **2.** Statistical approach in a time series to eliminate the effect of seasonal variation in a model.

SEASONAL FACTORY A factory that can deal with large fluctuations in product demand, employment, and capacity usage over the year (e.g., at Christmas and Thanksgiving periods).

SEASONALITY Product or service demand depends on the season of the year. It applies to variability in business activity occurring on a regular basis such as due to weather conditions or holidays. Examples are stronger demand for bathing suits during the summer months and strong demand for toys before Christmas.

SEC. *See* **SECURITIES AND EXCHANGE COMMISSION.**

SECOND WORLD The communist-bloc countries, primarily members of the Soviet bloc. *See also* **COMECON.**

SECONDARY BOYCOTT A refusal to do business with company X because it is doing business with company Y or a specific foreign country which is subject to the primary (original) boycott. For example, the United States passed a law in 1996 to abstain from doing business with any foreign country (e.g., French) doing business with a terrorist nation. Another example is individuals refusing to buy the products of a company that uses as its supplier one subject to a boycott. A final example is union members refusing to buy the merchandise or services of a company having a **JOINT VENTURE** with the employer.

SECONDARY DISTRIBUTION An additional stock offering through investment bankers for a multinational company that already has issued the same type of stock to the public. It is usually in the form of a block sale.

SECONDARY MARKET **1.** Market for resale of products or services. **2.** Market where previously issued securities (second hand securities) are traded between investors. Examples are stock exchanges and the **OVER-THE-COUNTER MARKET.**

SECONDARY PARTY A third party who is legally responsible for a debt of the debtor if there is nonpayment to the creditor.

SECTOR **1.** A specific group of stocks, typically by industry. An example is stocks of pharmaceutical companies. Investors may rotate from one sector to another depending on the trend in stock prices. **2.** A part of the economy (e.g., public sector).

SECTOR RECIPROCITY The easing of a country's tariff structure or trade restrictions in reciprocation of the easing of another country's import policies. It may apply to all items of trade between the countries or only to selected groups (e.g., electronics).

SECTORAL TRADE AGREEMENT An **INTERNATIONAL TRADE** arrangement for United States and foreign companies within the same industry.

SECURED BOND A bond backed up by **COLLATERAL**.

SECTION 482 The set of United States Treasury regulations governing transfer prices.

SECURITIZATION 1. The process of converting nonmarketable financial assets such as loans or mortgages into negotiable securities issued in the formal **CAPITAL MARKETS. 2.** The development of **FINANCIAL MARKETS** for a variety of new negotiable instruments so that borrowers and lenders are matched up.

SECURITY MARKET LINE (SML) The line in a graph that shows the relationship between risk as measured by beta and the required rate of return for individual securities. The equation is: Required return on a stock = **RISK-FREE RATE** + Stock's BETA x market risk premium.

SECURITY RISK 1. The risk associated with a financial instrument (e.g., stock, bond). For example, there is always uncertainty of a **STOCK MARKET** correction occurring lowering the price of a stock. **2.** The risk that **COLLATERAL** given for a loan will decrease in value because of adverse market conditions.

SEED MONEY Money invested or lent to a new company. There is high risk to such an equity interest or loan. The funds may be to assist in the startup phase until more permanent financing may be obtained.

SEGMENT MARGIN Profit margin of a subunit (e.g., subsidiary, affiliate, branch, division, department) of a multinational company.

SEGMENTATION STRATEGY 1. In marketing, a producer's introduction of different varieties of the same basic product under the same name so as to obtain recognition for it in consumers' minds. **2.** Concentrating advertising for a product or service in one targeted market segment. An example is promoting a new line of luxury cars to a wealthy consumer group.

SEGREGATION OF DUTIES The separation of responsibilities among employees for related tasks as an internal control measure. For example, the person handling the financial records should be different from the one having physical custody over the property. Segregation of functions prevents errors, theft, and other problems. The one approving payment on a bill should not write out the check. The one preparing the bank reconciliation should not be handling the cash.

SELECTIVE DISTRIBUTION A manufacturer's product distribution to selective wholesalers or retailers based on their agreeing to conform to specified manufacturer requirements (e.g., minimum price support, annual volume of purchases).

SELF-INSURANCE A multinational company bears the risk itself against losses due to theft, fire, flood, or other cause. This policy is only recommended for a financially strong company. A special fund is usually set up in which periodic deposits are made into. The purpose of self-insurance is to save on insurance costs.

SELF-SUSTAINED GROWTH A country's developmental state in which it can sustain economic growth without foreign assistance.

SELL-IN A multinational company's attempt to stimulate retailers to carry their product line such as through discounted prices and "free" advertising.

SELLER'S MARKET A market situation in which demand exceeds supply. In this situation, the seller has the upperhand and can charge a higher price and/or terms. This usually occurs in a certain sector of the economy (e.g., real estate market in California).

SELLING CLIMAX A sudden drastic decline in stock prices coupled with very significant demand due to investor panic to sell. After the climax, a buying opportunity may exist because of depressed prices. A graph illustrating a selling climax follows:

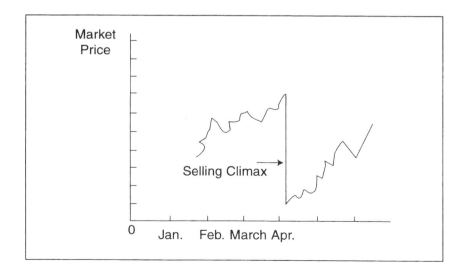

SELLING SHORT Selling something (e.g., stocks, foreign currencies) that a party does not own. This is for future delivery in anticipation of a drop in its price. This tactic is also used to hedge a **CURRENCY RISK.**

SELL-OFF The sale of property or securities experiencing a significant declining trend in prices before further losses are incurred.

SENIOR SECURITY A security having priority over other securities in the event of a company's bankruptcy or in the distribution of earnings. For example, bonds come before stock.

SENSITIVE PRODUCTS Domestic goods considered very susceptible to competition from foreign imports. An example is United States produced electronic equipment that faces stiff competition from Japanese produced products.

SEQUENTIAL ENTRY STRATEGY A sequence of market entry strategies used by **MULTINATIONAL CORPORATIONS** that involves relatively inexpensive steps such as exports or licensing and a development into joint venture ownership and/or full subsidiary ownership.

SEQUESTRATION The seizure of property and possessing it until earnings have covered the obligation owed.

SERVICES Actions of people transacted for compensation such as repairmen, accountants, and consultants.

SETOFF A counterclaim to offset in full or partially what is owed by a business to another or the the government. For example, if company A owes company B damages of $200,000 because of a product deficiency but in turn company B owes company A $150,000 for the failure to render quality services, the net due company B is $50,000.

SETTLEMENT A resolution through negotiation of a dispute between two parties such as an out-of-court settlement of a lawsuit.

SETTLEMENT DATE **1.** The date an order to buy or sell a stock or bond must be settled either by paying for the stock bought or delivering the stock sold and receiving the cash proceeds. The settlement date is 3 business days after the trade date. However, for options there is a one-day settlement date. **2.** The date a deed to real estate is transferred.

SEVEN SISTERS Also called the **MAJOR MULTINATIONALS,** the late 1980s world's giant oil companies, including Royal Dutch Shell, Exxon, Mobil, British Petroleum, Texaco, Chevron (Socal), and Amoco.

SEVERABLE CONTRACT A contract considered divisible into several independent agreements so the breach of one agreement does not negate the entire contract. Thus, damages only apply to that part actually breached.

SHAKEOUT **1.** An adverse financial environment causing marginal companies to go out of business. **2.** A sudden, drastic decline in securities prices forcing speculative investors to sell their securities at significant loss.

SHAKEUP A drastic change within a multinational company affecting managers and/or employees such as to result in cost savings through a downsizing program or to change corporate policies to achieve greater efficiencies. A lot of employee anxiety may result therefrom.

SHARK REPELLENT A company's attempt through some means to prevent being taken over by another company.

SHEKEL Israel's currency.

SHELTER ALLOWANCE A reimbursement to employees for their extra housing costs due to working in a foreign country compared to the United States

SHILLING Monetary unit of Kenya, Somalia, Tanzania, and Uganda.

SHIPMENT **1.** The cargo being transported by a common carrier. **2.** Merchandise sent from a manufacturer to a retailer.

SHIPPER'S EXPORT DECLARATION. *See* **EXPORT DECLARATION.**

SHIPPING TOLERANCES The maximum increase in physical or dollar amounts that may be shipped and still conform to the government approved export license.

SHOGUN BONDS Foreign currency-denominated bonds issued within Japan by Japanese corporations. This contrasts with **SAMURAI BONDS.**

SHORT LIFE CYCLE Merchandise having a short commercial life because of perishability, obsolescence, or flammability.

SHORT SUPPLY Products having demand substantially exceeding supply. A country may place export restrictions on such items to assure there is not a significant drain of the goods in the domestic market to compound the problem further. An example might be petroleum.

SHORTAGE COSTS. *See* **STOCKOUT COST.**

SHORT-TERM NATIONAL FINANCIAL MARKETS Money markets in different countries, markets for short-term instruments such as bank deposits and government bills in different nations. This contrasts with **LONG-TERM NATIONAL FINANCIAL MARKETS.**

SHORTAGE The demand for a product exceeds its supply resulting in a price increase.

SHUNTO The "spring wage offensive" in Japanese characterized by coordinated collective bargaining by **ENTERPRISE UNIONS** seeking wage increases and addressing cost-of-living and industry productivity issues.

SHUTDOWN POINT The point where a company is better off financially closing down a plant, product line, or the entire business than continuing to operate it. For example, by shutting down a branch the company may lose less money than it is now.

SIBOR. *See* **SINGAPORE INTERBANK OFFERED RATE.**

SIC. *See* **STANDARD INDUSTRIAL CLASSIFICATION.**

SIGHT DRAFT A document representing an order to pay an amount of money when presented to the drawee, i.e., payment is due upon sight. During the shipment of goods, a seller may use a sight draft when he/she wants to retain title to the goods until they reach their destination and are paid for. A **DRAFT** may also be payable after a shipment is received by the buyer. *See also* **ACCEPTANCE; TIME DRAFT.**

SIGHT DRAFT AND BILL OF LADING ATTACHED (S/D-B/L)

SIMEX. *See* **SINGAPORE INTERNATIONAL MONETARY EXCHANGE.**

SIMILAR GOODS Products having similar but not identical attributes and characteristics allowing for substitution.

SIMULATION An attempt to represent a real life system via a model to determine how a change in one or more variables affect the rest of the system, also called what-if analysis. Simulation will not provide optimization except by trial and error. It will provide comparisons of alternative systems or how a particular system works under specified conditions. It is a technique used for "what-if" scenarios. The advantages of simulation are: (1) when a model has been constructed, it may be used over and over to analyze different kinds of situations; (2) it allows modeling of systems whose solutions are too complex to express by one or several mathematical relationships; (3) it requires a much lower level of mathematical skill than do optimization models; and (4) it is usually cheaper than building the actual system and testing it in operation. Financial planning models that are used to generate pro forma financial statements and help answer a variety of "what-if" questions are an example of simulation. Simulation is usually done with the help of a computer. There are many English-like financial simulation languages such as Integrated Financial Planning System (IFPS).

SINGLE-COUNTRY FUNDS Mutual funds invested in securities of a single country. Single-country funds are the most focused and therefore by far the most aggressive foreign stock funds. Almost all single-country funds are **CLOSED-END FUNDS** (exceptions are the Japan Fund and French Fund). This exaggerates their aggressiveness because single-country (and regional) closed-end funds have been known to sell at both large discounts and premiums to their **NET ASSET VALUE.**

SINKING FUND A fund set aside for periodic payments, aimed at reducing or amortizing a financial obligation. A bond with a sinking fund provision is an example. The issuer makes periodic payments to the trustee. The trustee can retire part of the issue by purchasing the bonds in the open market. The trustee can invest the cash deposited periodically in the sinking fund in income-producing securities. The objective is to accumulate investments and investment income sufficient to retire the bonds at their maturity. A sinking fund may be established for other purposes such as for plant expansion.

SITC. *See* **STANDARD INTERNATIONAL TRADE CLASSIFICATION.**

SKIMMING PRICING The initial selling price is established high so as to recover costs of development. With time, the price decreases particularly in light of competitive factors. It occurs with new production introduction so as to optimize earnings.

SKUNK WORKS
A think-tank environment found in some **MULTINATIONAL CORPORATIONS** in which researchers and scientists are encouraged to explore new projects in small teams without too much bureaucracy from the mainstream business of the company.

SLACK   1. A slow period of activity. **2.** Free time in a network representing the length of time an activity or program can be delayed without interfering with the project completion. It is considered under the **PROGRAM EVALUATION AND REVIEW TECHNIQUE. 3.** Available time before the next stage of a production run.

SLACK MARKET There is an inactive market for securities and property with high spreads between bid and ask quotes. *See also* **TIGHT MARKET.**

SLIDING SCALE TARIFF A customs fee having the rate change depending on the value of the imported item. As prices decrease, so does the rate.

SLUMP A sudden decline in activity or performance for the economy as a whole or segment thereof, or in manufacturing activity.

SML. *See* SECURITY MARKET LINE.

SNAKE The agreement of many West European nations to stabilize their currencies by capping their exchange rates relative to the United States dollar to a range of 2.25 percent.

SOCIAL BENEFIT/COST RATIO The ratio of the social benefits to the social costs for all inputs for a project. Social benefits accrue to the society as a result of production or consumption, while social costs are the costs to the society as a result of activities performed by others (e.g., the costs of cleaning the water and air polluted by a manufacturing firm). If the ratio is above one, the project should be undertaken, from the host country's perspective.

SOCIAL DARWINISM "Survival of the fittest," which is Darwin' theory adaptation to the society in a societal context.

SOCIAL DUMPING A multinational company switching all or some of its operations and labor force from a country having stricter regulations and higher salary rates to a country with less restrictions and lower wage rates. A financially troubled company may do this to reduce its overall costs. A company with labor problems may also be prompted to do so.

SOCIALISM An economy partly controlled by the government such as when essential industries are government owned and operated. Nonessential industries may be privately owned. Socialism differs from communism in that the latter has prices, production, and distribution set only be government dictate for all industries.

SOCIEDAD ANONIMA DE CAPITAL E INDUSTRIA Spanish term for company of capital and industry.

SOCIEDAD ATINITTIA Spanish term meaning corporation. Societe Anonyme (French). For example, "S.A." must follow the firm name, indicating that it is a corporation.

SOCIETA A RESPONSABILITA LIMITADA Italian term for company with limited liability. Societe a Respotisabilite Limitee (French).

SOCIETAL CULTURE The totality of behavior patterns, values, norms, and institutions that are unique to a country, region, community, or society.

SOCIETE A RESPONSABILITE LIMITEE French term for company with limited liability.

SOCIETE ANONYME French term meaning corporation. For example, "S.A." must follow the firm name, indicating that it is a corporation.

SOCIETE DE PERSONNES A RESPONSABILITE LIMITEE Belgian term for company of persons with limited liability.

SOCIETE PER AZIONI (SPA) Italian term for public corporation. It must have at least two shareholders at formation; after formation, the requirement is reduced to one shareholder.

SOCIETY FOR WORLDWIDE INTERBANK FINANCIAL TELECOMMUNICATIONS (SWIFT) A dedicated computer **NETWORK** providing funds transfer messages between over 900 member banks around the world.

SOFT GOODS Products that feel soft and are nondurable. An example is sheets and towels.

SOFT MARKET A situation where supply exceeds demand for a product, service, property, or securities. It may be characterized by one or more of the following: significant decline, low trading activity, and increasing spreads between bid-ask prices.

SOLE PROPRIETORSHIP An unincorporated business with one owner having all the net worth. If the business goes bankrupt, the owner is personally liable for the debts remaining.

SOLVENCY The ability of a multinational company to pay its long-term obligations when due out of noncurrent assets. Consideration is given to the company's debt relative to its stockholders' equity, interest coverage, and earning power.

SOURCE ANALYSIS An appraisal of the profitability, growth, risk, etc., associated with the different phases of a multinational company's business. The purposes of the evaluation are to identify problem areas and take corrective action, or to take further advantage of positive situations and markets.

SOURCING POLICY The strategy set forth by a multinational company for the buying of raw materials, supplies, and components including the type and location of suppliers.

SOVEREIGN RISK. *See* **POLITICAL RISK.**

SOVEREIGNTY Also called national sovereignty, the power of each nation-state over the land within its border and over the people and business activities within its territory. It means control over the national economy. The threat to sovereignty reflects considerations over and above the sum of the net benefits or costs of individual international business activities.

SOVIET BLOC. *See* **COUNCIL FOR MUTUAL ECONOMIC ASSISTANCE.**

S&P500 STOCK COMPOSITE INDEX. *See* **STANDARD & POOR'S 500 STOCK COMPOSITE INDEX.**

SPA. *See* **SOCIETE PER AZIONI.**

SPAN OF CONTROL The number of employees that a supervisor can realistically and appropriately supervise. This worker number depends on several factors such as employees' education and experience, type of task to be performed, quality of resources provided, and geographic dispersion.

SPECIAL AND DIFFERENTIAL (S&D) TREATMENT Special consideration should be given to exports from developing countries to improve their economic and financial base such as lower or no **TARIFFS** and easing of **TRADE BARRIERS.**

SPECIAL BUYER CREDIT LIMIT A credit insurance ceiling for a particular buyer to cover the merchandise delivered by an exporter.

SPECIAL DRAWING RIGHTS (SDRs) A new form of international reserve assets, created by the **INTERNATIONAL MONETARY FUND (IMF)** in 1967. Its value is based on a weighted basket of five currencies: United States dollar, West German Mark, U.K Sterling, French Franc, and Japanese Yen. Unlike gold, SDRs have no tangible life of their own and take the form of bookkeeping entries in a special account managed by the IMF. They are used as the instruments for financing **INTERNATIONAL TRADE.**

SPECIAL MARKING Unique labeling of specified imported products so as to identify them for special attention or treatment such as by a particular government agency. An example is a marking of an imported agricultural product from Africa that the United States Department of Agriculture is concerned might cause a health problem.

SPECIAL PURCHASE A customer's purchase of merchandise at a lower than normal price such as when the product has some minor defect.

SPECIALIZED INTERNATIONAL A unit of an intergovernmental agency representing labor's interests and views within that agency.

SPECIALTY ADVERTISING A promotion strategy using novelties such as inscribed pens, flags, and calendars.

SPECIALTY GOODS Products appealing to selective customers such as IBM Think Pads.

SPECIALTY SELLING Products or services not usually sold in retail stores such as very expensive luxury furniture.

SPECIFIC DUTY **1.** A definite or explicit responsibility or requirement of an entity or person. For example, a multinational chemical company is obligated to take health precautions to safeguard factory workers. **2.** A particular, clearly stated governmental fee charged on specific imported goods.

SPECIFIC PERFORMANCE A judicial determination that the party who breached a contract must perform his contractual duties under it. This occurs only when a monetary damage or equitable remedy other than performance is not possible. An example is a specific piece of land the company believes is essential to its operations.

SPECIFICATION The stating of specific information such as about an order of merchandise or service (e.g., size, quality, delivery date).

SPECULATION The risk taken deliberately. Foreign exchange markets-as is also true of commodity, interest futures, and other markets-provide a mechanism for outright speculation. The speculator undertakes high risk in an attempt to earn a higher rate of return.

SPILLOVER BENEFITS The positive impact an activity or situation has on others indirectly involved. An example is the increased overseas sales of a multinational company in a foreign country in which either the foreign competitor is on strike or another problem exists (e.g., the meat scare in England in 1996).

SPIN-OFF The reorganization of a business in which the original firm transfers some of its assets to a newly formed one (usually a former subsidiary or division). The original company receives all of the issued stocks as consideration for the transfer.

SPLINTERED AUTHORITY Managers of business segments share their responsibilities in decision making.

SPLIT PAY The employee's salary for working overseas is in both United States dollars and in the foreign currency (e.g., French francs).

SPORADIC DUMPING The selling of temporarily surplus products overseas at prices less than in the United States.

SPOT RATE Also called **CASH RATE,** the exchange rate of one currency for another for immediate delivery. *See also* **EFFECTIVE EXCHANGE RATE.**

SPOT TRANSACTION Also called **CASH TRANSACTION.** Transaction involving the purchase and sale of commodities, currency, and financial instruments for immediate delivery. This contrasts with a forward transaction which provides the delivery at a future date.

SPRL. *See* **SOCIETE DE PERSONNES A RESPONSABILITE LIMITEE.**

SPREAD **1.** The difference between the bid (offer to buy) and ask (offer to sell) price of a financial security (e.g., stock), **COMMODITY,** or foreign exchange. For example, if XYZ stock has a bid price of $20 and an ask price of $21, the buyer would have to pay $21 per share and the seller would receive $20 per share. The spread of $1 per share goes to the dealer. The spread usually becomes wider with less volume traded in the security. **2.** The difference in price arising from **ARBI-TRAGE** of a security or a currency exchange rate in different markets. **3.** The difference between the low and high prices of a stock or **BOND** for a stated time period (e.g., one quarter). **4.** The difference between the rate of return earned and the cost of financing. **5.** The difference in yields of similar quality bonds with a different **MATURITY DATE. 6.** The difference in prices from combining a **CALL** option and **PUT** option in the same security. **7.** The difference between delivery months for a **FUTURES** contract in a **COMMODITY** in a market. **8.** The amount received as compensation by UNDERWRITERS representing the difference to the issuing company on a new issue of a security (e.g., $95 per share) and the amount paid by the public ($100 per share).

SQUARE POSITION 1. A position in foreign exchange that is always in balance, neither long nor short. 2. A situation in which sales and buys of an identical currency are equal so the exchange broker's position is in balance.

SQUEEZE 1. A multinational company is unable to pass on all or part of its increased costs to its customers in the form of higher selling prices. **2.** Investors who have sold short securities are forced to cover their positions ("short squeeze") to avoid larger losses because the prices of those securities are rising rather than falling. **3.** Tight money period resulting in higher interest rates. **4.** Exerting pressure on someone to do something.

STABILIZATION 1. An underwriter or **UNDERWRITERS** of a security enters into transactions designed to prevent a fall in its stock price by supporting it. **2.** A country's buying and selling of its currency to stabilize its exchange value. **3.** A nation's attempt to moderate the business cycle by changing aggregate demand and aggregate supply, or fiscal and monetary policies.

STAGFLATION Combination of **STAGNATION** and **INFLATION.** It is the existence of high unemployment and **RECESSION** and high rates of inflation at the same time.

STAGNATION A situation where output does not grow over a period of time. Such an economy is in a prolonged slump of the **BUSINESS CYCLE.**

STANDARD A commonly recognized and typical rule, model, guideline, manufacturing method, productivity, product or service characteristics, packaging, advertising, or labeling. It may be stipulated by an authoritative body in appraising performance or quality.

STANDARD ADVERTISING REGISTER The directories of advertisers and advertising agencies. Managers of multinational companies should refer to them in deciding how to best promote their products and services.

STANDARD COST A predetermined expected ("should be") cost for manufacturing a product or rendering a service. It is a targeted cost. If actual cost exceeds standard cost, an unfavorable variance arises that needs to be investigated and any corrective action taken. Variance analysis may be done by division, department, responsibility unit (e.g., cost center), product, service, customer, geographic area, etc. Standards may be derived in several ways such as time studies assessing normal operations.

STANDARD INDUSTRIAL CLASSIFICATION (SIC) A categorization norm applying to United States industry financial and statistical data related to goods and services. Numerical coding for industries ranges from two digits to seven digits.

STANDARD INTERNATIONAL TRADE CLASSIFICATION (SITC) U. S. Bureau of the Census categorization to describe and account for international trade by multinational companies. Companies are identified by industry.

STANDARD & POOR'S 500 (S&P 500) STOCK COMPOSITE INDEX The 500 Stock Composite Index computed by Standard & Poor's. It is different from the **DOW JONES INDUSTRIAL AVERAGE (DJIA)** in several respects. First, it is value-weighted, not priced-weighted. The index, thus, considers not only the price of a stock but also the number of outstanding shares. It is based on the aggregated market value of the stock, i.e., price times the number of shares. A benefit of the index over the DJIA is that **STOCK SPLITS** and **STOCK DIVIDENDS** do not have an impact on the index value. A drawback is that large capitalization stocks — those with a large number of shares outstanding — significantly influence the index value. The S&P 500 consists of four separate indices: the 400 industrials, the 40 utilities, the 20 transportation, and the 40 financial. It is used as a broad measure of market direction. These indices are also frequently used as proxies for market return when computing the **SYSTEMATIC RISK** measure (BETA) of individual stocks and portfolios. The S&P500 Stock Index, especially, is one of the United States Department of Commerce's 11 leading economic indicators. The purpose of the S&P 500 Stock Price Index is to portray the pattern of common stock price movement. The total market value of the S&P 500 represents nearly 90 percent of the aggregate market value of common stocks traded on the **NEW YORK STOCK EXCHANGE.** For this reason, many investors use the S&P 500 as a yardstick to help evaluate the performance of mutual funds.

STANDARD RATE A predetermined price per piece of material or per hour of labor. The expected rate is compared to the actual rate and the difference between the two is evaluated as to cause. For example, if the actual labor rate per hour is $10 and the standard labor rate per hour was $12, it may indicate less experienced workers were hired or the existence of an excess labor supply due to a poor economy.

STANDARDIZED PRODUCT A uniform good manufactured by a company to simplify the production of it so as to lower per unit cost and accomplish **ECONOMIES OF SCALE.**

STANDING ORDER The automatic reordering of merchandise on a recurring basis. Such order conforms to predetermined amounts.

STAPLE STOCK Merchandise having consistent demand and stocking over the years.

STATE DOCTRINE Government dogma or tenets expressing certain principles including foreign policy.

STATEMENT OF AFFAIRS A company's financial statements presenting assets and liabilities at their liquidation values. It is prepared by companies actually or in the process of becoming bankrupt. The Statement may also be requested for a "going concern" business to show the "worst-case" scenario using the most pessimistic figures for a company experiencing severe financial difficulties.

STATEMENT OF FINANCIAL ACCOUNTING STANDARDS (SFAS) NUMBER 52 A **FINANCIAL ACCOUNTING STANDARDS BOARD** pronouncement dictating the rules to account for foreign currency translation and transactions engaged in by multinational companies. In the translation process, a foreign subsidiary's financial statements must be first restated in accordance with United States **GENERALLY ACCEPTED ACCOUNTING PRINCIPLES** and secondly converted from the foreign currency to United States dollars. Assets and liabilities are translated at the current exchange rate at the balance sheet date. Revenue and expenses are translated at the weighted-average exchange rate for the year. The resulting translation gain or loss is presented separately in the parent company's stockholders' equity section. On the other hand, transaction gains and losses arise from changes in exchange rates between the foreign currency and the United States currency in which the transaction is expressed (e.g., a Mexican subsidiary has a receivable denominated in pesos). In effect, transaction gains and losses are produced from redeeming receivables/payables that are fixed in terms of amounts of foreign currency received/paid. Transaction gains and losses are reported separately in the income statement. A multinational company may hedge its exposure to the fluctuating **FOREIGN EXCHANGE RATE** by entering into a forward exchange contract which is an agreement to exchange at a specified future date currencies of different countries at a specified rate. Any significant changes in foreign exchange rates occurring after year-end but before the financial statements are released requires footnote disclosure.

STATIC BUDGET A budget based on one level of activity (e.g., one particular volume of sales or production). It has two characteristics: (1) it is geared toward only one level of activity; (2) actual results are compared against budgeted (standard) costs only at the original budget activity level. A **FLEXIBLE BUDGET** differs from a static budget on both scores. First, it is not geared to only one activity level, but rather, toward a range of activity. Second, actual results are not compared against budgeted costs at the original budget activity level. Managers look at what activity level was attained during a period and then turn to the flexible budget to determine what costs should have been at that actual level of activity.

STATUTORY NOTICE The time mandated by law for notice of a particular date to which something will happen. For example, a notice of an increase in tariff rates may require 30 days advance notice before its effective date.

STERILIZED INTERVENTION An interference by a third party (e.g., government) to improve or rectify a situation or dispute between contractual parties (e.g., multinational companies engaged in an international transaction).

STERLING Great Britain's currency. The monetary unit is the pound sterling.

STEVEDORE An individual or entity involved with the loading or unloading of cargo such as from a ship, airplane, or truck.

STEWARDS' COUNCIL Usually found in the United Kingdom, an elected group of labor representatives, not a union, to negotiate with management on labor agreements and workers' problems and issues.

STOCK MARKET An organized exchange where stockbrokers execute buy and sell orders of stock and other securities either on their own account or on behalf of their clients. Stock exchanges consist of physical buildings and locations where brokers, traders, market makers, et al., meet and execute buy and sell securities transactions. Among the financial instruments traded on the **NEW YORK STOCK EXCHANGE (NYSE)** are: common stock; preferred stock, bonds, notes; warrants, options; rights; etc. Examples of stock markets are the **NYSE, AMERICAN STOCK EXCHANGE,** and the Pacific Stock Exchange.

STOCKOUT COST Also called shortage costs, those costs incurred when an item is out of stock, also called stockout costs. These costs include the lost contribution margin on sales plus lost customer goodwill.

STRATEGIC BUSINESS UNIT (SBU) An operating unit in an organization that sells a distinct set of products or services to an identified group of customers in competition with a well-defined set of competitors. SBUs operate within the objectives and strategy set by top management. Within the framework, each SBU performs its own strategic management process. For example, SBUs of General Electric are aircraft engines, appliances, broadcasting, industrial, materials, power systems, technical, and capital services.

STRATEGIC CLUSTERS A multinational company physically located in proximity to its major customers or suppliers.

STRATEGIC MANAGEMENT The process by which top management determines the long-term direction and performance of the company by ensuring careful formulation, effective implementation, and continuous evaluation and improvement of the **STRATEGY.** It is concerned with analyzing and implementing the activities needed to develop, select, implement, and evaluate a firm's competitive strategy. This term is often used interchangeably with **STRATEGY AND POLICY FORMULATION, LONG-RANGE PLANNING,** and **BUSINESS POLICY.**

STRATEGIC OBJECTIVES A company's long-term goals-for example, enhance a firm's competitive superiority, achieve superior performance and growth, and improve its market value.

STRATEGIC PLANNING The long-term plan for future activities and operations, typically involving at least five years.

STRATEGY The way that a multinational company will pursue its goals, given the threats and opportunities in the environment and the resources and capabilities of the company.

STRENGTH WEAKNESS OPPORTUNITY AND THREAT (SWOT) An operating philosophy for a company.

STRENGTH WEAKNESS OPPORTUNITY AND THREAT ANALYSIS (SWOT ANALYSIS) Analysis of a company's strengths and weaknesses in light of the threats and opportunities presented by the environment. A SWOT analysis stresses that the organizational strategies must result in a proper fit between the organization's internal and external environments.

STRIKE Employees cease working so as to pressure a business to agree to labor demands in a new or existing contract. The issues may be about one or more key factors such as salary, fringe benefits, working environment, or other grievances.

STRIPPED BONDS Bonds created by stripping the coupons from a bond and selling them separately from the principal.

STRONG DOLLAR. *See* **APPRECIATION OF THE DOLLAR; REVALUATION.**

STRUCTURAL CHANGE A major modification or adjustment such as in the corporate organization of a multinational company.

STRUCTURE The set of reporting relationships among the responsible units within the organization, and the assignment of responsibilities among those units.

SUBCONTRACTING **1.** The process by which a general contractor allocates part of or the entire job on a project to a subcontractor. **2.** The process by which a manufacturer buys product components from other producers.

SUBLIMINAL ADVERTISING Sales promotion expressed so as not to be conscious. An example is a very brief statement or picture flashed during a television program.

SUBORDINATION **1.** Something of lesser importance, rank, or priority such as to an ownership interest, claim, or lien. **2.** Junior debt holders have a claim on a multinational company's assets after senior debt holders.

SUBPART F A special category of foreign "unearned" income, as defined in the United States tax code, that under certain conditions is currently taxed by the **INTERNAL REVENUE SERVICE** whether or not it is remitted back to the United States.

SUBPART F INCOME Income received from a **FOREIGN-BASED COMPANY.** *See also* **SUBPART F.**

SUBROGATION The substitution of one party for another obligated to act or make payment. An example is an insurance company paying citizens for injury due to accidents caused by the insured company's delivery trucks.

SUBSIDIARY A company in which a controlling interest in its stock is held by another company, called the parent company. After acquisition, the parent company accounts for its investment in the subsidiary company including intercompany eliminations such as for intercompany sales and purchases, and receivables and payables. *See also* **CONSOLIDATION.**

SUBSIDIES The financial assistance given directly or indirectly by a government to specified individuals, businesses, or industries. The subsidy may be in the form of direct grants, tax credits, low-cost financing, or other tax relief. The goal is to promote the subsistence, growth, or earnings of the affected parties such as to develop a new industry. An example is a low interest loan or lower taxes to a domestic industry so that it can be more competitive in the international market. Another example is the economic stimulus package to the disaster stricken agricultural industry.

SUBSTANTIAL SUPPLIER A major supplier of products or services to a multinational company. For example, a significant source of airplanes to American Airlines is Boeing.

SUCRE Ecuador's currency.

SUE AND LABOR PROVISION A stipulation in a marine insurance contract giving the one insured the right to be reimbursed for reasonable costs incurred so as to minimize exposure prior to obtaining the approval of the insurer for that loss.

SUNSET INDUSTRY An older and established industry near the end of its life cycle for the good or service. An example are typewriter manufacturers giving way to computer technology.

SUPERIMPOSED CLAUSE A reference on a bill of lading as to some defect in the shipment.

SUPPLIER CREDIT CAPITAL GUARANTEES. *See* **EXPORT-IMPORT BANK.**

SUPPLIER CREDITS An exporter's financing applicable to a bank's purchasing of notes deferred in payment to the exporter by a foreign buyer.

SUPPLY ACCESS An importer is assured of obtaining equal and reasonable volume and prices of imported goods from exporters without undue restrictions.

SUPPLY-SIDE ECONOMICS Aims at achieving efficiency through economic policies and measures designed to stimulate production, unlike **DEMAND-SIDE ECONOMICS** which focuses on regulating aggregate demand. Supply-side economics relies heavily on the direct use of incentives. For example, reductions in marginal tax rates - the taxes paid on the last dollar of taxable income-provide direct incentives to work, save, and invest, thereby stimulating aggregate supply rather than aggregate demand. Tight monetary control to curb inflation is another principal prescription of supply-side economics.

SUPPORT LEVEL The lowest price based on previous experience a particular security or an overall market index (e.g., Standard and Poor's 500) is expected to fall to. If the security goes down to the support level, it is a significant bearish indicator. A diagram follows:

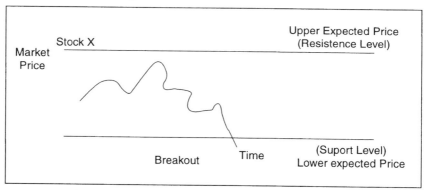

SURCHARGE The extra amount added to something such as on a fee, tax, or cost of an important product. It is typically an incremental amount on a customary or normal charge. An example is a surtax of 10 percent of the tax owed.

SURETY BOND **1.** An individual or entity agreeing to be held accountable in the event of another's contractual duties (e.g., performance, obligations). **2.** A contractual assurance to United States customs that full payment will be made of any **TARIFFS** and duties.

SURVEY **1.** To evaluate or consider something such as by obtaining information about a new product. **2.** To describe a property's measurements, attributes, and boundaries. Examples are appraising the physical condition of land to build a structure or examining a shipping vehicle as to suitability for a particular cargo.

SURVEY OF CURRENT BUSINESS A publication of the Bureau of Economic Analysis of the **UNITED STATES DEPARTMENT OF COMMERCE,** which is published monthly and contains monthly and quarterly raw economic data. It presents a monthly update and evaluation of the business situation, analyzing such data as Gross National Product, business inventories, personal consumption, fixed investment, exports, labor market statistics, financial data, and much more. For example, if personal consumption expenditures are broken down into subcategories, one would find expenditures on durable goods such as motor vehicles, parts, furniture, and equipment; nondurables would show food, energy, clothing, and shoes. Note: The survey can be extremely helpful for industry analysis as it breaks down data into basic industries. For example, data on inventory, new plant and equipment, production, and more can be found on such specific industries as coal, tobacco, chemicals, leather products, furniture, and paper. Even within industries such as lumber, production statistics can be found on hardwoods and softwoods right down to Douglas fir trees, Southern pine, and Western pine.

SUSHI BONDS EURODOLLARS, or other non-yen denominated, bonds issued by a Japanese company for sale to Japanese investors.

SUSPENSE ACCOUNT 1. Temporary account (i.e., not included in the financial statements) for recording part of a transaction, such as those involving receipts and payments, before final analysis or identification of that transaction. **2.** Entering an incomplete transaction awaiting final disposition (e.g., adjustment to price) such as in the case of a warranty claim.

SWAP 1. The exchange of assets or payments. It is a simultaneous purchase and sale of a given amount of securities, with the purchase being effected at once and the sale back to the same party to be carried out at a price agreed upon today but to be completed at a specified future date. Swaps include **INTEREST RATE SWAPS, CURRENCY SWAPS,** and **CREDIT SWAPS.** Interest rate swaps typically involve exchanging fixed interest payments for floating interest payments. Currency swaps is the exchange of one currency into another at an agreed rate and a reversal of that exchange at the same rate at the end of the swap contract period. **2.** A barter of goods or services.

SWAP RATE A forward foreign exchange quotation expressed in terms of the number of points by which the forward rate differs from the SPOT RATE.

SWEETENER Making a security more attractive to investors by adding to it some feature. An example is offering a stock warrant with a bond.

SWIFT. *See* **SOCIETY FOR WORLDWIDE INTERBANK FINANCIAL TELECOMMUNICATIONS.**

SWITCH TRADING In **INTERNATIONAL TRADE,** the import or export of merchandise via an **INTERMEDIARY** country. The intermediary country is not in fact the seller or the buyer. This arrangement may occur when the country to which the product is destined has insufficient United States dollars (e.g., Russia) and the intermediary country (e.g., Germany) has sufficient United States dollars and offers its services (often for a fee) to accept the destination country's currency as payment for the goods or services.

SWOT. *See* **STRENGTH WEAKNESS OPPORTUNITY AND THREAT.**

SWOT ANALYSIS. *See* **STRENGTH WEAKNESS OPPORTUNITY AND THREAT ANALYSIS.**

SYNDICATE 1. Temporary association of investment bankers for the purpose of selling securities of multinational companies. One investment banker in the group, typically the originating house, is selected to manage the syndicate. Most syndicates are of the undivided account type in which each member is liable for unsold securities up to the amount of its percentage participation regardless of the number of securities that investment banker has sold. Members typically share profits proportionately. **2.** Association of companies or individuals to engage in a **JOINT VENTURE** such as a project or new product line so as to obtain greater talents, efficiencies, synergy, cost savings, or **DIVERSIFICATION** to reduce risk.

SYNDICATED LOAN A big size loan made by a group of banks to a large multi-national corporation or government. It allows the group to spread the risk of loan default.

SYNERGY The combination of two or more separate businesses results in more than the total effect of the combining entities. For example, $1 + 1 = 2 \ 1/2$. An example is a business combination of two publishing companies that results in cost savings by downsizing and eliminating duplication.

SYSTEMATIC RISK A risk that results from forces outside of a firm's control, also called nondiversifiable, noncontrollable risk. Purchasing power, interest rate, and market risks fall in this category. This type of risk is assessed relative to the risk of a diversified portfolio of securities, or the **MARKET PORTFOLIO.** It is measured by the beta (b) used in the **CAPITAL ASSET PRICING MODEL.** The systematic risk is simply a measure of a security's volatility relative to that of an average security. For example, $b = 0.5$ means the security is only half as volatile, or risky, as the average security; $b = 1.0$ means the security is of average risk; and $b = 2.0$ means the security is twice as risky as the average risk. The higher the BETA, the higher the return required.

T

T/A. *See* **TRADE ACCEPTANCE.**

TAA. *See* **TRADE ADJUSTMENT ASSISTANCE.**

TAKE-OR-PAY CONTRACT A buyer-seller agreement in which the former agrees to a minimum price to pay or quantity to buy for a good or service. An example is Company X agreeing to buy for the year at least 5000 units of product A from Company Y.

TAKEOVER A form of acquisition usually followed by a merger. A takeover can be hostile or friendly. The public tender offer is a means of acquiring a target firm against the wishes of management. A friendly takeover is when the acquiring firm negotiates with the targeted company and common agreement is reached in an amiable atmosphere for subsequent approval by shareholders. A government may establish specified takeover regulations or restrictions. *See also* **PROXY FIGHT.**

TARGET AUDIENCE The potential customers to which promotion effort is concentrated on. It may be based on demographic factors such as income, sex, age, and number of children.

TARGET COMPANY A mutinational company that is of interest to another company for acquisition. An example was Mattel's purchase of Tyco Toys. If 5 percent or more of a company's stock is acquired, the acquirer must inform, in writing, the **SECURITIES AND EXCHANGE COMMISSION** of its intentions.

TARGET COSTING 1. A Japanese method of determining the maximum available cost of a product before it is designed, engineered, or produced by subtracting an acceptable rate of profit margin from a projected selling price. 2. The **TARGET PRICE** minus desired profit margin. 3. Sometimes used interchangeably with standard costing.

TARGET MARKET An attractive market for multinational company's products or services. It is expected that customers in that particular market would be apt to buy the goods and services offered. An example is undertaking an advertising campaign among young adults to buy a new fashion of clothing.

TARGET PRICE 1. Also called **TARGET RETURN PRICE,** a price that seeks to achieve a targeted rate of return on a firm's capital. The pricing formula can be stated as follows:

$$\text{Price} = \frac{\text{Total cost} + (\text{Target rate of return} \times \text{Total capital employed})}{\text{Sales volume in units}}$$

2. In a highly competitive market, a lower price offered by the competition for the similar quality product or service. This requires **TARGET COSTING** which seeks to determine the maximum available cost of a product before it is designed, engineered, or produced by subtracting an acceptable rate of profit margin from the competitive target price. 3. Selling price based on customers'

perceived value in use, constrained by competitors' prices of similar items, of a product or service.

TARGET-ZONE ARRANGEMENT An agreement by a multinational company with foreign companies in which each is allowed to concentrate their products in designated market segments.

TARIFF ANOMALY The duty applied to an imported item in final form is less than the combined duty on the raw materials or components of that product.

TARIFF BARRIER A duty assessed by an importing country to form an obstacle to imported products or services designed to protect domestic industries.

TARIFF ESCALATION The more processed imported items are the higher the tariff rates associated with them. In other words, tariffs are on a graduating scale as the processing moves toward final form (e.g., from raw materials to work-in-process to finished goods). One objective of such a structure is an importing country's desire to protect its processing industries.

TARIFF SCHEDULE **1.** Listing of tariffs by product. **2.** Stipulation in the **NORTH AMERICAN FREE TRADE AGREEMENT** between the United States, Canada, and Mexico phasing out tariffs among them by December 31, 2002.

TARIFF WALL The setting of a high tariff or tax on imports to protect domestic industries against foreign competition.

TARIFFS **1.** A tax (or taxes) on imports or exports, most often calculated as a percent of the price charged for the good by the foreign supplier. The money collected is duty. A tariff may be imposed as a source of revenue for the government. However, a more common purpose of tariffs is protection against foreign competition. By raising prices of imported goods relative to the prices of domestic goods, tariffs encourage domestic consumers to buy domestic rather than foreign products. **2.** Schedule of rates in the transportation industry. *See* **END-USE TARIFF.**

TAX CREDIT An amount that directly offsets tax liabilities (dollar-for-dollar) due the federal or local government. It is different than a tax deduction that only reduces the tax base. Credits may either reduce income taxes for the year, or operate as prepayments of a tax due for the year. Some credits are refundable meaning that the taxpayer receives a money refund from the tax authorities, while others are merely nonrefundable and simply reduce the taxpayer's tax liabilities. Examples of tax credits are: (1) targeted-jobs tax credit for hiring targeted groups stipulated by the government; (2) foreign taxes paid on the same income being taxed by the United States (called a **FOREIGN TAX CREDIT**).

TAX EQUALIZATION **1.** A process by which a company withholds from an employee the home country tax obligation payable to a host country so as to avoid double taxation on the part of the expatriate employee. **2.** The policy to amend the tax laws so that the tax burden applies to different groups of tax-payers based upon their ability to pay. For example, a tax equalization act may exempt certain types of income while simultaneously raising taxes on other forms of income so as to have no effect on overall tax revenues.

TAX HAVEN A country that has very low, or even no income taxes and that employs its favorable tax structure to entice foreign investment or financial dealing.

TAX PLANNING An appraisal of alternative tax options so as to legally reduce the overall tax obligation in current and future years. Some approaches to minimize taxes might be to delay the receipt of taxable income and accelerate tax deductions. Tax software may be used for tax planning purposes. Some techniques cover a short-term period while others cover longer periods of time. A short-term plan involves a year or two and attempts to reduce taxes such as by recording immediate gains when the taxpayer is in a lower tax bracket, by taking immediate tax deductible losses to reduce an entity's tax liability, or by taking tax losses or tax credits before they are about to expire. A long-term strategy generally covers two or more years and may include different methods of accounting.

TAX PROTECTION An employee of a multinational company working in a foreign country is reimbursed in full or in part for his or her income taxes paid to the foreign country and/or the United States

TAX RETURN ACT OF 1986 A 1986 tax legislation involving a major overhaul of the United States tax system. It eliminated many of the abuses in the tax code and at the same time lowered the overall tax rates. For example, it allowed a United States citizen to exempt the first $70,000 of foreign income from United States income taxes provided certain requirements are met (e.g., the time spent in actually working and living outside the United States).

TAXES (MULTINATIONAL COMPANIES) The tax cost applied by foreign jurisdictions to companies doing business in their territory. The tax cost of doing business in a foreign country will be different than that of the parent company's domicile because of differences in the host company's domestic economy, rate of **INFLATION,** tax structure, and **FOREIGN EXCHANGE RATES.**

TEAM BUILDING A developing of cooperation, trust, and productivity of members of a group so as to accomplish the multinational company's goals and objectives.

TEASER AD A short, interesting advertisement to stimulate public interest without disclosing either the sponsor or the product or service. The ad only provides a few "teasing" comments. Such an ad comes before a full fledged advertising effort. The objective is to get potential buyers curious and motivates them to want to learn more.

TEASER RATE An enticingly attractive initial rate of interest that is below the market rate.

TECHNICAL INVESTMENT ANALYSIS A study of the stock market using various indicators including an evaluation of the economic variables within the marketplace. Stock prices of companies tend to move with the market because they react to various demand and supply forces. The technical analysts try to predict short-term price changes and then recommend the timing of a purchase and sale. They attempt to uncover a consistent pattern in prices or a relationship between stock price changes and other market data. Technical analysts also look at charts and graphs of internal market data including prices and volume.

TECHNOLOGY ADVANTAGE The advantages enjoyed by the use of the latest scientific and technical methods and processes to manufacture of goods and services. It results from creation or obtaining of **PROPRIETARY TECHNOLOGY.** This advantage can only be brought about through research and development. Technology is perishable, and advantages can easily erode. It is crucial for the multinational company to maintain that advantage over time.

TECHNOLOGY INTENSITY The level of technology utilized relative to labor and capital in production of a goods or service.

TELECOMMUNICATIONS The transmission of information between computers at different locations including access to online commercial data bases on the **INTERNET.** Data are usually transmitted over telephone lines, but radio waves and satellites may also be used. A modem and telecommunications software are needed. A terminal may also be used. Communications packages usually reserve some of the computer memory as a buffer, awaiting future disposition (e.g., saving on disk, printing).

TELEMARKETING The selling or promoting of goods or services over the telephone. Examples are soliciting orders, obtaining responses to advertising, and consumer surveys.

TEMPORAL METHOD A translation method which is essentially the same as the **MONETARY-NONMONETARY METHOD** except in the treatment of physical assets that have been revalued. It applies the current exchange rate to all financial assets and liabilities, both current and long term. Physical, or nonmonetary, assets valued at historical cost are translated at historical rates. *See also* **CURRENT RATE METHOD.**

TEMPORARY ADMISSION CARNET A short-term permission given by an importing country to allow specified goods normally subject to tariff to pass duty free or at a lower tariff. This temporary admission privilege may be for all exporting countries or a selected few.

TEMPORARY TARIFF SURCHARGE A short-term increase in import **TARIFFS** assessed by a country for some reason such as in relaliation to tariff increases made by other countries.

TENDER An offer to pay or perform services to another to satisfy one's obligation and responsibilities.

TERM DOCUMENTARY DRAFT A financial instrument associated with export payments.

TERM (TIME) DRAFT A financial instrument having a specified due date from its issuance or after it is accepted.

TERMS OF TRADE Economic factors influencing a nation's foreign trade in goods and services, such as dependency on foreign sourcing and relative competitiveness in production. They imply (1) the real quantities of exports that are required to pay for a given amount of imports, (2) the weighted average of a nation's export prices relative to its import prices, (3) the weighted average exchange ratio between a nation's export prices and its import prices, used to measure gains from trade.

TEST MARKET A sampling of the population when bringing forth a new product or service. The sampling may be done demographically by type of consumer (e.g., age, sex) and/or geographically. Based on the results of the limited market tested the company can formulate a better overall marketing approach. For example, before a company goes nationally or globally with a new product it can test its success on a representative region (e.g., Midwest).

THE 10/70 RULE The rule applying to the deferral of income at the **CONTROLLED FOREIGN-CORPORATION (CFC)** level. If less than 10 percent of the income at the CFC (parent) level is **SUBPART F INCOME,** full deferral applies; if the percent is above 70 percent, there is no deferral. If the proportion is between 10 and 70 percent, income is allocated to Subpart F on this same ratio.

THIN MARKET A situation in which securities, property, or merchandise have only a few offers to purchase or sell. As a result of the inactivity in buys and sells, price volatility is much greater than in an active market.

THIRD WORLD Countries other than the Eastern-bloc countries, once dominated by the USSR and the **ORGANIZATION FOR ECONOMIC COOPERATION AND DEVELOPMENT** countries. They are the **LESS DEVELOPED COUNTRIES,** primarily in Latin America, Africa, and Asia that have relatively low per capita incomes and relatively high importance of primary products in their economies.

THIRTEENTH MONTH A form of compensation in some foreign nations in which a worker receives each year one month's additional pay.

THREE-WAY ARBITRAGE. *See* **TRIANGULAR ARBITRAGE.**

THROUGHPUT AGREEMENT A contract to have a specified amount of merchandise through production in the factory for a specified time period. If the facilities are not used, some compensation must be made.

TIE-IN PROMOTION The additional marketing strategies to support the recurring advertising efforts. Examples are unique displays, free samples, and prizes. The objective is to stimulate demand particularly for new products or services.

TIGHT MARKET The market for securities or property being active with little spreads between bid and ask prices. *See also* **SLACK MARKET.**

TIGHT MONEY 1. Less funds available to borrowers by lending institutions and creditors. This is a situation in which credit is difficult to obtain. This may be a phase of monetary policy when the supply of credit is restricted and interest rates are high. The object of such a policy is to reduce the general level of demand, or restrain its growth. **2.** A reduction in the dollars available for individual spending because of a decrease in the money supply. *See also* **EASY MONEY.**

TIME DRAFT A document representing an order for payment at a future date after its presentation to the drawee. A time draft is used when a seller does not mind receiving payment some time after the goods are delivered to the buyer. *See also* **SIGHT DRAFT.**

TIME MANAGEMENT The use of an employee's working time for maximum achievable productivity so operations are as efficient and utilized as best as possible.

TIME ORIENTATION The adjustment of how long it takes to perform a manufacturing operation or service activity based on a particular situation. For example, a "rush" order may require filling it in less time than is customary for a "normal" order.

TIME-AND-MOTION STUDY An analysis of how long it takes and the proces to perform a particular manufacturing or service activity. Such a study helps to improve employee productivity and lower production or operational costs.

TOKYO ROUND OF MULTILATERAL NEGOTIATION A **GENERAL AGREEMENT ON TARIFFS AND TRADE** meeting establishing a framework on tariff reductions and other obstacles to free trade among member countries.

TOKYO STOCK EXCHANGE (TSE) Major stock exchange in Tokyo, Japan. It lists stocks in Japanese companies. In the 1870s, the securities system was introduced and bargaining on public bonds was activated. Thus the establishment of a public trading institution was requested and the Stock Exchange

Ordinance was enacted in May 1878. Based on this ordinance, the Tokyo Stock Exchange Co., Ltd. was established on May 15, 1878, and trading began on June 1. In March 1943, the Japan Securities Exchange Law was enacted to reorganize the stock exchange as a war-time control institution. On June 30, 1943, 11 stock Exchanges throughout Japan were unified and a quasi-public corporation, the "Japan Securities Exchange", was established (dissolved in April, 1947).

TOPPING OUT The price of a specific stock, industry group, or stock market index that has reached its upper (ceiling) price level and thus the expectation is for either a price decline or for the price to remain at that level.

TOTAL DOLLAR RETURN The excess of selling price over cost for a security, property, good, or service. For example, if an investor bought a stock for $50,000 and sold it for $60,000, the total dollar return is $10,000 while the percentage return is 20 percent.

TRACER 1. Tracing a shipment which is lost and an attempt is made to find it or hastening its delayed delivery. **2.** Tracing the shipment of an item to determine its status.

TRADE 1. A domestic or international transaction (exchange) between companies or between a company and its customers for products or services. **2.** Businesses in an industry selling similar types of products or services after receiving discounts from suppliers. They usually belong to trade associations (e.g., chemical companies). **3.** Conducting business activities. **4.** Barter (non-monetary) exchanges between companies for goods and services. **5.** Act of buying or selling a security such as a stock or bond. **6.** Type of business or profession a multinational company or individual is engaged in.

TRADE ACCEPTANCE (T/A) A **TIME DRAFT** or **DATE DRAFT** similar to a **BANKER'S ACCEPTANCE,** the difference being that a bank is not a party. The exporter presents the draft to the importer (the buyer or drawee) for its acceptance to pay the amount stated at maturity. Trade acceptances cannot become bankers' acceptances or be guaranteed by a United States bank.

TRADE ADJUSTMENT ASSISTANCE (TAA) A United States government policy, authorized by the 1974 Trade Act. It offers aid to workers laid off because of competition from imported goods. This mechanism attempts to alleviate the burden on people who are adversely affected by the operation of comparative advantage in international trade, which leads to contraction of some domestic industries and expansion of others. Assistance includes instruction, job placement and relocation support, and reemployment services for those displaced by imports. TAA for companies is under the direction of the **UNITED STATES DEPARTMENT OF COMMERCE;** The United States Department of Labor handles employee issues.

TRADE ADVERTISING A manufacturer's promotion of its product line so as to obtain wholesaler and/or retailer interest in carrying its goods.

TRADE AGREEMENT A contractual understanding between importer and exporter.

TRADE BALANCE. *See* **BALANCE OF TRADE.**

TRADE BARRIERS Barriers that hinder free trade and competition. The United States Trade Representative categorizes trade barriers into eight groups: (1) import policies (**TARIFFS** and other import charges, quantitative restrictions, import licensing, and customs barriers); (2) standards, testing, labeling, and certification; (3) government procurement; (4) export subsidies; (5) lack of intellectual property protection; (6) service barriers; (7) investment barriers; and (8) other barriers (e.g., barriers encompassing more than one category or barriers affecting a single sector).

TRADE CREATION 1. A situation that exists when the elimination of internal trade barriers increase the volume of trade by making lower cost goods and services available. This contrasts with **TRADE DIVERSION. 2.** A situation created when imported goods or services are at such lower prices that domestic manufactures and service providers are displaced.

TRADE CREDIT The credit given from one business to another business for the purchase of goods. A partial payment may or may not be made. It is credit arising from **OPEN ACCOUNT** purchases. A cash discount may be offered for early payment.

TRADE CYCLE The cyclicality in trade caused by economic conditions. For example, if the economy is improving there is a greater demand for imported products and services, and vice versa. The pattern of trade should be examined over a period of time.

TRADE DEFICIT An unfavorable balance of trade, that is the excess of imports of goods (raw materials, agricultural and manufactured products, and capital and consumer products) over the exports of goods, resulting in a negative balance of trade. Trade surplus is the reverse. The difference is often called trade gap. The balance of trade is distinguished with the balance of payments which consists of the current account which includes services as well as merchandise trade and other invisible items such as interest and profits earned abroad. Factors that affect a country's balance of trade include the strength or weakness of its currency value in relation to those of the countries with which it trades and comparative advantage in key manufacturing areas.

TRADE DEFLECTION Imports directed into countries having lower tariffs than higher tariffs.

TRADE DIVERSION A situation that occurs when less efficient makers inside the market area replace more efficient external manufacturers since the outsider still faces external tariffs. The degree to which trade diversion occurs will hinge on the severity of the external **TARIFFS.**

TRADE DRAFT A **DRAFT** drawn on a business firm.

TRADE FINANCING Credit extended to an importer by the exporter, or a bank or some other financial intermediary that assists the importer in paying for the export merchandise. Two types of trade financing exist: **PRETRADE FINANCING** and **POST-TRADE FINANCING.**

TRADE GAP. *See* **TRADE DEFICIT.**

TRADE LEADS The potential domestic or foreign markets for a company's products or services. The list may include possible joint ventures, distributors, wholesalers, and retailers. Revenue may be in the form of direct sales or the franchising of the product or activity.

TRADE LIBERALIZATION The easing of tariffs and other barriers to importation by a country so as to promote trade.

TRADE NAME. *See* **BRAND NAME.**

TRADE POLICY Government policy aimed at improving the competitive position of a domestic industry and/or domestic firm in the global market. Six main instruments of trade policy are: **TARIFFS, SUBSIDIES, IMPORT QUOTAS, VOLUNTARY EXPORT RESTRAINTS,** local content requirements, and administrative policies.

TRADE PREFERENCES The advantages and concessions such as lower **TARIFFS** and less restrictions granted to select countries on their exported goods and services into the country. Such preferences may be afforded to "friendly" countries.

TRADE RATE 1.Discounted price given by manufacturers, wholesalers, or distributors to retailers. 2. Special price a seller grants to other companies in the same or similar industry.

TRADE SECRET Any aspect of production activity (e.g., manufacturing processes, mechanisms, formulas) of a company that gives it a competitive edge since such secret is unknown to external parties.

TRADE SHOW The presentation at a meeting of a company's merchandise or services to potential customers, clients, and other interested parties. Competing companies in the same industry will often be present. In most cases, the exhibit is shown at a convention hall where space is leased for the display. A trade show is smaller in scope and size than a trade fair.

Multinational companies may exhibit their products annually in trade shows in different countries.

TRADE TERMS The provisions in the agreement between importer-exporter concerning the goods or services as well as each others' duties and responsibilities.

TRADEMARK A legal right of a name, symbol, or other attribute of a good. It has in effect no expiration date because the trademark may be renewed indefinitely over 20 year periods. The cost of a trademark includes filing and attorney fees. The cost of trademarks (and all intangible assets) are amortized equally over the period benefited not exceeding 40 years per Accounting Principles Board Opinion 17.

TRADER A business or individual who purchases and sells merchandise, services, property, or securities (stocks and bonds) to earn a profit. This includes retailers, wholesalers, dealers, and brokerage houses.

TRADING HOUSE A business entity specializing in the import-export business.

TRADING PAPER The financial instruments of the **EUROMARKETS**.

TRADING RANGE **1.** High-low price range for a particular security (stock or bond) or the overall **STOCK MARKET**. **2.** Limit established by a futures exchange for a particular **COMMODITY** (e.g., wheat). The price of that commodity may not exceed or go below the predetermined limit for that trading day or period.

TRADING-WITH-THE-ENEMY ACT A United States law that keeps United States companies from doing business with enemy nations such as North Korea, Cuba, and Vietnam.

TRADITIONAL ECONOMIC SYSTEM. *See* **ECONOMIC SYSTEM**.

TRADITIONAL SECTOR The old, rudimentary form of a dual economy that is based on farming, hunting, or fishing, and is weakly connected to the market sector or the industry.

TRANCHE An installment payment on a bank loan or on account to a supplier.

TRANSACTION COSTS. *See also* **EFFICIENT MARKET**.

TRANSACTION EFFICIENCIES Efficiencies achieved by operation of **MULTINATIONAL CORPORATIONS** because they are often more cost effective than smaller, uninational firms.

TRANSACTION EXPOSURE The potential gains or losses on the future settlement of outstanding obligations that are denominated in a foreign currency. An example would be a United States dollar loss after the French Franc devalues, on payments received for an export invoiced in Francs before that devaluation.

TRANSACTION RISK The risk resulting from **TRANSACTION EXPOSURE** and losses from changing foreign currency rates.

TRANSACTION STATEMENT A contractual agreement specifying the terms of trade among the exporter and importer.

TRANSACTION VALUE The worth of the products and services being traded among companies in different countries. It is the price agreed to by the parties.

TRANSFER PAYMENT **1.** Amount paid to or from the United States parent and foreign subsidiary for services or equipment. **2.** Payment made by a business to another without obtaining a service or product such as charitable contributions. **3.** Federal or local government payments to individuals that are not in the form of compensation such as unemployment benefits.

TRANSFER PRICE The price charged when one division of a company provides goods or services to another division of the company. A good transfer price will help us evaluate the performance of the divisions. Under ideal circumstances, the transfer price will promote congruence between the goals of divisions and the company as a whole. Unfortunately, there is no single transfer price that may accomplish all these goals. Because the divisions are evaluated as independent investment centers, their managers may use transfer prices that are not in the best interest of the company as a whole. *See also* **TRANSFER PRICING.**

TRANSFER PRICING Pricing the goods or services that are exchanged between various divisions (or subsidiaries) of a decentralized organization. A major goal of transfer pricing is to enable divisions that exchange goods or services to act as independent businesses. Various transfer pricing schemes are available, such as market price, cost-based price, or negotiated price. Unfortunately, there is no single transfer price that will please everybody-that is, top management, the selling division, and the buying division-involved in the transfer. However, usually the best transfer price is the outside market price less costs saved by dealing within the company (e.g., transportation costs, advertising, salesperson salaries). If the two division managers-buying division and selling division-cannot agree on a price, one will be arbitrated by upper management. When an outside market price is not available, budgeted cost plus profit markup may be used so that cost efficiencies at the selling division are still maintained. A transfer price may depend on such factors as degree of competition, autonomy, and political considerations.

TRANSFERABLE LETTER OF CREDIT A **LETTER OF CREDIT (L/C)** under which the beneficiary (exporter) has the right to instruct the paying bank to make the credit available to one or more secondary beneficiaries. No L/C is transferable unless specifically authorized in the credit. Further, it can be transferred only once. The stipulated documents are transferred alone with the L/C.

TRANSHIPPING 1. Movement of cargo among carriers. **2.** The transferring of cargo between vehicles or ships of the same carrier.

TRANSIT TARIFF A levy or fee on merchandise transported over a country going from a selling nation to a buying nation.

TRANSLATION EXPOSURE. *See* **ACCOUNTING EXPOSURE.**

TRANSLATION GAIN OR LOSS An accounting gain or loss resulting from changes caused by changes in foreign currency based receivables, payables, or other assets or liabilities.

TRANSLATION PROFIT OR LOSS. *See* **EQUITY METHOD.**

TRANSLATION RISK. *See* **ACCOUNTING EXPOSURE.**

TRANSPARENCY The degree to which a multinational company's policies and strategies are clearly stated, measurable, and appropriate.

TREE DIAGRAM A diagram illustrating various stages of the decision-making process on the branches of a decision tree. This is used widely for expected value analysis of decision making under uncertainty.

TRIAL OFFER A potential buyer is permitted for a short time (e.g., 30 days) to use and appraise the suitability of a product to him before buying or returning it. The product may be at a discounted price to the first-time buyer. An example is a publisher offering three issues of a magazine on a trial basis.

TRIANGULAR ARBITRAGE Also called three-way arbitrage, a form of arbitrage seeking a profit as a result of price differences in foreign exchange among three currencies. This form of arbitrage occurs when the **ARBITRAGEUR** does not desire to operate directly in a two-way transaction, due to restrictions on the market or for any other reason. In this case, the arbitrageur moves through three currencies, starting and ending with the same one.

TRICKLE-DOWN ECONOMICS The concept that if you give tax breaks and benefits to big business and the wealthy it will find its way down to the middle-class and poor, through capital expansion, increased productivity, and increased employment. It was a popular concept in the Reagan years and espoused by Prime Minister Margaret Thatcher. The trickle-down concept was used in **REAGANOMICS** as a means to fight **INFLATION.** However, during times of inflation it tended to have the reverse effect. The newspapers and journals labeled it the "horse and sparrow theory," that is, "feed a horse oats and the sparrow could live off of the dropping." It tended to increase the tax burden on the middle-class and the poor working class, in order to cover the lost taxes from the wealthy, thus having the effect of reducing discretionary spending.

TRICULTURAL SETTING The total cultural environment in which the multinational company is encountering threefold cultures-its own corporate culture, the home country culture, and the host country culture.

TRIGGER POINT The price of an imported product that is far less than that charged within the exporting country. For such a low-priced good, the importing country may place restrictions or higher tariffs on it such as to protect domestic industries.

TRIGGER PRICE 1. The price established internationally by a global organization for a good or service. **2.** The estimated cost of producing each steel product in Japan, the world's low-cost steel product maker.

TRIGGER PRICE MECHANISM A system used by the United States during the period 1978-82 to restrict imports of Japanese steel products. Firms undertaking to import at prices lower than the **TRIGGER PRICES** were penalized for **DUMPING** in the United States market.

TRILATERAL TRADE Commercial trade among three nations.

TROUGH The lowest point in an economic downturn. A recovery is expected.

TRUST RECEIPT An instrument that acknowledges that the borrower holds specified property in trust for the lender. The lender retains title. This type of financing is used for equipment dealers, automobile dealers, and the like, involved in durable expensive goods. It is also used for clearance of perishable goods through United States customers and/or the Food and Drug Administration. The goods are subject to repossession by the bank. The trust receipts are always used when merchandise is financed via acceptances under a **LETTER OF CREDIT.** When the lender receives the sale proceeds, title is given up.

TSE. *See* **TOKYO STOCK EXCHANGE.**

TURNAROUND 1. A reversal in the financial condition of a business or securities market, or in the state of the economy. An investor can profit significantly if he times properly when a turnaround will occur. **2.** A return trip to the originating point of a delivery vehicle after unloading at its destination.

TURNING POINT An upward movement in the economy, securities market, or a particular security from the trough or a downward movement in the economy, securities market, or a particular security from its peak.

TURNKEY PROJECT. *See* **TURNKEY VENTURE.**

TURNKEY VENTURE **1.** Also called a turnkey project, a foreign project or facility which a firm agrees to plan, set up, and operate for a specified period of time, after which the keys (i.e., ownership and control) are turned over to a foreign client. The firm receives a fee for its services but usually retains no ownership interest. This is one way in which firms can engage in international business without making **FOREIGN DIRECT INVESTMENT** commitments. **2.** An arrangement in which a seller agrees to furnish a complete product or service to the buyer.

TURNOVER **1.** Number of times an asset such as inventory, receivables, and fixed assets turn over during the year. The higher the turnover, the better because it indicates less risk (e.g., less obsolescence risk in inventory, less collection risk in receivables). The freed cash can be invested for a return. Inventory turnover equals cost of goods sold divided by average inventory. Accounts receivable turnover equals credit sales divided by average accounts receivable. Fixed asset turnover equals sales divided by average fixed assets. **2.** Number of shares traded in a security. Actively traded securities have greater **LIQUIDITY.** **3.** Number of workers leaving the company. It may reflect employee discontent.

TWO-TIER FOREIGN EXCHANGE RATES Two sets of exchange rates

U

UCC. *See* **UNIFORM COMMERCIAL CODE.**

UNBIASED PREDICTOR A predictor whose expected value equals the true population parameter is said in statistics to be unbiased.

UNBUNDLING **1.** A practice to transfer liquid assets across borders by mixing one or more of a variety of techniques such as dividend remittances, royalty payments and fees, transfer prices, and fronting loans. By using this practice, a multinational company can recover funds from its foreign subsidiaries without piquing host-country sensitivities with large "dividend drains." **2.** A strategy of governments to try to force **MULTINATIONAL CORPORATIONS** into sharing more of their benefits with the local country in the form of shared ownership, required technology transfer, and local content requirements.

UNCONFIRMED LETTER OF CREDIT (L/C) A **LETTER OF CREDIT** issued by one bank and not confirmed by another. Therefore, an unconfirmed L/C is the obligation of only the issuing bank.

UNCTAD. *See* **UNITED NATIONS CONFERENCE ON TRADE AND DEVELOPMENT.**

UNDERCAPITALIZATION An insufficiency in capital for a business to conduct its usual and customary operational activities.

UNDERDEVELOPED COUNTRY A lesser developed, poorer country such as indicated by relatively low per capita real income.

UNDERSELLING **1.** A foreign company's products are at lower prices than similar goods of domestic companies. **2.** A company's selling price for a good or service is below that of a competitor.

UNDERVALUATION **1.** A security, **COMMODITY,** or currency is underpriced in the market. **2.** Assets are understated in the **BALANCE SHEET.**

UNDERWRITERS **1.** A securities firm agreeing to market an issue of securities (e.g., stocks, bonds) to the public and buying any part remaining unsubscribed. The underwriter's **SPREAD** is the difference between the price paid to the issuing company and the amount received from investors. This spread depends on such factors as the amount and quality of the issue, terms of issue, and type of security. **2.** An insurance company's assumption of liability in the event of an insurable loss (e.g., fire, theft) to the insured. **3.** A business entity's undertaking a risk for compensation.

UNDP. *See* **UNITED NATIONS DEVELOPMENT PROGRAM.**

UNFAIR COMPETITION **1.** Selling a product or service below its cost. **2.** Deceptive practices and representations to mislead consumers such as erroneous advertisements and making untrue derogatory statements about a competitor. The agrieved party may be able to sue for fraud.

UNIFORM COMMERCIAL CODE (UCC) The authoritative body of laws applying to commercial transactions entered into within the United States by multinational companies. These laws govern the sale or purchase of merchandise or services, personal property dealings, and banking arrangements.

UNILATERAL TRANSFER A one-way movement of currency from one nation to another, such as straight grant-in-aid without any strings attached.

UNIT **1.** Responsibility center or segment of a business such as a department, division, product line, or service line. **2.** Minimum trading unit of a security (e.g., one bond stated in a $1,000 denomination). **3.** Class of securities packaged together such as in a new Initial Public Offering (IPO) of one share and two warrants in XYZ Company. **4.** A unit of quantity (e.g., each manufactured product). **5.** Quantity division used as a measurement norm or of exchange (United States dollar). **6.** One person or single group in a population. **7.** Distinct element with a particular purpose.

UNITARY TAX A tax expressed in percentage terms of a business entity's global activities.

UNITED NATIONS CONFERENCE ON TRADE AND DEVELOPMENT (UNCTAD) Established in 1964 as a permanent intergovernmental body,

UNCTAD is the principal organ of the United Nations General Assembly in the field of trade and development. It is the focal point within the United Nations for the integrated treatment of development and interrelated issues in the areas of trade, finance, technology, investment and sustainable development. The main goals are to maximize the trade, investment and development opportunities of developing countries, and to help them face challenges arising from globalization and integrate into the world economy, on an equitable basis. UNCTAD pursues its goals through research and policy analysis, intergovernmental deliberations, technical cooperation, and interaction with civil society and the business sector. There are currently 188 member States. Many intergovernmental and non-governmental organizations have observer status and participate in its work. The Secretariat is located in Geneva, Switzerland; the 394 staff members form part of the United Nations Secretariat.

UNITED NATIONS DEVELOPMENT PROGRAM (UNDP) A fund established on a voluntary basis to provide money to assist countries, particularly developing ones, with worthy projects. Funds may be available for purchase of facilities (e.g., laboratories), training workers, purchase of high-tech equipment (e.g., latest computers), technical advice, and correcting environmental problems (e.g., pollution). A prime obligation of the fund is to improve the well being of the population in the country, particularly those who are poor. *See also* **AFRICAN DEVELOPMENT BANK.**

UNITED STATES BUREAU OF CENSUS Established in 1902, Congress established the Bureau of Census as a separate organization within the Department of Interior with the responsibility of collecting national demographic and other related data every ten years. In addition, the taking of interim censuses and surveys was also mandated. The United States Bureau of Census was transferred to the **UNITED STATES DEPARTMENT OF COMMERCE** and the United States Department of Labor in 1903 and then to the separate Department of Commerce in 1913. Currently, the Bureau of the Census is required by the United States Constitution to report state population counts to the President by January 1 of the year following the taking of the full census for the purpose of apportioning seats in the House of Representatives. Population totals for all counties, cities, and political and statistical subdivisions are submitted to each respective state legislature after the census date. The states use this information for drawing up or modifying current legislative and other district boundaries.

UNITED STATES CUSTOMS SERVICE **1.** The agency of the of United States government responsible for assessing and collecting all duties, taxes, or tariffs levied on imported goods brought in the country. **2.** Agency that checks individuals at airports, American ports of call, etc., to insure that all persons entering the United States have fully declared all the goods required by law that necessitate the assessment of custom duties.

UNITED STATES DEPARTMENT OF COMMERCE Federal Department

whose primary objective is to promote and stimulate domestic and foreign trade. The United States Department of Commerce also plays an important role in the negotiation and establishment of international trade agreements as well as the enforcement of trade restrictions assessed by the government.

UNITED STATES STATE DEPARTMENT Independent department of the executive branch of the federal government whose principal responsibility is the conduct of foreign policy for the purpose of advancing the interests and security of the United States. Overall foreign policy is established by the President and implemented and interpreted by the State Department. Contact between all foreign nations and the United States is maintained by the State Department through ambassadors and representatives of foreign governments that are accredited to this country through diplomatic and consular offices of the United States Foreign Service. The State Department is administered by the Secretary of State who is appointed by the President with the approval of the Senate.

UNIVERSAL MIS A **MANAGEMENT INFORMATION SYSTEM** that is common and universal to all levels of business operations, whether it is the subsidiary or parent.

UNSTERILIZED INTERVENTION A state of interfering with the affairs of another.

UNSYSTEMATIC RISK Risk in a portfolio that can be eliminated by diversification. *See also* **SYSTEMATIC RISK; BETA COEFFICIENT.**

UPLIFT A bonus paid to a worker because of some danger or hardship associated with the overseas assignment.

UPSTREAM PRICING The steps in deriving the market value for commodities resulting in additional main or by-products. An example is oranges which then result in orange juice. The pricing structure goes from the source to the final product. *See also* **DOWNSTREAM PRICING.**

UPSTREAM SUBSIDIZATON When a federal or local government gives a manufacturer a subsidy or **SUBSIDIES,** and that manufacturer sells the subsidized product to another company which additionally processes it and sells it overseas.

URGENT CONSIGNMENTS Imported goods needing immediate approval by customs because of such reasons as perishability and obsolescence.

URUGUAY ROUND First convened in 1986 in Uruguay, this latest in a series of **GENERAL AGREEMENT ON TARIFFS AND TRADE** trade negotiations seeks to settle trading differences in agriculture, services, and intellectual-property rights.

V

VALUABLE PAPERS INSURANCE Protection against the loss in intrinsic value if important records are damaged or destroyed. The insurance policy will require that the papers be secured in a locked place.

VALUABLE ADDITIVITY PRINCIPLE Important addition to a processed product enhancing its value such as incorporating a highly technological component.

VALUATION 1. The process of determining the intrinsic value of an asset, such as a security, business, or a piece of real estate. The process of determining security valuation involves finding the present value of an asset's expected future cash flows using the investor's required rate of return. Thus, the basic security valuation model can be defined mathematically as follows:

$$V = \sum_{t=1}^{n} \frac{C_t}{(1+r)^t}$$

where V = intrinsic value or present value of an asset
C_t = expected future cash flows in period $t = 1, ..., n$
r = investor's required rate of return

2. Assessing the value of imported goods by customs to assess the appropriate duty charge.

VALUE-ADDED TAX (VAT) An indirect percentage tax levied on products or services at various stages of production and distribution. The actual value added to the product, including raw materials, labor and profit, is determined at each stage or state of production and the tax is computed upon the increase in value. It is basically a tax allocated among the economic units responsible for the production and distribution of goods and services. Collection of VAT takes place at the product's ultimate destination, therefore VAT is not charged on export sales. VAT is charged on all domestically sold products regardless of the country of origin. Thus, VAT is designed to provide an incentive to export and of course a disincentive to import.

VALUE DATE 1. A **SETTLEMENT DATE** of a security, **COMMODITY,** or **FOREIGN CURRENCY TRANSACTION.** For example, the settlement date for buying a stock or bond is three days after the trade date. 2. The effective date of a deposit in an account.

VALUE DATING 1. SETTLEMENT DATE or delivery date. **2.** Date money is first available to a depositor.

VARIABLE BUDGETING. *See* **FLEXIBLE BUDGET.**

VARIABLE COSTING. *See* **DIRECT COSTING.**

VARIABLE INTEREST RATE The interest rate on a loan fluctuates based on a change in some specified measure or index such as the prime interest rate or the interest rate on a six-month Treasury bill.

VARIABLE PRICE 1. Selling price of a product or service fluctuates based on some predetermined factor such as volume ordered. **2.** Negotiated selling price between seller and buyer.

VARIANCE 1. The difference of revenues, costs, and profit from the planned amounts. One of the most important phases of responsibility accounting is establishing standards in costs, revenues, and profit and establishing performance by comparing actual amounts with the standard amounts. The differences (variances) are calculated for each responsibility center analyzed, and unfavorable variances are investigated for possible remedial action. *See also* **VARIANCE ANALYSIS. 2.** In statistics, a measure of a dispersion of a distribution. It is a squared standard deviation.

VAT. *See* **VALUE-ADDED TAX.**

VERTICAL ANALYSIS Also called Common-size analysis. A financial statement item used as a base amount. All other financial statement accounts are compared to it. For example, total assets represents 100 percent in the balance sheet. If total assets are $800,000 and cash is $160,000, cash is 20 percent of total assets. In the income statement, net sales represents 100 percent. If sales are $1,000,000 and gross profit is $300,000, gross profit is 30 percent of sales.

VERTICAL INTEGRATION The extension of activity by a firm into business directly related to the production or distribution of the firm's end products. It typically combines a parent firm and the suppliers of its raw materials or purchasers of its finished product. Vertical merger involves extending the lines of distribution or production, either backward toward the source or forward toward the end-user. A firm controlling the entire production process is considered totally integrated vertically. This compares with **HORIZONTAL INTEGRATION.**

VERTICAL MANAGEMENT STRUCTURE An organizational scheme of a business in which there is a declining ranking order of responsibility and authority.

VISA A valid passport which has been reviewed and certified.

VISIBLE TRADE Synonymous with the **BALANCE OF TRADE.** It represents foreign trade in merchandise.

VOLATILE A very unstable and fluctuating condition in something such as the prices of property and securities, political or economic makeup of a foreign country, or workforce.

VOLUNTARY EXPORT RESTRAINTS (VERs) An exporting country agrees on its own to restrict the amount of its exports of specified products. The voluntary offer may be designed to establish good relations with countries it normally trades with. Such a policy may enhance mutual respect and accommodation.

VOLUME The quantity of securities (stock, **BOND**), **COMMODITIES,** products, etc. transacted. In investment analysis, an increase or decrease in price of a security is considered more important when accompanied by significant volume.

VOLUNTARY IMPORT EXPANSIONS A country giving into pressure from another country to increase its imports from it or otherwise face trade restrictions or barriers (e.g., increased **TARIFFS, QUOTAS**).

VOLUNTARISM A philosophy that prevailed in Britain that the interests in unions is workers' basic rights and that they will respect each individual's right to work or not work.

VOLUNTARY QUOTA An **EXPORT QUOTA,** by a mutual agreement, pegged to the exports to some predetermined level or some percentage of the exporting country's market.

VOTING COMMON STOCK Equity shares in a publicly or privately held corporation. Each share of stock has certain rights and privileges that can be restricted by contract when the shares are issued. For an enumeration of those fundamental rights, *see* **COMMON STOCK.** If the right to vote for the Board of Directors is not specifically restricted (i.e., the right to share in the management of the corporation), then the common stock is voting common stock.

VOTING STOCK The shares owned by an investor in a company entitling that investor to vote in company matters. For example, **COMMON STOCK** typically carries with it voting rights. However, a class of common stock may be designated with no or restricted voting rights. Preferred stock does not usually having voting privileges.

W

WACC. *See* **WEIGHTED AVERAGE COST OF CAPITAL.**

WAITING LINE THEORY. *See* **QUEUING THEORY.**

WAIVER CLAUSE **1.** A contractual provision voluntarily surrendering some right or claim of a party. **2.** An insurance provision dictating that the insured should take all reasonable steps to minimize loss.

WAN. *See* **WIDE AREA NETWORK.**

WAREHOUSE RECEIPT A document evidencing title listing items stored at a warehouse facility. If the items are sold it may still be kept at the warehouse by transferring the warehouse receipt to the new owner. For legal considerations, reference may be made to the Uniform Warehouse Receipts Act.

WARRANTY An assurance that merchandise sold or services rendered are suitable for the use intended in terms of performance and quality for a specified time period. If not, the items may be returned, replaced, kept with an allowance given, or repaired free of charge. The warranty period and terms vary but exclude damage from unauthorized use.

WATS. *See* **WIDE AREA TELEPHONE SERVICE.**

WAY BILL A document of the delivery carrier specifying the delivery cost and how delivery will be made to the receipt point. It usually is included with the shipment itself.

WEAK DOLLAR. *See* **DEPRECIATION OF THE DOLLAR.**

WEAK MARKET Declining prices of securities, property, products, or services due to very poor demand.

WEAKEST LINK THEORY The entire or complete function, project, or team is only as good as its component elements including the weakest item or member. For example, the successful working of a constructed facility also depends on the weakest support structure.

WEAROUT FACTOR **1.** The effectiveness of a sales promotion no longer exists. It may occur from oversaturation of ads, poor communication, poor approach to targeted consumers, and overexaggerated assertions. **2.** The employee productivity is in a state of decline because of poor working conditions including working excessive hours. **3.** The failure to properly maintain machinery accelerates its deterioration.

WEIGHT AGREEMENT A contractual provision specifying the weight of the shipment.

WEIGHTED-AVERAGE EXCHANGE RATE The exchange rate used in translating income and expense accounts at the end of a fiscal period. It takes into consideration the relative change of exchange rates during the period and adjusts the consolidated statement with this weighted average rate.

WHAT-IF SCENARIO. *See* **EXECUTIVE INFORMATION SYSTEM.**

WHIPSAWED An investor experiencing significant losses because of widely fluctuating prices for real or financial assets held. For example, the investor sells just before stock prices increase and he buys just before stock prices decrease.

WHITE KNIGHT A targeted company seeks another "more friendly" acquirer to take it over.

WHOLESALER The **INTERMEDIARY** between the manufacturer and distributor or retailer. The wholesaler typically buys large quantities of merchandise at low prices for resale.

WIDE AREA NETWORK (WAN) A computer network comprising of a large geographic area.

WIDE AREA TELEPHONE SERVICE (WATS) The use of long distance telephone lines for business purposes at lower rates. It includes "800" telephone numbers.

WIDGET A hypothetical unit of a manufactured good used to illustrate a production or selling point.

WINDING UP The process of liquidating a failing business by selling its assets, paying its liabilities, and distributing any excess to its stockholders.

WINDOW DRESSING A company artificially makes itself look better financially than it really is. Although legal, it may be designed to mislead creditors and investors. A thorough financial analysis may be needed to uncover such attempts. An example is:

A few days before year-end a company had current assets and current liabilities of $1,000,000 and $500,000, respectively. Therefore, its current ratio is:

$$\text{Current Ratio} = \frac{\text{Current Assets}}{\text{Current Liabilities}} = \frac{\$1,000,000}{\$\ 500,000} = 2$$

The company wants to obtain a bank loan. The bank will request its December 31 year-end balance sheet. To artificially make its **LIQUIDITY** look much better by year-end the company pays off $400,000 of current liabilities with cash (a current asset). Thus, by year-end its current ratio becomes:

Current Ratio = $\dfrac{\text{Current Assets}}{\text{Current Liabilities}}$ = $\dfrac{\$600,000}{\$100,000}$ = 6

A financial analyst could uncover such window dressing activity by comparing a company's year-end debt to its average debt during the year. In this case, the $100,000 of current liabilities is excessively understated relative to its average balance for the year. The average might be based on either quarterly or monthly figures.

WINDOW OF OPPORTUNITY Favorable circumstances that arise to be taken advantage of. An example is when a United States multinational company (e.g., General Motors) attains a competitive advantage including new customers when employees of foreign companies selling the same items (e.g., autos) are on strike.

WITHOUT RECOURSE When a company factors (sells) its accounts receivable to a third party and customers in fact do not pay their balances, the third party cannot go against the seller for payment. Because of the risk involved, the factor will charge a high finance rate.

WORKING CAPITAL **1.** Net working capital (net assets) equal to current assets less current liabilities. **2.** Gross working capital representing the money invest in current assets.

WON South Korea's currency.

WORKS COUNCIL An elected group of labor representatives that have legal rights to some company information and that determine together with management certain issues (for example, employee work safety). The Works Council is more popular in Europe.

WORLD BANK. *See* **INTERNATIONAL BANK FOR RECONSTRUCTION AND DEVELOPMENT.**

WORLD WIDE WEB (WWW) Internet system for world-wide hypertext linking of multimedia documents, making the relationship of information that is common between documents easily accessible and completely independent of physical location. It is simply the matrix of graphical information stored on servers connected to the Internet.

WWW. *See* **WORLD WIDE WEB.**

Y

YANKEE BONDS Dollar-denominated bonds issued within the United States by a foreign corporation. *See also* **FOREIGN BONDS.**

YELLOW GOODS High-priced household items held by homeowners for a long time. They are usually profitable merchandise. Examples are dishwashers and refrigerators.

YEN Japanese currency.

YIELD (Rate of Return) Also called **RETURN.** **1.** The income earned on an investment, usually expressed as a percentage of the market price. **2.** The percentage return earned on a common stock or preferred stock in dividends. It is figured by dividing the total of dividends paid in the preceding 12 months by the current market price. For example, a stock with a current market value or $40 a share which has paid $2 in dividends in the preceding 12 months is said to return 5 per cent ($2/$40). If an investor paid $20 for the stock five years earlier, the stock would be returning him/her 10 per cent on his/her original investment. *See also* **DIVIDEND YIELD.** **3.** In the case of bonds, the **CURRENT YIELD** or **YIELD TO MATURITY.** **4.** The money earned on a loan, which is determined by multiplying the **ANNUAL PERCENTAGE RATE** by the amount of the loan over a stated time period.

YIELD TO MATURITY (YTM) Sometimes called long-term yield to maturity or effective yield, this measure takes into consideration the stated rate of interest on the bond as well as any discount or premium that may have been generated when issued. The YTM or effective yield is sometimes viewed as the rate of interest demanded by creditors in the market at a given point in time. If a bond is issued at a discount then the bond's stated rate is less than the effective yield and therefore the bond will sell at less par. On the other hand, if the bond was issued at a premium, then the bond's stated rate exceeds the effective yield and it will sell at more than par. The exact method of computing YTM is somewhat complex and is not presented here. A formula for computing an estimate of YTM when a bond is issued at a discount follows:

$$\frac{\text{Stated Amount of Interest} + \dfrac{\text{Discount}}{\text{Years to Maturity}}}{\dfrac{\text{Current Price of Bond} + \text{Maturity Value}}{2}}$$

A formula for computing an estimate of the YTM when a bond is issued at a premium is modified slightly and presented below.

$$\frac{\text{Stated Amount of Interest} - \dfrac{\text{Premium}}{\text{Years to Maturity}}}{\dfrac{\text{Current Price of Bond} + \text{Maturity Value}}{2}}$$

EXAMPLE
Compute the YTM on a $1,000, 20-year bond, 8 percent bond that was issued at a price of $777.77. The YTM that could be earned on this bond assuming it was held to maturity is estimated on the following page:

$$\text{Stated Amount of Interest} + \cfrac{\cfrac{\text{Discount}}{\text{Years to Maturity}}}{\cfrac{\text{Current Price of Bond} + \text{Maturity Value}}{2}}$$

Let's compute the numerator of the formula of first and then the denominator.

The numerator is calculated below:

$$80 + \frac{(\$1,000 - \$777.77)}{20} =$$

$$80 + \frac{\$222.23}{20} =$$

$$\$80 + \$11.11 = \$91.11$$

The numerator computes to $91.11

The denominator follows:

$$\frac{\$777.77 + \$1000}{2} =$$

$$\frac{\$1777.77}{2}$$

$$\$888.89$$

The YTM on this bond is $= \cfrac{\$91.11}{888.89}$

The YTM on this bond is = 10.25 percent

Since the bond was issued at a discount, its YTM is greater than the stated rate of 10 percent being offered.

YIELD-TO-CALL The annual percentage return on a note or bond called (redeemed) by the issuer at the first available call (redemption) date.

YTM. *See* **YIELD TO MATURITY.**

YUAN China's currency.

Z

ZAIBATSU The pre-World War II Japanese economic groups that dominated the Japanese economy. These groups are made up of centralized, family-controlled, monopolistic holding companies.

ZAIRE The currency of Congo (Kinshasa) and Zaire.

ZBB. *See* **ZERO BASE BUDGETING.**

ZERO-BASE BUDGETING (ZBB) A planning and budgeting tool that uses cost/benefit analysis of projects and functions to improve resource allocation in an organization. Traditional budgeting tends to concentrate on the incremental change from the previous year. It assumes that the previous year's activities and programs are essential and must be continued. Under zero base budgeting, however, cost and benefit estimates are built up from scratch, from the zero level, and must be justified. The basic steps to effective zero base budgeting are: (1) describe each company activity in a "decision" package; (2) analyze, evaluate, and rank all these packages in priority on the basis of cost/benefit analysis; and (3) allocate resources accordingly.

ZERO COUPON BOND A bond sold at a deep discount. The interest instead of being paid out directly is added to the principal semiannually and both the principal and the accumulated interest are paid at maturity. Although a fixed rate is implicit in the discount and the specific maturity, they are not fixed income securities in the traditional sense because they provide for no periodic income. Although the interest on the bond is paid at maturity, accrued interest, though not received, is taxable yearly as ordinary income. Zero coupon bonds have two basic advantages over regular coupon-bearing bonds: (1) A relatively small investment is required to buy these bonds; and (2) A specific yield is assured throughout the term of the investment.

ZERO SUM GAME A situation in which an economic gain by one nation results in an economic loss by another.

ZERO TAX HAVEN A country that has either no or a minimal tax on business income. Multinational companies set up offices in such areas as part of its tax planning policy. An example of a tax haven is the Cayman Islands.

ZONE FACILITIES The space available in foreign trade zones to accommodate such functions as warehousing, distribution, repackaging, maintenance, assembling, inspecting, relabeling, and repackaging.

ZONE PRICING Also called delivered pricing. A type of pricing under which the seller divides the economy into zones or regions and charges the same delivered price within each zone, but different prices between zones sufficient to cover average freight costs as a whole. In theory, the seller's average net is the same in every zone. If the seller's price zones are the same as the freight-rate zones, this type of pricing is the same as **FREE ON BOARD** pricing, no legal problems are involved.

ZOONEN Dutch word for sons.

APPENDIX

AGEXPORTER
United States Department of Agriculture
Foreign Agricultural Service
Information Division, Room 4638-S
Washington, D.C. 20520-1000
Phone: 202/720-3329
Price: $17.00 per year (domestic delivery), $21.00 per year (international delivery)
Magazine on international trade and trade opportunities overseas. Published by the Department of Agriculture.

BUSINESS AMERICA
U.S. Government Printing Office
Superintendent of Documents
Washington, DC 20402
Phone: 202/783-3238 or contact the Government
Printing Office in your area.
Price: $61.00 per year; $2.50 each issue
Magazine on international trade issues and business opportunities overseas. Published bi-weekly by the U.S. Department of Commerce.

EXPORT TODAY
733 15th Street, N.W., Suite 1100
Washington, D.C. 20005
Phone: 202/737-1060   FAX: 202/783-5966
Price: $49.00 per year
The "how to" international business magazine for U.S. exporters. Published ten times a year.

THE EXPORTER
34 West 37th Street
New York, NY 10018
Phone: 212/563-2772   FAX: 212/563-2798
Price: $144.00 per year
Monthly reports on the business of exporting.

FOREIGN TRADE MAGAZINE
6849 Old Dominion Drive, #200
McLean, VA 22101
Phone: 703/448-1338   FAX: 703/448-1841
Price: $45.00 per year (10 editions)
Features trade briefs, information on financing, shipping, air cargo, trucks and rails, and current legislation.

GLOBAL TRADE MAGAZINE
North American Publishing Company
401 North Broad Street
Philadelphia, PA 19108
Phone: 215/238-5300
Price: $45.00 per year
Information on international finance, transportation and commerce.

INTERNATIONAL BUSINESS MAGAZINE
American International Publishing Corporation
500 Mamaroneck Avenue, Suite 314
Harrison, NY 10528
Phone: 914/381-7700   FAX: 914/381-7713
Price: $48.00 per year
Reports on overseas opportunities, global strategies, trade and political developments to assess impact on U.S. imports, exports, joint ventures/acquisitions.

JOURNAL OF COMMERCE
Two World Trade Center, 27th Floor
New York, NY 10048
Phone: 212/837-7000
Price: $295.00 per year
Information on domestic and foreign economic developments, export opportunities, agricultural trade leads, shipyards, export ABCs and trade fair information. Feature articles on tariff and non-tariff barriers, licensing controls, joint ventures and trade legislation in foreign countries.

JOURNAL OF COMMERCE SHIPYARD
Two World Trade Center, 27th Floor
New York, NY 10048
Phone: 212/837-7000
Price: $295.00
Shipyards is a supplement to the Journal of Commerce. It lists scheduled sailings of vessels worldwide.

SHIPPING DIGEST
Geyer-McAllister Publications
51 Madison Avenue
New York, NY 10010
Phone: 212/689-4411
Price: $42.00 per year
Explores current topics related to international transportation.

WORLD TRADE MAGAZINE
Taipan Press, Inc.
500 Newport Center Drive
Newport Beach, CA 92660
Phone: 714/640-7070   FAX: 714/640-7770
Price: $24.00 per year
Profiles of successful exporters and reports on international trade developments.

DO'S AND TABOOS AROUND THE WORLD

Roger E. Axtell
The Benjamin Company
One Westchester Plaza
Elmsford, NY 10523
ISBN: 0-471-85356-9
Phone: 914/592-8088
Describes worldwide protocol, customs and etiquette. Especially of use to the business traveler.

DEPARTMENT OF COMMERCE
ECONOMIC BULLETIN BOARD (EBB)

U.S. Department of Commerce 14th and Constitution Avenue,
N.W.
Washington, D.C. 20230
Phone: 202/482-1986   FAX: 202/482-2164 or try EBB as a guest user by dialing 202/482-3870 with PC and modem (2400 baud, 8 bit words, no parity, 1 stop bit) EBB is a personal computer-based electronic bulletin board providing trade leads and up-to-date statistical releases from the Bureau of Census, the Bureau of Economic Analysis, the Bureau of Labor Statistics, the Federal Reserve Board and other federal agencies.

NATIONAL TRADE DATA BANK (NTDB)

U.S. Department of Commerce
14th and Constitution Avenue, N.W.
Washington, D.C. 20230
Phone: 202/482-1986   FAX: 202/482-2164
Price: $35.00 per disk or $360.00 for one year
The NTDB is an international trade data bank compiled by 15 U.S. government agencies. It contains the latest census data on U.S. imports and exports by commodity and country, the complete CIA World Factbook, current market research, the Foreign Traders Index and many other data series. The NTDB is available at over 900 federal depository libraries, or can be purchased on CD-ROM for personal PC use. Offices of Africa, Near East and South Asia 202/482-1064. Categories include general and country information (Nigeria and South Africa). For the Office of the Near East, categories include general and country information (Algeria, Bahrain, Egypt, Iran, Iraq, Israel, Jordan, Kuwait, Lebanon, Libya, Morocco, Oman, Qatar, Saudi Arabia, Syria, Tunisia, United Arab Emirates and Yemen). Categories for the Office of South Asia include general and country information (Afghanistan, Bangladesh, Bhutan, India, Nepal, Maldives, Pakistan and Sri Lanka).

HOTLINE NUMBERS

THE EXPORT OPPORTUNITY HOTLINE
The Small Business Foundation of America
1155 15th Street, N.W.
Washington, D.C. 20005
Phone: 1-800-USA-XPORT, 1-800-243-7232
In Washington, DC: 202/223-1104
Answers questions about getting started in exporting. Advice on product distribution; documentation; licensing and insurance; export financing; analyzing distribution options; export management firms; customs; currency exchange systems and travel requirements.Presented by AT&T and the Hotline Referral Network in cooperation with the U.S. Department of Commerce. The Export Hotline, a corporate-sponsored nationwide fax retrieval system provides international trade information for U.S. businesses. Its purpose is to help find new markets for U.S. products and services.

SBA ON-LINE
Electronic Bulletin Board
From Washington, D.C. — 202/205-7265
Toll free — 1-800-859-4636 for a 2400 baud modem; 1-800-697-4636 for a 9600 baud modem. Set communications software protocol for N (no parity), 8 (data bits), and 1 (stop bit). This is a 24-hour-a-day service with information on SBA export and financial assistance, speakers, SBA's women's mentor program, minority programs and a mail box for electronic conversations.

U.S. AGENCY FOR INTERNATIONAL DEVELOPMENT
Center for Trade and Investment Services (CTIS). Tailored country-specific information. 9:00-5:30 EST Monday through Friday 202/663-2660; 1-800-USAID-4-U FAX 202/663-2670

U.S. DEPARTMENT OF AGRICULTURE
Trade Information: 202/720-7420

U.S. CUSTOMS
Customs will help you identify your product's code under the Harmonized System (HS). Call 202/927-0370 for the phone number of the Customs office nearest you. U.S. Customs has a
NAFTA hotline, too. Call 202/927-0066.

U.S. DEPARTMENT OF COMMERCE
Trade Information Center
1-800-872-8723   TDD 1-800-833-8723

U.S. CENTER FOR STANDARDS AND CERTIFICATION INFORMATION ON PRODUCT STANDARDS, TESTING AND CERTIFICATION.
301/975-4040

EXPORT-IMPORT BANK OF THE UNITED STATES 1-800-424-5201

OVERSEAS PRIVATE INVESTMENT CORPORATION 1-800-336-8799.

FLASH FACTS — TO GET EXPORT INFORMATION INSTANTLY

For several areas of the world, the information is at your fingertips from the U.S. Department of Commerce, if you have a touch-tone telephone and a fax. Dial the number, follow instructions and the requested information will automatically be faxed to you. The Automated Fax Delivery System Flash Facts are available 24 hours-a-day, seven days a week, free of charge.

Flash Facts are available for the following regions:

EASTERN EUROPE BUSINESS INFORMATION CENTER (EEBIC)

202/482-5745. Information is available on specific Eastern European countries including Albania, Bosnia-Hercegovina, Bulgaria, Croatia, Czech Republic, Estonia, Hungary, Latvia, Lithunia, Macedonia, Poland, Romania, Slovak Republic and Slovenia.

DOING BUSINESS IN MEXICO

202/482-4464.

Current trade-related documents concerning Mexico are available. Information is also available on the North American Free Trade Agreement; tariffs, permits and customs regulations; marketing, distribution and finance; investment; statistics and demographics. The same type of information is available for Canada by calling 202/482-3101.

OFFICE OF THE PACIFIC BASIN

202/482-3875 or 202/482-3646.

Categories include general export information, regional and country information (Australia, Cambodia, Indonesia, Korea, Laos, Malaysia, New Zealand, Philippines, Singapore, Taiwan, Thailand and Vietnam).

BUSINESS INFORMATION SERVICE FOR THE NEWLY INDEPENDENT

STATES (BISNIS) 202/482-3145. Categories include U.S.-Newly Independent States trade statistics, current export and investment opportunities and upcoming trade events, general investment and defense conversion opportunities, World Bank and European Bank for Reconstruction and Development (EBRD) opportunities, export and trade opportunities and BISNIS publications.

APPENDIX C
STATISTICAL INFORMATION

FEDERAL
- U.S. Bureau of the Census
- Federal Trade Commission (FTC)
- International Economic Policy (IEP) Country Officers
- International Trade Administration (ITA)
- U.S. Department of Labor-Foreign Labor Trends
- U.S. Export Assistance Centers (USEACs)
- U.S. International Trade Commission (USITC)
- U.S. Small Business Administration (SBA)

INTERNATIONAL ORGANIZATIONS
- Japan External Trade Organization (JETRO)
- United Nations

PRIVATE SECTOR
- Journal of Commerce - PIERS

STATE OF CALIFORNIA
- California Trade & Commerce Agency - Export Development (Long Beach)

APPENDIX D
INTERNET ON INTERNATIONAL BUSINESS AND TRADE

THE BALTICS ONLINE: FINANCIAL ONLINE
http://www.viabatt.ee/Financial/indexhtml
This site carries business news from the Baltic region.

BUSINESS INFORMATION SOURCES ON THE INTERNET
http://www.dis.strath.ac.uk/business/
This British site has an astounding number of links to other Web business sites, primarily in England and Europe.

BUSINESS LINE (INDIA)
http://www.indiaserver.com/news/bline/
This site has up-to-date business news from the Indian subcontinent, including information about Indian companies and industries.

THE BUSINESS RIMES
http://www.asia1.com.sg/biztimes/
This is an exceedingly thorough site providing business-related information from the Far East, including Taiwan.

THE ECONOMIST
http://www.economist.com/
This is an online site for an excellent international business journal.

EXPORTNET
http://www. exporttoday.com/
This site offers tips for businesses that want to trade internationally. Not a free service.

EXPORT USA
http://www.exportusa.com/
This is a consultancy that addresses selling and marketing overseas.

FOREIGN EXCHANGE RATES
gopher:// una.hh.iib.umich.edu/OO/ebb/monetary/tenfx.frb
This drab site has fairly up to-date foreign exchange rates.

GLOBAL TRADE CENTER
http://www.tradezone.com/tz/
This site includes many business links, as well as listings of international business opportunities.

INTERNATIONAL BUSINESS FORUM
http://www.ibf.com/
For entrepreneurs who want to participate in the international marketplace. Included are extensive lists of resources in various countries, postings of opportunities, and information about various associations.

THE INTERNATIONALIST
http://www.internationalist.com/
An excellent source for information on a wide range of international issues.

INTERNATIONAL TRADE ADMINISTRATION
http://www.ita.doc.gov/
A division of the Department of Commerce, the ITA offers help to companies that wish to export their wares. It has information about export opportunities for specific industries, as well as information about specific nations. The Trade Information Center (http://www.ita.doc.gov/tic) provides advice on financing, marketing abroad and the Gold Key program.

NEWSPAGE: TRADE REGULATION & TARIFFS
http://www.newspage.com/newspage/cgibin/walk.cgi/newspage/info/d10/d5/d6/
Part of a much larger news site, this page provides excellent coverage of international trade issues. This site is updated daily, and you must register to use it.

WORLD INDEX OF CHAMBERS OF COMMERCE & INDUSTRY
http://www.usa1.com/%eibnet/chamshp.html
A thorough listing of chambers of commerce from around the world.

WWW HOME SERVERS GUIDE FOR THE COMPANIES IN JAPAN
http://www.jicst.go jp/dir-www/com.html
Looking for the Web site of a Japanese company? Look no further. This Web site has it.

FOREIGN LANGUAGE TRANSLATION
http://www.travlang.com
English may be the global tongue for business, but knowing a few words of other languages can make international business life easier. Produced by Travlang president Michael Martin, this web site allows users to type in about 200 phrases—like "Where can I find..."—for translation into 33 languages, including European tongues, Japanese, Korean and more.

Country, Island or Territory	Currency	Symbol
Afghanistan	afghani	Af
Albania	lek	s
Algeria	dinar	DA
American Samoa	dollar	$
Angola	kwanza	Kz
Anguilla	dollar	EC$
Antarctica	krone	NKr
Argentina	peso	double-dashed
Australia	dollar	A$
Austria	schilling	S
Bahamas	dollar	B$
Bahrain	dinar	BD
Bangladesh	taka	Tk
Barbados	dollar	BdS$
Belgium	franc	BF
Belize	dollar	BZ$
Benin	franc	CFAF
Bhutan	ngultrum	Nu
Bolivia	peso	$b
Botswana	pula	P
Bouvet Island	krone	NKr
Brazil	Real	
British Indian Ocean Territory	rupee	Mau Rs
British Virgin Islands	dollar or pound	$ or £
Brunei	ringitt	B$
Bulgaria	lev	Lv
Burkina Faso	franc	CFAF
Burundi	franc	FBu
Cameroon	franc	CFAF
Canada	dollar	Can$
Canton and Enderbury Islands	dollar	$
Cape Verde Island	escudo	C.V.Esc.
Central African Republic	franc	CFAF
Chad	franc	CFAF
Chile	peso	Ch$
China	yuan	Y
Christmas Island	dollar	A$

Cocos (Keeling) Islands	dollar	A$
Cook Islands	dollar	NZ$
Niue	dollar	NZ$
Colombia	peso	Col$
Comoros	franc	CF
Congo	franc	CFAF
Costa Rica	colon	slashed C
Cyprus	pound	£C
Czech Republic	koruna	CK
Denmark	krone	Dkr
Djibouti	franc	DF
Dominica	dollar	EC$
Dominican Rep.	peso	RD$
Dronning Maud Land	krone	NKr
Ecuador	sucre	S/
Egypt	pound	£E
El Salvador	colon	¢
Equatorial Guinea	ekwele	
Ethiopia	birr	Br
European Union	European Currency Unit	ecu
Faro Islands	krone	Dkr
Falkland Islands	pound	£F
Fiji	dollar	F$
Finland	markka	Fmk
France	franc	F
French Guiana	franc	F
French Polynesia	franc	CFPF
New Caledonia	franc	CFPF
Gabon	franc	CFAF
Gambia	dalasi	D
Germany	deutsche mark	DM
Ghana	cedi	¢
Gibraltar	pound	£
Greece	drachma	Dr
Greenland	krone	Dkr
Grenada	dollar	EC$
Guadeloupe	franc	F
Guam	dollar	$
Guatemala	quetzal	Q
Guinea-Bissau	peso	PG
Guinea	syli	
Guyana	dollar	G$
Haiti	gourde	G
Heard and McDonald Islands	dollar	A$

Honduras	lempira	L
Hong Kong	dollar	HK$
Hungary	forint	Ft
Iceland	krÛna	IKr
India	rupee	Rs
Indonesia	rupiah	Rp
Iran	rial	Rls
Iraq	dinar	ID
Ireland	pound or punt	£Ir
Israel	new shekel	IS
Italy	lira	Lit
Ivory Coast	franc	CFAF
Jamaica	dollar	J$
Japan	yen	¥
Johnston Island	dollar	$
Jordan	dinar	JD
Kampuchea	riel	CR
Kenya	shilling	K Sh
Kiribati	dollar	A$
Korea, North.	won	Wn
Korea, South	won	W
Kuwait	dinar	KD
Laos	kip	KN
Latvia	Lats	Ls
Lesotho	loti, pl., maloti	L, pl., M
Liberia	dollar	$
Libya	dinar	LD
Liechtenstein	franc	SwF
Luxembourg	franc	LuxF
Macao	pataca	P
Madagascar	franc	FMG
Malawi	kwacha	MK
Malaysia	ringgit	RM
Maldives	rufiyaa	Rf
Mali	franc	CFAF
Malta	lira	£m
Martinique	franc	F
Mauritania	ouguiya	UM
Mauritius	rupee	Mau Rs
Midway Islands	dollar	$
Mexico	peso	Mex$
Monaco	franc	F
Mongolia	tugrik	Tug
Montserrat	dollar	EC$
Morocco	dirham	DH
Mozambique	metical	Mt

Myanmar	kyat	K
Nauru	dollar	A$
Namibia	rand	R
Nepal	rupee	NRs
Netherlands		
Antilles	guilder	Ant.f.
Netherlands	guilder	f.
New Zealand	dollar	NZ$
Nicaragua	cordoba	C$
Niger	franc	CFAF
Nigeria	naira	double-dashed N
Norfolk Island	dollar	A$
Norway	krone	NKr
Oman	rial	RO
Pakistan	rupee	PRs
Panama	balboa	B
Panama Canal Zone	dollar	$
Papua New Guinea	kina	K
Paraguay	guarani	slashed G
Peru	inti	I/
Philippines	peso	dashed P
Pitcairns Island	dollar	NZ$
Poland	zloty	Z dashed l
Portugal	escudo	Esc
Puerto Rico	dollar	$
Qatar	riyal	QR
Reunion	franc	F
Romania	franc	RF
San Marino	lira	Lit
Saudi Arabia	franc	CFAF
Seychelles	rupee	SR
Sierra Leone	leone	Le
Singapore	dollar	S$
Slovakia	koruna	Sk
Solomon Island	dollar	Sl$
Somalia	shilling	So. Sh.
South Africa	rand	R
Spain	peseta	Ptas
Sri Lanka	rupee	SLRs
St. Kitts and		
Nevis	dollar	EC$
St. Lucia	dollar	EC$
St. Vincent and		
Grenada	dollar	EC$
Sudan	pound	LSd
Suriname	krone	NKr
Swaziland	ilangeni,	pl., L, pl., E
	emalangeni	

Sweden	krona	Sk
Switzerland	franc	SwF
Syria	pound	LS
Taiwan	dollar	T$
Tanzania	shilling	TSh
Thailand	baht	Bht or Bt
Togo	franc	CFAF
Tokelau	dollar	NZ$
Tonga	pa'anga	PT
Trinidad and		
Tobago	dollar	TT$
Tunisia	dinar	D
Turkey	lira	LT
Turks and Caicos		
Islands	dollar	$
Tuvalu	dollar	A$
Uganda	shilling	USh
United Arab		
Emeriates	dirham	Dh
United Kingdom	pound	£
United States of		
America	dollar	$
Uruguay	new peso	NUr$
Vanuatu	vatu	VT
Vatican	lira	Lit
Venezuela	bolivar	Bs
Viet Nam	dong	D
Virgin Islands	dollar	$
Wake Island	dollar	$
Wallis and Futuna		
Islands	franc	CFPF
Western Sahara	peseta	Ptas
Western Samoa	tala	WS$
Yemen	rial	YRls
Yugoslavia	dinar	Din
Zaire	zaire	Z
Zambia	kwacha	K
Zimbabwe	dollar	Z$

Sources for assistance in conducting business
contact the following organizations:

U.S. DEPARTMENT OF COMMERCE
14th and Constitution Avenue NW
Washington, DC 20230

Office of Canada, (202) 377-3103
Office of Mexico. (202) 482-4464
Latin America/Caribbean Business Development Center, (202) 482-0841
Trade Info. Center, (800) USA-TRADE
(Industry related questions will be referred to Industry Desks)

NAFTA HELP DESK
U.S. Department of Customs
(202) 927-0066

U.S. TRADE AND DEVELOPMENT AGENCY
(LATIN AMERICA)
SA-16, Room 309
Washington. DC 20523 (703) 875-4357

OFFICE OF THE U.S. TRADE REPRESENTATIVE
600 17th St. NW Washington, DC 20506
(202) 395-3230

CANADIAN COUNCIL FOR THE AMERICAS
145 Richmond St. W., 3rd floor
Toronto, ON Canada M5H 2L2
(416) 367-4313

OFFICES OF THE TRADE COMMISSION OF MEXICO:
New York (212) 826-2916
Chicago: (312) 856-0316
Dallas: (214) 688-4095
Beverly Hills: (213) 655-6421
Atlanta: (404) 522-5373
Miami: (305) 372-9929
Seattle: (206) 441-2833

MEXICAN CHAMBER OF COMMERCE
(202) 296-5198

AMERICAN ECONOMIC ASSOCIATION
JOURNAL OF ECONOMIC LITERATURE
Economic Literature Index
P.O. Box 7320
Pittsburgh, PA 15213
(412) 268-3869

INTERNATIONAL TRADE COMMUNICATIONS
GROUP/WORLD INFORMATION NETWORK
Department of External Affairs (Canada)
Canada-U.S. Free Trade Agreement
125 Sussex Dr.
Ottawa. ON Canada KIA 0G2
(613) 944-4000

THE ECONOMICS INTELLIGENCE UNIT
111 W. 57th St. New York, NY 10019
(212) 554-0600

JOURNAL OF COMMERCE, INC.
TRADE INFORMATION SERVICE
2 World Trade Center, 27th floor.
New York. NY 10048
(212) 837-7000

TRADE DATA REPORTS, INC.
THE EXPORTER
34 W. 37th St.
New York, NY 10018
(212) 563-2772

Source: *Global Competitor,* Spring 1994, p. 63.